D1571201

ALFRED NORTH WHITEHEAD:

A PRIMARY-SECONDARY BIBLIOGRAPHY

BIBLIOGRAPHIES OF FAMOUS PHILOSOPHERS

The Philosophy Documentation Center is publishing a series of "Bibliographies of Famous Philosophers," edited by Richard H. Lineback. **HENRI BERGSON: A BIBLIOGRAPHY** was the first bibliography in the series. **JEAN-PAUL SARTRE AND HIS CRITICS: AN INTERNATIONAL BIBLIOGRAPHY** (1938-1975) was the second and **ALFRED NORTH WHITEHEAD: A PRIMARY-SECONDARY BIBLIOGRAPHY** is the third.

ALFRED NORTH WHITEHEAD

A PRIMARY-SECONDARY BIBLIOGRAPHY

Barry A. Woodbridge, Editor

Jay McDaniel and Marjorie Suchocki,
Associate Editors

Published by

PHILOSOPHY DOCUMENTATION CENTER
BOWLING GREEN STATE UNIVERSITY
BOWLING GREEN, OHIO 43403
U.S.A.

0146723

90342

Library of Congress Card Number: 77-72822

ISBN 0-912632-34-8

CONTENTS

SECTION I

THE MANY BECOME ONE, AND THE INCREASE BY THE ONE: AN INTRODUCTION

The very existence of this work attests to the expanding influence Alfred North Whitehead is having on twentieth century thought. As Whitehead's vision of a unifying cosmology for all disciplines is finding actualization, it is becoming increasingly difficult to keep informed of the Whiteheadian discussion. Various professional societies provide working seminars on Whitehead; the journal *Process Studies* offers a forum for Whiteheadian scholarship; and two major centers on the Continent and in the United States provide the resources and opportunity for research and interchange on Whitehead's thought.[1] This volume, then, originates from the need to collect and organize the interdisciplinary proliferation of Whiteheadian scholarship. Physicists, educators, artists, mathematicians, theologians, biologists, historians, and philosophers alike will find this bibliography directed to the issues being illumined by Whiteheadian conceptuality in their disciplines.

While the purpose of an introduction to a bibliography is not so much to present yet another critical introduction to the author represented (for the reader will find many of those listed in the text), it may be appropriate to provide an introduction to the structure of this bibliography and its history. Whitehead's philosophy of organism demonstrates how the many become one and in fact are increased by the one. In the case of this volume, the editor would like to show how the many contributions invested in it became one unique entity, and how this new entity may potentially increase the many in their work on Whitehead.

A. The Many Contributions

The greatest reward a Whitehead bibliographer can receive from his or her labors (besides the joy of actually having the work used!) is to see the work "concresce" in a Whiteheadian manner. It inherits much from the past and becomes one unique entity by organizing that past in novel ways. In this case, the "many" of the past are rich and varied. They represent previous Whitehead bibliographies, as well as three years of largely "labors of love" on the part of librarians, student research assistants, computer programmers and operators, and many others. Since it is the diversity of these contributions which makes the one work what it is, it is most appropriate and Whiteheadian that each be acknowledged in its own right.

The costs involved in the acquisition, cataloguing, reading, translating, abstracting, and finally computer indexing of all the materials listed here were formidable. Throughout the three year duration of this project, the Center for Process Studies, with its director, John Cobb, and executive director, David Griffin, has generously funded this work and supplied the staff to complete it. Old Dominion University has also provided a research grant to fund a portion of these labors. The editor is indeed grateful for their sustaining support.

In 1971 David Griffin and Gene Reeves, then bibliographical editors of *Process Studies*, published the prototype of the secondary bibliography apearing in this work.[2] At that time they envisioned that someday that literature would be subject indexed. Meanwhile, Victor Lowe, a longstanding biographer and bibliographer of Whitehead's, had recently discovered several new entries for a primary bibliography on Whitehead and consented to their being published with an expanded and indexed secondary bibliography. Thus the present editor acquired the initial data for a novel project of a rather large scope. (This work includes 1868 entries which are retrievable from a 3,200 term index listing over 12,744 occurrences of those descriptors in the secondary literature.)

Sheila Davaney and Janis Rafferty, bibliographical assistants at the Center for Process Studies, invested much time in verifying and cataloguing the secondary literature. Where the accuracy of this bibliography has improved from earlier bibliographies on Whitehead, they deserve much of the credit. Where information is still lacking or inaccurate, the editor assumes responsibility. (Actually, some 35 Whitehead scholars were consulted in the preparation of this volume, and their cumulative knowledge confirmed or disproved the existence of many a document with a fleeting reference.) Also contributing to the identification and location of such elusive documents were inter–library loan librarians Helen Hardy (Honnald Library of the Claremont Colleges), Elsie Freudenberger, and Jean Cobb (both of the School of Theology at Claremont library).

Another kind of contribution was made by Peggy Sever, who became acquainted with the descriptor system used in this project and wrote the computer program which stored and sorted the data to produce the index of the terms, persons, and disciplines appearing in the secondary literature. Sarah Wyant and Tom Hofeller also made important program revisions which enhanced the accuracy and readability of the final index.

Near the completion of this project, the Seaver Computer Center of the Claremont Colleges made generous extensions of the editor's normal allotment of computer and staff time to allow for the completion of the index manuscript. Without this extension, the project would have been too costly to undertake. Cathy Foster and her staff there worked long and very irregular hours to produce, correct, and reschedule program runs of the data input as the editor and his staff approached the deadline for the completion of the manuscript.

To be sure, the most significant and often sacrificial contribution to this work was made by two very dedicated associate editors, Marjorie Suchocki and Jay McDaniel. They are the ones who actually read each entry, decided upon the descriptor terms most pertinent to it, and frequently wrote an annotation clarifying its contents or stating its thesis. With 1763 entries in the secondary bibliography, this became a very laborious but illuminating procedure. Perhaps no one else in the history of Whiteheadian scholarship has had the opportunity to read as much about Whitehead as they have. In general they divided the labor so that McDaniel read the monographs and dissertations while Suchocki read periodical literature. In their reading and abstracting they were backed up by a group of specialists in the use of Whitehead in non–English materials.

Guiseppe Riconda assisted with the Italian entries. Jon Berthrong covered the Chinese literature on Whitehead. Jan Van der Veken and Andre Cloots read and abstracted the Dutch literature. Vibiana Andrade prepared the entries for the literature in Spanish. The editor read and prepared the entries for the literature in German and French. Dean Fowler read and abstracted the literature in the field of physics and mathematics which involved extensive use of mathematical notation.

The editor is deeply grateful for the kind of supererogatory effort his associate editor Jay McDaniel and assistant David Vergin invested in the final proofreading of the manuscript and computer index. Assisting him in that phase of the project was Ernest Simmons, Assistant Director of the Center for Process Studies and proofreader for the journal *Process Studies*.

Finally, the editor wishes to thank the general editor of the *Bibliographies of Famous Philosophers* series, Richard H. Lineback, for the helpful suggestions he has made during the preparation of the manuscript. His knowledge of the descriptor system and the computer programming of such descriptor indices has greatly facilitated the writing of the program for this work.

B. The One—Organization of this Work

The many and varied contributions described in the preceding section have given rise to an entity with its own unique internal constitution. The reader's use of this bibliography will be facilitated by a general acquaintance with its principles of organization.

The primary bibliography contains the 107 pieces of literature Whitehead is known to have written. In several cases the annotations note new discoveries by Victor Lowe which have not been previously published in a primary bibliography on Whitehead. The editor is most appreciative of Victor Lowe's contributions and his permission to publish them here. The reader should be aware that while this primary bibliography is complete at the present time, there is another genre of Whitehead literature which is just being compiled and does not strictly fall under a primary or secondary category. A number of notes on Whitehead's lectures at Harvard are extant and in time will be correlated and prepared for use. Copies of them are on file at the Harvard library and hopefully will be available at the library of the Center for Process Studies in Claremont, California.

The primary bibliography is organized chronologically, with works published in the same year being arranged alphabetically within that year. No descriptors are used for the primary literature; hence they are not listed in the index, which is on secondary literature alone. The complete descriptor indexing of all Whitehead's works awaits another publication—a concordance to the Whiteheadian corpus. The editor hopes that the computerized indexing system used in this work and organized on the word frequency of the Whiteheadian vocabulary would lend itself to the preparation of such a concordance in the near future.

The principles of organization and the criteria for selection of material in the secondary bibliography are somewhat more elaborate. The obvious criterion for selection was that a given piece of material actually treated Whitehead's thought. In practice, however, that criterion was at times difficult to implement. There were many works, for example, which were devoted to process philosophy in general and were influenced by Whiteheadian conceptuality but which never mentioned nor treated Whitehead explicitly. (Some of the writings of Charles Hartshorne, Bernard Meland, and Norman Pittenger, for instance, fall into that category.) Similarly, there were others which approached and solved a problem in a Whiteheadian manner, using a conceptuality remotely inspired by Whitehead, but still were not strictly a work about Whitehead or the application of his thought. In some of these borderline cases where the influence of Whitehead was at least vaguely discernible, such works were included (usually with an annotation noting their applicability to certain related topics in Whitehead's own thought). In other cases—for instance where Bergson or Alexander were being discussed and Whitehead only mentioned by name in passing without any discussion or comparison of his thought—the material was not included. In all cases, the editors have strived not to eliminate any materials which might be of even negligible value to those studying Whitehead and the application of his thought to various disciplines. Therefore, the secondary bibliography can be used with the confidence that virtually everything meeting this criterion and published by June 1976 appears in it. Of course, the editor will appreciate hearing from readers who discover any additions meeting the criterion employed. (In several cases literature which had appeared in previous secondary bibliographies on Whitehead was omitted here because after consultation with publishers, librarians, and sometimes even the author him or herself, it was decided that no such publication had in fact existed.)

Each secondary entry is divided into two sections, with an optional third section for an annotation. The first section is the citation string. The citations are usually straightforward, using a form adapted from the Turabian bibliographical form. It is hoped that this information will be complete and sufficient enough to enable the reader to obtain the material listed. Naturally, some of the material is very obscure and difficult to locate. The library of the Center for Process Studies contains most of the secondary literature in this bibliography and now has a record of where the literature it does not own may be obtained. Inquiries about the location or availability of copies of secondary literature listed in this work may be directed to the editor and sent to the Center for Process Studies, 1325 N. College Ave., Claremont, CA 91711.

The second section includes a series of descriptors for the technical terms, persons, and disciplines appearing in the work. The use of this bibliography will be greatly enhanced by an understanding of the descriptor system and its organization. Each complete descriptor is separated from others by a semi-colon. Descriptors involving two or more words are *usually* listed with the noun first, followed by any modifiers. Examples are "abstraction, extensive", "God, primordial nature of", and "Whitehead, Alfred North; philosophical development of". Where

Whiteheadian vocabulary has normalized the order of a particular expression, a modifier may be listed and then indexed first, but in that case the index includes a cross reference under the noun too. An example of this is "perception in the mode of causal efficacy", where there is an entry under "causal efficacy", along with a cross reference to "perception". Where there are two or more modifiers for one main descriptor in the text, they are listed after a full colon—"Value: intrinsic, moral, and time".

The order in which the descriptors are listed in the text will tell the reader much about their relative importance in the work being described. There are three categories of descriptors used: technical terms, persons, and schools of thought or other disciplines. A glance at a large descriptor listing will easily reveal these divisions. Within each of the three divisions in the more lengthy listings, an attempt has been made to place at the beginning the ones most frequently used in the work being described.

In a few cases where a work could not be obtained for abstracting, its descriptors merely reflect its title. This should not be confused with other occurrences where the work's title in fact contained its most revealing description.

Sometimes when a work contained a lengthy discussion about a discipline per se, the order of the three kinds of descriptors was interrupted so that the discipline appeared first as the most important descriptor. The same is true if a person and the comparison of his or her thought with Whitehead's was the central topic; therefore, the person's name would appear first, followed by technical terms, other persons, and other disciplines.

Some explanation needs to be provided for the origination of the descriptors themselves. Very early we decided not to make all vocabulary in the secondary literature conform to a finite list of subject headings but whenever possible to use each author's own language in our descriptors and index. In this sense, our descriptor system and index is not a subject index but a compilation of the way Whitehead's conceptuality is actually being used and a catalog vocabulary generated through its use. Therefore, we list technical terms which Whitehead himself would never have used but which are meaningful to those interpreting his thought. This makes our index more lengthy but also more representative of contemporary Whiteheadian scholarship.

In examining all the literature written about Whitehead, the editors soon became aware of how much of it fell under the category of an interpretive introduction to Whitehead's thought. This genre of literature includes both short encyclopedia articles on Whitehead and larger works devoted to the exposition of Whitehead's philosophy (such as Sherburne's *A Key to Process and Reality.*) All of this kind of literature falls into one of two categories in the descriptor index—"process philosophy, summary of" or "Whitehead, Alfred North; introduction to his thought".

The third and optional section of each entry is the annotation. An annotation has been provided whenever the literature lent itself to a one or two sentence summary or when some editorial notation was called for. In the former case, the editors have tried to preserve the author's own language as much as possible and to excerpt a thesis statement from the work. In the latter case, since what appears as an annotation is not related to the author's own language, the annotation appears within a parenthesis.

In some cases the editors were inclined to forewarn the reader of faulty scholarship or complete misrepresentation of Whitehead. They have usually sublimated this urge to append critical comments to the annotations and have instead noted in a more neutral language that the author uses Whitehead for his or her own purposes. It would have been possible to include more critical editorial comments, but the diversity of interpretation of Whitehead and the freedom of the reader to draw his or her own conclusions seemed an even higher priority.

C. The Potential Increase by the One

The question arises, finally, whether a bibliography on and about Whitehead constitutes a very "Whiteheadian" enterprise. That is, among the ranks of Whiteheadians there is considerable discussion and fear that the study of Whitehead may be becoming so scholastic and preoccupied with the correct technical usage of Whitehead's conceptualities that it ceases to be processive. Certainly a bibliography on and about Whitehead would seem to be more fuel for the scholastic passion. More and more pedants could become involved in the heresy hunt for those who have not employed Whitehead's thought in a consistent manner. On the other hand, Whitehead himself was quick to point out that novelty depends on a certain amount of order, that adventure and zest arise from a new turn taken while treading the familiar path, and most importantly that generalization in scholarship depends upon a mastery of the rhythm of precision. Therefore, those of us who have invested so much time and energy on the preparation of this bibliography would like to envision it as a lure toward novel feelings. Some of these will arise through the legitimate scholastic task of filling in the gaps and inconsistencies in Whitehead's thought. Others will emerge through the incitement to employ Whitehead's thought to new disciplines, where old impasses await some new unifying vision.

As the reader uses this research tool for either of the purposes noted above or for gaining some general introduction to Whitehead and the employment of his thought in other disciplines, the various factions and rallying points in the Whiteheadian camp will come into clear relief in the secondary literature. This is as it should be. Whitehead himself contended that the real zest in all occasions of experience and interpretation comes from the intensity of heightened contrasts. We have taken the many contrasts we have located and have presented them within this one bibliography. We now reach our satisfaction in making the one available for the increase of the many.

Barry A. Woodbridge
January, 1977
Claremont, California

NOTES

1. The Center for Process Studies, located in Claremont, California, was

instituted by John Cobb in 1973 for this purpose. After visiting that Center and acquiring copies of many of its library resources, Jan Van der Veken organized the Documentation Center for Process Thought in Leuven, Belgium.

2. David R. Griffin and Gene Reeves, "Bibliography of Secondary Literature on Alfred North Whitehead." *Process Studies*, 1 (1971), 2–83.

SECTION II

PRIMARY BIBLIOGRAPHY

1   "Editorials." *Shirburnian Magazine.* Dorset, England: Sherborne School, 1879–1880. A number of unsigned editorials were written by Whitehead as editor of his school magazine.

2   "A Celebrity at Home. The Clerk of the Weather." *Cambridge Review,* 7, February 10, 1886, 202–203.

3   "Davy Jones." *Cambridge Review,* 7, May 12, 1886, 311–312.

4   "On the Motion of Viscous Incompressible Fluids. A Method of Approximation." *Quarterly Journal of Pure and Applied Mathematics,* 23, 1888, 78–93.

5   "Second Approximations to Viscous Fluid Motion. A Sphere Moving Steadily in a Straight Line." *Quarterly Journal of Pure and Applied Mathematics,* 23, 1888, 143–152.

5a   "A Visitation." *Cambridge Fortnightly,* 1, March 6, 1888, 81–83. This new addition to Whitehead's bibliography was discovered and contributed by Victor Lowe. In it Whitehead reflects on the way visitors are given a tour of Cambridge and in particular what he tells them about the religion of the chapel there.

6   "The Fens as Seen from Skates." *Cambridge Review,* 12, February 20, 1891, 212–213. (This addition to Whitehead's bibliography was contributed by Victor Lowe. He notes that it is signed "W" and most likely authentic, although its authenticity has not been confirmed by editorial correspondence between Whitehead and the editor.)

7   "Proposed Extension of the Paddocks." Co–authored with J. Ward and R. J. Glazebrook, March 4, 1895, and R. St. J. Parry, March 7, 1895. (This is a three part document concerning the land owned by Trinity College, Cambridge, which was printed but probably not published.)

8   "On Ideals: with Reference to the Controversy Concerning the Admission of Women to Degrees in the University." *Cambridge Review,* 17, May 14, 1896, 310–311. (Victor Lowe contributed this addition to the Whitehead bibliography. Although he notes that it is signed "W" and most likely authentic, its authenticity has not been confirmed by editorial correspondence between Whitehead and the editor.)

9   "The Geodesic Geometry of Surfaces in Non–Euclidean Space." *Proceedings of the London Mathematical Society,* 29, 1897–1898, 275–324.

10   *A Treatise on Universal Algebra.* Cambridge: Cambridge University Press, 1898.

Reviews

Couturant, Louis. *Revue de Métaphysique et de Morale*, 8, 1900, 323–362.

Mathews, G. B. *Nature*, 58, 1898, 385–386.

McFarlane, A. *Science*, 9, 1899, 324–328.

Vacca, Giovanni. *Revue de Mathematico*, 6, 1896–1899, 101–104.

11   "Sets of Operations in Relation to Groups of Finite Order." Abstract only. *Proceedings of the Royal Society of London*, 64, 1898–1899, 319–320.

12   "Memoir on the Algebra of Symbolic Logic." *American Journal of Mathematics*, 23, 1901, 139–165, 297–316.

13   "On Cardinal Numbers." *American Journal of Mathematics*, 24, 1902, 367–394. Except for some of the notes, Section III is, according to the Preface, "entirely due to Russell, and is written by him throughout."

14   "The Logic of Relations, Logical Substitution Groups, and Cardinal Numbers." *American Journal of Mathematics*, 25, 1903, 157–178.

15   "The University Library." Co–authored with Ernest W. Barns. *Cambridge Review*, 24, May 14, 1903, 295. (This addition, a letter to the editor of the *Cambridge Review*, was contributed by Victor Lowe.)

16   "Theorems on Cardinal Numbers." *American Journal of Mathematics*, 26, 1904, 31–32.

17   "Note." *Revue de Métaphysique et de Morale*, 13, 1905, 916–917. This was written to correct Boutroux's interpretation in the same issue of Whitehead's views on the relation of Logic to Analysis.

18   *The Axioms of Projective Geometry.* (*Cambridge Tracts in Mathematics and Mathematical Physics.*) Cambridge: Cambridge University Press, 1906. New York: Hafner Publishing Company, 1971.

18a   "Liberty and the Enfranchisement of Women." Cambridge: Cambridge Women's Suffrage Association, 1906. This new addition to the Whitehead bibliography was discovered in 1976 by John S. Slater of the University of Toronto, who noticed its listing in a secondhand bookseller's catalogue from England, obtained it, and brought it to the attention of Victor Lowe. It is a pamphlet of a remarkable address Whitehead gave on November 5, 1906 in which he pleads that progress in science, in thought, and in civilization is ultimately bound up with the enfranchisement of women in England.

19   "On Mathematical Concepts of the Material World." *Philosophical Transactions of the Royal Society of London*, series A, 205, 1906, 465–525.

20   *The Axioms of Descriptive Geometry.* (*Cambridge Tracts in Mathematics and Mathematical Physics.*) Cambridge: Cambridge University Press, 1907. New York: Hafner

Publishing Company, 1971. The Preface states that this tract is written in conjunction with *The Axioms of Projective Geometry*, 1906.

21   "Axioms of Geometry." In Division VII of article, "Geometry," *Encyclopedia Britannica*, 11, 1910, 730–736.

22   "Non–Euclidean Geometry." Co–authored with Bertrand Russell, in Division VI of article, "Geometry," in *Encyclopedia Britannica*, 11, 1910, 724–730.

23   *Principia Mathematica*. Volume 1. Co–authored with Bertrand Russell. Cambridge: Cambridge University Press, 1910, 1925. (Note: Since reviews of *Principia Mathematica* often reviewed more than one volume, reviews for all three volumes appear here under volume 1.)

Reviews

Bernstein, B. A. *Bulletin of the American Mathematical Society*, 32, 1926, 711–713.

Carnap, Rudolf. *Erkenntnis*, 2, 1931–1932, 73–75.

Church, Alonzo. *Bulletin of the American Mathematical Society*, 34, 1928, 237–240.

Cohen, Morris R. *Philosophical Review*, 21, 1912, 87–91.

Dufumier, H. *Revue de Métaphysique et de Morale*, 20, 1912, 538–566.

Jourdain, P. E. B. *Jahrbuch über die Fortschritte der Mathematik*, 41, 1910, 83–84.

Jourdain, P. E. B. *Cambridge Review*, 33, 1911, 7–9.

Jourdain, P. E. B. *Cambridge Review*, 33, 1911–1912, 381.

Jourdain, P. E. B. *Jahrbuch über die Fortschritte Mathematik*, 43, 1912, 93–94.

Jourdain, P. E. B. *Cambridge Review*, 34, 1913–1914, 435–436.

Jourdain, P. E. B. *Journal of the Indian Mathematical Society*, 5, 1913, 20–23.

Unsigned. *Athenaeum*, No. 4462, May 3, 1913, 497.

Translation

(Introduction only) *Einführung in die mathematische Logik* (die *Einleitung der 'Principia Mathematica'*). Trans. Hans Mokre. Munich: Drei Masken, 1932.

24   *An Introduction to Mathematics*. (Number 15 in the *Home University Library of Modern Knowledge*.) London: Williams and Norgate. New York: Henry Holt and Company, 1911. London: Oxford University Press, Inc., 1948, 1958, 1969.

Review

Unsigned. *Athenaeum*, 2, 1911, 48–49.

Translations

Einführung in die Mathematik. Trans. Berthold Schenker. Vienna: Humbolt, 1948.

Introduzione all matematica.   Trans.   Gian   Mario   Crespi.
Florence: Sansoni, 1953.

Muqaddima   li–al–riyadijat.   Trans.   Muhyi   al–Din   Yusuf.
Baghdad: Matb. al–Rabita, 1952.

Staerfraedin.   Trans.   Gudmundur   Finbogason.   Reykjavik:
Isafoldarprentsmidja H. F., 1931.

Sûgaku nyûmon.   Trans.   Kôno   Isaburô.   Tokyo: Sôgensha, 1953.

Vvedeniye v matematiku.   Petrograd, 1916.

Wstep do matematyki.   Trans.   Wladyslaw   Wojtowicz.   Warsaw:
E. Wende i Ska., undated.

25   "The Philosophy of Mathematics."   *Science Progress in the
Twentieth Century*, 5, October, 1910, 234–239.   (This new
addition to Whitehead's bibliography was discovered by Ivor
Grattan–Guinness and brought to the editor's attention by
Victor Lowe, who notes that it is an unfavorable review of
Hastings Berkeley's *Mysticism in Modern Mathematics*, and
the only review Whitehead is known to have published in his
life.)

26   "Mathematics."   *Encyclopedia Britannica*, 17, 1911, 878–883.

27   *Principia Mathematica.*   Volume 2.   Co–authored with Bertrand
Russell.   Cambridge: Cambridge University Press, 1912, 1927.

28   *Principia Mathematica.*   Volume 3.   Co–authored with Bertrand
Russell.   Cambridge: Cambridge University Press, 1912, 1927.

29   "The Place of Mathematics in a Liberal Education."   *Journal of
the Association of Teachers of Mathematics for the
Southeastern Part of England*, 1, 1912.

30   "The Principles of Mathematics in Relation to Elementary
Teaching."   *Proceedings of the Fifth International Congress of
Mathematicians.*   Cambridge,   August   22–28,   1912,   2,
Cambridge: Cambridge University Press, 1913, 449–454.
Translation
"Les principes mathématiques et l'enseignement élémentaire."
L'Enseignment Mathematique, 15, 1913, 111–112.

31   "Presidential Address to the London Branch of the Mathematical
Association."   *Mathematical Gazette*, 7, March, 1913, 87–94.

32   "Report of the Council of the Royal Society of London."
Year–Book of the Royal Society, 1914, 177–187.

33   "Report of the Council of the Royal Society of London."
Year–Book of the Royal Society, 1915, 176–185.

34   "Space, Time, and Relativity."   *Proceedings of the Aristotelian
Society*, 16, 1915–1916, 104–129.

35   "The Aims of Education. A Plea for Reform."   *Mathematical
Gazette*, 8, January, 1916, 191–203.

36   "The Organisation of Thought."   *Report of the 86th Meeting of
the British Association for the Advancement of Science*, 1916,
355–365.

37   "La Théorie Relationniste de L'Espace." *Revue de Métaphysique et de Morale*, 23, May, 1916, 423–454.

38   "Letter to the Editor." *Mathematical Gazette*, 9, January, 1917, 14. This letter, dated November, 1916, is signed on behalf of the Mathematical Association by A. N. Whitehead, President, and A. W. Siddons, Chairman of the Teaching Committee.

39   *The Organisation of Thought, Educational and Scientific.* London: Williams and Norgate, 1917. Philadelphia: J. B. Lippincott Company, 1917.

Reviews

Jourdain, P. E. B. *Mind*, 27, 1918, 224–247.

Keyser, C. J. *Science*, 47, 1918, 171–173.

40   "Technical Education and Its Relation to Science and Literature." *Technical Journal*, 10, January, 1917, 59–74.

41   "Graphical Solution for High–Angle Fire." *Proceedings of the Royal Society of London*, Series A, 94, 1918, 301–307.

42   "Address on Founder's Day." (At Stanley Technical Trade School, South Norwood, London, February, 1, 1919.) South Norwood, S. E., England: Coventry and Son, 1919. "Printed for private circulation only."

43   *An Enquiry Concerning the Principles of Natural Knowledge.* Cambridge: Cambridge University Press, 1919, 1925.

Reviews

Broad, C. D. *Hibbert Journal*, 18, 1920, 397–406, and *Mind*, 29, 1920, 216–231.

Costello, H. T. *Journal of Philosophy*, 17, 1920, 326–334.

Hicks, G. D. *Nature*, 105, 1920, 446–448.

De Laguna, T. *Philosophical Review*, 29, 1920, 269–275.

Translation

Ricerca sui principi della conoscenza naturale. Trans. Giovanni Gignami. Milan: Lampugnanie Nigri Editore, 1972.

44   "Fundamental Principles in Education." *Report of the 87th Meeting of the British Association for the Advancement of Science*, Bournemouth, 1919, 361. (Whitehead's opening remarks before the section on education are printed in abridged form here.)

45   "A Revolution in Science." *Nation*, 26, November 15, 1919, 232–233. Also in *Educational Review*, 59, 1920, 148–153. (This is a discussion of the confirmation of Einstein's prediction about the path of light waves in a gravitational field, as evidenced by recent photographs of the eclipse of the sun.)

46   "Symposium: Time, Space, and Material: Are They, and if so in What Sense, the Ultimate Data of Science?" Co–authored with Sir Oliver Lodge, J. W. Nicholson, Henry Head, Mrs. Adrian Stephen, and H. Wildon Carr. *Aristotelian Society, Supplementary Volume 2*, "Problems of Science and

Philosophy," 1919, 44–108. Pages 44–57 are Whitehead's contribution.

47 *The Concept of Nature.* Cambridge: Cambridge University Press, 1920, 1926, 1930, 1955, 1964, 1971. (This material was originally delivered as the Tarner Lectures at Trinity College in November, 1919.)

Reviews

Birkhoff, G. D. *Bulletin of the American Mathematical Society*, 28, 1922, 219–221.

Carr H. Wildon. *Philosophy Magazine*, 40, 1920, 389–392.

Crespi, G. M. *Rivista Critica di Storia della filosofia*, 6, 1951, 237–240.

Driesch, Hans. *Kant Studien*, 26, 1921, 204–205.

McGilvary, E. B. *Philosophical Review*, 30, 1921, 500–507.

Selvaggi, F. *Gregorianum*, 31, 1950, 313–314.

Taylor, A. E. *Mind*, 30, 1921, 76–83.

Watson, J. A. *Actes 8 Congress of International Philosophy*, 1936, 903–909.

Translations

El concepto de naturaleza. Trans. J. Díaz. Madrid: Gredos, 1968.

Il Concetto della natura. Trans. Massimo Meyer. Turin: Einaudi, 1948.

48 "Einstein's Theory; An Alternative Suggestion." *London Times Educational Supplement*, February 12, 1920, 83.

49 "Report of a Committee: Appointed by the Prime Minister to Inquire into the Position of Classics in the Educational System of the United Kingdom." Co-authored with Marquess of Crewe and other members of the committee. London: His Majesty's Stationery Office, 1921.

50 "Science in General Education." *Proceedings of the Second Congress of Universities of the Empire.* London: G. Bell & Sons, 1921, 31–39.

51 "Discussion: The Idealistic Interpretation of Einstein's Theory." Co-authored with H. Wildon Carr, T. P. Nunn, and Dorothy Wrinch. *Proceedings of the Aristotelian Society*, 22, 1921–1922, 123–138. (Whitehead's criticism of Carr's contribution appears on pages 130–134.)

52 "The Philosophical Aspects of the Principle of Relativity." *Proceedings of the Aristotelian Association*, 22, 1921–1922, 215–223.

53 *The Principle of Relativity, with Applications to Physical Science.* Cambridge: Cambridge University Press, 1922.

Reviews

Broad, C. B. *Mind*, 32, 1923, 211–219.

Sanger, Charles Percy. *New Statesman*, 20, 1923, 546–548.

Unsigned. *Nature,* 3, 1923, 697–699.

54   "The Rhythm of Education." London: Christophers, 1922. (This address, originally delivered to the Training College Association, was later incorporated as chapter 2 in *The Aims of Education and Other Essays.*)

55   "Some Principles of Physical Science." Lecture in honor of Professor Charlotte Angas Scott. Bryn Mawr College, April 18, 1922. (This address was also published as chapter 4 of *The Principle of Relativity.*)

56   "Uniformity and Contingency." *Proceedings of the Aristotelian Society,* 23, 1922–1923, 1–18. (Whitehead originally delivered this as an inaugural address as President of the Aristotelian Society, November 6, 1922.)

57   "The First Physical Synthesis." *Science and Civilization.* Edited by F. S. Marvin. London: Oxford University Press, 1923, 161–178.

58   "Letter to the Editor." *New Statesman,* 20, February 17, 1923, 568. (This is a reply to Charles Percy Sanger's review of *The Principle of Relativity* in *New Statesman,* 20, February 10, 1923, 546–548.)

59   "The Place of Classics in Education." *Hibbert Journal,* 21, 1923, 248–261. Also in *The Aims of Education and Other Essays,* chapter 5.

60   "The Rhythmic Claims of Freedom and Discipline." *Hibbert Journal,* 21, 1923, 657–668. Also in *The Aims of Education and Other Essays,* chapter 3.

61   "Symposium—The Problem of Simultaneity: Is There a Paradox in the Principle of Relativity in Regard to the Relation of Time Measured and Time Lived?" Co–authored with H. Wildon Carr and R. A. Sampson. *Aristotelian Society, Supplementary Volume 3. Relativity, Logic, and Mysticism,* 1923, 15–41.

62   "The Importance of Friendly Relations Between England and the United States." *Phillips Bulletin,* 19, 1925, 15–18. (This was originally delivered as an address at Phillips Academy in Andover, Massachusetts, February 22, 1925.)

63   "Religion and Science." *Atlantic Monthly,* 136, 1925, 200–207. Also in *Science and the Modern World,* chapter 12.

64   *Science and the Modern World.* Lowell Institute Lectures, 1925. New York: Macmillan Company, 1925. Cambridge: Cambridge University Press, 1926. New York: The Free Press, 1967.
      Reviews
      Alexander, S. *Nature,* 117, 1926, 847–850.
      Braithwaite, R. B. *Mind,* 35, 1926, 489–500.
      Dewey, John. *New Republic,* 45, 1926, 360.
      Henderson, L. J. *Quarterly Review of Biology,* 1, 1926, 289–294.
      Hummel, C. *Neue Schweizer Rundschau,* 20, 1952, 434–437.

Read, H. *Criterion*, 4, 1926, 581–586.

Russell, B. *Nation and Athenaeum*, 39, 1926, 206–207.

Smith, G. B. *Journal of Religion*, 6, 1926, 308–315.

Stebbing, L. S. *Journal of Philosophical Studies*, 1, 1926, 380–385.

Swabey, W. C. *Philosophical Review*, 35, 1926, 272–279.

Translations

De natuurwetenschap in de moderne wereld. Trans. Jan van Rheenen. Utrecht–Antwerp: Aula–Boeken, 1959.

"Die Abstrakion" in Max Bense, *Zwischen beiden Kriegen: Die Philosophie.* Frankfurt: Suhrkamp Verlag, 1951.

"Gott" in Arthur Hübscher, *Denker Unserer Zeit.* Munich: Piper Verlag, 1956.

Gwahag gwa hyeondae. Trans. Kim Chin–sup. Seoul: Eulyoo, 1956.

Kagaku to kindai sekai. Trans. Ueda Yasuharu and Murakami Shikô. Tokyo: Sôgensha, 1954.

La ciencia y el mundo moderno. Trans. Marina Ruiz Lago and J. Rovira Armengol. Buenos Aires: Losada, 1949.

La science et le monde moderne. Trans. A. d'Ivery and P. Hollard. Paris: Payot, 1930.

La scienza e il mondo moderno. Trans. Antonio Banfi. Milan: Bompiani, 1945. (2nd edition) Edited with an introduction by E. Paci, 1959.

"Tzu–jan chih wei yu–chi–t'i." (Nature as Organism.) trans. Ts'ai Yuan–huang. *Chinese Cultural Renaissance Monthly*, 8, 1975, 35–40.

Wissenschaft und moderne Welt. Trans. Gertrud Tschiedel and Francois Bondy. Zürich: Morgarten, Conzett and Huber, 1949.

65 "The Education of an Englishman." *Atlantic Monthly*, 138, 1926, 192–198. (Whitehead reflects on his years at Sherborne School.)

66 "Principia Mathematica." *Mind*, 35, 1926, 130. (Whitehead wrote this letter to the editor, clarifying that all revisions and additions to the second edition of *Principia Mathematica* were undertaken by Bertrand Russell alone.)

67 *Religion in the Making.* Lowell Institute Lectures, 1926. New York: Macmillan Company, 1926. Cambridge: Cambridge University Press, 1926, 1936.

Reviews

Moore, G. E. *Nation and Athenaeum*, 40, 1927, 664.

Stebbing, L. S. *Journal of Philosophical Studies*, 2, 1927, 234–239.

Taylor, A. E. *Dublin Review*, 181, 1927, 17–41.

Tennant, F. R. *Mind*, 36, 1927, 221–228.

Wieman, H. N. *Journal of Religion*, 7, 1927, 487–490.

Wieman, H. N. and Miller, D. S. *New Republic*, 49, 1927, 361–363.

Translations

Il divenire della religione. Trans. F. Cafaro. Turin: Paravia, 1963.

La devenir de la religion. Trans. Philippe Devaux. Paris: Montaigne, 1939.

68   "Time." *Proceedings of the Sixth International Congress of Philosophy.* New York and London: Longmans, Green, & Co., 1927, 59–64. (Whitehead discusses the problems of simultaneity, objective immortality, and the epochal character of time.)

69   "England and the Narrow Seas." *Atlantic Monthly*, 139, 1927, 791–798.

70   *Symbolism, Its Meaning and Effect.* Barbour–Page Lectures, University of Virginia, 1927. New York: Macmillan Co., 1927. London: Cambridge University Press, 1928. New York: G. P. Putnam's Sons, 1959.

Reviews

Carbonara, C. *Logos*, 13, 1930, 373–376.

Hartshorne, Charles. *Hound & Horn*, 1, 1927, 148–152.

Murphy, A. E. *Journal of Philosophy*, 26, 1929, 489–498.

Ratner, J. *New Republic*, 55, 1928, 23–24.

Russell, L. J. *Journal of Philosophical Studies*, 3, 1928, 527–530.

Smart, H. R. *Philosophical Review*, 37, 1928, 388–389.

Weiss, Paul. *Nation*, 126, 1928, 128–129.

Translations

El simbolismo, su significado y efecto. Mexico: Unam, 1969.

Il simbolismo, suo significato e sue consequenze. Trans. F. Cafaro. Turin: Paravia, 1963.

Shôchô sayô; kaka no kenkyû; Yoken ni tsuite. Trans. Ichii Saburô. Tokyo: Kawade Shobo, 1955.

71   "Universities and Their Function." *Atlantic Monthly*, 141, 1928, 638–644. Also in *Harvard Business School Alumni Bulletin*, 5, 1928, 9–14; *The Aims of Education and Other Essays*, chapter 7. (This was delivered at the meeting of the American Association of the Collegiate Schools of Business, May 1927.)

72   *The Aims of Education and Other Essays.* New York: Macmillan Company, 1929. London: Williams & Northgate, 1929, 1936.

Reviews

Fisher, H. A. L. *Nation and Athenaeum*, 45, 1929, 401.

Gauss, Christian. *New Republic*, 59, 1929, 157–158.

Translations

Gyoyug eui mogjeog. Trans. Yu Hyeong–chin. Seoul: Eulyoo, 1960.

I Fini dell'educazione e altri saggi. Trans. F. Cafaro. Florence: La Nuova Italia, 1960.

Kyôiko no mokuteki. Trans. Motono Yoshikatsu. Tokyo: Kyoiko Shorin, 1955.

Os fins da educačao e outros ensaios. Trans. Leonidas Gontijo de Carvalho. São Paulo: Ed. Nacional, 1969.

73 *The Function of Reason.* Louis Clark Vanuxem Foundation Lectures, Princeton University, March, 1929. Princeton: Princeton University Press, 1929. Boston: Beacon Press, 1958.

Review

Aaron, R. I. *Mind*, 39, 1930, 488–492.

Translations

Enzo Paci (p. 1–7) included in *Il pensiero scientifico contemporaneo*, Florence: Sansoni, 1950.

La funzione della ragione. Trans. F. Cafaro. Florence: La Nuova Italia, 1958.

74 *Process and Reality. An Essay in Cosmology.* Gifford Lectures Delivered at the University of Edinburgh During the Session 1927–1928. New York: Macmillan Company, 1929. Cambridge: Cambridge University Press, 1929. New York: Social Science Bookstore, 1941. New York: Harper & Bros., 1960. (A corrected edition of *Process and Reality*, complete with notes and extended index, has been prepared by David Griffin, Ivor Leclerc, and Donald Sherburne. Publication is forthcoming from The Free Press, 1977.)

Reviews

Belgion, M. *Criterion*, 9, 1929–1930, 557–563.

Carr, H. W. *Personalist*, 11, 1930, 157–163.

Fjellman, C. *Lutheran Quarterly*, 13, 1961, 371–372.

Guzzo, A. *Filosofia*, 16, 1965, 821.

Moore, M. H. *Philosophical Review*, 40, 1931, 265–275.

Murphy, A. E. *Christian Centenial*, 47, 1930, 303–304.

Nagel, E. *Symposium*, i, 1930, 392–398.

Northrop, F. S. C. *Saturday Review of Literature*, 6, 1930, 621.

Stebbing, L. S. *Mind*, 39, 1930, 466–475.

Taylor, A. E. *Theology*, 31, 1930, 66–79.

Wieman, H. N. *Journal of Religion*, 10, 1930, 137–139.

Translations

Il processo e la realta. Trans. N. Bosco. Milan: Bompiani, 1965.

Proceso y realidad. Trans. J. Rovira Armengol. Buenos Aires: Losada, 1956.

75 "An Address." Delivered at the Celebration of the Fiftieth

Anniversary of the Founding of Radcliffe College. *Radcliffe Quarterly*, 14, 1930, 1–5.

76   "Prefatory Note." *The Practice of Philosophy.* Susanne K. Langer. New York: Henry Holt & Company, 1930, vii.

77   "On Foresight." *Business Adrift.* W. B. Donham. London: George Routledge & Sons, 1931, xi–xxix. (These introductory remarks were originally delivered at the Harvard Graduate School of Business Administration.)

78   "Objects and Subjects." *Philosophical Review*, 41, 1932, 130–146. Also in *Proceedings & Addresses, American Philosophical Association*, 5, 1931, 130–146; *Adventures of Ideas*, chapter 11. (This was originally delivered as Whitehead's presidential address at the Eastern Division of the American Philosophical Association meeting in New Haven, Connecticut, December, 1931.)

79   *Symposium in Honor of the Seventieth Birthday of Alfred North Whitehead.* Cambridge, Massachusetts: Harvard University Press, 1932. (Whitehead responds to the presentations about him on pages 22–29.)

80   *Adventures of Ideas.* New York: Macmillan Company, 1933. Cambridge: Cambridge University Press, 1933, 1938.

Reviews

Agosti, V. *Giornale di Metafisica*, 18, 1963, 294–296.

Becker, C. *American Historical Review*, 39, 1933, 87–89.

Burns, C. D. *International Journal of Ethics*, 44, 1933, 166–168.

Cohen, M. R.   *Yale Review*, 23, 1933, 173–177; enlarged in Cohen, *Faith of a Liberal*, Holt, 1946, Ch. 44.

De Saint–Seine, P. *Archiv fuer Philosophie*, 10, 1934, 65–76.

Dewey, J. *New Republic*, 74, 1933, 285–286.

Emmet, D. M. *Hibbert Journal*, 32, 1934, 175–183.

Garrison, W. E. *Christian Centenial*, 50, 1933, 424–425.

Hooper, S. E. *Philosophy*, 8, 1933, 326–344.

Huxley, J. *Spectator*, 150, 1933, 611.

Translations

Abenteuer der Ideen. Trans. E. Bubers. Frankfurt: Suhrkamp, 1971.

Aventuras de las ideas. Trans. Carlos Botet. Barcelona: Miguza, 1947.

Aventure d'Idee. Trans. G. Gnoli. Milan: Bompiani, 1961.

Shôchô sayô; Kako no kenkyû; Yoken mi tsuite . Trans. Ichii Saburô. Tokyo: Kawade Shobô, 1955 (Includes "Foresight" bound with the above listed translation of Science and the Modern World).

81   "The Study of the Past—Its Uses and Its Dangers." *Harvard Business Review*, 11, 1933, 436–444. Also in *Educational Record*, 14, 1933, 454–467. (This was originally delivered at a

meeting commemorating the twenty–fifth anniversary of the founding of Harvard Business School, April 13, 1953.)

82 "Foreword." *The Farther Shorne: An Anthology of World Opinion on the Immortality of the Soul*, with a preface to each selection by the editors. Edited by Nathaniel Edward Griffin and Lawrence Hunt. Boston and New York: Houghton Mifflin Co., 1934, xvii. (This addition to Whitehead's bibliography was contributed by Victor Lowe.)

83 "Foreword." *A System of Logic*. Willard Van Orman Quine. Cambridge, Massachusetts: Harvard University Press, 1934, ix–x. London: Oxford University Press, 1934.

84 "Indication, Classes, Numbers, Validation." *Mind*, 43, 1934, 281–297. (A corrigenda to the above appears in the same volume on page 543.)

85 *Nature and Life.* Chicago: University of Chicago Press, 1934. Cambridge: Cambridge University Press, 1934. Also in *Modes of Thought*, chapters 7 and 8.

Reviews

Hooper, S. E. *Philosophy*, 9, 1934, 465–472.

Murphy, A. E. *Journal of Philosophy*, 31, 1934, 329.

Romanell, P. *Journal of Philosophy*, 41, 1944, 585–586.

Schiller, F. C. S. *Mind*, 44, 1935, 245–246.

Translations

Natura e vita. Trans. G. M. Crespi. Milan: Bocca, 1951.

Naturaleza y vida. Trans. Risieri Frondizi. Buenos Aires: Universidad de Buenos Aires, 1941.

86 "The Aim of Philosophy." *Harvard Alumni Bulletin*, 38, 1935, 234–235. Also in *Modes of Thought* as the epilogue.

87 "In Memoriam." *Bernard Bosanquet and His Friends.* Edited by J. H. Muirhead. London: George Allen & Unwin, Ltd., 1935, 316.

88 "Minute on the Life and Services of Professor James Haughton Woods." Co–authored with Ralph Barton Perry and other members of the Harvard arts and sciences faculty. *Harvard University Gazette*, 30, 1935, 153–155.

89 "Harvard: The Future." *Atlantic Monthly*, 158, 1936, 260–270.

Translation

"Harvard: El futoro." *Revista de filosofia de la Universidad de Costa Rica*, 2, 1961, 45–46. Trans. Ligia Herrera.

90 "Letter to Charles Hartshorne." *Alfred North Whitehead: Essays on His Philosophy.* Edited by George L. Kline. Englewood Cliffs, New Jersey: Prentice–Hall, 1963, 196–199. Also in *Whitehead's Philosophy: Selected Essays, 1935–1970.* Edited by Charles Hartshorne. Lincoln, Nebraska: University of Nebraska Press, 1972, ix–xii. (This is a personal letter which Whitehead wrote to Charles Hartshorne on January 2, 1936.)

91   "Memories." *Atlantic Monthly*, 157, 1936, 672–679.

92   "Remarks." *Philosophical Review*, 46, 1937, 178–186. Also in *Proceedings & Addresses, American Philosophical Association*, 10, 1936, 178–186. (Whitehead's response here was to John Dewey, A. P. Ushenko, and Gregory Vlastos, members of Eastern Division of the American Philosophical Association's symposium on Whitehead's philosophy, held at Harvard on December 29, 1936.)

93   *Modes of Thought*. Six lectures delivered at Wellesley College, 1937–1938 and two lectures at the University of Chicago, 1933. New York: Macmillan Company, 1938. Cambridge: Cambridge University Press, 1938.

Reviews

DeBurgh, W. G. *Philosophy*, 14, 1939, 205–211.

Emmet, D. M. *Mind*, 48, 1939, 385–386.

Hartshorne, C. *Review of Religion*, 3, 1939, 494–496.

Schermerhorn, R. A. *Christian Century*, 55, 1938, 1506.

Tsanoff, R. A. *Philosophical Review*, 49, 1940, 246–265.

Wieman, H. N. *Journal of Religion*, 19, 1939, 237–239.

Translations

I modi del pensiero. Trans. Pier Aldu Rovatti. Rome: Il Saggiatore, 1972.

Modos de pensamiento. Trans. Joaquain Xirau. Buenos Aires: Losada, 1944.

94   "An Appeal to Sanity." *Atlantic Monthly*, 163, 1939, 309–320. (Whitehead discusses international foreign policy, with special reference to that of England, central Europe, and Palestine.)

95   "John Dewey and His Influence." *The Philosophy of John Dewey*. Edited by Paul Arthur Schilpp. Evanston and Chicago: Northwestern University Press, 1939, 477–478.

96   "The Issue: Freedom." *Boston Daily Globe*, December 24, 1940, 12. (This is a letter to the editor of the *Daily Globe*.)

97   "Autobiographical Notes." *The Philosophy of Alfred North Whitehead*. Edited by Paul Arthur Schilpp. Evanston and Chicago: Northwestern University Press, 1941, 1–14. Cambridge: Cambridge University Press, 1943. New York: Tudor Publishing Company, 1951.

98   "Immortality." The Ingersoll Lecture for 1941. *The Philosophy of Alfred North Whitehead*. Edited by Paul Arthur Schilpp. Evanston and Chicago: Northwestern University Press, 1941, 682–700. Cambridge: Cambridge University Press, 1943. New York: Tudor Publishing Company, 1951. (This sermon was originally delivered at the Harvard memorial Church on April 22, 1941. Also in *Harvard Divinity School Bulletin*, 39, 1941–1942, 5–21.)

Translation

"Immortalité." *La Philosophique organique de Whitehead.* Trans. F. Cesselin. Paris: Presses Universitaires de France, 1950, 225–226.

99 "Mathematics and the Good." *The Philosophy of Alfred North Whitehead.* Edited by Paul Arthur Schilpp. Evanston and Chicago: Northwestern University Press, 1941, 666–681. Cambridge: Cambridge University Press, 1943. New York: Tudor Publishing Company, 1951. (This was originally delivered at Harvard, December 15, 1939.)

Translation

"Les Mathematiques et le bien." *La philosophique organique de Whitehead.* trans. F. Cesselin. Paris: Presses Universitaires de France, 1950, 220–225.

100 "Statesmanship and Specialized Learning." *Proceedings of the American Academy of Arts and Sciences,* 75, 1942, 1–5. Also in revised form as "The Problem of Reconstruction" in *Atlantic Monthly,* 169, 1942, 172–175.

101 "Preface." "The Organization of a Story and a Tale." William Morgan. *Journal of American Folklore,* 58, 1945, 169. (Whitehead responds to Morgan's use of concepts from *Process and Reality* to explain the growth of a folk–tale.)

102 "James Haughton Woods." *Undercurrents in Greek Philosophy.* James Haughton Woods. Privately printed pamphlet, 1945, 5. (This addition to Whitehead's bibliography was contributed by Victor Lowe. He notes that although it contains no place of publication, a copy of it is in the collection of James Haughton Woods' papers at the Harvard University Archives.)

103 "The Wit and Wisdom of Whitehead." A. H. Johnson. *Philosophy of Science,* 13, 1946, 223–251. (Pages 224–251 contain brief quotations from Whitehead about the nature and function of philosophy, as well as comments about science, morality, social philosophy, the philosophy of history, religion, and education.)

104 *Essays in Science and Philosophy.* New York: Philosophical Library, 1947. London: Rider & Company, 1948.

Reviews

Cesselin, F. *Revue de Métaphysique et de Morale,* 53, 1948, 81–84.

Hansen, H. *Survey Graphic,* 36, 1947, 300–302.

Hooper, S. E. *Philosophy,* 23, 1948, 89–93.

Kattsoff, L. O. *Philosophy and Phenomenological Research,* 9, 1948, 334–346.

Lowe, V. *Cronos,* 1, 1947, 36–38.

Murphy, A. E. *Philosophical Review,* 56, 1947, 709–711.

Premartin, J. *Revista de Filosofia,* 7, 1948, 593–604.

Whittaker, E. *Nature,* 160, 1947, 415–416.

Translations

"Hua–te–hai Tzu–chuan."   *Ta–hsüeh Sheng–huo* (University Life), 8, 1941, 23–30.   Trans. Yü Yung–chia.

Philosophie und Mathematik.   Trans.   Felizitas   Ortner. Vienna–Stuttgart: Humboldt, 1949.

Scienze e filosofia.   Trans. I. Bona.   Milan: Il Saggiatore, 1966.

105   *The Wit and Wisdom of Whitehead.*   Edited by A. H. Johnson. Boston: Beacon Press, 1947.   Toronto, Canada: S. J. Reginald Saunders & Company, Ltd., 1947.   (Pages 35–102 contain a revised collection of the quotations from Whitehead originally published in the author's article under the same title, *Philosophy of Science*, 13, 1946, 223–251.

Reviews

Gross, M. W.   *Journal of Philosophy*, 45, 1948, 214–216.

Hartshorne, C.   *Christian Register*, 126, 1947, 446.

SECTION III

SECONDARY BIBLIOGRAPHY

106   Abbagnano, Nicola. "Whitehead." *Storia della Filosofia*, 3, 1950, 611–616.

Whitehead, Alfred North, evaluation of; pantheism.

Whitehead's philosophy may be categorized as a romantic pantheism.

107   Abbagnano, Nicola. "Whitehead e il concetto della ragione." *Revue Internationale de Philosophie*, 15, 1961, 204–216.

The *Function of Reason*; reason; philosophy, speculative; Bergson, Henri; Huxley, T. H.; biology; neo–vitalism.

(The author presents an expository and critical commentary on Whitehead's *The Function of Reason*.)

108   Abe, Masao. "Mahayana Buddhism and Whitehead: A View by a Lay Student of Whitehead's Philosophy." *Philosophy East and West*, 25, 1975, 415–428.

God: as principle of limitation, transcendence of, as nontemporal; dualism; conjunction, of disjunction; emptiness; dependent coorigination; Nagarjuna; Buddhism, Mahayana.

Creative dialogue between Whiteheadians and Mahayana Buddhists must take account of deep structural differences between the two systems, notably dualistic implications following from Whitehead's distinctions between God and the world.

109   Actis, Perinetti L. "Filosofia e scienza nella 'filosofia natura' di Whitehead." *Filosofia*, 3, 1952, 251–266.

Philosophy: of nature, of science; space–time; mathematics.

110   Actis, Perinetti L. *Cosmologia e assiologia in Whitehead. Studi e Ricerche di Storia della Filosofia*, number 12. Turin, 1954.

Empiricism; rationalism; metaphysics, and cosmology; cosmology, and theory of values; Descartes; Kant.

111   Actis, Perinetti L. "Studi su Whitehead." *Filosofia*, 5, 1954, 191–214.

Experience; epistemology; cosmology; feelings, theory of; symbolic reference.

112   Actis, Pernetti Ludovico. "Cosmologia e Assiologia in Whitehead." *Filosofia*, 5, 1954, 658–674.

Cosmology; value; beauty; truth; aesthetics, and religion; dualism, metaphysical; Descartes, Rene; Locke, John; Hume, David; empiricism; rationalism.

113   Actis, Perinetti L. "Whitehead." *Encyclopedia Filosofica*, 1957–1958, Volume 4, 1751–1756.

Process philosophy, summary of.

114   Adell, Arvid W.   "The Transcendence of God in Whitehead's
        Metaphysics."   Unpublished   Ph.D.   dissertation,   Boston
        University, 1970.

        God: transcendence of, primordial nature of, functions of, and
        order, and categoreal scheme, Whitehead without; Plato;
        Aristotle; theology.

        Since the primordial nature of God does not receive conceptual
        experience from its physical relationship to the world, it
        violates the categoreal scheme.

115   Adhin, Herman S.   *Whitehead en de wereld.   Een
        mathematico–logische, natuur–en cultuurfilosofische inleiding.*
        Delft, Belgium: Waltman, 1963.

        Philosophy, speculative; bifurcation, of nature; education; logic;
        mathematics.

        (This work sketches the main aspects of Whitehead's work on
        logic, mathematics, philosophy of science, and metaphysics; and
        studies the influence of Whitehead's thinking in England, the
        United States, and other countries. It stems from the author's
        dissertation written in 1963 at Delft.)

116   Agar, W. E.   "Whitehead's Philosophy of Organism: An
        Introduction for Biologists."   *Quarterly Review of Biology*, 11,
        1936, 16–34.

        Process philosophy, summary of; mind–body problem;
        causation: final, efficient; nexūs; biology.

        Features of process philosophy which are particularly significant
        for theoretical biology include the concept of the uniformity of
        experience as the basis of reality, the concept of efficient and
        final causation, and the notion of nexūs.

117   Agar, W. E.   "The Concept of Purpose in Biology."   *The
        Quarterly Review of Biology*, 13, 1938, 255–273.

        Purpose; evolution; causation, teleological; process, microscopic
        and macroscopic; cells; Gestalt; Darwin, Charles; biology.

        Biology must account not only for the single purpose of a
        single agent, but also for the purposes of nexūs. This entails
        consideration of both short and long–range goals.

118   Agar, W. E.   *A Contribution to the Theory of the Living
        Organism.*   Victoria, Australia: Melbourne University Press,
        1951.

        Evolution: and genetics, and natural selection, and embryonic
        development, and human existence; agency; nature, and
        subjectivity; organism; whole and part; cells; eye; Lamarck, J.
        B.; Darwin, Charles; biology; psychology: physiological, Gestalt;
        physiology.

        Living organisms, including those which are constituents or
        sub–agents of larger organisms, can be characterized as
        perceptive and purposive agents. The Lamarckian theory of
        evolution accounts for the causal factor in evolution, but

cannot account for organisms directing their actions to goals which have remote biological consequences.

119   Agassi, Joseph. "Positive Evidence in Science and Technology." *Philosophy of Science*, 32, 1970, 261–270.

Induction; method, scientific; Popper, Karl; Kant, Immanuel; philosophy, of science; sociology; positivism.

We may project the future success of science on the basis that the success is built into our social institutions and is partially safeguarded by institutions.

120   Akeley, Lewis E. "Wholes and Prehensive Unities for Physics and Philosophy." *Journal of Philosophy*, 24, 1927, 589–608.

Wholes; eternal objects: as abstractive hierarchy, as universals, as relational, relational essence of; unity, prehensive; physics.

Application of Whitehead's principles of abstraction shows that in every whole there is a uniform significance for the universals that characterize it. The relational essence of these universals yields possibilities for human creation of new wholes.

121   Al–Azm, Sadik J. "Whitehead's Notions of Order and Freedom." *Personalist*, 48, 1967, 579–591.

Freedom and determinism; subjective aim, initial phase of; order; disorder; novelty; causa sui.

Since the initial aim of an occasion contains all which the occasion must become, there is no genuine freedom in Whitehead's philosophy.

122   Alderisio, F. "Il realismo e il razionalismo di Whitehead." *Saggi di Filosofia contemporanea*, 1952.

Realism; rationalism.

123   Alexander, Samuel. "Some Explanation." *Mind*, 30, 1921, 409–428. A translation is published in *Neue Auslese aus dem Schrifttum der Gegenwart*, 3, 1948, 85–88.

Metaphysics: as science, as descriptive, as concrete; space–time: as motion, as events; relations; mind–body problem; enjoyment; God, as ideal; Alexander, Samuel, and Whitehead; Broad, C. D.; Whitehead, Alfred North, method of; metaphysics; physics.

(In the process of explaining his philosophy in light of C. D. Broad's criticism, Alexander elucidates his methodological differences from Whitehead.)

124   Alexander, Samuel. "Qualities." *Encyclopedia Brittanica*, fourteenth edition, 18, 1937, 810–813.

Qualities: primary, secondary, tertiary, emergence of, reality of, interrelationships of; subjectivity; space–time; sensible; valuation; Locke, John; Berkeley, George; James, William; Kant, Immanuel; Alexander, Samuel.

The philosophical problem of qualities concerns differentiation of types of qualities, the interrelationships between the types, and the mode of reality ascribed to each.

125   Alexander, Samuel. "Alfred North Whitehead." *Neue Auslese aus dem Schrifttum der Gegenwart*, 3, 1948, 85–88.
Whitehead, biography of.

126   Allan, George. "A Whiteheadian Approach to the Philosophy of History." Unpublished Ph.D. dissertation, Yale University, 1963.
History, nature of; philosophy, of history.

A Whiteheadian approach to history demonstrates the reality of historical transition; it indicates the extent, limits, and objective reality of causal influence; and it argues that the objects exhibited by history can most fruitfully be understood and explained in terms of an analysis of the structural and genetic characteristics of social order.

127   Allan, George. "The Aims of Societies and the Aims of God." *Journal of the American Academy of Religion*, 35, 1967, 149–158. The article is republished in *Process Philosophy and Christian Thought*. Edited by Delwin Brown, Ralph E. James, and Gene Reeves. Indianapolis: Bobbs–Merrill Company, Inc., 1971, 464–474.

Aims: societal, institutional, individual, divine; order: social, teleological, axiological; institutions; norms, transpersonal; God: as purposive, as acting in history; theology; religion; sociology.

The interrelationships between institutional and individual aims indicate a corollary interrelationship between salvation of the individual and of the social order.

128   Allan, George, and Allshouse, Merle. "Current Issues in Process Theology: Some Reflections." *Christian Scholar*, 50, 1967, 167–175.

Philosophy and theology; language; God: doctrine of, as persuasive power, as good, as deus ex machina; history and theology; Crosby, Donald; Reinelt, Herbert; Ford, Lewis; Sherburne, Donald; Parsons, Howard; Hocking, Richard; Griffin, David; theology; christology.

(Essays in this issue discuss the manner in which process theology deals with problems concerning God, language, history, and christology.)

129   Allan, George. "Reply." *The Christian Scholar*, 50, 1967, 320–322.

Metaphysics, and religion; class: of particulars; Christian, William A.; metaphysics; religion.

A claim for the autonomy of metaphysical and theological principles of judgment cannot be based on the claim that each deals with a distinct and separate subject matter. (Reply to William A. Christian, "The New Metaphysics and Theology," *Christian Scholar*, 50, 1967, 304–315.)

130   Allan, George. "The Gods Above, the Stones Beneath: An Essay on Historical Existence." *Soundings*, 51, 1968, 448–464.

History: as conflict, as dialectical, as teleological; dialectic: of history, of need, of abundance, of selection; teleology; freedom; Sartre, Jean-Paul; Marx, Karl; Hegel, G. W. F.; existentialism. The rhythm of dialectic and teleology which lifts up civilizations and promotes new intensities also makes possible the fall of cultures and the destruction of riches.

131   Allshouse, Merle F. "Reply." *The Christian Scholar*, 50, 1967, 328–331.

Relativism; dogmatism; dialectic; language: ordinary, theological, metaphysical; Christian, William A.; Allan, George; Sherburne, Donald W.; language; theology.

Dialectic between experience and speculation is required for clarification of theological language and avoidance of relativism and dogmatism. (Reply to William Christian, "The New Metaphysics and Theology," *Christian Scholar*, 50, 1967, 304–315.)

132   Alonso, A. "La existancia d'Dios en la philosofia de Alfred North Whitehead." Unpublished Ph.D. dissertation, Fribourg, 1969.

God: Whitehead's arguments for, function of, primordial nature of, consequent nature of, nature of, and time.

133   Alston, William P. "Internal Relatedness and Pluralism in the Philosophy of Whitehead." Unpublished Ph.D. dissertation, University of Chicago, 1951.

Relations, internal; relatedness; immanence, mutual; future, relations to; God; pluralism; monism.

Whitehead's doctrine of internal relations is difficult to reconcile with his attempt to develop a metaphysical pluralism. The doctrine of internal relations, especially as it is expressed in the notion of mutual immanence, should be modified.

134   Alston, William P. "Whitehead's Denial of Simple Location." *Journal of Philosophy*, 48, 1951, 713–721.

Location: fallacy of simple, single, multiple; immanence, mutual; region; space–time: absolute, relative.

The fallacy of simple location is more accurately stated as the fallacy of single location.

135   Alston, William P. "Internal Relatedness and Pluralism in Whitehead." *Review of Metaphysics*, 5, 1952, 535–558.

Relatedness, internal; pluralism; immanence, mutual; interconnectedness; pluralism, linear; temporality; prehensions, of future; objectification; monism.

The principle of internal relatedness logically entails the denial of pluralism. Neither Whitehead's concept of time nor his concept of the abstractions of objectification are sufficient to preserve his doctrine of pluralism.

136   Alston, William P. "Simple Location." *Review of Metaphysics*, 8, 1954–1955, 334–341.

Location, simple; immanence, mutual; ingression; objective

immortality; concreteness, misplaced (fallacy of); bifurcation of nature; Lawrence, Nathaniel; materialism, scientific.

Whitehead's denial of simple location is based upon his theory of mutual immanence, and is therefore untenable.

137   Altizer, Thomas J. J.   "Dialectical vs. Di–Polar Theology." *Process Studies*, 1, 1971, 29–37.

Consciousness, as locus of reality; negation: of particular, of self, of otherness; God: consequent nature of, and christology; and eschatology; objective immortality; apotheosis; Hegel, G. W. F.; Cobb, John B. Jr.; christology; eschatology; theology.

By stressing the primacy of the particular, di–polar theology closes itself to an encompassing vision. However, by interpreting objective immortality as self–negation and the consequent nature as christologically grounded, a vision of universality emerges in di–polar theology which is akin to that of dialectical theology.

138   Altizer, Thomas J. J.   "Method in Dipolar Theology and the Dipolar Meaning of God."   *Philosophy of Religion and Theology Section Papers of The American Academy of Religion*, 1972, 14–21.

Method, theological; God: and christology, Cobb's interpretation of, as dipolar, and world; Cobb, John B., Jr.; theology; christology.

Cobb undertakes his theological project in full recognition of historical and cultural relativity. In consistency, he should ground the abstractly formulated primordial nature of God in history. "Spirit," as an historical transformation of consciousness in Christ for both God and humanity, provides this ground.

139   Altizer, Thomas J. J.   "The Buddhist Ground of the Whiteheadian God." *Process Studies*, 5, 1975, 227–236.

Buddhism; God: and world, transcendence of, of classical theism; metaphysics.

Whitehead's conception of God is not necessarily the God of Christianity or the western tradition because it calls into question the central doctrine of transcendence. Because the language and structures of Buddhist thought allow for the possible coinherence of contraries and polarities it may be more helpful as a metaphysical ground for Whitehead's conception of God.

140   Ambrose, A.   "The Problem of Linguistic Inadequacy." *Philosophical Analysis*. Edited by Max Black. Englewood Cliffs, New Jersey: Prentice–Hall, 1963, 14–35.

Language: and metaphysics, inadequacy of, limitations of, metaphysical.

141   Ames, Edward Scribner.   "Humanism Fulfilled." *Christian Century*, 54, 1937, 1075–1076.

Humanism; Hartshorne, Charles; theology, natural.

In Hartshorne's philosophy, human beings are organically related both to God and to nature, and are not left groping between the two as in the old supernaturalism and humanism. Hartshorne thus goes beyond humanism in order to fulfill it rather than to reject it. (Written in review of Charles Hartshorne, *Beyond Humanism.*)

142   Anderson, Susan A. "Evolutionary Futurism in Stapledon's *Star Maker.*" *Process Studies*, 5, 1975, 123–128.

Literature; eschatology; person, and society; evolution; peace; Stapledon, W. Olaf; Marxism.

The evolutionary aspects of Whitehead's thought permeate the science fiction novel *Star Maker* by W. Olaf Stapledon. The novelist develops a notion of personality–in–community using Whitehead's themes of harmony and peace.

143   Anshen, R. N. *Alfred North Whitehead: His Reflections on Man and Nature, Selected and with Prologue.* New York: Harper and Bros., 1961.

Nature, and human existence.

144   Ariel, Robert Andrew. "Recent Empirical Disconfirmation of Whitehead's Relativity Theory." *Process Studies*, 4, 1974, 285–287.

Relativity, theory of; gravitation; curvature; geometry; Einstein, Albert; Newton, Isaac; relativity physics.

Whitehead's theory of relativity, in contrast to Einstein's, demands a prior geometry for space. Recent experimentation fails to show a variation required by the geometrical assumptions, thus disconfirming Whitehead's theory.

145   Arnold, Charles H. *Near the Edge of Battle.* Chicago: Divinity School Association of the University of Chicago, 1966.

Chicago school, of process theology; Foster, George B.; Mathews, Shailer; Smith, Gerald B.; Case, Shirley J.; Ames, Edward S.; Haydon, Albert H.; Wieman, Henry Nelson; Williams, Daniel D.; Meland, Bernard E.; Loomer, Bernard M.; theology, process.

(A short history of the Divinity School at the University of Chicago and the 'Chicago School of Theology'.)

146   Arregui de dell'Oca, C. *Principio de communidad de los entes en la filosofía de Alfred North Whitehead.* Montevideo: Universidad de la Republica, Faculdad de humanidades y ciencias, 1963.

Relatedness; community; nexus; actual entities.

147   Assunto, Rosario. "Sull'estetica di Whitehead." *Rassenga di Filosofia*, 1955.

Aesthetics: and aesthetic experience, and philosophy; art; form.

148   Assunto, Rosario. "La forma e l'arte." *Rassegna di Filosofia*, 4,

1955, 107–130, 233–244; 5, 1956, 41–55, 252–265, 319–337; 6, 1957, 42–67.

Art: and science, and nature, and form, and social life; beauty; truth, civilization; Kant, Immanuel.

In outlining the aesthetics and philosophy of art found in Whitehead, one may determine his relevance for contemporary aesthetics and poetics. In so doing, a critical comparison emerges between Whitehead's aesthetics and Kant's critique of judgment.

149   Atkins, Anselm. "Religious Assertions and Doctrinal Development." *Theological Studies*, 27, 1966, 523–552.

Language, theological; doctrine: and error, development of, as harmonization; falsification principle; prehensions, negative; anathema; harmonization: as subordination, as novel synthesis; Flew, Antony; Newman, Henry Cardinal; Rahner, Karl; Catholicism; dogma, history of; linguistic analysis; positivism.

Counterassertions function analogously to negative prehensions, and are a means whereby orthodox concepts are subject to progressively clearer expression and broader comprehension.

150   Aubrey, Edwin Ewart. "The Naturalistic Conception of Man." *Journal of Religion*, 19, 1939, 189–200.

Naturalism: mechanistic, biological, psychological; nature: continuity, discontinuity; man: origin of, social genesis of; sin: as disobedience, as resistance to natural law, as maladjustment; freedom; destiny; immortality; naturalism; pragmatism; religion; anthropology.

The naturalistic view of human existence holds that human beings are integral to nature, and that they realize their destiny as they contribute value to the cosmic drama.

151   Augustyn, Jerry A. "An Outline of the Philosophy of Alfred North Whitehead." Unpublished Ph.D. dissertation, University of Zurich, 1962. East Hartford, Connecticut: United Aircraft Corporation, 1962.

Simple location; bifurcation, of nature; language, and philosophy; abstraction, extensive; time; objects; feelings; propositions; perception; God, nature of; psychology.

152   Axtelle, George E. "Alfred North Whitehead and the Problem of Unity." *Educational Theory*, 19, 1969, 129–153.

Unity: individual, social, of systems of thought, and cultural pluralism; individuality, and community; values, criteria of; creativity, as supreme value; beauty; philosophy, of history; education; sociology.

Whitehead's speculative philosophy can be summarized through an analysis of the concept of unity. Particular attention can then be given to the application of Whiteheadian philosophy to the philosophy of history, to social organization, and to educational thought.

153   Azar, Larry. "The Meaning of Essence in the Philosophy of Alfred North Whitehead." Unpublished Ph.D. dissertation, University of Toronto, 1953.

Essence.

154   Azar, Larry. "Esse in the Philosophy of Whitehead." *New Scholastic*, 37. 1963, 462–471.

Creativity, and being; God: and being, and creativity; Thomas Aquinas; Thomism; theology.

Creativity is Whitehead's counterpart to the Thomistic esse. The difference between Whitehead and Thomas lies in the fact that, for Whitehead, creativity is ontologically prior to God, whereas, for Thomas, God and esse are the same.

155   Azar, Larry. "Whitehead: Challenging a Challenge." *Thomist*, 30, 1966, 80–87.

Receptacle, Platonic; matter, prime; creativity; Thomas Aquinas; Stokes, Walter; Hegel, G. W. F.; Thomism.

It is by misrepresenting Plato's receptacle, Aquinas' prime matter, and Whitehead's creativity, and by failing to see the influence of Hegelian ways of thinking on Whitehead, that Walter Stokes can construe Whitehead's philosophy to be a challenge to the principles of Thomism.

156   Bagby, P. H. "Whitehead: A New Appraisal." *Beyond the Five Senses*. Edited by E. Garrett. Philadelphia: J. B. Lippincott and Company, 1957, 279–297.

Perception; Whitehead, Alfred North, evaluation of.

157   Bahm, Archie J. "Philosophy of Organism." *Philosophy: An Introduction*. New York: John Wiley & Sons, Inc., 1953, 255–272. Bombay: Asia Publishing House, 1964; Madras, India: Bureau of Tamil Publications, 1967.

Process philosophy, summary of.

Whitehead's efforts towards organicism retain tendencies toward a double reductionism—that of reducing the being of actual occasions to their becoming, and that of reducing the nature of actual occasions to eternal objects.

158   Bakan, Mildred B. "On the Subject–Object Relationship." *Journal of Philosophy*, 55, 1958, 89–101.

Subject: as experiencing itself, as self–evolving historical unity; subject–object; appetite: as anticipation, as evaluation, as emotion, as realization; awareness; unity: of subject, of self, of occasion, historical; object, knowledge of; epistemology.

In contradistinction to Whitehead's view, the subject is a self–evolving historical unity.

159   Baker, John Robert. "A Critical Analysis of Selected Contemporary American Christologies." Unpublished Th.D. dissertation, Southwestern Baptist Theological Seminary, 1969.

Christology; process philosophy, summary of; Pittenger,

Norman; Meland, Bernard E.; Ogden, Schubert; Hartshorne, Charles.

Theologians need to apply in a thoroughgoing way the systems of Whitehead and Hartshorne to christology, and in this way the technical achievements of a contemporary philosophical system could be brought to bear upon certain christological problems.

160   Ballard, Edward G. "Kant and Whitehead, and the Philosophy of Mathematics." *Tulane Studies in Philosophy*, 10, 1961, 3–29.

Mathematics: as science, as logical deduction, as pure, as applied, as eternal objects, as forms, as constructions; propositions: analytic, synthetic; conventionalism; subjectivist principle; abstraction; mathematician; Kant, Immanuel; Poincare, H.; Descartes, Rene; philosophy: of mathematics, of science; mathematics.

Both Whitehead and Kant in different ways recognize the dependence of mathematics upon certain prior demands imposed by human experience.

161   Baltazar, Eulalio. "Evolutionary Perspectives and the Divine." *Traces of God in a Secular Culture*. Edited by George F. McLean. Staten Island, New York: Alba House, 1973, 143–165.

God, and nature; evolution.

162   Balz, Albert G. A. "Whitehead, Descartes, and the Bifurcation of Nature." *Journal of Philosophy*, 31, 1934, 281–297.

Bifurcation; subject: as knower, as perceiver, as psychical, as thinking; cogito ergo sum; soul; matter; Descartes, Rene; philosophy: modern, of science; theology; physics.

In order to avoid the bifurcation of nature, a philosophy of nature must absorb within its field questions concerning relations between perceivers and perceptions.

163   Balz, Albert G. A. "Matter and Scientific Efficiency: St. Thomas and the Diversity of Matter." *Journal of Philosophy*, 31, 1934, 645–664.

Matter: as indefinite dimensionality, as independent of form, as diversity, as prime, as potentiality, and form; creation: as order, as expression of divine wisdom, as world–set, as compossibles, as illimitable; Thomas Aquinas; Aristotle; metaphysics; philosophy: medieval, of science.

The Thomistic analysis of matter as potentiality provides a preparatory basis for centuries of scientific inquiry, leading directly to the Whiteheadian interplay between scientific inquiry and philosophical reflection.

164   Band, William. "Dr. A. N. Whitehead's Theory of Absolute Acceleration." *Philosophical Magazine*, 7, 1929, 434–440.

Cosmology; space–time; acceleration; velocity; coordinate

systems; motion; Einstein, Albert; Broad, C. D.; Eddington, A. S.; Temple, G.; physics; mathematics; geometry.

An appeal to empirical problems arising from Whitehead's theory concerning planetary revolutions around the sun suggests inconsistencies in his theory of relativity and renders problematic his belief that there is one universe within which diverse observers can express absolute (rather than relative) acceleration.

165   Band, William. "A Comparison of Whitehead's with Einstein's Law of Gravitation." *Philosophical Magazine*, 7, 1929, 1183–1186.

Relativity, theory of; impetus; metric tensor; orbits; motion, of comets; Schwarzschild metric; Einstein, Albert; Temple, G.; physics; mathematics.

Whitehead's equation for the field around a single point mass is only approximate in comparison with the Schwarzschild solution to the Einstein field equations. (Note: Whitehead carries out a similar solution in *The Principle of Relativity*, 1922)

166   Band, William. "Is Space–Time Flat?" *Physical Review*, 61, 1942, 698–701.

Relativity, theory of; space–time; simultaneity; causality; acceleration; velocity; motion; physics.

(The author criticizes Whitehead's position that space–time is flat and the correlated notion that accelerations are absolute.)

167   Banfi, Antonio. "Prefazione." *La scienza e il mondo moderno.* Trans. and edited by Antonio Banfi. Milan: Bompiani, 1945.

Whitehead, Alfred North, work of.

168   Barbour, Ian G. *Issues in Science and Religion.* Englewood Cliffs, New Jersey: Prentice–Hall, Inc., 1966. New York: Harper and Row, 1971.

Religion, and science; process philosophy, summary of; God: and nature, as persuasive power, primordial nature of, and novelty, consequent nature of, as creator, and creatio ex nihilo; experience, religious; epistemology, realist; self–creativity; subjective aim, in nature; panpsychism; Hartshorne, Charles; Teilhard de Chardin; existentialism; theology, neo–orthodoxy; linguistic analysis; theology, process.

While neo–orthodoxy and existentialism have important insights concerning the basis of the human knowledge of God, they are deficient at the point where process philosophy makes a distinctive contribution: the development of metaphysical categories in terms of which divine activity can be related to the structure of nature as it is understood in scientific thought.

169   Barbour, Ian G. "Science and Religion Today." *Science and Religion: New Perspectives on the Dialogue.* Edited by Ian G. Barbour. New York: Harper and Row, 1968, 193–215.

Birch, Charles; science, and religion.

170   Barbour, Ian G. "Teilhard's Process Metaphysics." *Journal of
      Religion*, 49, 1969, 136–159. Also in *Process Theology: Basic
      Writings*. Edited by Ewert H. Cousins. New York: Newman
      Press, 1971, 323–350.

      Reality, as temporal process; "within," the; freedom and
      determinism; creation, as continuing; God: and time, and evil,
      as future, as primordial, as consequent, as Omega; eschatology;
      world: history of, future of; Teilhard de Chardin; metaphysics.

      Despite his tendency toward monism, Teilhard's process
      metaphysics shows striking similarities with Whitehead's,
      especially in his views of temporality, interdependence,
      continuity, and the "within."

171   Barbour, Ian G.   *Science and Secularity: The Ethics of
      Technology*. New York: Harper and Row, 1970, 46–57.

      Secularity; nature, and value; God: sovereignty of, and nature,
      and order, and novelty, and evil; language, religious; causation:
      efficient, final; science; religion; process philosophy; theology,
      process.

      Process thought contributes to an understanding of the relation
      between God and nature in that it yields a theology of nature,
      illuminates the problem of evil, and encourages an affirmation
      of the world.   Process thought is problematic in that it may
      compromise the autonomy of nature over God, as well as the
      sovereignty of God, and neglect the noncognitive functions of
      religious language.

172   Barnes, M. W. "Concept Structure in Cassirer and Whitehead."
      Unpublished Ph.D. dissertation, Northwestern University, 1961.

      Concept; structure.

173   Barnhart, J. E. "Incarnation and Process Philosophy." *Religious
      Studies*, 2, 1967, 225–232.

      Incarnation; empathy; immanence, mutual; Jesus: as man, as
      Christ, as objectified in God; Logos; Brightman, E. S.;
      theology, natural.

      The constitutive effect of relationships suggests that incarnation
      be understood as the empathetic relationship mutually
      influencing the identity of both God and Jesus.

174   Barnhart, J. E.   "Bradley's Monism and Whitehead's
      Neo–Pluralism."   *Southern Journal of Philosophy*, 7, 1969,
      395–400.

      Monism; pluralism: metaphysical, neo–pluralism, organic;
      relations: as self–contradictory, as real, as appearance; God: as
      absolute, infinity of; reality, as harmony; immanence, mutual;
      Bradley, F. H.; Leibniz, G. W.; philosophy: monistic, pluralistic.

      Bradley's monism derives from his conclusion that no finite
      entity is self–contained. Whitehead reverses the conclusion by
      arguing from mutual immanence to an organic pluralism.

175   Bar–On, Zvie A.   "Whitehead's Philosophical Development" (in Hebrew). *Iyun*, 8, 1957, 167–178.

Process philosophy, summary of.

176   Bar–On, Zvie A.   "Whitehead's Platonism" (in Hebrew). *Iyun*, 8, 1957, 214–236.

Platonism; *Adventures of Ideas.*

177   Bar–On, Zvie A.   "Whitehead and the Heritage of Modern Philosophy" (in Hebrew). *Iyun*, 13, 1962, 13–29. Revised, trans., and reprinted in *International Philosophical Quarterly*, 4, 1964, 48–67.

Substance; causality; interconnectedness; time; subjectivity; causal efficacy; presentational immediacy; cogito ergo sum; Descartes, Rene; Hume, David; Husserl, Edmund; philosophy, modern.

Whitehead develops his theory of the fundamental structure of experience and his revision of the categories of substance and causality in critical continuity with the heritage of modern philosophy.

178   Bates, Leslie M.   "Alfred North Whitehead's Doctrine of Divine Prehension."   Unpublished Ph.D. dissertation, Yale University, 1951.

God: as actual entity, religious ·availability of, as persuasive; Christianity; theology, philosophical.

While the philosophical functions of Whitehead's God can be described without explicit reference to religion, the religious functions of Whitehead's God are best described in terms of the Christian tradition.

179   Battalia, F. and Abbagnano, Nicolai.   *Filosofia e sociologia.* Bologna: Il Mulino, 1954.

Philosophy, of sociology; religion; sociology.

180   Baxter, Gerald D. and Kennedy, Bart F.   "Whitehead's Concept of Concrescence and the Rhetorical Situation."   *Philosophy and Rhetoric*, 8, 1975, 159–164.

Eternal objects: subjective, objective, propositional; rhetoric: situation of, and rhetor; subject; occasion; philosophy, of language; language.

Whitehead's treatment of eternal objects and a concrescent theory of criticism afford a view of the rhetorical situation.

181   Beardslee, William A., editor.   *America and the Future of Theology.* Philadelphia: Westminster Press, 1967.

Theism, American; theology, radical; social sciences; aesthetics; religion.

(These papers were originally presented at a conference held at Emory University, Atlanta, Georgia, November, 1965.)

182   Beardslee, William A.   "The Motif of Fulfillment in the Eschatology of the Synoptic Gospels."   *Transitions in Biblical*

Scholarship. Edited by J. C. Rylaarsdam. Chicago: University of Chicago Press, 1968, 171–191.

Future: meaning of, inherent in present, openness of, as reward, relations to; eschatology: present, as process, realized; hope: phenomenology of, eschatological; fulfillment; God, consequent nature of; Q material; Mark, gospel of; Schweitzer, Albert; biblical studies.

Whiteheadian categories can be used in a framework of thought that is analogous to eschatology in that it is grounded in the future rather than in the past.

183   Beardslee, William A.   "Hope in Biblical Eschatology and in Process Theology."   *Journal of the American Academy of Religion,* 38, 1970, 227–239.

Hope: function of, truth of, modes of; eschatology: apocalyptic, as reversal, and history; history: relativity of, as totality; existence, structure of Christian; New Testament; Pannenberg, Wolfhart; Moltmann, Jürgen; Altizer, Thomas J. J.; Cobb, John B., Jr.; philosophy and theology; biblical studies.

The compatibility of the frames of reference of process theology and apocalyptic eschatology provide grounds for a fruitful process reinterpretation of Christian hope.

184   Beardslee, William A.   *A House for Hope.*   Philadelphia: Westminster Press, 1972.

Hope; creativity; infinity; secularism; life, eternal; Christ, as Logos; eschatology; christology; biblical studies.

Hope in a process perspective is not hope for a final, literal end but a trust in the future in which God calls humans to participate.

185   Beardslee, William A.   "Narrative Form in the New Testament and Process Theology."   *Encounter,* 36, 1975, 301–315.

New Testament; symbols; myths; biblical studies.

Process thought may be useful for the interpretation of narrative through its understanding of symbolism, its use of contrasts, and its possibilities for interpreting the narrative symbol of the end.

186   Beardslee, William A.   "Sex: Biological Basis of Hope."   *Religious Experience and Process Theology.*   Edited by Harry J. Cargas and Bernard Lee.   New York: Paulist Press, 1976, 175–194.

Hope; sexuality; God, as source of initial aim; evolution; morality; sociology.

Whitehead's metaphysical system can provide a framework for integrating hope and the physical processes of the world, especially sexual relationships.

187   Beer, S. H.   *The City of Reason.*   Cambridge, Massachusetts: Harvard University Press, 1949.

Philosophy, political; civilization; political science; ethics; reason; freedom.

Whitehead's thought provides a framework through which the relationship between human reason and freedom can be understood. Politics should strive for a society in which reason in both personal and public life is protected.

188 Belaief, Lynne. "The Ethics of Alfred North Whitehead." Unpublished Ph.D. dissertation, Columbia University, 1963.

Freedom; value: as objective, as subjective; love; justice; tragedy; evil; person: and personal identity, and personal immortality; God, consequent nature of; philosophy: method of, aim of; Hegel, G. W. F.; Bradley, F. H.; Royce, Josiah; Buchler, Justus; neo–Hegelianism; idealism; realism; ethics.

An ethical theory can be derived which emphasizes novelty in ethical vision rather than permanent ethical standards.

189 Belaief, Lynne. "Whitehead and Private–Interest Theories." *Ethics*, 76, 1965–1966, 277–286.

Self: as relational, as substance, as personal society; value: aesthetic, ethical; morality; self–interest; happiness; good; evil; novelty; tragedy; egoism; altruism; ethics.

The charge that Whitehead's philosophy leads to an ethics of private interest is based on an erroneous understanding of his metaphysical analysis of the self. Concern for others and a continuous openness to the possibility of revision of moral judgment is required by a relational selfhood.

190 Belaief, Lynne. "A Whiteheadian Account of Value and Identity." *Process Studies*, 5, 1, 1975, 31–45.

Value: moral, theory of, ethical, hierarchy of; evil; novelty; eternal objects; negative prehensions; ethics; morals.

191 Belth, Marc. "Education in the Universe of Whitehead." *Teachers College Record*, 58, 1957, 323–328.

Relatedness: of fact and value, of church and religion, of abstractions and nature; progressivism; education.

Whiteheadian education must be in the present, in awareness of the connectedness of events. This leads to a strictly traditional curriculum.

192 Bendall, R. Douglas. "'On Mathematical Concepts of the Material World' and the Development of Whitehead's Philosophy of Organism." Unpublished dissertation, Graduate Theological Union, 1973.

"On Mathematical Concepts of the Material World"; space, relational theory of; geometry; mathematics.

193 Bender, R. "Whitehead's Implied Social Ethics." *Philosophy Forum*, 10, 1952, 22–31.

Ethics, social; society, human; morality.

194 Benjamin, A. Cornelius. "La philosophie en Amérique entre les deux guerres." *L'Activité philosophique contemporaine en France et aux États–Unis.* Edited by Marvin Farber. Paris: Presses Universitaires de France, 1950, 1–29.

Whitehead, and American philosophy; feeling; concreteness, fallacy of misplaced; Peirce, Charles S.; idealism; pragmatism.

195 Bennett, John B. "Whitehead's Philosophy of Personal Experience." Unpublished Ph.D. dissertation, Yale University, 1969.

Person: and experience, and personal identity; memory, as hybrid physical prehension; freedom; decision; agency; subjective aim; God, and experience; subjective aim, initial phase of; Cobb, John B., Jr.; Descartes, Renes; Browning, Douglas; Pols, Edward; theology; religion: and belief, and community.

Personal identity, freedom, and agency are elucidated by Whitehead's thought in a way more adequate than that of substance conceptuality.

196 Bennett, John B. "Process or Agent: A Response." *Philosophy of Religion and Theology Section Papers of The American Academy of Religion*, 1972, 146–159.

Unity: of self, of occasion, of subject; agency; freedom; Kirkpatrick, Frank; Pols, Edward.

The unity which Whitehead's philosophy allows to the self is more adequate than Kirkpatrick's alternative account of agency. (Written in response to Frank Kirkpatrick, "Process or Agent: Two Models for Self and God.")

197 Bennett, John B. "Whitehead and Personal Identity." *The Thomist*, 37, 1973, 510–521.

Identity; order, personal; inheritance, serial; conformal feelings; prehensions, hybrid; characteristic, defining; dispositions; memory; action, intentional; Cobb, John B., Jr.

A correcting alternative to Cobb's interpretation of personal identity is possible within Whiteheadian philosophy by renewed attention to the importance of serial inheritance and the immanence of the past in the present.

198 Bennett, John B. "Ecology and Philosophy: Whitehead's Contribution." *Journal of Thought*.

Ecology.

199 Bense, Max. "Bertrand Russell und Alfred North Whitehead." *Die Philosophie*. Frankfurt: Suhrkamp Verlag, 1951, 86–104.

Whitehead, biography of; relations, theory of; mathematics; geometry.

Whereas for Russell, philosophy is essentially a critique of language, for Whitehead it remains a metaphysical task concerned with entities and their relations. (Note: pages 333–352 contain an excerpt from the German translation of *Science and the Modern World*, *Wissenschaft und moderne Welt*, Zürich: Morgarten Verlag, 1949.)

200 Bense, Max. "Kosmologie und Literatur: Über Alfred N.

Whitehead und Gertrude Stein." *Texte und Zeichen: Eine literarische Zeitschrift,* 3, 1957, 512–525.

Whitehead, Alfred North, relation with Gertrude Stein; art; form; structure; pattern; rhythm; text; language; adjective; aesthetics, critique of; literature; Stein, Gertrude.

Gertrude Stein's use of language is grounded in the nature of reality which Whitehead describes in *The Concept of Nature* and *Process and Reality.*

201 Bera, Marc–André. *A. N. Whitehead (Un philosophie de l'expérience).* Paris: Hermann et Cie Éditeurs, 1948.

Mysticism; romanticism; empiricism; rationalism; Platonism.

202 Bergeron, R. "Un exemple de christologie organique: W. N. Pittenger." *Revue de Sciences Religieuses,* 48, 1971, 1–24.

Christology; Pittenger, Norman.

203 Bergmann, Hugo. "Der Physiker Whitehead." *Keatur,* 2, 1928, 356–363.

Philosophy, of science; abstraction; concretion; relations, as I–Thou; nature; Weltanschaaung, materialistic; God, as principle of concretion; Buber, Martin; Russell, Bertrand; physics.

204 Berstein, B. A. "Remark on Nicod's Reduction of *Principia Mathematica.*" *Journal of Symbolic Logic,* 2, 1937, 165–166.

Deduction; Nicod, J. G. P.; logic; mathematics.

The theory of deduction based on Nicod's postulates and included in the revised *Principia* requires further revision.

205 Bertolini, Piero. "Aspetti e problemi dell'educazione in A. N. Whitehead." *Aut Aut,* 28, 1955, 323–340.

Education, theory of; adventure; harmony; peace; Dewey, John; Hegel, G. W. F.

In studying the interrelation of the theoretical philosophy of Whitehead and his theory of education, a comparison can be made with the development of Dewey's theory of education.

206 Besancon, R. "The Problem of God and Evil in the Thought of Representative Contemporary Philosophers." Unpublished dissertation, Northern Baptist Theological Seminary, 1959–1960.

God: and evil, primordial nature of, consequent nature of, and world; evil.

207 Bianchi, Eugene C. "A Holistic and Dynamic Development of Doctrinal Symbols." *Anglican Theological Review,* 55, 1973, 148–169.

Symbols, religious; myths; value, maximization of; God, holistic doctrine of; reality, dynamic concept of; dualism; incarnation; crucifixion; resurrection; eucharist; Hartshorne, Charles; Tillich, Paul; Catholicism.

Process theology provides a context in which the symbolic

power of doctrines to disclose meaning and value may be renewed.

208   Bidney, D.   "The Problem of Substance in Spinoza and Whitehead." *Philosophical Review*, 45, 1936, 574–592.

Substance; accidents; dualism; monism; God, as absolute; existence, and perfection; actuality; potentiality; Spinoza, B.; Plato; Aristotle; Leibniz, G. W.; scholasticism; metaphysics.

There is a conflict of philosophical traditions at the basis of the metaphysics of Spinoza and Whitehead. All the problems of Spinoza's metaphysics recur in Whitehead's works in a more acute form.

209   Bigger, Charles P.   "Speculative Demonstration." *Journal of Philosophy*, 58, 1961, 785–796.

Language: demonstrative, and reality, descriptive, and conceptual stability; nature; extension; isomorphism; Plato; Weedon, William; philosophy, linguistic; phenomenology; semantics.

The rediscovery of Socratic demonstration by Whitehead and William Weedon respectively provides a solution to the relation between perceived nature and discourse, or phenomenology and semantics.

210   Bigger, Charles P.   *Participation: A Platonic Enquiry.*   Baton Rouge, Louisiana: Louisiana State University Press, 1968.

Forms, participation; Plato; Platonism; philosophy, process.

(Although the work does not contain a sustained discussion of Whitehead's philosophy, various parallels between Plato and Whitehead are mentioned in passing. The author is sympathetic to Whitehead's interpretations of Plato, and interprets Plato in a similar manner.)

211   Bigger, Charles P.   "Becoming and Time."   *Akten des XIV Internationalen Kongresses fuer Philosophie* (Vienna), Band 3, 1969, 578–580.

Becoming, and time; time; epochal theory of, and transition.

212   Biller, Alan D.   "Whitehead's Conception of Speculative Philosophy."   Unpublished Ph.D. dissertation, Columbia University, 1971.

Philosophy: speculative, method of, and imagination, theoretical content of, and natural science; adequacy; coherence.

213   Birch, L. Charles.   "Interpreting the Lower in Terms of the Higher." *The Christian Scholar*, 37, 1954, 402–407.

Mechanism; meaning; values, potential; evolution; God, experience of; physics; chemistry; biology; zoology.

Since matter is life–like, the universe is more like a life than a mechanism.

214   Birch, L. Charles.   "Creation and the Creator."   *Journal of Religion*, 36, 1957, 85–98. The article is republished in *Science*

and Religion: New Perspectives on the Dialogue. Edited by
Ian G. Barbour. New York: Harper and Row, 1968, 193–215.

Evolution: natural selection and random mutation; creation: as
continuous process, as mechanistic, as revelation; God:
creativity of, experience of, as persuasive; evil; suffering;
Brunner, Emil; Hartshorne, Charles; Dobzhansky, T.; religion;
science; genetics; biology.

Unlike the neo–orthodox views represented by Emil Brunner,
process metaphysics provides a reconciliation of science and
religion on the issue of creation and evolution.

215   Birch, L. Charles. *Nature and God.* Philadelphia: Westminster
        Press, 1965.

Nature: and value, and subjectivity; God: and nature, as
creator, and science, as persuasive; evolution; poetry, and
nature; Christ; Darwin, Charles; Wordsworth, William;
Tennyson, A. L.; Hartshorne, Charles; Tillich, Paul; Teilhard
de Chardin; science, and religion; biology; theology.

Process philosophy and theology offer a way in which religion
and science can be reconciled, each to the benefit of the other.
The biblical understanding of creation can then be understood
in light of evolution.

216   Birch, L. Charles. "Purpose in the Universe: A Search for
        Wholeness." *Zygon*, 6, 1971, 4–27.

Evolution: as creative, as cosmic, as biological, as social;
purpose: human, cosmic; order; value; God: and order, as
source of value; chaos; Hartshorne, Charles; Darwin, Charles;
Teilhard de Chardin; Cobb, John B., Jr.; metaphysics; religion;
biology; anthropology; ecology; psychology.

The facts of science and human experience require an overall
view of the unity of creation.

217   Birch, ˌL. Charles. "Participatory Evolution: The Drive of
        Creation." *Journal of the American Academy of Religion*, 40,
        1972, 147–163.

Evolution: as conscious participatory, as cosmic, as organic, as
cultural, as mechanical; society: high grade, low grade, human;
future; possibilities; persuasion; harmony; God: as unitary
actuality, as love; Darwin, Charles; LeConte, Joseph;
Hartshorne, Charles; neo–Darwinism; metaphysics; biology;
physics; religion.

Cultural evolution provides the key to biological evolution,
indicating that the universe is to be conceived in terms of
processes that are influenced from what has gone on before
and that anticipate potentialities of the future.

218   Birch, L. Charles. "Biology and the Image of Man." *The
        Modern Churchman*, 98, 1973, 3–7.

Biology, and process; anthropology.

219   Birch, L. Charles.   "A Biological Basis for Human Purpose."
           Zygon, 8, 1973, 244–260.

           Purpose, basis for; evolution: biological, cultural; nature:
           intrinsic worth of, instrumental worth of; science; Darwin,
           Charles; Dobzhansky, Theodosius; biology; ecology; genetics;
           ethics.

           Biology may be on the one hand a destroyer of cherished
           values and their foundations, and on the other the harbinger
           of a new approach to human purpose.

220   Birch, L. Charles and Cobb, John B., Jr.   "God's Love, Ecological
           Survival and the Responsiveness of Nature."   *Anticipation*, 16,
           1974, 32–34.

           Nature: devaluation of, and human existence, ethic of, and
           biblical theology; values: intrinsic, instrumental; God:
           primordial nature of, consequent nature of, as love;
           anthropocentrism; Von Rad, Gerhard; dualism; ethics;
           mechanism; ecology.

           Human beings are continuous with and responsible for their
           environment.

221   Birch, L. Charles.   "Chance, Necessity and Purpose."   *Studies in
           the Philosophy of Biology*.   Edited by F. Ayala and T.
           Dobzhansky.   New York: Macmillan Company, 1974, 225–239.

           Freedom, and determinism; chance; necessity; purpose; biology;
           evolution.

222   Birch, L. Charles.   "What Does God Do in the World?"   *Union
           Seminary Quarterly Review*, 30, 1975, 75–83.

           Science, and religion; causation: mechanical, efficient; God: as
           sustaining, as creating, as persuasive lure, as primordial, as
           consequent, as love; order: explicate, implicate; Darwin,
           Charles; Williams, Daniel Day; Hartshorne, Charles, Bohm,
           David; Newton, Isaac; mechanism; biology; physics, religion.

           Mechanism as an understanding of causation must be
           supplemented with the notion of subjective response.   God acts
           in the world through persuasive influence relative to subjective
           response.

223   Birro, C.   *The Ways of Enjoyment: A Dialogue Concerning
           Social Science*.   New York: Exposition Press, 1957.

           Science, social.

224   Bixler, Julius S.   "Whitehead's Philosophy of Religion."   *The
           Philosophy of Alfred North Whitehead*.   Edited by Paul A.
           Schilpp.   La Salle, Illinois: Open Court Publishing Company,
           1941, 487–511.

           Religion: and value, and process; God: Whitehead's arguments
           for, nature of; teleology; value: objective, subjective, intrinsic;
           adventure; peace.

           Whitehead's philosophy of religion is distinctive in the manner
           in which it defends religion against the attacks of scientific

positivism, encourages religious tolerance, argues against religious dogmatism, and interprets religion as an experience of growth.

225   Bjelland, Andrew G.   "Bergson's Dualism in 'Time and Free Will'."   *Process Studies*, 4, 1974, 83–106.

Location, fallacy of simple; concreteness, fallacy of misplaced; Bergson, Henri.

Analysis of Bergson's philosophy reveals that he anticipated Whitehead's critiques of the vacuous actuality of simply–located entities and of those fallacies of misplaced concreteness which have pervaded much of Western thought.

226   Black, M.   *The Nature of Mathematics: A Critical Survey.*   New York: Harcourt and Brace, 1933.

Mathematics.

227   Blackwell, Richard J.   "Whitehead and the Problem of Simultaneity."   *Modern Schoolman*, 41, 1963, 62–72.

Simultaneity: absolute, relative, instantaneous, durational; causal efficacy; presentational immediacy; potentiality; time, epochal theory of; continuum, extensive; concreteness, fallacy of misplaced; Einstein, Albert; Newton, Isaac; physics, relativity; physics, classical; epistemology; geometry.

Whitehead argues against Einstein and Newton for a community of discourse which runs through the whole of nature, expressed in the notion of a simultaneity within an extended duration.   However, there is a problem in accounting for the unity of the causally independent world of contemporaries.

228   Blaikie, R. J.   "Being, Process, and Action in Modern Philosophy and Theology."   *Scottish Journal of Theology*, 25, 1972, 129–154.

Unity; dualism; forms, static; dynamism; agent; action; acts; events; logic; Macmurray, John; Kant, Immanuel; Descartes, Rene; rationalism; empiricism; idealism; theology; physics.

Unlike Macmurray's personalist philosophy, Whitehead's organic philosophy of events is without an empirically rooted basis in experience, and hence does not answer the problems of dualism and static forms in modern thought.

229   Blanshard, Brand.   "Wisdom on the Wing."   *Saturday Review*, 37, May 8, 1954, 13, 33.

Whitehead, Alfred North, biography of; Price, Lucien.

(This is a review of Price's Dialogues of *Alfred North Whitehead*.)

230   Blyth, John W.   "On Mr. Hartshorne's Understanding of Whitehead's Philosophy."   *Philosophical Review*, 46, 1937, 523–528.

Qualities, secondary; relativism, objective; prehensions; feelings, universality of; contemporaneity; universe, solidarity of; Hartshorne, Charles; metaphysics.

Hartshorne's interpretation of Whitehead is unfounded in reference to secondary qualities and to the unqualified inclusiveness of prehensions.

231   Blyth, John W. *Whitehead's Theory of Knowledge.* New York: Brown University Press, 1941.

Epistemology; ontological principle; relativity, principle of; subjectivist. principle; extensive continuum; space, relational theory of; time; presentational immediacy; propositions.

In attempting to combine the principle of relativity, the ontological principle, and the subjectivist principle, serious inconsistencies arise in Whitehead's metaphysics. (This is the author's Ph.D. dissertation submitted to Brown University in 1936.)

Reviews

Gross, M. W. *Journal of Philosophy,* 39, 1942, 419–420.

Hartshorne, C. *Philosophy and Phenomenological Research,* 3, 1943, 372–375.

232   Boas, George. *Dominant Themes of Modern Philosophy.* New York: Ronald Press Co., 1957.

Novelty; temporalism; creativity; self–creativity; God, as principle of concretion; Bergson, Henri.

Questions must be raised concerning the legitimacy of novelty in Whitehead's system.

233   Bochenski, I. M. *Europaeische Philosophie der Gegenwart.* Berne: A. Francke, 1947, 1951. English trans.: *Contemporary European Philosophy.* Berkeley: University of California Press, 1956, 226–237.

Materialism, criticism of; mechanism, organic; immanence; God, knowledge of; process philosophy, summary of; epistemology; metaphysics; psychology.

(*Science and the Modern World* is used as the basis for a summary of process philosophy.)

234   Bodkin, Maud. "Physical Agencies and the Divine Persuasion." *Philosophy,* 20, 1945, 148–161.

God: persuasive power of, as ideal lure, as future; immanence; evil; action, social; Santayana, George; Buber, martin; Hartshorne, Charles; ethics; religion; theology.

Whitehead's analysis of God as the lure toward the ideal promises great fruitfulness for religious use.

235   Bodnar, Ján. "Process Philosophy—Filozofia Subjektívneho Idealizmu." *Slovensky Filizofický Casopis,* 9, 1954, 252–262.

Process philosophy, summary of; mathematics.

236   Bodnar, J. "Teoria organicizmu, urovni a finitizmu v sucasnej filozofii prirdonych viewd ("The Theory of Organism: Levels

and Finitism in the Contemporary Philosophy of the Natural Sciences")." *Otazky Marxistickey Filozofia*, 18, 1963, 215–228.

Organism, theory of; natural sciences; finitude.

237   Böhme,   Gernot.   "Whiteheads   Abkehr   von   der Substanzmetaphysik: Substanz und Relation." *Zeitschrift für philosophische Forschung, 24, 1970, 548–553.*

Metaphysics, of substance; substance; relations; prehension; predicate; being; Aristotle.

238   Bogomolov, A. S.   "A. N. Uaitkhed i yevo 'filosofiya protsessa'." *Ideya razvitiya v burzhuanznoi filosofii XIX i XX vekov.* Moscow: Izdatel'stvo Moskovkovo Universiteta, 1962. *Filosofiya anglo–amerikanskovo   realizma.   * Moscow: Izdatel'stvo Moskovskovo   Universiteta,   57–58.   Also   in   *Filosofiya anglo–amerikanskovo   realizma.   * Moscow: Izdatel'stvo Moskovskovo Universiteta, 1962.

Process philosophy.

239   Bonevac, Daniel.   "The Existential Implications of Whitehead's Metaphysics."   *Undergraduate Journal of Philosophy*, 6, 1974, 17–29.

Consciousness, as affirmation–negation contrast; knowledge; decision;   presentational   immediacy;   loneliness;   Peace; existentialism.

The affirmation–negation contrast is inherent in consciousness; the insecurity of knowledge can never be eliminated; constant decision–making is inevitable; isolation of the individual persists perpetually.   These existential problems may lead to anguish or to peace.

240   Bonfantini, M.   *Introduzione a Whitehead.*   Bari: Laterza, 1972.

Whitehead, Alfred North: introduction to his thought.

241   Boodin, J. E.   *Three Interpretations of the Universe.*   New York: Macmillan Company, 1934.

Cosmology.

242   Boodin, J. E.   "Fictions in Science and Philosophy II."   *Journal of Philosophy*, 40, 1943, 701–716.

Experience; relatedness; consciousness; method; Moore, G. E.; Hume, David; Descartes, Rene; Leibniz, G. W.; mathematics; psychology.

Whitehead errs in his substantival conception of experience, in his extension of experience to nature, and in applying mathematical methods to metaphysical problems.

243   Borghi, L.   "Aspetti religiosi e morali del pensiero americano contemporaneo."   *Il saggiatore rivista di cultura filosofica e pedaggogica*, 3, 1953, 37–61.

Religion; morality.

244   Bosco, N. "Introduzione a Whitehead, 'il processo e la relata'." *Filosofia*, 14, 1963, 481–494.   Also in *Il processo e la realta.* Milan: Bompiani, 1965.

Whitehead, Alfred North: introduction to his thought; *Process and Reality.*

245   Bowden, Daniel J.   "The Teleological Arguments for the Existence of God as Found in the Writings of F. R. Tennant, L. T. Hobhouse, and A. N. Whitehead." Unpublished Ph.D. dissertation, Yale University, 1937.

God, teleological argument for; Tennant, F. R.; Hobhouse, L. T.

246   Bowman, Carroll R.   "Time and the Religious Consciousness." *Southern Journal of Philosophy,* 11, 1973, 73–82.

Time, triumph of; temporalism; modernism; culture, contemporary; church, contemporary; consciousness, religious; permanence; Augustine; religion.

Contemporary thought is dominated by temporalism, requiring the corrective of an insight into permanence such as is achieved by A. N. Whitehead.

247   Boyle, Marjorie O'Rourke.   "Interpoints: A Model for Divine Spacetime." *Process Studies,* 5, 1975, 191–194.

God: and world, and time; space–time, and God; theism: classical, process; simultaneity; time, and temporality.

What is required for understanding divine space–time in process perspective is a logic which does not situate judgment restrictively in front of things and in sequence, as if the universal stuff were solids extended seriatim in rigid, empty space, but rather allows access to plenitude and simultaneity.

248   Braham, Ernest G.   "The Place of God in A. N. Whitehead's Philosophy." *London Quarterly Holborn Review,* 164, 1939, 63–69.

God: religious adequacy of, and creativity.

Despite the rich suggestiveness of Whitehead's concept of God, the concept fails lamentably for Christian use insofar as Whitehead subordinates God to the metaphysical principles.

249   Brantl, G. E.   "The Tragic Commitment: An Essay in Existentialist Metaphysics." Unpublished Ph.D. dissertation, Columbia University, 1957.

Existentialism; tragedy; metaphysics.

250   Breuvart, J. M.   "Place et rôle de la religion dans la pensée d'Alfred North Whitehead." *Melanges de Science Religieuse,* 27, 1970, 96–114.

Religion, foundations of; religion, and metaphysics.

251   Breuvart, J. M.   "A. N. Whitehead et G. W. Leibniz ou une certaine 'mort de Dieu'." *Melanges de science religieuse,* 28, 1971, 89–111.

God: death of, as actual entity, and the world, as dipolar, transcendence of, as persuasive, primordial nature of, consequent nature of; monads; eternal objects; res verae; facts: of experience, of reason; objects, of thought; truths, necessary;

"On Mathematical Concepts of the Material World"; Leibniz, G. W.; Locke, John; Russell, Bertrand; dynamism; empiricism; theism; mathematics.

In accepting the dynamistic aspects of Leibnizian philosophy while rejecting its substantialist aspects, Whitehead can differentiate the death of God from the death of the semantic representation of God.

252   Bright, Laurence, O. P. *Whitehead's Philosophy of Physics.* New York: Sheed and Ward, 1958.

Philosophy, and science; causal efficacy; presentational immediacy; bifurcation, of nature; relations, internal; space; time; events, unity of; organism; concreteness, misplaced; duration; science, physical.

(This work is designed to introduce physical scientists to the general aspects of Whitehead's philosophy of nature.)

Reviews

Colnort, B. S. *Archives Internationales d'Historie des Sciences,* 14, 1961, 367.

253   Brightman, Edgar S. *Person and Reality: An Introduction to Metaphysics.* Edited by Peter A. Bertocci in collaboration with Jannette E. Newhall and Robert S. Brightman. New York: Ronald Press Company, 1958.

Person, as datum for philosophy; experience, as datum for philosophy; time, and present experience; actuality, and potentiality; subjective aim; eternal objects, as essences; God, and time.

(The author discusses various aspects of Whitehead's thought within the context of a personalistic metaphysics.)

254   Brinkley, Alan B. "Whitehead on Symbolic Reference." *Tulane Studies in Philosophy,* 20, 1961, 31–45.

Symbolic reference; symbolism; causal efficacy; presentational immediacy; symbols; perception; analysis, conceptual; error; epistemology.

The inconsistencies regarding direct recognition and error in Whitehead's theory of perception may be corrected within the scope of his system.

255   Broad, C. D. "The External World." *Mind,* 30, 1921, 385–408.

Objects, of perception; sense data; qualities: primary, secondary; Alexander, Samuel; Russell, Bertrand; world; epistemology; perception.

Whitehead, Alexander, and Russell contribute to philosophical discussion of the question: what is the status of sensa in nature and how are they related to physical objects?

256   Broad, C. D. *Scientific Thought.* New York: Harcourt, Brace and Company, Inc., 1927.

Abstraction, extensive; space, timeless; objects, scientific; event; science.

257   Broad, C. D.   "Alfred North Whitehead (1861–1947)."   *Mind*, 57, 1948, 139–145.

Whitehead, Alfred North: biography of.

(Particular   attention   is   given   to   Whitehead's   work   in mathematics and physics.)

258   Bross, Helen H.   "The Problem of Bifurcation in Whitehead's Philosophy of Science."   Unpublished Ph.D. dissertation, Yale University, 1952.

Bifurcation, of nature; sense–perception; objects, of science; experience, and scientific theory; science.

While Whitehead does not avoid bifurcation in his later philosophy of science, he avoids his early criticism of the unverifiability of such a bifurcated science by accepting a new criterion of verification.   He no longer holds that the fundamental entities of science should themselves be disclosed in sense–experience, but believes they are to be derived from experience in a broad metaphysical sense.

259   Brotherston, Bruce W.   "The Wider Setting of 'Felt Transition'." *Journal of Philosophy*, 39, 1942, 97–104.

Feelings, transmission of; prehensions; past, immanence of; James, William; Dewey, John; Lowe, Victor; empiricism, radical; rationalism; psychology.

The radical empiricism which underlies William James' analysis of conjunctive experience cannot support Whitehead's further development into atomistic entities of experience.

260   Brown, Alan Willard.   *The Metaphysical Society: Victorian Minds in Crisis, 1869–1880.*   New York: Columbia University Press, 1947.

Whitehead, Alfred North: biography of.

(While this work does not discuss Whitehead directly, it is nevertheless of importance to the Whitehead scholar and biographer because it provides information on the "Apostles," an undergraduate society to which Whitehead belonged while at Cambridge.)

261   Brown, Delwin.   "God and Process: A Study of the Systematic Theological Alternatives in the Process Philosophy of Alfred North Whitehead."   Unpublished Ph.D. dissertation, Claremont Graduate School, 1964.

Process theology; God: of classical theism, as dipolar, and world; theology, method of; Cobb, John B. Jr.

262   Brown, Delwin.   "Recent Process Theology."   *Journal of the American Academy of Religion*, 35, 1967, 28–41.

Johnson, A. H.; Leclerc, Ivor; Mays, Wolfe; Christian, William; Cobb, John B. Jr.; Lowe, Victor; Wilcox, John T.; Williams, Daniel Day; Sherburne, Donald W.; Lawrence, Nathaniel; Hartshorne, Charles; Gibson, A. Boyce; Stokes, Walter E.;

Wieman, Henry Nelson; Meland, Bernard E.; Loomer, Bernard
M.

(The essay is a synopsis of critical works in process theology
from 1950 through 1967.)

263 Brown, Delwin. "God's Reality and Life's Meaning: A Critique
of Schubert Ogden." *Encounter*, 28, 1967, 256–262.

Questions, limiting; belief; meaningfulness; secularism; Ogden,
Schubert; Toulmin, Stephen; ethics.

The question of life's meaning is the primary focus for religious
discourse, particularly in the context of asserting the reality of
God.

264 Brown, Delwin; James, Ralph E. Jr. and Reeves, Gene, editors.
Process Philosophy and Christian Thought. Indianapolis,
Indiana: Bobbs–Merrill Company, Inc., 1971.

Reviews

Axel, L. E. *Religious Education, 66, 1971, 394–398.*

Christian, W. A. *Interpretation*, 26, 1972, 120–121.

Kantonen, T. A. *Religion in Life*, 40, 1971, 573–574.

Morris, E. *Theology*, 74, 1971, 379–380.

Neville, R. *Journal of American Academy of Religion*, 41, 1973.

Pailin, D. *Religious Studies*, 6, 1972.

Pittenger, W. N. *Journal of Theological Studies*, 23, 1972,
562–564.

Process philosophy; God; Christ; christology; human existence,
and society; theology, and philosophy.

265 Brown, Delwin. "Process Philosophy and the Question of Life's
Meaning." *Religious Studies*, 7, 1971, 13–29.

Purpose; knowledge, factual; God: as persuasive power, as love,
objective immortality in; verifiability; tragedy; Flew, Antony;
Baier, Kurt; philosophy, analytical; theodicy.

Process philosophy provides a constructive approach to the
question of life's meaning in light of the possibilities and
questions raised by analytic philosophers.

266 Brown, Delwin and Reeves, Gene. "The Development of Process
Theology." *Process Philosophy and Christian Thought.* Edited
by Delwin Brown, Ralph E. James, and Gene Reeves.
Indianapolis, Indiana: Bobbs–Merrill Company, Inc., 1971,
21–64.

Process Theology, summary of.

267 Brown, Delwin. "Freedom and Faithfulness in Whitehead's God."
Process Studies, 2, 1972, 137–148.

God: as an actual entity, as a society, satisfaction of,
primordial vision of, freedom of, faithfulness of; subjective aim,
in God; Ford, Lewis S.; Christian, William A.; theology.

In its notion of repeated freedom, the societal view of God

more adequately accounts for the religious intuition of God's faithfulness than does the entitative view.

268   Brown, Delwin. "The World and God: A Process Perspective." *Philosophy of Religion: Contemporary Perspectives.* Edited by Norbert O. Schedler. New York: Macmillan, 1974, 423–440.
Process philosophy, summary of; God: and cosmic order, nature of, and world.

269   Brown, Delwin. "Hope for the Human Future: Neibuhr, Whitehead and Utopian Expectation." *Iliff Review,* 32, 1975, 3–18.
Utopianism; history; nature; progress, as unguaranteed; existence, human; death; God, and world; chaos; eschatology.
History is open to the possibility of dramatic progress, and in spite of human sin, the divine presence in history makes the pursuit of such progress a rational undertaking.

270   Brown, Delwin. "What Is a Christian Theology?" *Religious Experience and Process Theology.* Edited by Harry J. Cargas and Bernard Lee. New York: Paulist Press, 1976, 41–52.
Jesus: as God's decisive act, as unique, work of; causal efficacy; presentational immediacy; prehension; christology; epistemology.
Whitehead's epistemology is relevant for clarifying and resolving the normative problems in christology.

271   Brown, Patricia B. "An Analysis of the Theories of John Dewey and Alfred North Whitehead on the Qualitative Aspect of Experience and the Relation of these Theories to Education." Unpublished Ph.D. dissertation, New York University, 1962.
Experience; feeling; qualities: primary, secondary, tertiary; propositions; Dewey, John; education; aesthetics.
There are areas of agreement between Whitehead and Dewey on educational principles even though these areas are not explicitly described by Whitehead in his formal philosophy.

272   Browning, D. "Whitehead's Theory of Human Agency." *Dialogue,* 2, 1963–1964, 424–441.
Responsibility, moral; agent; agency; self–identity; causation: efficient, final; ethics.
Whitehead's theory of human agency is insufficient on the grounds that it provides no doctrine of the persistence of the agent.

273   Browning, D., editor. *Philosophers of Process.* New York: Random House, 1965.
Process, philosophy.

274   Browning, Don S. "Psychological and Ontological Perspectives on Faith and Reason." *Journal of Religion,* 45, 1965, 296–308. Also in *Process Philosophy and Christian Thought.* Edited by Delwin Brown, Ralph E. James, Jr. and Gene Reeves. Indianapolis, Indiana: Bobbs–Merrill Company, Inc., 1971, 128–142.

Faith, and reason; response, valuational; symbolic form; coherence, internal and external; God, experience of; self–concept; distortion; sin; revelation; Emmet, Dorothy; Rogers, Carl; ontology; epistemology; psychology.

Conditions of self–worth prohibit a positive valuational response to the ontologically given experience of God, thus inhibiting adequate reasoning about God.

275   Browning, Don S. *Atonement and Psychotherapy.* Philadelphia: Westminster Press, 1966, 160–167.

Religion, and psychology; psychotherapy; God, language about; perception, and psychotherapy; Emmet, Dorothy; Hartshorne, Charles.

The psychotherapist's empathic acceptance of the patient can serve as an analogy to God's acceptance of the world. The position of Dorothy Emmet, in her simplification and slight reinterpretation of Whitehead's thought, can give insight into the nature of this analogy. (This is the author's Ph.D. dissertation submitted to the University of Chicago in 1964–1965.)

276   Brumbaugh, Robert S. and Lawrence, Nathaniel M. *Philosophers on Education: Six Essays on the Foundations of Western Thought.* Boston: Houghton Mifflin Company, 1963, 154–184.

Education: aim of, physical, and relativity theory; rhythm: romance, precision, generalization; dipolarity, and education; mind, mind–body problem; teacher, function of; curriculum; Rousseau, Emile.

For Whitehead the aim of education is to combine the collective resources of society in order to help in the rhythmic process of self–production in the individual.

277   Bryan, L. D. "The Understanding of Jesus Christ in the Theology of John B. Cobb, Jr.: A Study of the Position of Christology within a Christian Adaptation of Whiteheadian Organismic Philosophy." Unpublished Ph.D. dissertation, Northwestern University, 1973.

Christology; Jesus, as Christ.

278   Bubser, Eberhard. "Die speculative Philosophie Alfred North Whitehead." Unpublished dissertation, University of Göttingen, 1958.

Philosophy, speculative; language; metaphysics.

279   Bubser, Eberhard. "Sprache und Metaphysik in Whiteheads Philosophie." *Archiv für Philosophie,* 10, 1960, 79–106.

Language, and metaphysics; propositions: and meaning, and statements, and judgments, conformal, and truth, environment of; Urban, Wilbur M.

(This article represents a chapter from the author's dissertation, "Die spekulative Philosophie Alfred North Whitehead," and is written in response to Wilbur Urban's "Whitehead's Philosophy of Language and its Relation to his Metaphysics.")

280   Buchler, Justus. *The Metaphysics of Natural Complexes.* New York: Columbia University Press, 1966, 48–51.

Actualities, atomic; reality; ultimacy; individuality; atomism, metaphysical.

Whitehead errs in attributing special reality to atomic actualities.

281   Buchler, Justus. "On a Strain of Arbitrariness in Whitehead's System." *Journal of Philosophy*, 66, 1969, 589–601.

Categoreal scheme; generalization, descriptive; reality, degrees of; ontological principle; concreteness; eternal objects; concrescence; dramatization.

There are two opposing trends within Whitehead: a dramatic evaluation of metaphysical priorities, and a more reliable analytical description.

282   Buehrer, Edwin T. "Mysticism and A. N. Whitehead." *Mysticism and the Modern Mind.* Edited by Alfred P. Stiernotte. New York: Liberal Arts Press, 1959, 60–70.

Mysticism: cosmic, social; togetherness; process; flux; convergence; peace; tragedy; Einstein, Albert; Schweitzer, Albert.

Cosmic and social mysticism are necessarily implied in Whitehead's philosophy of organism.

283   Burch, George Bosworth, and Stewart, Dwight C. "Whitehead's Harvard Lectures, 1926–1927." *Process Studies*, 4, 1974, 199–206.

Eternal objects, ingression of; God, as actual entity; Descartes, critique of; metaphysics, six principles of; Demos, R.; Hartshorne, Charles.

A large set of class notes, papers, and clippings indicate Whitehead's direct teachings of fundamental themes in his philosophy.

284   Burgers, J. M. *Experience and Conceptual Activity: A Philosophical Essay Based Upon the Writings of A. N. Whitehead.* Cambridge: M. I. T. Press, 1965.

Reviews

Mays, W. *Philosophical Quarterly*, 17, 1967, 271–272.

Palter, R. *Science*, 154, 1966, 1156.

Stevenson, I. *Virginia Quarterly Review*, 43, 1967, 504.

Activity, conceptual; mind; subjectivity; novelty; spontaneity; subjective form; subjective aim; purpose; value; creativity, as principle of novelty; future; many, become one; relatedness; play; rhythm; body; matter; past, and causal efficacy; determinism; memory; order; societies; evolution; mutation; Darwin, Charles; Waddington, Charles H.; science; biology; physics.

Using Whitehead's metaphysics, a system of thought can be developed in which notions of value find a place along with the ideas of causal relationships that are applied in the physical sciences. The claim is that, in every act occuring in the universe, experience derived from that which has gone before is integrated with conceptions concerning possibilities in the future.

285   Burgers, J. M.   "Comments on Shimony's Paper." *Boston Studies in the Philosophy of Science*, Volume 2. Edited by R. S. Cohen and M. W. Wartofsky. New York: Humanities Press, 1965, 331–342.

Philosophy, of science; physics, quantum.

286   Burgers, J. M.   "The Measuring Process in Quantum Theory." *Reviews of Modern Physics*, 35, 1963, 145–150.

Quantum; apparatus, measuring; eigenstate; eigenvalue; causality; relatedness, forms of; process, in physics; von Neumann, J.; Everett, Hugh, III; Groenewald, H. J.; Komar, A.; physics.

Certain demonstrations in physics indicate the possibility of teleological forces in nature.

287   Burgers, J. M.   "Causality and Anticipation." *Science*, 189, 1975, 194–198.

Causality: context of, limitations of; teleology; anticipation; freedom; memory; quantum mechanics; biology; physics, quantum.

Analysis of the concept of anticipation can contribute to the philosophy of biology.

288   Buri, E.   "Existential–Ontologie und neue Metaphysik als christliche natürliche Theologie." *Gott in Amerika: Amerikanische Theologie seit 1960.* Bern: Paul Haupt, 1970, 95–135.

Theology, natural; existentialism; ontology; metaphysics.

289   Burke, T. E. B.   "Whitehead's Philosophy of Nature." Unpublished dissertation, Trinity College, Dublin, 1955.

Philosophy, of nature; nature.

290   Burke, T. E. B.   "Whitehead's Conception of Reality." *Hermathena*, 93, 1959, 3–15.

Criterion: of genuineness, of existence; self–creativity; order; God; empiricism.

Whitehead resolves the subject–object dilemma with his descriptive criterion of reality, but misuses the criterion in his discussion of God.

291   Burkle, Howard R.   "God's Relation to the World: The Issues Between St. Thomas Aquinas and Charles Hartshorne." Unpublished Ph.D. dissertation, Yale University, 1954.

God, and world; Aquinas, Thomas; Hartshorne, Charles.

(This study examines Charles Hartshorne's critique of the classical view of God as exemplified in the thought of Thomas Aquinas.)

292   Burkle, Howard R.   *The Non-Existence of God: Antitheism from Hegel to Duméry.*   New York: Herder and Herder, 1969, 204–205.

Theism; God, as persuasive; Hartshorne, Charles.

A theist cannot accept Hartshorne's and Whitehead's theory of divine persuasion because it places God in dependence upon the world for actuality.   As long as the world is part of God's being, there is not anything for God to persuade.

293   Burnett, Joe R.   "The Educational Philosophy of Alfred North Whitehead."   Unpublished Ph.D.   Dissertation, New York University, 1958.

Value; knowledge; learning; rhythm; romance; precision; generalization; perception; civilization; truth; beauty; adventure; art; peace; education, philosophy of; religion; aesthetics.

Although Whitehead's educational philosophy stresses the individual human being's nature, whereas his formal philosophy stresses a cosmological approach to the nature of reality, the two philosophies can be correlated.

294   Burnett, Joe R.   "Whitehead's Concept of Creativity and Some of Its Educational Implications."   *Harvard Educational Review,* 27, 1957, 220–234.

Creativity; creative advance; purpose; values; growth; individual; society; civilization; Dewey, John; pragmatism; empiricism; education.

The metaphysics of creativity suggests educational guidelines for optimum development of individual and societal creativity.

295   Burnett, Joe R.   "Alfred North Whitehead (1861–1947)."   *Educational Theory,* 11, 1961, 269–278.

Whitehead, Alfred North: introduction to his thought; philosophy, of education.

296   Burnett, Joe R.   "Whitehead on the Aims of Schooling."   *Educational Theory,* 11, 1961, 269–278.

Learning; philosophy, of education.

297   Burns, C. Delisle.   "Philosophy in the University of Cambridge."   *International Journal of Ethics,* 34, 1923, 27–36.

Nature: relatedness of, as process, and values; significance; substance; events; Broad, C. D.; Johnson, W. E.; McTaggart, J. M.; ethics; philosophy, social; science.

In the Cambridge of 1923, a new philosophical outlook was emerging in the logical reconstructions of reality developed respectively by McTaggart, Whitehead, Broad, and Johnson.

298   Burrell, D. B.   "The Possibility of a Natural Theology."   *Encounter,* 29, 1968, 158–164.

Theology, natural.

299   Burtt, E. A. *Types of Religious Philosophy.* New York: Harper & Row, 1939, 422–427.

Process philosophy, summary of; God: as principle of order, as lure for feeling; order, moral; experience, religious.

Religious, moral experience provides confirmation for the philosophical notion of God as the principle of ordered value.

300   Cafaro, F. *Il pensiero educativo de A. N. Whitehead.* Bologna: Leonardi, 1969.

Rhythm; philosophy, of education.

301   Cailliet, Emile. *The Christian Approach to Culture.* New York: Abingdon–Cokesbury Press, 1953.

Christianity, and culture; religion, and science; God, and science.

Whitehead's religious postulates exhibit the fact that, in science and philosophy, principles of faith and working hypotheses exist in intimate interrelation.

302   Calkins, M. W. *The Persistent Problems of Philosophy.* New York: Macmillan Company, 1933, 407 n., 413 n., 423, 437, 586.

Philosophy, in America; Whitehead, Alfred North: and American philosophy.

303   Campbell, Harry M. "Emerson and Whitehead." *Proceedings of the Modern Language Association,* 75, 1960, 577–582.

Nature; harmony; unity; evolution, as creative; individual; over–soul; self–enjoyment; God; evil; Jesus; immortality; Emerson, Ralph Waldo; transcendentalism; pragmatism; rationalism, analytical; romanticism.

Parallels between Whitehead and Emerson establish the two as leaders in a religious revolt against analytical rationalism.

304   Capek, Milic. "Bergson's Theory of Matter and Modern Physics." *Revue Philosophique,* 77, 1953. Reprinted in *Bergson and the Evolution of Physics.* Edited by P. A. Y. Gunter. Knoxville, Tennessee: University of Tennessee Press, 1969.

Matter, vibratory theory of; becoming: discontinuity of, continuity of; energy; Bergson, Henri; physics.

(In discussing Bergson the author suggests that Whitehead and Bergson agree with one another in accepting a vibratory theory of matter. Like Whitehead, Bergson defines materiality as a succession of elementary events possessing an almost vanishing duration.)

305   Capek, Milic. "Note about Whitehead's Definitions of Co–Presence." *Philosophy of Science,* 24, 1957, 79–86.

Co–presence; simultaneity; space; time; relativity, special theory of; past, causal; independence, causal; Newton, Isaac; Lorentz; physics: classical, relativity.

The notion of co–presence in *The Principle of Relativity*
clarifies misleading statements in *The Concept of Nature*
concerning simultaneity.

306   Capek, Milic. *The Philosophical Impact of Contemporary
        Physics.* New York: Van Nostrand Press, 1961.

Space: classical view of, relational theory of; time: classical
view of, relativity view of; becoming; event; relativity, general
theory of; Einstein, Albert; Bergson, Henri; Euclid; physics.

(Although the work does not contain a sustained discussion of
Whitehead's thought, there are numerous references to
Whitehead's criticisms of classical physics and to Whitehead's
theories of space, time, and becoming.)

307   Capek, Milic. "The Elusive Nature of the Past." *Experience,
        Existence and the Good: Essays in Honor of Paul Weiss.*
        Edited by Irwin C. Lieb. Carbondale, Illinois: Southern Illinois
        University Press, 1961.

Time, and past; location, fallacy of simple.

The relation which a past event has to the present is not an
external feature of that past event, but rather a constitutive
part of its nature. By virtue of the perpetual emergence of
novelty, this relation is continually changing. In this sense the
past continually changes with the addition of subsequent
entities.

308   Capek, Milic. "Simple Location and Fragmentation of Reality."
        Process and Divinity. Edited by W. R. Reese and Eugene
        Freeman. LaSalle: Open Court, 1964, 79–100. The article is
        republished in *Monist*, 48, 1964, 195–218.

Simple location; atomism; concreteness, fallacy of misplaced;
consciousness, stream of; asymmetry, temporal; independence,
causal; Descartes, Rene; Hume, David; James, William;
Bergson, Henri; Hartshorne, Charles; Newton, Isaac; Faraday,
M.; Maxwell, J. C.; Mach, E.; Spinoza; Leibniz; Ehrenfels;
Köhler, Wolfgang; Ward, James; Brentano, Franz;
associationism; psychology, Gestalt.

Whitehead's denial of simple location culminates a long history
within physics and psychology during which slow advances
were made against the artificial fragmentation of reality.

309   Capek, Milic. *Bergson and Modern Physics: A Reinterpretation
        and Re–evaluation.* Dordrecht, Holland: D. Reidel Publishing
        Company, 1971.

Past, immortality of; matter, and Bergson; self–creativity;
relativity, theory of; possibility; continuity, becoming of;
simultaneity; location, fallacy of simple; instants; Langevin's
paradox; Bergson, Henri; Kant, Immanuel; Russell, Bertrand;
physics.

(This work consists of numerous essays on Bergson, many of
which discuss relations between the thought of Bergson and
that of Whitehead.)

310   Capps, Walter H. "'Being and Becoming' and 'God and the World': An Analysis of Whitehead's Account of their Early Association." *Revue Philosophique de Louvain*, 63, 1965, 572–590.

Philosophy: as structure, and theology, and religion; being, becoming; God; world; Nicea; Chalcedon; trinity; christology; asymmetry; Plato; Aristotle; Augustine; metaphysics; theology; religion.

Theological expressions exhibit complex relationships between philosophy as structure and religious affirmation as content.

311   Caraway, James E. "God as Dynamic Actuality: The Reality of God in the Theologies of John B. Cobb, Jr. and Schubert M. Ogden." Unpublished Ph.D. dissertation, Emory University, 1969.

God: as actual entity, and categoreal scheme; temporality, as mystery; subjective aim, initial phase of; Cobb, John B. Jr.; Ogden, Schubert M.

312   Cargas, Harry James and Lee, Bernard, editors. *Religious Experience and Process Theology*. New York: Paulist Press, 1976.

Process theology; prayer; Church; Holy Spirit; hope; truth, religious; revelation; freedom; commitment; sexuality.

(This collection of essays focuses on a process understanding of the Church, its ministry, and pastoral responsibility. See individual entries under Beardslee, Brown, Cobb, Cooper, Doud, Fleming, Fontinell, Ford, Griffin, Hartshorne, Janzen, Lee, Loomer, Mellert, Ogden, Pittenger, Van der Veken.)

313   Carmody, John. "A Note on the God–World Relation in Whitehead's *Process and Reality*." *Philosophy Today*, 15, 1971, 302–312.

God: as dipolar, primordial nature of, consequent nature of, religious availability of, and classical theism; Christianity.

Whitehead's failure to emphasize the claims of Jesus is the major inadequacy of his thought for the Christian.

314   Carr, H. Wildon. "Professor Whitehead's World-Building." *The Personalist*, 11, 1930, 157–163.

Experience; eternal objects; God, as deus ex machina; Plato; Hume, David; idealism; realism.

Process and Reality contains much that is obscure and arbitrary.

315   Castiglione, Robert L. "The Reality of the Past: A Comparison of the Philosophies of Alfred North Whitehead and Paul Weiss." Unpublished Ph.D. dissertation, Catholic University of America, 1971.

Time: as past, and past actual entities, and relevance of the past; God, in relation to past; possibility; solidarity of world;

transition; concrescence; process: as microscopic and macroscopic; Weiss, Paul.

316   Castuera, Ignacio. "The Theology and Practice of Liberation in the Mexican American Context." *Perkins Journal*, 29, 1975, 2–11.

Praxis; oppression; liberation: Chicano, women; ecumenism; love; fundamentalism; machismo; God, as call forward; Freire, Paulo; Cobb, John B. Jr.; Ghandi; theology, liberation.

The practice of liberation requires theological foundations. Process views of God and of love contribute to this praxis situation.

317   Cauthen, Kenneth. "Process and Purpose: Toward a Philosophy of Life." *Zygon*, 3, 1968, 183–204.

Creativity; life; evolution: as cosmic, as biological, as cultural; values; self–transcendence; self–enjoyment; evil; Teilhard de Chardin; Tillich, Paul; metaphysics; science; physics.

A comprehensive vision of the cosmos must incorporate scientific knowledge into a metaphysics in which life becomes the central category.

318   Cauthen, Kenneth. *Science, Secularization, and God: Toward a Theology of the Future.* New York: Abingdon Press, 1969.
Review
Overman, R. H. *Process Studies*, 1, 1971, 60–63.

God: as being, as becoming, as principle of concretion, as worthy of worship; cosmos, as organism; philosophical, theology; redemption; Christ: as Logos, as Messiah; Teilhard de Chardin; Tillich, Paul; Hartshorne, Charles; Christian theology; Christology; science, and religion.

(In developing a theology inclusive of the insights of science and philosophy, the author makes use of Whitehead's doctrines of God and organism.)

319   Caws, Peter. "Conmemoración de Whitehead." *Actas Segundo Congreso Extraordinario Interamericano de Filosofía, 22–26 Julio 1961.* San José, Costa Rica: Imprenta Nacional, 1963, 145–155.

Whitehead, Alfred North, introduction to his thought.

(This is an opening address at the section on Whitehead at the Interamerican Conference on Philosophy in 1961, where the hundredth anniversary of Whitehead's birthday was honored.)

320   Centore, F. F. "Whitehead's Conception of God." *Philosophical Studies* (Ireland), 19, 1970, 148–171.

God: as primordial, as consequent, as superjective, as principle of concretion, as deus ex machina; Plato; Descartes, Rene; Leibniz, G. W.

Whitehead's conception of God is insufficient on grounds of 1) infinite regress; 2) *deus ex machina*; 3) dualism; 4) incoherence.

321   Cesselin, Félix. *La philosophie organique de Whitehead.* Paris:
        Presses Universitaires de France, 1950.
        Review
        Lentin, A. *Pensée,* 45, 1962, 141.

        Philosophy, of organism; actual occasions; eternal objects;
        perception; causality; God; person; value; freedom; Aristotle;
        Alexander, Samuel; Bergson, Henri; Hartshorne, Charles;
        Heidegger, Martin; James, William; Plato; sociology; cosmology;
        platonism.

        (Includes a bibliography of French translations of Whitehead's
        major works, plus excerpts from his two essays on "Les
        mathematiques et le bein" and "Immortality.")

322   Cesslin, Félix. *La philosophie organique de Whitehead.* Paris:
        Presses Universitaires de France, 1950.

        Process philosophy, summary of; events; occasions, actual;
        objects, eternal; relations, spacio–temporal; causality;
        perception; value; immortality; Whitehead, Alfred North,
        biography of; morality; cosmology; sociology; mathematics.

323   Cesslin, Félix. "La bifurcation de la nature." *Revue
        Metaphysique et de Morale,* 55, 1950, 30–49.

        Events: theory of, spatio–temporal structure of; objects: of
        perception, of science, physical; space; time, relativity view of;
        nature, bifurcation of; Newton, Isaac; Einstein, Albert; Galilie,
        Galileo; Descartes, Rene; Leibniz, G. W.

324   Chang, Yen–Ling. "The Problem of Emergence: Mead and
        Whitehead." *Kinesis,* 2, 1970, 69–80.

        Creativity; emergence; novelty; causality; symbol, function of;
        time, epochal; self–creation; relations, internal; Mead, George
        Herbert; Hume, David; Zeno; metaphysics; epistemology;
        psychology, social; pragmatism; realism.

        The metaphysical realism of Whitehead and epistemological
        pragmatism of Mead yield significant differences in their
        respective use of the notion of emergence.

325   Chao, I–Wei. "Huait–te–hai ti Wen–hua Che–hsüen
        ("Whitehead's Philosophy of Culture")." *Ta–lu Tsa–chih
        (Mainland Magazine,* Shanghaï), IV, 3, 10–13.

        Culture, philosophy of.

326   Chao, I–Wei. "Huai–te–hai Yu–chi Shih–tsai–lun chien–chieh ("A
        Brief Introduction to Whitehead's Organic Theory of
        Reality")." *San–mi Chu–i Pan–yueh– K'an (The Three
        People's Principles Fortnightly,* number 3, 8–13.

        Whitehead, Alfred North, introduction to his thought.

327   Chao, I. "Huai–Te–Hai Che–Hsueh Kai–Shu ("An Examination
        of Whitehead's Philosophy")." *Hsueh–Shu Chi–K'an,* 3,
        number 1, 52–61.

        Process philosophy, summary of.

328   Chappell, Vere C.   "The Philosophy of Process."   Unpublished
        Ph.D. dissertation, Yale University, 1957.

        Time, continuity of; motion; change; becoming; substance;
        Zeno's paradox; Parmenides; Bergson, Henri.

        In responding to Zeno's paradox Whitehead and Bergson each
        develop views of time which reduce to absurdity.

329   Chappell, Vere C.   "Whitehead's Metaphysics."   *Review of
        Metaphysics*, 13, 1959, 278–304.

        Atomicity;   continuum,   extensive;   extension,   temporal;
        ontological principle; eternal objects; God; satisfaction; past,
        givenness of; Leclerc, Ivor; Christian, William A.

        Whitehead's metaphysical system is presented in a linear
        method by Leclerc, and in an organic, circular method by
        Christian.

330   Chappell, Vere C.   "Whitehead's Theory of Becoming."   *Journal
        of Philosophy*, 58, 1961, 516–528.   Reprinted in *Alfred North
        Whitehead: Essays on his Philosophy*.   Edited by George L.
        Kline.   Englewood Cliffs, New Jersey: Prentice–Hall, 1963,
        70–80.

        Time, epochal theory of; extension, temporal; concrescence;
        transition;   Zeno,   dichotomy   of;   Aristotle;   Simplicius;
        philosophy: analytical, speculative.

        An epochal theory of time is not only untenable within the
        Whiteheadian system, but also unnecessary.

331   Chappell, Vere C.   "Time and Zeno's Arrow."   *Journal of
        Philosophy*, 59, 1962, 197–213.   Also in *Bergson and the
        Evolution of Physics*.   Edited by P. A. Y. Gunter.   Knoxville,
        Tennessee: University of Tennessee Press, 1969, 253–274.

        Zeno's paradox, flying arrow; time; space; motion; time:
        epochal, as continuous, as indivisible; Zeno; Weiss, Paul;
        Bergson, Henri; Russell, Bertrand.

        With problematic degrees of success, Whitehead, Weiss, Bergson
        and Russell appeal to Zeno's Flying Arrow argument to justify
        their respective views on time.

332   Chiaraviglio, Lucio.   "Abstraction and Temporality: A Study of
        Whitehead's Metaphysics."   Unpublished Ph.D. dissertation,
        Emory University, 1961.

        Abstraction, extensive; analysis, coordinate; time; language, and
        logic; logic.

333   Chiaraviglio, Lucio.   "Strains."   *Journal of Philosophy*, 58, 1961,
        528–534.

        Definiteness; position; strain–feelings; strain–locus; flat loci;
        eternal   objects;   abstraction,   extensive;   points;   volume;
        geometry.

        The theory of feelings in connection with the theory of
        extensive abstraction yields definitions of "definiteness" and

"position" which elucidate the reproduction of geometric eternal objects in physical feelings.

334   Chiaraviglio, Lucio.   "Whitehead's Theory of Prehensions." *Alfred North Whitehead: Essays on his Philosophy.* Edited by George L. Kline. Englewood Cliffs, New Jersey: Prentice–Hall, Inc., 1963.

Prehension; position; definiteness; strain feelings; nexus; eternal object; ontological principle; prehension, hybrid physical.

(The author articulates Whitehead's theory of prehensions through set theory and posits an alternative to Whitehead's theory in which the notion of eternal object is called into question.)

335   Chiaraviglio, Lucio.   "Extension and Abstraction." *Process and Divinity: Philosophical Essays in Honor of Charles Hartshorne.* Edited by William L. Reese and Eugene Freeman. La Salle, Illinois: Open Court Publishing Company, 1964.

Causation, efficient; extension, and causation; novelty, and causation; freedom, and determinism.

Whitehead's philosophy of organism attempts to explain causal determination and novelty by assuming (a) that there exist properties and relations of actual entities which are independent of position, (b) that the extensive relations which hold among actual entities govern the manner in which causal transmission occurs, but do not govern what is transmitted, and (c) that physical feelings are the only agency of causal transmission. Set theory can elucidate these assumptions.

336   Chiesa, E. L.   "La doctrina de la immortalidad objéctiva en la filosofía de Alfred North Whitehead." Unpublished M. A. dissertation, University of Puerto Rico, 1967.

Eternal objects: as abstractions, as forms, as forms of definiteness, ingression, in objectification, as pure possibilities, structure of.

337   Christian, William A. Jr.   "Whitehead's Organic Pluralism: A Study of Transcendence and Immanence in Alfred North Whitehead's Theory of Actual Occasions." Unpublished Ph.D. dissertation, Yale University, 1942.

Actual occasion: as present in others, as transcending others; objectification; regions, overlapping of; substance; novelty; God, as source of initial aim; Hume, David.

(This study deals with Whitehead's descriptions of how any actual occasion transcends, or is 'other than', other occasions, and how any occasion is immanent in, or 'present in', other occasions. The author argues that Whitehead revises but does not reject the notion of substance.)

338   Christian, William A.   "God and the World." *Journal of Religion,* 28, 1948, 255–262.

God: sovereignty of, as love; freedom; evil; language; philosophy, and theology; theology.

Philosophical alternatives are explored for their adequacy in depicting the relationship between God and the world in light of religious experience, thought, and language.

339 Christian, William A. "The Mutual Exclusiveness of Whitehead's Actual Occasions." *Review of Metaphysics*, 2, 1949, 45–75.

Actual occasions; exclusiveness, mutual; objectification; subjective immediacy; objective immortality; independence, causal; prehensions: indirect, hybrid; presentational immediacy; feeling, transmission of; Blyth, John W.; Hartshorne, Charles; Weiss, Paul; metaphysics.

Evidence for the general assertion that no two actual occasions share any immediacy of feeling is explained and examined.

340 Christian, William A. *An Interpretation of Whitehead's Metaphysics*. New Haven, Connecticut: Yale University Press, 1959.

Reviews

Anonymous. *Revue de Metaphysique et de Morale*, 65, 1960, 363.

Barry, R. M. *New Scholasticism*, 33, 1959, 526–528.

Bogie, T. M. *Revue Philosophique*, 84, 1959, 1137.

Chappell, V. C. *Review of Metaphysics*, 13, 1959–1960, 278–304.

Collins, J. *Cross Currents*, 10, 1960, 157–158.

Faleiro, B. *Revista Portugesa di Filosofia*, 18, 1962, 97.

Heineman, F. H. *Hibbert Journal*, 58, 1960, 397.

Johnson, A. H. *Philosophy and Phenomenological Research*, 20, 1960, 427–428.

Kline, G. L. *Ethics*, 70, 1960, 337–340.

Leclerc, I. *Journal of Philosophy*, 57, 1960, 138–143.

Leroy, A. L. *Revue Philosophique*, 87, 1962, 552–555.

Lowe, V. *Philosophical Review*, 70, 1961, 114–116.

Schaper, E. *Philosophy*, 37, 1962, 365–366.

Thornton, L. S. *Journal of Theological Studies*, 12, 1961, 159–161.

Actual occasions; eternal objects: ingression, as pure possibilities, and universals, and Platonic forms, as forms of definiteness, and creativity; God: and world, and categoreal scheme, primordial nature of, consequent nature of, and ontological principle, and negative prehensions, immanence of, transcendence of, as superject, and classical theism, Whitehead's arguments for, satisfaction of, and evil; novelty; past, and present; extension; regions; substance; causation: efficient, final; objectification; subjective form; subjective aim; feelings: simple physical, conceptual.

(This work is a systematic interpretation of Whitehead's later philosophy. It is divided into three major sections—the first dealing with the theory of actual occasions, the second with the theory of eternal objects, and the third with God and the world.)

341 Christian, William A. "Whitehead's Explanation of the Past." *Journal of Philosophy*, 58, 1961, 534–543. Reprinted in *Alfred North Whitehead: Essays on his Philosophy*. Edited by George L. Kline. Englewood Cliffs: Prentice–Hall, Inc., 1963, 92–101.

Past; causal efficacy; categoreal scheme; language, Whitehead's use of; ontological principle; God, and givenness of past.

The category of the past is not required by the categoreal scheme. God is an essential condition of the effectiveness of the past in the present.

342 Christian, William A. "Some Uses of Reason." *The Relevance of Whitehead*. Edited by Ivor Leclerc. New York: Humanities Press Inc., 1961, 47–89.

Philosophy: and religion, method of; aesthetics, as data for philosophy; religion.

Whitehead's philosophy procedes from religious as well as philosophical interests.

343 Christian, William A. "Truth–claims in Religion." *Journal of Religion*, 42, 1962, 52–62.

Truth–claims, criteria for; language: uses of, religious, and common reference, and referent, and predication; religion; linguistic analysis; logic.

Significant truth–claims may be made in the language of religion.

344 Christian, William A. "Whitehead's Conception of Speculative Philosophy." *Nous*, 10, 1962, 1–15.

Philosophy: speculative, method of, task of.

345 Christian, William A. "On Whitehead's Explanation of Causality: A Reply." *International Philosophical Quarterly*, 2, 1962, 323–328.

Causality, efficient; categoreal scheme; objectification; past, givenness of; conformal feelings; language, Whitehead's use of; Gustafson, D. F.; realism; language.

Whitehead's development of causal objectification and conformal feelings allows a coherent theory of efficient causation. (Written in reply to D. F. Gustafson, "Christian on Causal Objectification in Whitehead," *International Philosophical Quarterly*, 1, 1961, 683–696.)

346 Christian, William A. "The Concept of God as a Derivative Notion." *Process and Divinity: Philosophical Essays Presented to Charles Hartshorne*. Edited by William L. Reese and Eugene Freeman. LaSalle, Illinois: Open Court Publishing Company, 1964, 181–203.

God, concept of; notions: derivative, pre–systematic;

explanation, category of; obligation, category of; categoreal scheme; reversion, conceptual; contingency.

The concept of God must be studied from the way it is introduced, and not merely the way it is used, in Whitehead's system. God is required by the categoreal scheme and is therefore categorically necessary instead of categorically contingent.

347 Christian, William A. "A Discussion on the New Metaphysics and Theology." *The Future of Theology in America.* Edited by William A. Beardslee. Philadelphia: Westminster, 1967, 94–111. Also in *Christian Scholar,* 50, 1967, 304–315.

Philosophical theology; being; ultimacy, religious; Platonism, and Christian tradition; God: and the world, immutability of, doctrine of; Plato; metaphysics; theology.

Although metaphysics and theology grow from separate roots, methods may be developed for their creative interchange.

348 Clark, G. A. "The Problem of Two Bodies in Whitehead's Theory." *Proceedings of the Royal Society of Edinburgh,* Series A, 64, 1954, 49–56.

Body; mathematics; physics.

349 Clark, George A. "Intimations of Philosophy in Whitehead's Introduction to Mathematics." *Actas Segundo Congreso Extraordinario Interamericano de Filosofía, 22–26 Julio 1961.* San José, Costa Rica: Imprenta Nacional, 1963, 157–161.

Introduction to Mathematics; dynamics; science, method of; Galilie, Galileo; mathematics.

Whitehead's *Introduction to Mathematics,* in its intimations of classically conflicting cosmologies, represents an integration of mathematics and physics, marked with a delicate sense of their cultural implications.

350 Clarke, Bowman L. "Whitehead's Cosmology and the Christian Drama." *Journal of Religion,* 39, 1959, 162–169.

Drama; kerygma; creativity, phases of; objective immortality, in God; salvation, as catharsis; Aristotle; cosmology.

The correspondence between the dramatic structures of the Christian kerygma and of the four creative phases of the universe suggest that drama may be a vehicle for uniting Whiteheadian philosophy and historical Christianity.

351 Clarke, Bowman L. "Language and Whitehead's Conception of Speculative Philosophy." *Process and Divinity: Essays in Honor of Charles Hartshorne.* Edited by William L. Reese and Eugene Freeman. La Salle, Illinois: Open Court Publishing Company, 1964, 217–234.

Language; philosophy, speculative; logic, symbolic; algebra.

Whitehead's cosmological scheme can be articulated in terms of a monadic functional logic.

352   Clarke, Bowman L. *Language and Natural Theology.* Paris: Mouton and Company, 1966.

Language: formal, religious, and logic, and meaning; metaphysics; philosophy, method of; abstraction, extensive; coherence; adequacy; necessity; God: proofs of, language about; Anselm; Aquinas, Thomas; Wittgenstein, Ludwig; Carnap, Rudolph; Ramsey, Ian T.; Findlay, J. N.; Quine, Willard Van Orman; Goodman, Nelson; Salamucha, Jan; Hartshorne, Charles; philosophy, analytical; linguistics; logic; religion; theology, natural.

(Although the work explicitly concerns language and natural theology rather than Whitehead's philosophy, it uses Whitehead's view of metaphysics to show the relation between formal and religious language.)

353   Clarke, Bowman L. "Religion and the Human Situation." *Philosophy Forum,* 8, 1970, 3–31.

Secularism; culture; language; God, concept of; Van Buren, Paul; Cox, Harvey; Tillich, Paul; religion; science; technology.

The need to speak of God is particularly crucial in our day, demanding a constructive dialogue between religion and contemporary scientific and technological culture.

354   Clarke, W. Norris, S. J. "A New Look at the Immutability of God." *God Knowable and Unknowable.* Edited by Robb Roth, S. J. New York: Fordham University Press, 1973, 43–72.

God: immutability of, and being, being of, as loving, relations of, perfection of, and temporality; and the world; causality; Thomas Aquinas, Aristotle; Thomism; theology, process; metaphysics.

Thomistic metaphysics allows development of a new dimension of intentional process and time in God which leaves intact, while transcending, the entire Aristotelian dimension of real change and immutability.

355   Clarke, Norris. "Reply." *Christian Scholar,* 50, 1967, 319–320.

God: knowledge of, and world; Christian, William A.; Thomas Aquinas; metaphysics.

Knowledge of God through the world does not require a dependency of God upon the world. (Reply to William A. Christian, "The New Metaphysics and Theology," *Christian Scholar,* 50, 1967, 304–315.)

356   Clarke, William F. "The Idea of God in a Philosophy of Events." *Monist,* 38, 1928, 620–629.

God: as principle of limitation, and order, as source of values, immanence of, as worthy of worship.

The view of God as principle of order leads to a view of God as will toward order.

357   Cloots, Andre. "Charles Hartshorne's Bipolar Theism." Unpublished M. A. thesis, Leuven, 1972.

Hartshorne, Charles.

358   Cobb, John B. Jr. "Theological Data and Method." *Journal of Religion*, 33, 1953, 212–223.

Relativity, cultural; criteria: theological, philosophical; God, doctrine of; experience, Christian; hermeneutics, problems of; Schleiermacher, Friedrich; Wieman, Henry Nelson.

Theological procedures must and can be revised in light of problems posed by the relativity of knowledge.

359   Cobb, John B. Jr. "Toward Clarity in Aesthetics." *Philosophy and Phenomenological Research*, 18, 1957, 169–189.

Prehensions; causal efficacy; subjective aim; subjective form; transmutation; presentational immediacy; symbolism; beauty; intensity; emotion; relationships, patterned; discovery; pleasure; Ducasse, Curt John; Lee, Vernon; aesthetics; painting; music; poetry; literature; sculpture.

Objective and subjective dimensions of aesthetic experience can be analyzed in terms of form and function.

360   Cobb, John B. Jr. "The Philosophic Grounds of Moral Responsibility; A Comment on Matson and Niebuhr." *Journal of Philosophy*, 56, 1959, 619–621.

Responsibility, moral; freedom; self–determination; society, personally ordered; Niebuhr, Reinhold; Matson, W. I.; Kant, Immanuel; ethics; determinism; positivism; libertarianism.

Whitehead's grounds of moral responsibility overcome the assertions of Matson and Niebuhr that moral responsibility is philosophically unintelligible.

361   Cobb, John B. Jr. "Some Thoughts on the Meaning of Christ's Death." *Religion in Life*, 28, 1959, 212–222.

Atonement, theories of; sin; forgiveness; Aulén, Gustaf; theology.

A literal meaning can be given to the doctrine that Christ in his death won a victory over transpersonal forces of evil.

362   Cobb, John B. Jr. "Nihilism, Existentialism, and Whitehead." *Religion in Life*, 30, 1961, 521–533.

Nihilism; existentialism; subjectivism; objectivism; God, as source of value; Heidegger, Martin; Tillich, Paul; Husserl, Edmund.

Whitehead overcomes the alienation of subjectivistic philosophy from our total knowledge of the world in which we live.

363   Cobb, John B. Jr. "'Perfection Exists': A Critique of Charles Hartshorne." *Religion in Life*, 32, 1963, 294–304.

Argument, ontological; God, perfection of; theism, neoclassical; Hartshorne, Charles; theology, and philosophy.

In *The Logic of Perfection*, Hartshorne has shown that the ontological argument can be formulated without violating any established principle of logic.   However, some ontological positions capable of serious defense must be rejected if the argument is to be effective.

364   Cobb, John, B. Jr. "Whitehead's Philosophy and a Christian Doctrine of Man." *Journal of the American Academy of Religion*, 32, 1964, 209–220.

Man, Christian doctrine of; sin; freedom, and responsibility; immortality, personal; identity, self; Niebuhr, Reinhold; ethics; existentialism.

Whitehead's philosophy allows meaningful formulation of the traditional Christian doctrines that a person is a responsible sinner, and that personal existence is not limited to this life.

365   Cobb, John B. Jr. "From Crisis Theology to the Post–Modern World." *Centennial Review*, 8, 1964, 174–188. Also in *Toward a New Christianity: Readings in the Death of God Theology*. Edited by Thomas J. J. Altizer. New York: Harcourt, Brace & World, 1967, 241–252. *The Meaning of the Death of God*. Edited by Bernard Murchland. New York: Random House, 1967, 138–152. *Radical Theology: Phase Two*. Edited by C. W. Christian and Glenn R. Wittig. Philadelphia: J. B. Lippincott Company, 1967, 191–206.

Theology, radical; God, death of; relativism; relations; truth; self.

When we combine a Whiteheadian doctrine of God with his triumph over nihilistic relativism, we are able to see that the truth we seek is already real.

366   Cobb, John B. Jr. "Ontology, History, and Christian Faith." *Religion in Life*, 34, 1965, 270–287.

History; ontology; past, status of; Jesus, historical; God, as acting in history; theology, and history.

The Christian historian must determine the ontological status of the past, and rigorously interpret the past using illuminating categories derived from both faith, and objective data.

367   Cobb, John B. Jr. *A Christian Natural Theology: Based on the Thought of Alfred North Whitehead*. Philadelphia: Westminster, 1965.

Reviews

Ferre, F. *Christian Century*, 82, 1965, 712–713.

Ford, L. S. *Journal of Bible and Religion*, 34, 1966, 60–64.

Guy, F. *Andrews University Seminary Studies*, 4, 1966, 107–134.

Gilkey, L. B. *Theology Today*, 22, 1965–1966, 530–545.

Perkins, R. L. *Library Journal*, 90, 1965, 1723.

Schmidt, P. F. *Zygon*, 2, 1967, 206–209.

God: Whitehead's arguments for, functions of, and creativity, and categoreal scheme, as living person, as source of initial aim, and novelty, as creator, primordial nature of, consequent nature of, superjective nature of, and reversal of poles, religious availability of, and eternal objects, and creatio ex nihilo;

novelty; creativity: and God, as material cause, and Aristotle's prime matter, and actuality, as substantial activity; subjective aim, initial phase of; human existence; soul; person: as series of experiences, as enduring object, and personal identity, and memory, and personal immortality; occasion, dominant; morality, and moral responsibility; value; beauty; adventure; peace; prehensions, hybrid physical; societies; consciousness; unconscious; Whitehead, Alfred North: introduction to his thought; Hartshorne, Charles; Edwards, Jonathon; theology, natural.

A Christian natural theology can be developed on the basis of Whitehead's philosophy such that the notions of God and soul are rendered intelligible and religiously meaningful to modern culture.

368   Cobb, John B. Jr. "Christian Natural Theology and Christian Existence." *Christian Century*, 82, 1965, 265–267. Trans. as "Natürliche Theologie und christliche Existenz." *Theologie im Umbruch: Der Beitrag Amerikas zur gegenwärtigen Theologie.* Munich: Chr. Kaiser Verlag, 1968, 42–48.

Existence, Christian; phenomena, paranormal; Jesus, work of; theology, natural.

A Christian natural theology is indispensable for reflection on God, and what it means to affirm the work of God in Jesus Christ, both in the past and in the present.

369   Cobb, John B. Jr. "Christianity and Myth." *Journal of Bible and Religion*, 33, 1965, 314–320.

Myth: language of, meaning of, possibility of; sacred, and profane; language, of religion; Altizer, Thomas J. J.; metaphysics; religion.

In order to believe in God, God will have to be met on terms which conform to contemporary profane consciousness. This indicates a need to reject the language of myth, replacing its function with profane metaphysics.

370   Cobb, John B. Jr. "Can Natural Theology Be Christian?" *Theology Today*, 23, 1966, 140–142.

Theology, and philosophy; language, univocal; Gilkey, Langdon; theology, natural.

Natural theology is but a part of the total task of theology, and must rest its case on philosophical argument rather than an appeal to biblical and traditional authority. (Written in response to Gilkey's critical review of *A Christian Natural Theology*.)

371   Cobb, John B. Jr. "The Finality of Christ in a Whiteheadian Perspective." *The Finality of Christ*. Edited by Dow Kirkpatrick. Nashville: Abingdon, 1966.

Christology; history, and nature; existence: structures of, structure of Christian; prehension, hybrid physical; unconscious;

causation, efficient; perception, non–sensory; God, as source of initial aim; Jesus, as Christ.

The Christian claim that Jesus is immediately present in the lives of those who follow him depends on a view of causation wherein a present event can be influenced by a non–contiguous past event. Whitehead's notion of unmediated prehensions of the past provides a framework in which such causality—and hence the presence of Jesus—can be understood.

372   Cobb, John B. Jr.   The Structure of Christian Existence. Philadelphia: Westminster Press, 1967.

Human existence; history; evolution; culture; civilization; Christianity; existence, structures of; symbolism; psyche; consciousness; person; self, and self–transcendence; dominant occasion; unconscious; Buddhism; Hinduism; Judaism; India; Israel; Greece; Jesus; Homer; Socrates; theology; Christology.

(Although the work is not on Whitehead's philosophy, much of Whitehead's conceptuality is employed in order to display various 'structures of existence' which have existed in human history. The use of Whitehead's technical vocabulary is consciously minimized.)

373   Cobb, John B. Jr.   "Speaking About God." Religion in Life, 36, 1967, 28–39.

Language, about God; God: concepts of, transcendence of, as personal; linguistic analysis; theology, radical.

Whitehead's philosophy points to a solution of the problem of the meaningfulness of language about God; further, it provides us with categories for thinking about God which can overcome the negative implications of traditional thought without losing what is positive in it.

374   Cobb, John B. Jr.   "The Possibility of Theism Today." The Idea of God: Philosophical Perspectives. Edited by E. Madden, R. Handy, and M. Farber. Springfield, Illinois: Charles C. Thomas, Publishers, 1968, 98–123.

Theism; vision, of reality; Matson, W. I.; Flew, Antony; philosophy, analytic; empiricism.

The rejection of theism is chiefly related to a perception of reality which is closed to ontological, cosmological, and causal questions. Whitehead's success in developing an alternative vision of reality, his adoption of a theistic doctrine, and his creative contribution to the doctrine of God are encouraging and helpful guides to further theistic reflection.

375   Cobb, John B. Jr.   God and the World. Philadelphia: Westminster Press, 1969. Christlicher Glaube nach dem Tode Gottes: Gegenwartiges Weltverstandnis im Licht der Theologie. Trans. by Hans Weissgerber. Munich: Claudius Verlag, 1971.

Reviews

Best, Ernest. Methodist Theological School, 4, 1970, 45–48.

Burke, Ronald. *Theological Studies*, 32, 1971, 147–148.

Eller, Vernard. *Religion in Life*, 39, 1970, 129–131.

Mcclendon, J. W. Jr. *Interpretation*, 24, 1970, 258–261.

Meilach, Michael D. *Cord*, 19, 1969, 23–24.

Mueller, David L. *Review and Expositor*, 68, 1971, 274–275.

Ross, James. *Journal of the American Academy of Religion*, 38, 1970, 310–315.

Towne, Edgar A. *Encounter*, 33, 1972, 207–208.

Vick, Edward W. H. *Andrews Union Seminary Studies*, 12, 1974, 143.

Williamson, C. M. *Process Studies*, 3, 1973, 68–70.

God: as call forward, and world, death of, as source of initial aim, and evil, primordial nature of, consequent nature of, as persuasive power; experience, religious; Altizer, Thomas J. J.; Wieman, Henry Nelson; Dewey, John; Bonhoeffer, Dietrich; Bultmann, Rudolph; Teilhard de Chardin.

Whitehead's concept of God as the One Who Calls the world forward can aid in the development of a new Christian vision which continues the theological advances of Bultmann, Teilhard, Bonhoeffer, and Altizer.

376   Cobb, John B. Jr. "Freedom in Whitehead's Philosophy: a Response to Edward Pols." *Southern Journal of Philosophy*, 7, 1969–1970, 409–413.

Freedom; causa sui; becoming, epochal; time, epochal theory of; self–determination.

(This is a critical review of Pols' *Whitehead's Metaphysics: A Critical Examination of Process and Reality*.)

377   Cobb, John B. Jr. "The Population Explosion and the Rights of the Subhuman World." *IDOC–International American Edition*, 9, September 12, 1970, 41–63.

Nature, value of; value, and man (humans); individual; nature: rights of, and subhuman world; evolution, theory of; Kant, Immanuel; Descartes, Rene; Teilhard de Chardin.

Whitehead's philosophy provides a more adequate account of experience, one in which the subhuman world is real, valuable, and related to our actions.

378   Cobb, John B. Jr. "A Whiteheadian Christology." *Process Philosophy and Christian Thought*. Edited by Delwin Brown, Ralph E. James and Gene Reeves. Indianapolis, Indiana: Bobbs–Merrill Company, Inc., 382–398.

Christology; Jesus, God's presence in, as Christ, as unique, work of; self; causal efficacy.

Jesus introduced into history a radical and unsurpassable structure of human existence.

379   Cobb, John B. Jr., and Ford, Lewis S. "The Prospect for Process Studies." *Process Studies*, 1, 1971, 3–8.

Process philosophy: application of, criticisms of; culture, contemporary; ecology.

Process Studies seeks to provide a forum to explore the pertinence of process philosophy to contemporary culture and to a broad spectrum of academic disciplines.

380   Cobb, John B. Jr. *Is It Too Late?: A Theology of Ecology.* Beverly Hills, California: Bruce, 1971.

Ecology; nature: as alive, devaluation of, and ecology, ethic of, exploitation of, and human existence, theology of; theology.

(Using aspects of Whitehead's thought the author develops a theology of ecology designed to be an adult religious education program.)

381   Cobb, John B. Jr. "Alfred North Whitehead." *Twelve Makers of Modern Protestant Thought.* Edited by George L. Hunt. New York: Association Press, 1971.

God; actual occasions; religion, and science; theology, process.

In the modern theological climate there has been a tension between those who cling to the past and those who would cut loose from that past and live purely out of the future. Whitehead offers an alternative to this tension in his suggestion that novelty arises in a creative appropriation of the past rather than in a rejection of it.

382   Cobb, John B. Jr. "The Whitehead Without God Debate: The Critique." *Process Studies,* 1, 1971, 91–100.

God: Whitehead without, function of, and eternal objects, as source of initial aim; standpoint; region; Sherburne, Donald.

Donald Sherburne's failure to distinguish the question of whether God prehends contemporaries from that of whether God is extended caused him to attribute to his argument against regional inclusion an illusory decisiveness. Sherburne's arguments for Whitehead without God fail.

383   Cobb, John B. Jr. "Man in Process." *Concilium,* 1972.

Human existence; future; hope; anthropology.

384   Cobb, John B. Jr. "What is the Future?" *Hope and the Future of Man.* Edited by Ewert Cousins. Philadelphia: Fortress Press, 1972. "Was ist die Zukunft?" Trans. by Barbara Link–Ewert. *Evangelische Theologie,* 32, 1972, 372–388.

Future; hope; God: primordial nature of, consequent nature of; spirit; history; eschatology; Bultmann, Rudolf; existentialism; ecology.

385   Cobb, John B. Jr. "Regional Inclusion and the Extensive Continuum." *Process Studies,* 2, 1972, 277–282, 288–294.

Regions; inclusion, regional; extensive continuum; God, and the world; prehensions: contiguous, noncontiguous, hybrid; potentiality: real, general, and extensive continuum; Sherburne, Donald W.

Regions as such do not originate with the becoming of

occasions. A region is a potentiality for division preceding the actuality of division by actual entities; this allows the possibility of regional inclusion of standpoints as God's mode of prehending the world.

386   Cobb, John B. Jr. "A New Christian Existence." *Neues Testament und christliche Existenz.* Edited by H. D. Betz and L. Schottroff. Tübingen: J. C. B. Mohr, 1973, 79–94.

Existence, structure of Christian; New Testament; Jesus, as Christ; vision, of reality; community; eschatology; christology.

A new vision of Christian existence must see God as a relational process at work in all things, calling them to creative self–transcendence. It must see an open future with threats of catastrophe, but also offering the possibility of joy.

387   Cobb, John B. Jr. "Natural Causality and Divine Action." *Idealistic Studies*, 3, 1973, 207–222.

Causation: efficient, as real influence, as grounds for prediction, Hume on, formal, material, final; freedom; God, power of; Hume, David; Wieman, Henry Nelson; Tillich, Paul; Pannenberg, Wolfhart.

Real influence, as a fruitful notion of efficient causality, applies to God's relation to the world and supports freedom.

388   Cobb, John B. Jr. and Takeda, Ryusei. "'Mosa–Dharma' and Prehension: Nagarjuna and Whitehead Compared." *Process Studies*, 4, 1974, 26–36.

Prehensions: and mosa–dharma, negative, and distortion, valuation of; creativity, and Buddhist dependent co–origination; creative advance, and Buddhist sunyata; Peace, and Buddhist sunyata; God, consequent nature of; Nagarjuna; Buddhism: Mahayana, Shin.

Fundamentally similar ontological doctrines in Nagarjuna and Whitehead nevertheless give rise to profoundly different religious attitudes, perhaps stemming in part from the differing valuations given to negative prehensive activity. (Note: Missing line on p. 33 should read: "Whitehead, on the other hand, takes the universal dependent co–origina–.")

389   Cobb, John B. Jr. "The Christian Concern for the Non–Human World." *Anticipation*, 16, 1974, 23–24.

Nature: desacralized, rights of, in Christianity; Derr, Thomas S.; ecology.

Christianity must acknowledge the inadequacy of its past view toward nature, and then proceed to develop in the direction of a wider concern. (Written in response to Thomas S. Derr, "How Loudly Should a Christian Say, 'Man is Unique'.")

390   Cobb, John B. Jr. and Birch, Charles. "God's Love, Ecological Survival and the Responsiveness of Nature." *Anticipation*, 16, 1974, 32–34.

Nature: devaluation of, man continuous with, ethic of, biblical views of; values: intrinsic, instrumental; God, primordial nature of, consequent nature of, as love; anthropocentrism; Von Rad, Gerhard; dualism; ethics; mechanism; ecology.

Man is continuous with and responsible to his environment.

391   Cobb, John B. Jr. *Christ in a Pluralistic Age.* Philadelphia: Westminster Press, 1975.

Reviews

Anonymous. *Choice,* June, 1976, 307–308.

Boers, Hendrikus W. *Chandler Review,* May, 1976.

Rosenau, Alan. *Living Church,* November 14, 1976, 15–16.

TeSelle, Eugene. *Perkins Journal,* 30, 1976, 35–39.

Vogel, Arthur A. *Anglican Theological Review,* 58, 1976, 401–403.

Zuck, John E. *Theology Today,* 33, 1976, 211–212.

Christ: as Logos, as creative transformation, and hope; initial aim; God: and Christology, as source of initial aim, primordial nature of, consequent nature of, objective immortality in; novelty; Kingdom of God; heaven; death; resurrection; Buddhism, and love; self, as different from psyche; past, as field of force in present; art, and Christ; Jesus Christ; Pannenberg, Wolfhart; Teilhard de Chardin; Soleri, Paolo; theology, process.

The primordial nature of God can be interpreted as a principle of creative transformation which the Christian names Christ, or the Logos. Through receptivity to this principle, the Christian tradition is called to an openness to all faiths which leads to its own internal transformation.

392   Cobb, John B. Jr. and Griffin, David R. *Process Theology: An Introductory Exposition.* Philadelphia: Westminster Press, 1976.

Christology; cosmology; doctrine, Christian; church; eschatology; God: as actual entity, as becoming, as dipolar, primordial nature of, consequent nature of, superjective nature of, and world; human existence; ontology; peace; relativity; societies, personally–ordered; space; time; unity; metaphysics; philosophical theology; ecology; biology; anthropology; psychology; theology.

(An introductory explanation of process thought, especially theology, which is intended for non–technical Whiteheadian readers. This volume also contains an extensive appendix which gives a chronological survey of the Whiteheadian literature.)

393   Cobb, John B. Jr. "Spiritual Discernment in a Whiteheadian Perspective." *Religious Experience and Process Theology.* Edited by Harry J. Cargas and Bernard Lee. New York: Paulist Press, 1976, 349–367.

God, as lure for feeling; decision; prayer.

A Whiteheadian understanding of God's action in us and in

our world can give helpful direction to a new form of spiritual discipline.

394 Cobb, William S. "Whitehead's Twofold Analysis of Experience." *Modern Schoolman*, 47, 1970, 321–330. .

Perception: causal efficacy, presentational immediacy, symbolic reference; feelings: propositional, comparative.

Process and Reality includes two separate analyses of experience: modes of perception, and comparative and propositional feelings. Despite criticism to the contrary, the two analyses are not incompatible, but are complementary.

395 Cohen, Morris R. *American Thought: A Critical Sketch.* Glencoe, Illinois: Free Press, 1954.

History, American intellectual; philosophy, of history; religion, in American thought; aesthetics, in American thought; Hegel, G. W. F.

(Whitehead's role in American thought is analyzed, with attention given to his philosophy of history, aesthetics, and metaphysics.)

396 Colbert, James G. "Dios en la filosofía de Whitehead." *Anuario Filosófico* (Pamplona), 1, 1968, 23–35.

God: primordial nature of, consequent nature of, concept of.

397 Colbert, James G. "La jerarquía de saberes en Whitehead." *Anuario Filosófico*, 2, 1969, 13–25.

Science: and metaphysics, and philosophy, method of; philosophy: task of, method of, and natural science; materialism, scientific; concreteness, misplaced (fallacy of); epoch, cosmic.

Whitehead fails to distinguish between philosophical and scientific knowledge and their respective methodologies. As a result, Whitehead's thought is a chaotic mixture of highly technical terminology and poetic metaphor.

398 Colbert, James G. "Whitehead y la historia de la filosofía." *Anuario Filosófico*, 4, 1971, 10–29.

Whitehead, Alfred North, influences on; Plato; Aristotle; Leibniz, G. W.

399 Collingwood, R. G. *The Idea of Nature.* New York: Oxford University Press, 1945, 1970, 165–174.

Nature; organism; eternal object; mind, and nature; location, simple; Alexander, Samuel; Moore, G. E.; Santayana, George.

Whitehead does not fully account for the differences between mind and nature. By calling insentient matter a mere abstraction, Whitehead falls into the subjectivism he sought to avoid.

400 Collins, James. "Metaphysics in an Empirical Climate." *Giornale di Metafisica*, 2, 1947, 338–351.

Philosophy: method of, and science; metaphysics; nature, and experience; Dewey, John; Murphy, Arthur; Emmet, Dorothy; Lowe, Victor; empiricism.

While Whitehead is right to seek similarities between human experience and non–human events in nature, the manner and degree of this similarity is left undetermined.

401   Comstock, W. Richard. "Naturalism and Theology." *Heythrop Journal*, 8, 1967, 181–190.

Theology: and philosophy, and culture, radical, natural; dualism, revolt against.

Secular and radical theologies are evidence of theology's search for an adequate contemporary philosophic form in which to express its distinctive kerygmatic content. Process philosophy is faithful to major elements of our contemporary experience and of the biblical tradition, and thus is most promising for theological use.

402   Connelly, George E. "The Existence and Natures of God in the Philosophy of Alfred North Whitehead." Unpublished Ph.D. dissertation, St. Louis University, 1962.

God: primordial nature of; consequent nature of, superjective nature of, Whitehead's arguments for; Hartshorne, Charles.

403   Connelly, George E. "Whitehead and the Actuality of God in his Primordial Nature." *Modern Schoolman*, 41, 1964, 309–323,

God: primordial nature of, as principle of concretion, as source of initial aim, and order; metaphysics.

The primordial nature of God is genuinely metaphysical rather than simply cosmological in scope, since the primordial nature is the ground of order for any and every cosmic epoch.

404   Connely, Robert J. "Negative Prehension in Whitehead." Unpublished Ph.D. dissertation, St. Louis University, 1970.

Prehensions, negative; God, and negative prehensions; concrescence; analysis, genetic; actual entities, in the past; objectification; contrast; time, as past; eternal object: individual essence of, relational essence of; creativity, as eternal object; feeling: physical, conceptual; pole: physical, mental; Hartshorne, Charles.

Whitehead's few explicit comments on negative prehensions can be clarified and developed in light of other concepts in his system.

405   Coolidge, Mary L. "Purposiveness Without Purpose in a New Context." *Philosophy and Phenomenological Research*, 4, 1943–1944, 85–93.

Value: aesthetic, theory of; Good; beauty; purpose; Kant, Immanuel; aesthetics.

Whitehead's notion of the Good and of Beauty is similar to Kant's notion of Beauty as "purposiveness without a purpose."

406   Cooper, Burton. "The Idea of God: A Whiteheadian Critique of

Thomas Aquinas' Concept of God." Unpublished Ph.D. dissertation, Union Theological Seminary, 1968.

God: as trinity, perfection of, and divine knowledge, religious availability of, and evil, simplicity of, and creativity; Thomas Aquinas; Plato; Cappadocian fathers; Augustine; theology.

Whitehead's view of God is more adequate than that of Thomas Aquinas for the understanding of redemption in Christian theology.

407   Cooper, Robert M.   "God as Poet and Man as Praying." *Personalist*, 49, 1968, 474–488.

Prayer, philosophy of; poetry; vision, poetic; God: as poet, as lure.

Prayer can be understood to be analogous in function to the primordial and consequent natures of God; as such, prayer is both an ideal vision and an ingredient in the process of the world.

408   Cooper, Robert M.   "A Note on Lionel S. Thornton: An Early Process Theologian." *Anglican Theological Review*, 55, 1973, 182–188.

Thornton, Lionel S.: personality of, works of, methodology of, and Biblical theology.

Thornton's critics have failed to see the great value of *The Incarnate Lord* as a methodology for Biblical theology. Thornton appropriated the methods which Whitehead had used with respect to science, and applied them to the study of the Bible.

409   Cooper, Robert M.   "God as Poet and Persons at Prayer." *Religious Experience and Process Theology*.   Edited by Harry J. Cargas and Bernard Lee.   New York: Paulist Press, 1976, 411–427.

God: as poet, as lure for feeling; concrescence, phases of; prayer; poetry.

God as poet of the world enables a poetic prayer in which one prays to, with, and beyond God.

410   Cormier, Ramona T.   "The Understanding of the Past." *Tulane Studies in Philosophy*, 10, 1961, 47–58.

History: scientific, and nature; reason: practical, speculative; time, and past actual entities; past: giveness of, and present.

Whitehead's cosmology furnishes an ontological basis for both scientific and universal methods of studying history. Whitehead's analysis of practical and speculative reason justifies the distinction between the two methods of doing history.

411   Cornelissen, M. R.   "Final Cause and Its Pre–Eminence in the Philosophy of Alfred North Whitehead." *Saint–Louis Quarterly*, Baguio City, Phillippines, 3, 1965, 595–608.

Causation, final.

412   Cory, Daniel. "Dr. Whitehead on Perception." *Journal of Philosophy*, 30, 1933, 29–43.

Perception; causal efficacy; presentational immediacy; consciousness; Santayana, George; epistemology.

Neither personal observation nor physiology supports Whitehead's view of causal efficacy as a primary level of perception.

413   Costa, M. "Whitehead y la función de la razón." *Cuadernos de Filosofía*, 9, 1969, 283–287.

Reason, function of; rationality.

414   Cotton, J. Harry. "The Meaning of 'God' in Whitehead's Philosophy." *Encounter*, 29, 1968, 125–140.

Process philosophy, summary of; God: Whitehead's arguments for, and time, religious availability of; philosophy, and religion; positivism.

Many of Whitehead's assertions, particularly concerning God, have programmatic rather than cognitive meaning, pointing to the need for further inquiry.

415   Cousins, Ewert H. "Truth in St. Bonaventure." *American Catholic Philosophical Association, Proceedings*, 43, 1969, 204–210.

Relatedness; creativity; exemplarism, Platonic; trinity, dynamic; truth: as creative expression, as ideal norm; Bonaventure; metaphysics.

Process philosophy's affirmation of the values of creativity and relatedness can find sympathetic resonance in the thought of St. Bonaventure.

416   Cousins, Ewert H., editor. *Process Theology: Basic Writings.* New York: Newman Press, 1971.

Process theology; God, and world; Christ; evolution; redemption; Teilhard de Chardin.

(This is an anthology of writings by a number of different "process" authors which provides not only a variety of applications of process thought but also indicates the diversity within the process approach.)

417   Cousins, Ewert H. "Teilhard, Process Thought and Religious Education." *Religious Education*, 68, 1973, 331–338.

Teilhard, and Catholic education; education, religious; culture, contemporary; Teilhard de Chadin; education.

As can be dimonstrated through the relation of Teilhard to Catholic education, process thought can assist religious education to become acclimated to cultural change, and to develop the content of religious teaching in contemporaneous forms.

418   Cousins, Ewert. "Introduction: Process Models in Culture, Philosophy, and Theology." *Process Theology.* Edited by Ewert Cousins. New York: Newman Press, 1971.

Process theology; process, principle of; God: and the world, Whitehead's doctrine of, and Christ; Teilhard de Chardin; eschatology.

Out of modern man's experience of the dynamism of nature, the reality of time and the possibility of novelty as well as the theory of evolution the process vision has emerged. The two leading spokesmen in the twentieth century for this process perspective are Teilhard de Chardin and Alfred North Whitehead, both of whom were concerned about God's relation to the world.

419   Craven, Gus J.   "A Comparative Study of Creativity in Education in Whitehead and Others."   Unpublished Ph.D. dissertation, University of Texas, 1952.

Education: and creativity, and concrescence, and personality development; Dewey, John.

Whitehead's doctrine of creativity provides a framework in which the nature and aim of education can be discussed.

420   Creegan, Robert F.   "The Actual Occasion and Actual History." *Journal of Philosophy*, 39, 1942, 268–273.

History: descriptive, lived, dimensions of; philosophy, of history; James, William; history.

Whitehead's identification of his phenomenology of aesthetic realization with experienced history is inadequate; however, his system allows a more adequate alternative based on analysis of dimensions of history.

421   Crespi, A.   *A. N. Whitehead: l'ultimo dei platonisti inglesi.   Il Ponte*, 4, 1948, 1139–1144.

Platonism; Whitehead, Alfred North, works of.

422   Crespi, G. M.   "La filosofia di Whitehead."   *Revista di Filosofia Neoscolastica*, 40, 1948, 293–331.

Whitehead, Alfred North, work of.

423   Crocker, D. A.   "A Whiteheadian Theory of Intentions and Actions."   Unpublished dissertation, Yale University, 1970.

Intentionality; action theory.

424   Crosby, Donald A.   "Language and Religious Language in Whitehead's Philosophy."   *Christian Scholar*, 50, 1967, 210–221.

Language: religious use of, limitations of, emotional tone of, and metaphysics; philosophy, of language.

Whitehead's metaphysics and philosophy of language will not allow for a hard–and–fast distinction between referential and emotive utterances; the two uses are frequently entwined. The emotive tones can make referential meanings more explicit.

425   Crosby, Donald A.   "Whitehead on the Metaphysical Employment of Language."   *Process Studies*, 1, 1971, 38–54.

Language, Whitehead's use of; metaphor; etymology; poetry; metaphysics.

Whitehead used at least six criteria in the derivation of his technical terminology. A principle consideration was the imaginative force and metaphorical impact the terms could have for the reader.

426   Crosby, Donald A. "Religion and Solitariness." *Journal of the American Academy of Religion*, 40, 1972, 21–35.

Solitariness: and freedom, and awareness of God, and self–evaluation, and world–consciousness; religion, communal; rightness, essential; *Religion in the Making*.

In *Religion in the Making*, Whitehead provides a theory of the origin, focus, and purpose of religion. Religion's origin is in the mood of solitary self–evaluation, from whence it broadens into a sense of the inherent worth of all men and a consciousness of the world as a community of value.

427   Curtis, Charles J. "Philosophy and Ecumenical Dialogue." *Ecumenist*, 4, 1966, 76–78.

Ecumenism; theology, natural; secularism; Cobb, John B., Jr.

Process thought provides a fruitful ground for Christian ecumenical dialogue because it corresponds most nearly to contemporary experience.

428   Curtis, Charles J. "Choose Your Trinity." *Anglican*, 22, 1966, 2–11.

God, as trinity; trinity, doctrine of.

429   Curtis, Charles J. "'The Living God' Theology." *Ecumenist*, 5, 1966, 1–3.

Theology, radical; theologians, "God is dead"; Altizer, Thomas J. J.; Söderblom, Nathan.

Theological and philosophical work is available which contains all the dimensions necessary for a philosophical theology that can go beyond "God is dead."

430   Curtis, Charles J. "Ecumenism and Process Theology." *Hartford Quarterly*, 7, 1967, 34–42.

Ecumenism; concrescence, social application of; unity, Christian.

A more adequate notion of Christian unity must begin with the recognition that something genuinely novel emerges in the process of acheiving ecumenicity.

431   Curtis, Charles J. *The Task of Philosophical Theology.* New York: Philosophical Library, 1967.

Christianity; God: death of, and divine knowledge, and nature; angels; baptism; bible; conscience; death; history; person, and personal immortality; judgment; eucharist; ministry; miracle; prayer; soul; suffering; revelation; Christ; philosophical theology.

Whitehead's philosophy can update many of the traditional theological ideas of Christianity by furnishing theology with a new vocabulary. Christian theologians should affirm Whitehead's thesis that reality is rationally explicable.

432   Curtis, Charles J. "Prayer in Process Theology." *Crane Review*, 10, 1967, 28–31.

Prayer: as feeling, as process of concrescence, goal of.

Prayer is openness to and active participation in the process of feeling that binds God and the world together in the inseparable unity of relatedness.

433   Curtis, Charles J. *Contemporary Protestant Thought.* New York: Bruce Publishing Company, 1970, 51–62.

Whitehead, Alfred North: biography of; theology, process; ecumenism; Bradley, Francis H.; Bergson, Henri; Cobb, John B. Jr.

(This is a general introduction to Whitehead, outlining his life, and indicating areas in which his thought may be relevant for Christian theology.)

434   Curtis, Charles J. "From Traditionalism to Process Theology." *Cord*, 18, 1968, 310–313.

God; metaphysics; Meilach, Michael D.

Traditional theologies lack contemporary and ecumenical relevance. Process theology is the most adequate base available for the contemporary ecumenical task of theological reconstruction.

435   Cushen, W. E. "The Physical Cosmology of Alfred North Whitehead." Unpublished dissertation, University of Edinburgh, 1951.

Cosmology; nature.

436   D'Abro, A. *The Evolution of Scientific Thought.* New York: Dover Publications, Inc., 1958.

Science: and religion, and humanism; philosophy, of science.

437   Dalton, Wayne A. "The Status of Artistic Illusion in Concrescence." *Process Studies*, 4, 1974, 207–211.

Art; music; propositions: conformal, nonconformal, as lure for feeling; symbol; contrast; Langer, Susanne K.; aesthetics.

Organic philosophy explains the phenomenon of aesthetic experience through the final integrative contrast of art.

438   Das, Rasvihary. *The Philosophy of Whitehead.* New York: Russell and Russell, 1928, 1964.

Creativity: as ultimate, as eternal object, as surd; eternal objects, functioning of: God: primordial nature of, consequent nature of; actual entity: as present in others, grades of; relatedness; substance; feelings; perception; presentational immediacy; causal efficacy; symbolic reference; propositions; truth, and beauty; extensive continuum; philosophy: method of, aim of; Whitehead, Alfred North; introduction to his thought.

Whitehead's emphasis on process and relation dominates the entirety of his metaphysics. Since reason is directed to categories such as being and substance, his thought is intrinsically difficult to interpret. The merit of his thought lies in its attempt to combine being and becoming, permanence and change, mind and matter, and unity and multiplicity. The combination of such categories is the aim of all philosophy which seeks to do justice to every aspect of experience.

439   David, Richard S.   "Whitehead's Moral Philosophy." Unpublished Ph.D. dissertation, Washington University, 1971.

Value; society; civilization; individual; subjectivity; emotion; evil; good; person, and personal identity; decision, moral; Plato; Aristotle; Kant, Immanuel; Dewey, John; utilitarianism; ethics; aesthetics; science; religion; art.

440   Davis, M. C.   "The Concept of Transcendence in the Philosophy of Alfred North Whitehead."   Unpublished Ph.D. dissertation, University of Chicago, 1963.

Transcendence.

441   Daya, Khrisna.   The Nature of Philosophy.   Calcutta: Prachi Prakashan, 1955.

Philosophy: method of, task of.

442   Dean, William D.   Coming to A Theology of Beauty. Philadelphia: Westminster Press, 1972.

Reviews

Cary, N. R.   Christianity and Literature, 23, 1974, 45–55.

Howard, T.   Christian Scholar Review, 3, 1973, 201–202.

Indinopulos, T. A.   Process Studies, 3, 1973, 118–120.

Kort, W. A.   Journal of American Academy of Religion, December 1974, 784–785.

Rygh, G. L.   Augsbury Publishing House Book News Letter, December 1972.

Vos, N.   Christian Centenial, 89, 1972, 1192.

Wilkey, J. W.   Review and Expositor, Winter 1974, 119.

Young, M.   Library Journal, July 1972.

Beauty: and goodness, and God, and the holy, and truth, and religion; God: and beauty, as source of initial aim; subjectivity; subjective aim; appearance, and reality; contrast; aesthetics, and aesthetic experience; novelty; propositions, as lure for feeling; symbolism; Cox, Harvey; Miller, David L.; Neale, Robert E.; Keen, Sam; Sherburne, Donald; Cobb, John B. Jr.; theology, of beauty.

The substance of religion lies in aesthetic response and imagination. Whitehead's philosophy helps to interpret religion as thus construed.

443   Dean, William D.   Love Before the Fall.   Philadelphia: Westminster Press, 1976.

Love: as aesthetic, as agape, as eros, and sexuality, and social justice; contemporaries; causality; aesthetics: and religion, and ethics; beauty; relations, causal; Plato; Jesus; Tillich, Paul; Buber, Martin; Williams, Daniel Day.

Whereas the more classical forms of love, such as eros and agape, impose a solitude of individuality, due to the causal and temporal relations between lover and beloved, "aesthetic love" points to a social bondedness which is nonindividual, noncausal, and nontemporal.

444   Deboe, Cornelius M. "The Distinction between the Primordial and Consequent Natures of God in the Philosophy of Professor Alfred North Whitehead." Unpublished Ph.D. dissertation, Princeton University, 1939.

God: primordial nature of, consequent nature of, and time, and evil; creativity; religion, in relation to individual.

445   DeBoer, Lawrence P. "Valuation and Judgments in Metaphysics and Religion: A Study of the Philosophy of Alfred North Whitehead." Unpublished Ph.D. dissertation, Columbia University, 1967.

Concrescence; judgment, intuitive; consciousness; valuation, conceptual; logic; inference; imagination; feeling, conceptual; propositions; contrast; truth, propositional; God, primordial nature of, consequent nature of; theology.

Theological concepts such as faith, hope, love, and peace can be understood in terms of intuitive judgments.

446   De Hovre, F. "Professor Alfred North Whitehead: Wiskundige, Natuurkundige, Wijsgeer en Paedegoog." *Vlaams Opvoedkundig Tijdschrift* (Antwerp), 28, 1948, 161–171.

Whitehead; biography of, works of.

(This is a memorial article following Whitehead's death.)

447   De Laguna, Grace A. "Existence and Potentiality." *Philosophical Review*, 60, 1961, 155–176.

Universals, status of; individuals; eternal objects: as multiplicity, as ideal continuum; potentiality; metaphysics.

Whatever exists includes, as essential to its existence, potentiality. Conversely, the realm of essences has being only through its correlative ingredience in a world of existence.

448   De Laguna, Grace A. *On Existence and the Human World.* New Haven, Connecticut: Yale University Press, 1966, 46–50, 51–52.

Potentiality: and existence, and actuality; eternal objects: as potentials, relational essence of, individual essence of; ontological principle; continuity, as potential; God, and eternal objects; Peirce, Charles.

The conception of an ideal continuum, not composed of discrete individuals, is a viable alternative to Whitehead's conception of a realm of eternal objects.

449   De Laguna, Theodore. "Extensive Abstraction: A Suggestion." *Philosophical Review*, 30, 1921, 216–218.

Abstraction, extensive; *Concept of Nature*; set, vanishing; *Principles of Natural Knowledge*.

The method of extensive abstraction employed by Whitehead in his *The Principles of Natural Knowledge* and *The Concept of Nature* can be simplified and strengthened if, instead of the indefinable relation of whole and part, we assume the relation of 'containing' in the sense of completely enveloping.

450   Deleu, Paul. "Alfred North Whiteheads opvatting over speculative filosofie." Unpublished M. A. dissertation, Katholieke Universiteit te Leuven, 1974.

Philosophy, speculative; reason: practical, speculative; adequacy; coherence; sensationalist principle; consciousness; causal efficacy; presentational immediacy; Kant, Immanuel.

(Whitehead's epistemology is compared with that of Kant in order to elucidate the nature of metaphysics as Whitehead conceives it.)

451   Deregibus, A. *Ragione e natura nella filosofia di Whitehead*. Milan: Marzorati, 1972.

Nature: bifurcation of, and freedom and necessity, as organic unity, and order.

452   Derr, Thomas S. "How Loudly Should a Christian Say: 'Man is Unique'." *Anticipation*, 16, 1974, 20–23.

Process theism, biblical critique of; nature: and freedom, and God, and ecology, and biblical theology, and process theology; ecology.

Process thought is inherently ecological, since it does not separate man from nature. However, its weak view of a limited God separates it from Christianity.

453   Derr, Thomas S. "Nature: Value or Rights?" *Anticipation*, 16, 1974, 24.

Nature: and value, rights of; ecology.

Nature's value is derived from God. The rights of animals differ from the rights of man, since the latter have societal and metaphysical overtones inappropriate to animals.

454   Derr, Thomas S. "The Human Drama and God's Gift of the Earth." *Anticipation*, 16, 1974, 30–32.

Value: hierarchy of, of man, of nature, and God; man, uniqueness of; anthropocentrism, biblical; Griffin, David R.; ecology.

(Many of Griffin's ecological differences from Derr are semantic rather than substantive in nature. Written in response to David R. Griffin, "Human Liberation and the Reverence for Nature.")

455   Desch, P. "The Transcendence of God in Whitehead's Philosophy." *Philosophical Studies* (Ireland), 11, 1961–1962, 7–27.

God: transcendence of, and world.

456   Devaux, Philippe. "Une nouvelle phase du réalisme anglo–saxon. A propos de 'Science and the Modern World'." *Archives de la Société Belge de Philosophie*, 1, 1928–1929, 9–24.

Realism; idealism; philosophy, method of.

457   Devaux, Philippe. "Experience et formalisme." *Archives de la Société Belge de Philosophie*, 2, 1930, 30–41.

Experience; formalism.

458   Devaux, Philippe. *Lotze et son influence sur la philosophie anglo–saxonne: contribution à l'étude historique et critique de la notion de valeur.* Brussells, 1932.

Value, theory of; Lotze, Rudolf H.

459   Devaux, Philippe. "L'esprit du néo–réalisme anglais." *Revue Internationale de Philosophie*, 15, 1971, 250–282.

Doctrine, development of; history: and historical research, of philosophy; actuality, order of; value, order of; space–time; Alexander, Samuel; Bergson, Henri; Russell, Bertrand; Moore, G. E.; neo–realism; science, philosophy of.

460   Devaux, Philippe. "Le bergsonisme de Whitehead." *Revue Internationale de Philosophie*, 15, 1961, 217–236.

Dualism; substance, philosophy of; relativity; Whitehead, Alfred North, relation to Bergson; Carr, Wildon; Northrop; F. S. C.; Cesslin, Félix; Alexander, Samuel.

Whitehead is frequently referred to as the "Bergson of Britain," and their two process philosophies show points of similarity in their dealing with creativity and process. Some have speculated that Wildon Carr was responsible for much of Bergson's influence on Whitehead.

461   Dewey, John. "Whitehead's Philosophy." *Philosophical Review*, 46, 1937, 170–177. Also in *Problems of Men*. New York: Philosophical Library, 1946, 410–418.

Method, philosophical; generalization, descriptive; model, mathematical; empiricism; rationalism.

Whitehead appears to have adopted a mathematical model for his method of descriptive generalization, although he also allows the alternative model of a genetic–functional view. The latter would be more fruitful for the continuing development of his thought.

462   Dewey, John. "The Objectivism–Subjectivism of Modern Philosophy." *Journal of Philosophy*, 38, 1941, 533–542.

Subject–object; empiricism; epistemology; objectivism; subjectivism.

Philosophy will become truly modern only when "objectivism–subjectivism" is seen to be the cooperative interaction of two distinguishable but complementary sets of conditions.

463   Dewey, John. "The Philosophy of Whitehead." *The Philosophy*

of Alfred North Whitehead. Edited by Paul A. Schilpp. La Salle, Illinois: Open Court Publishing Company, 1941, 641–661.

Experience, and nature; experience, as datum for philosophy; philosophy, task of; actual occasion; empiricism.

By uniting the facts of scientific observation with those of human experience Whitehead has opened a fruitful path for subsequent philosophy. However, his own movement of thought is sometimes blocked by an excessive appeal to mathematics and to the philosophical tradition.

464   Dicken, Thomas. "Process Philosophy and the Real Presence." *Journal of Ecumenical Studies,* 6, 1969, 68–75.

Sacrament; eucharist; church; Jesus Christ; theology.

Since process philosophy suggests how events have both physical and spiritual aspects, it eliminates the need for the distinction between the 'real' and 'spiritual' presence of Christ in the eucharist.

465   Didsbury, H. F. "Man and God in History According to Whitehead." *IQBAL* (Pakistan), 15, 1966, 1–7.

History; God: and history, and world, as acting in history; anthropology.

466   Dilley, Frank B. "Metaphysics, Language and Theology." Unpublished Ph.D. dissertation, Columbia University, 1961.

Language: analogical, limitations of, metaphysical, and philosophy, and reality, and subject–predicate mode of expression, symbolic, Whitehead's use of.

467   Dilley, Frank B. *Metaphysics and Religious Language.* New York: Columbia University Press, 1964, 62–66.

Metaphysics, method of; language, religious; religion.

468   Dilworth, David A. "The Platonism–Pragmatism Polarity in Whitehead's Thought." Unpublished Ph.D. dissertation, Fordham University, 1963.

Experience; mind; feeling; emotion; eternal object; relativity; relations; concreteness, misplaced; Plato; James, William; Bradley, F. W.; Hegel, G. W. F.; pragmatism; empiricism; idealism; Platonism.

Whitehead's philosophy synthesizes Platonism and pragmatism.

469   Doan, Frank M. "On the Construction of Whitehead's Metaphysical Language." *Review of Metaphysics,* 13, 1960, 605–622.

Language: metaphysical, Whitehead's use of; metaphor; philosophy, and language.

Whitehead's attitude towards language provides a constructive test case against which to assess the cluster of questions related to language and metaphysics raised by twentieth century philosophers of language.

470   Doud, Robert E. "Identity and Commitment." *Religious Experience and Process Theology.* Edited by Harry James

.

Cargas and Bernard Lee. New York: Paulist Press, 1976, 387–395.

Commitment; identity; route, historic; process, microscopic and macroscopic; hope; decision; person, living; freedom, and human existence.

Commitment is a hope structure, a patterning of one's own changing and changable trajectory.

471   Drennan, D. A.   "Whitehead and the Idea of Education." *Proceedings of the American Catholic Philosophical Association*, 41, 1967, 100–109.

Education: aim of, stages of; philosophy, of education.

472   Dretske, F. I.   "Space, Time and Substance: A Philosophical Inquiry."   Unpublished Ph.D. dissertation, University of Minnesota, 1960.

Substance; space; time.

473   Dubois, Ronald L.   "Reason in Ethics: A Whiteheadian Perspective."   Unpublished Ph.D. dissertation, St. Louis University, 1971.

Reason; value; civilization; natural law; morality; adventure; eros; propositions; philosophy, speculative; virtue; justice.

A natural law moral theory can be derived from Whitehead's metaphysics.

474   Dudman, V. H.   "Frege on Definition."   *Mind*, 82, 1973, 609–610.

Definition: contextual, metalinguistic status of; connectives, truth–functional; *Principia Mathematica*; Frege, G.; logic, symbolic; mathematics.

475   Dugan, Daniel O.   "The Gratuity of the Creative Act: A Whiteheadian View."   Unpublished Ph.D. dissertation, Vanderbilt University, 1972.

God: as creator, and creatio ex nihilo, and world, as persuasive, and divine freedom; being, in Thomas Aquinas; Thomas Aquinas; Hartshorne, Charles; Cobb, John B. Jr.; Ogden, Schubert; theology, process.

Despite Whitehead's intentions to reject the doctrine of creatio ex nihilo, a Whiteheadian doctrine of creatio ex nihilo can be sketched by stressing the primordial nature of God.

476   Dunham, Albert M.   "Animism and Materialism in Whitehead's Organic Philosophy."   *Journal of Philosophy*, 29, 1932, 41–47.

Prehensions, negative; relativity, theory of; panpsychism; animism; materialism; organism, philosophy of.

Change and time are dependent upon negative prehensions, but the theory of negative prehension rests on an unjustifiable animism.   Without the theory of negative prehensions, Whitehead's philosophy is inadequate; with the theory, it is incoherent.

477   Dunkel, Harold B.   *Whitehead on Education.*   Athens, Ohio: Ohio State University Press, 1965.

Education: aims of, and learning, and curriculum, in cosmological perspective; knowledge; value; rhythm; philosophy, of education.

The aim of education for Whitehead is to enable the human organism to effect, through adventure, that sort of self–creation which will be a good patterning of the data available in that epoch and which will constitute a creative advance into novelty.

478   Dunkel, Harold B. "Free Romance." *Elementary School Journal*, 68, 1967, 53–60.

Romance; philosophy, of education.

479   Duraisingh, C. "Meaning of God in Process Perspectives." *Indian Journal of Theology*, 21, 1972, 92–106.

God, concept of.

480   Duraisingh, C. "Science, Whitehead, and New Perspectives on Reality." *Bangalore Theological Forum*, 4, 1972, 31–54.

Whitehead, Alfred North, introduction to his thought; science.

481   Dwight, Charles A. S. "Whitehead the Inscrutable." *Personalist*, 32, 1951, 26–30.

Whitehead, Alfred North, evaluation of.

Whitehead has left us a few unworkable formulae—but a great philosophy; his inscrutability is our inspiration.

482   Dyer, J. A., and Schild, A. "The Center of Mass Motion in a Conservative Gravitational Theory of Whitehead's Type." *Journal of Mathematical Analysis and Application*, 4, 1962, 328–340.

Relativity, theory of; gravitation; acceleration; motion; space–time; force; Einstein, Albert; physics.

Whitehead's theory of action at a distance in flat space–time can be correlated with Einstein's predictions concerning acceleration and the center of mass.

483   Early, Thomas H. "Creativity and Value: An Elucidation of the Metaphysical Status of Value in Whitehead's Philosophy." Unpublished Ph.D. dissertation, Boston College, 1972.

Value; creativity; being, and value; time, and value; God, and value.

484   Easton, D. "What Dr. Whitehead Finds in John Locke." *Philosophy Forum*, 1, 1943, 11–18.

Perception; Locke, John; epistemology.

485   Eddington, A. S. "A Comparison of Whitehead's and Einstein's Formulae." *Nature*, 113, 1924, 192.

Relativity, theory of; Einstein, Albert; physics.

486   Eddington, A. S. *The Nature of the Physical World*. Cambridge: Cambridge University Press, 1928.

Philosophy: of science, of nature; mathematics; physics.

(Originally delivered as the Gifford Lectures, 1927)

487   Edwards, Rem B. "The Human Self: An Actual Entity or a
           Society?" *Process Studies*, 5, 1975, 195–203.

           Self: as series of experiences, as society; God, as actual entity;
           perishing; Pols, Edward; Hartshorne, Charles; Christian,
           William A.; Cobb, John B. Jr.

           Using Whitehead's notion of God as a single actual entity,
           alternatives to Whitehead's notion of the self as a society can
           be explored.

488   Eisendrath, C. R.   *The Unifying Moment: The Psychological
           Philosophy of William James and Alfred North Whitehead.*
           Cambridge, Massachusetts: Harvard University Press, 1971.

           Experience: subjective aspects of, and time; togetherness; time,
           and human experience; concrescence; causation: efficient, final;
           perception, and causation; self: as series of experiences, process
           model of; freedom; will; self–creativity; God: nature of, and
           nature; civilization; value.

           James' theory of will and personality can be integrated with
           Whitehead's theory of concrescence to the benefit of both.
           The result is an extension of James and an exegesis of
           Whitehead which illuminates the nature of perception, time,
           space, causality, natural laws, God, and civilization. (This is
           the author's Ph.D. dissertation at Harvard University in 1971.)

489   Ely, Stephen L. *The Religious Availability of Whitehead's God:
           A Critical Analysis.*   Madison, Wisconsin: University of
           Wisconsin Press, 1942.

           God: religious availability of, and evil, functions of;
           philosophical theology; Hartshorne, Charles; religion.

           The God that Whitehead derives from metaphysical analysis is
           not the God of religions. Whatever religious value Whitehead's
           God may have depends on aspects of God that lie beyond
           reason. Whitehead's use of the word 'God' is inappropriate.

           Reviews

           Bowers, D. F. *Journal of Philosophy*, 39, 1942, 612–613.

           Fries, H. S. *Journal of Liberal Religion*, 5, 1943, 96–97.

           Hartshorne, C. *Journal of Liberal Religion*, 5, 1943, 55.

           Loomer, B. M. *Journal of Religion*, 24, 1944, 162–179.

           Lowe, V. *Review of Religion*, 7, 1943, 409–415.

490   Emmet, Dorothy. *Whitehead's Philosophy of Organism.* London:
           Macmillan Company, 1932.   New York: St. Martin's Press,
           1966.

           Whitehead, Alfred North: introduction to his thought; reason:
           and rationality, and logos, practical, speculative; philosophy:
           method of, aim of; extensive abstraction; generalization;
           ontological principle; categoreal scheme; obligation, categories
           of; process; change; creativity; God; organism; atomism;
           experience; concrescence; prehensions; real internal constitution;
           eternal objects: as forms, as potential, subjective species of,

objective species of; perception; propositions; Plato; Aristotle; Descartes, Rene; Leibniz, Gottfried; Kant, Immanuel; James, William; Russell, Bertrand; Taylor, A. E.

(This is an interpretation of Whitehead's metaphysics, originally published in 1932. In the preface to the second edition, published in 1966, the author cites passages from letters Whitehead wrote to her in response to her original interpretations, and indicates respects in which she diverges from her earlier views. Whitehead's remarks concern causal immanence, subjective form, consciousness, and sense–perception.)

491   Emmet, Dorothy M. *The Nature of Metaphysical Thinking.* London: Macmillan and Co. Ltd., 1945. New York: St. Martin's Press, 1961.

Epistemology; prehension; feelings: physical, conceptual; consciousness; awareness; perception; sense–perception; importance; mind, mind–body problem; symbolism; projection; Heidegger, Martin.

There is a wider gap than Whitehead allows between physiological conditions of sensation and the conscious perceptions in which sensa are elements. In minimizing the significance of consciousness, Whitehead creates difficulties for his account of conscious awareness.

492   Emmet, Dorothy M. "On The Idea of Importance." *Philosophy*, 21, 1946, 234–244.

Importance; value: criteria for, theory of.

"Importance" can be a generic term for value, since it can be subdivided so as to express both its relational and its absolutist aspects.

493   Emmet, Dorothy. "Alfred North Whitehead: 1861–1947." *Proceedings of the British Academy: 1947.* London: Oxford University Press, 1947.

Whitehead, Alfred North: obituary of, biography of; logic; mathematics; philosophy, of nature; metaphysics.

(The author traces aspects of Whitehead's life and works in an obituary.)

494   Emmet, Dorothy. "A. N. Whitehead: The Last Phase." *Mind*, 57, 1948, 265–274.

Objective immortality; feelings, universality of; Whitehead, Alfred North, philosophical development of.

Whitehead's work can be read as a series of attempts to hold together two sides: the abstract schemes, and the concrete flow of experience. Objective immortality is the key thought in his later developments.

495   Emmet, Dorothy M. *Function, Purpose, and Powers.* Philadelphia: Temple University Press, 1958, 1972, 35–37, 57–59.

Organism; society; morality; sociology; religion.

In order to clarify the notion of organic order Whitehead distinguishes between uniform and non–uniform objects. The former endure in time, but have the same characteristics at any instant. The latter develop their characteristics only over an extended time span.

496   Emmet, Dorthy M. "Whitehead, Alfred North." *The Concise Encyclopedia of Western Philosophy and Philosophers.* Edited by J. O. Urmson. Hawthorn, 1960, 388–390.

Whitehead, Alfred North: evaluation of, biography of, philosophical development of.

497   Emmet, Dorothy M. "Whitehead, Alfred North." *Encyclopedia of Philosophy.* Edited by Paul Edwards. New York: Macmillan Company, 8, 1967, 290–296.

Whitehead, Alfred North: evaluation of, biography of, philosophical development of, introduction to his thought.

498   Emmet, Dorothy M. "Whitehead, Alfred North." *International Encyclopedia of the Social Sciences.* Edited by D. L. Sills, 16, 1968, 532–536.

Whitehead, Alfred North: evaluation of, biography of, introduction to his thought, philosophical development of.

499   Empereur, J. "An Introduction to Process Theology." National Catholic Reporter, 1974, 4–5.

Theology, process.

500   Enjunto, D. Gorge. *Terminologie de Whitehead.* Unpublished dissertation, University of Paris, 1966.

Actual entity; eternal objects; prehensions, theory of; nexus; societies; Whitehead, bibliography of.

(In expositing Whitehead's fundamental ideas, this work provides an extensive lexicon of French renderings for Whitehead's vocabulary and neologisms).

501   Enjuto–Bernal, Jorge. "La filosofía de A. N. Whitehead: una breve introduccíon." *Boletín Informativo del Seminario de Derecho Político,* 32, 1964, 101–121.

Process philosophy, summary of; actual entities; eternal objects; God; Whitehead, Alfred North: biography of.

502   Enjuto–Bernal, Jorge. "La teoria de los objetos eternos en la filosofía de A. N. Whitehead." *Aporia,* 5, 1966.

Eternal objects: as potential, as forms of definiteness, ingression.

503   Enjuto–Bernal, Jorge. "La teoria de los nexos y sociedades en la filosofía de Alfred North Whitehead." *Diálogos,* 5, 1966.

Societies, theory of; nexus.

504   Enjuto–Bernal, Jorge. *La filosofía de Alfred North Whitehead.* Madrid: Editorial Tecnos, 1967.

Actual entities; division: genetic, coordinate; eternal objects:

objective species of, subjective species of, as potential, relational essence of, individual essence of; prehensions: positive, negative, physical, conceptual; societies; nexus; God: primordial nature of, consequent nature of, superjective nature of; actuality; creativity; appetition; concrescence; extensive continuum; contemporaneity; subjective form; Whitehead, Alfred North: biography of, bibliography of, introduction to his thought.

(This introduction to Whitehead's metaphysics includes a systematic discussion of key concepts, a glossary of terms, and a selected bibliography.)

505   Enjuto–Bernal, Jorge. "Alfred North Whitehead y la metafísica." *Dianoia*, 15, 1969, 79–86.

Metaphysics; Whitehead, Alfred North: introduction to his thought.

506   Eslick, Leonard J. "Substance, Change and Causality in Whitehead." *Philosophy and Phenomenological Research*, 18, 1958, 503–513.

Substance; change; causality; concrescence; actual entities; events; Aristotle.

Whitehead grossly misunderstands Aristotle's theory of substance. His substance–less cosmology does not adequately account for the facts of change and causality, for there can be no genuine efficient causality without enduring substances.

507   Eslick, Leonard J. "Some Remarks in Reply to Professor Hartshorne." *Philosophy and Phenomenological Research*, 18, 1958, 521–522.

Causa sui; change; causality, efficient; Hartshorne, Charles.

True efficient causality demands a vital intersubjective contact, but it can exist only between contemporaries. Whitehead does not allow this, and hence gives no intelligible account of change. (Written in response to Charles Hartshorne, "Whitehead on Process: A Reply to Professor Eslick.")

508   Eslick, Leonard J. "Existence and Creativity in Whitehead." *American Catholic Philosophical Association, Proceedings*, 35, 1961, 151–163.

Prehensions, negative; creativity; ultimate, category of; existence: in Aquinas, in Whitehead; Thomas Aquinas; Plato; Spinoza; pluralism; metaphysics; Thomism.

Negative prehensions are the primary instrument of creativity. Analogies with Thomistic philosophy indicate possibilities of a fruitful encounter between Thomism and process thought.

509   Eslick, Leonard J. "The Material Substrate in Plato." *The Concept of Matter in Greek and Medieval Philosophy.* Edited by Ernan McMullin. Notre Dame, Indiana: University of Notre Dame Press, 1963, 39–58.

Creativity: and the material substrate in Plato, as generative; Plato, and creativity.

In Plato there exists an idea of matter which combines the roles of existential actuation and differentiation. Whitehead's notion of creativity functions in a similar manner.

510   Eslick, Leonard J. "God in the Metaphysics of Whitehead." *New Themes in Christian Philosophy.* Edited by R. M. McInerny. Notre Dame: Notre Dame University Press, 1968, 64–81.

God: primordial nature of, consequent nature of, superjective nature of, as deus ex machina; ontological principle; relativity, principle of.

The exigency in Whitehead's metaphysics is for a God who can remedy the metaphysical defects of all other actual entities, rendered impotent by the categoreal descriptions of them. The Whiteheadian God is deus ex machina.

511   Evans, D. E. "Platon Ac A. N. Whitehead." *Efrydiau Athronyddol,* 5, 1942.

Plato; platonism.

512   Fabro, C. "Concrescence or Dispersion of God into the World (Whitehead)." *God in Exile: Modern Atheism.* New York: Newman Press, 1968, 804–835.

Process theism, summary of; God: immanence of, Hartshorne's interpretation of; atheism; Hartshorne, Charles; Cohen, Morris. Whitehead's doctrine of God is one of the last and most vigorous efforts of modern thought to evade the atheistic bias of the principle of immanentism. However, Whitehead's own dispersion of God into the world threatens the very foundations of theism. (Translated from the author's Italian edition of *Introduzione All' Ateismo Moderno.* Rome: Editrice Studium, 1964.)

513   Falk, Arthur E. "A Many–sorted Ontology and the Progress of Science: An Interpretation of Whitehead's Early Philosophy of Nature as a Proposal for Language Reform." Unpublished Ph.D. dissertation, Yale University, 1965.

Nature; language, formal; objects: of science, of perception; logic; Sellars, Wilfrid; science.

Whitehead's early philosophy of nature lends itself to the formulation of a formal language for thinking about nature.

514   Fararo, Thomas J. "Whitehead and Parsons: A Working Paper on the Foundation of Action Theory." *Essays in General Theory: In Honor of Talcott Parsons.* Edited by J. Loubser, et. al. New York: Free press, 1974.

Action theory; Parsons, Talcott.

515   Fararo, Thomas J. and Conviser, R. "Sociology, History, and the Abstract Perspective." *Quality and Quantity,* 7, 1973, 157–170.

Sociology; history; social sciences.

516   Farley, William E. "The Most High: A Study of the Doctrine of the Transcendence of God in Contemporary Philosophical

Theology." Unpublished Ph. D. dissertation, Columbia University, 1957–1958.

God: transcendence of, sovereignty of.

517   Farley, William E. *The Transcendence of God.* Philadelphia: Westminster Press, 1960, 130–153.

Cosmology; God: as absolute, as relative, transcendence of; dipolarity; nature; reality, as social; Hartshorne, Charles.

518   Farrer, A. "The Prior Actuality of God." *Reflective Faith: Essays in Philosophy.* Grand Rapids, Michigan: Eerdmans, 1974.

God: nature of.

519   Feibleman, James. *The Revival of Realism: Critical Studies in Contemporary Philosophy.* Chapel Hill, North Carolina: University of North Carolina Press, 1946, 46–83.

Eternal objects: as universals, as potentials; realism, vs. nominalism; objectivity, vs. subjectivity; ontological principle; actual entities, and eternal objects; prehensions: physical, negative, conceptual; nexus; Plato; Aristotle; Locke, John; Spinoza, Benedict; Platonism.

In joining his doctrine of eternal objects with the ontological principle, Whitehead wavers between realism and nominalism.

520   Feibleman, J. K. "Realism from Plato to Peirce." *An Introduction to Peirce's Philosophy.* London: Allen & Unwin, 1961, 459–463.

Nominalism, repudiation of; Peirce, Charles: similarities to Whitehead; pragmatism.

Peirce and Whitehead demonstrate how two philosophers who have been subjected to similar influences and environments may, without knowledge of each other, come to strikingly similar conclusions.

521   Feibleman, James K. "Notes for a Commentary to Whitehead's *Science and the Modern World.*" *Darshana International,* 1, 1961, 44–55.

Science and the Modern World; philosophy, and science.

Whitehead undertakes to balance a highly charged idealism, for essence, and strongly developed nominalism, for existence.

522   Felt, James W. "Whitehead's Early Theory of Scientific Objects." Unpublished Ph.D. dissertation, St. Louis University, 1965.

Nature; objects, of science; objects, of perception; perception, and nature; abstraction, extensive; inference, in science; time; space, relational theory of; extension; duration; epistemology, in Whitehead's early writings; science.

In dealing with the problem of scientific objects Whitehead is driven toward epistemology and metaphysics, and toward an explanation of the 'complete fact' which includes the perceiving as well as the perceived.

523   Felt, James W.   "Whitehead and the Bifurcation of Nature."
           Modern Schoolman, 45, 1968, 285–298.

           Bifurcation, of nature; objects, scientific; abstraction; mind, and
           nature.

           Whitehead uses the term "scientific object" in two senses in
           his middle–period philosophy of nature: as a being in nature,
           and as being the mental concepts by which we denote the
           permanences in nature.   This tends toward the bifurcation he
           was intent to avoid.

524   Felt, James W.   "The Temporality of Divine Freedom."   *Process
           Studies*, 4, 1974, 252–262.

           God: and the world, freedom of, love of, emotional intensity of,
           temporality of, consequent nature of; subjective form:
           qualitative pattern of, intensive quantity of; Ford, Lewis S.;
           Brown, Delwin; theology.

           The dimension of temporal freedom in God consists in the
           spontaneous intensity of emotion by which God's propositional
           feelings toward particulars are clothed.

525   Ferrater Mora, J.   "Whitehead."   *Diccionario de Filosofia*, 1958,
           1425–1426.   5th Edition, 1965, Volume 2, 931–932.

           Whitehead, Alfred North, introduction to his thought.

526   Ferré, Frederick.   *Basic Modern Philosophy of Religion.*   New
           York: Charles Scribner's Sons, 1967, 430–435.

           God: as principle of limitation, and value, as persuasive power,
           and Christology; philosophy, of religion; theology, process.

           Whitehead's doctrine of God may be adequate for a general
           theistic religion of creativity, but its adequacy to the
           Christological claims of Christianity is more problematic.

527   Ferré, Frederick.   "Reply."   *Christian Scholar*, 50, 1967, 322–324.

           Philosophy, speculative: God, and world; metaphysics, and
           theology.

           (Written in response to William Christian's "The New
           Metaphysics and Theology.")

528   Ferré, Frederick.   "Science and the Death of 'God'."   *Science and
           Religion: New Perspectives on the Dialogue.*   Edited by I.
           Barbour.   New York: Harper and Row, 1968.   London: SCM,
           1968, Chapter 7.

           Religion: and science, and reason; language: religious, scientific,
           theological; God, death of; verifiability; theism; Christianity, in
           the twentieth century; Van Buren, Paul; theology,
           philosophical.

           Theological reform in the twentieth century must involve
           alterations of doctrine on the basis of critical norms, the
           development of a new tentativeness appropriate to the
           uncertainty of many religious beliefs, and the acceptance of
           genuine pluralism.   Such reform within Christian thinking must
           also be open to nontheistic religious positions.

529   Ferre, Nels F. S.   *The Christian Understanding of God.*   New York: Harper and Brothers Publishers, 1951.

God: nature of, and the world, and time, sovereignty of, as creator, of classical theism, and becoming, and Christology; theology, philosophical.

(The author employs numerous concepts from Whitehead's cosmology to interpret the Christian understanding of God.)

530   Ferre, Nels F. S.   *The Living God of Nowhere and Nothing.* London: Epworth Press, 1966.

God: of classical theism, as eternal; substance; Buddhism; process, philosophy.

In emphasizing becoming to the exclusion of being, process philosophy is closer to Buddhism than Christianity.   By virtue of this emphasis it fails to arrive at an adequate understanding of God.

531   Ferre, Nels F. S.   "Beyond Substance and Process."   *Theology Today,* 24, 1967, 160–171.

Being, and becoming; love; New Testament; theology.

Substance thinking has never succeeded in arriving at a unity of sameness that also allows for real distinction and change; process thinking provides no view of God as the eternal identity.   The New Testament categories of Spirit and Love go beyond substance and process, and may fulfill without their faults the basic aims of both.

532   Ferre, Nels F. S.   *The Universal Word: A Theology for a Universal Faith.*   Philadelphia: Westminster Press, 1969.

God: and process, and tragedy, and Christology; Buddhism, as process philosophy; tragedy; substance; Hartshorne, Charles.

For Whitehead's God, experience is ultimately tragic insofar as the finite must continually frustrate the divine vision and cause it to remain unfulfilled.

533   Feuer, Lewis S.   "What is Philosophy of History?"   *Journal of Philosophy,* 49, 1952, 329–340.

Method, historical; philosophy, of history; Marx, Karl; Toynbee, Arnold J.; history.

Whitehead, Marx, and Toynbee demonstrate the thesis that philosophies of history, as projective value systems, are defensive measures against historical anxiety.

534   Feuer, Lewis S.   "Causal Necessities."   *Philosophical Review,* 63, 1954, 479–499.

Causation, efficient; necessity, senses of.

535   Fisch, M. H.; Murphy, A. E.; and Schneider, H. W.   "One Hundred Years of American Philosophy."   *Philosophical Review,* 56, 1947, 351–389.

Philosophy, in America.

536   Fitch, Frederic B. "The Consistency of the Ramified 'Principia'."
        Journal of Symbolic Logic, 3, 1938, 140–149.

        Principia Mathematica; logic, mathematical; Russell, Bertrand;
        mathematics.

537   Fitch, Frederic B. "Combinatory Logic and Whitehead's Theory
        of Prehensions." *Philosophy of Science*, 24, 1957, 331–335.

        Prehensions, theory of; propositions; epistemology; logic.

        Combinatory logic is appropriate to a Whiteheadian theory of
        prehensions, since the latter involves the non–spatio/temporal
        presence of one entity in another. Hence a Whiteheadian
        epistemology and value theory can be formalized in
        postulational form in the notation of such logic.

538   Fitch, Frederick B. "Sketch of a Philosophy." *The Relevance of
        Whitehead.* Edited by Ivor Leclerc. New York: Humanities
        Press Inc., 1961, 93–103.

        Logic, symbolic; space–time; universals; propositions; substance.

        Whitehead assumes an antecedent plenum of space–time
        regions which are potentials for occupation by actual entities,
        but he never gives an adequate account of the metaphysical
        status of these regions.

539   Fitch, Frederic B. "Propositions as the Only Realities."
        American Philosophical Quarterly, 8, 1971, 99–103.

        Propositions; actual occasions, as propositions; propositions,
        property of; Russell, Bertrand.

        All entities are reducible to propositions, which remain as the
        final irreducible realities; no other entities qualify as ultimate
        realities in the same degree as propositions.

540   Fitzgerald, Janet A. "A Study of Alfred North Whitehead's
        Method of Extensive Abstraction as a Mathematical Model."
        Unpublished Ph.D. dissertation, St. John's University, 1971.

        Abstraction, extensive; philosophy, of mathematics; philosophy,
        of science; space, relational theory of; time; objects, of science;
        perception; event; duration; mathematics; science.

541   Fleming, David A. "God's Gift and Man's Response: Toward a
        Whiteheadian Perspective." *Religious Experience and Process
        Theology.* Edited by Harry J. Cargas and Bernard Lee. New
        York: Paulist Press, 1976, 215–228.

        God: consequent nature of, primordial nature of, activity of, as
        love; grace, of God; prayer; philosophical theology.

        Whitehead proposes a "one–world" metaphysics in contrast to
        the classical natural/supernatural distinction. This allows for
        the presence of God in history in ways that reflect divine
        grace.

542   Fogg, Walter L. "Experience and Order in Blanshard and
        Whitehead." Unpublished Ph.D. dissertation, Boston
        University Graduate School, 1963.

Order; experience; universal; particular; eternal objects, individual essence of, relational essence of; Blanshard, Brand. Blanshard and Whitehead each conceive the relation between the universal and its instances as one between potentiality and actuality.

543   Foley, Leo A. *A Critique of the Philosophy of Alfred North Whitehead in Light of Thomistic Philosophy.* Washington D. C.: Catholic University of American Press, 1946.

Being; God: as cause, and creativity; substance; actuality; epistemology; Thomas Aquinas.

Whitehead's philosophy fails because its comprehension of potency and act is incomplete. The notions of actual entity, relation, and causality in Whitehead's thought imply a doctrine of substance which is lacking in the philosophy of organism. God, properly speaking, should be Pure Act rather than an actual entity.

Reviews

Blyth, J. W. *Philosophical Review*, 58, 1949, 86–88.

Ghyka, M. *Personalist*, 28, 1947, 209–211.

Johnson, A. H. *Philosophy and Phenomenological Research*, 8, 1948, 728–731.

Mazzantini, C. *Rivista di Filosofia*, 39, 1948, 275–285.

544   Foley, Leo A. "Cosmos and Ethos." *New Scholasticism*, 41, 1967, 141–158.

Philosophy, Greek; Teilhard de Chardin; cosmology.

Whitehead and Teilhard de Chardin may be restoring the Greek vision of the cosmos to contemporary thinking, for they approach the universe through human existence.

545   Folse, Henry J., Jr. "The Copenhagen Interpretation of Quantum Theory and Whitehead's Philosophy of Organism." *Tulane Studies in Philosophy*, 23, 1974, 32–47.

Quantum theory: of action, Copenhagen interpretation of; hypotheses: physical, metaphysical; nature, as field of experience; knowledge; Bohr, Niels; Heisenberg, Werner; metaphysics; physics.

The philosophy of organism provides a natural context for the acceptance of the Copenhagen Interpretation of quantum theory, especially with respect to the ideas of Bohr and Heisenberg. It further eliminates the paradoxical quality which mechanistic materialism gives to quantum theory.

546   Fontinell, E. "Transcendent Divinity and Process Philosophy." *Proceedings of the Catholic Theological Society of America*, 23, 1968, 70–84. Also in *New Theology Number 7*. Edited by Martin E. Marty and Dean G. Peerman. New York: Macmillan and Company, 1970.

God: as transcendent, immanence of, relations of; Dewey, John; pragmatism.

The words "otherness" and "presence" may help us acknowledge certain features of reality which some in the past have associated with transcendent divinity.

547   Fontinell, Eugene.   "Pragmatism, Process and Religious Education." *Religious Education*, 68, 1973, 322–331.

Education, religious; beliefs, Christian; scriptures; symbols; James, William; Dewey, John; pragmatism; education.

A pragmatic metaphysic of process leads to an open educational approach to all institutions and beliefs, offering the possibility of continuance in a radically transformed manner.

548   Fontinell, Eugene.   "Process Theology: A Pragmatic Version." *Religious Experience and Process Theology*.   Edited by Harry J. Cargas and Bernard Lee.   New York: Paulist Press, 1976, 23–39.

Pragmatism; existence, human; Dewey, John; philosophical theology; religion; cosmology.

The role of religion serves as a point of comparison between Whitehead's process thought and other processive philosophies deriving from pragmatism.

549   Ford, Lewis S.   "Divine Persuasion and the Triumph of Good." *Christian Scholar*, 50, 1967, 235–250.   Also in *Process Philosophy and Christian Thought*, 287–304.   Edited by Delwin Brown, Ralph E. James and Gene Reeves.   Indianapolis, Indiana: Bobbs–Merrill Company, Inc., 1971.

God: of classical theism, as persuasive power, power of, and evil, and world, and good, primordial nature of, consequent nature of, as source of value; evil; beauty; good; subjective aim; Madden, Edward H.; Hare, Peter H.; Cobb, John B. Jr.; Thomas, George F.

Construing omnipotence in terms of coercive power, classical theism provides a guarantee that good will triumph in the world.   Process theism suggests that the triumph of good in the world can take place only if God and the world work together, with God supplying the initial aims and the world responding in faith.

550   Ford, Lewis S.   "Boethius and Whitehead on Time and Eternity."   *International Philosophical Quarterly*, 8, 1968, 38–67.

Time: and timelessness; eternity; temporality; God: simplicity of, and time; Boethius.

In including the temporal within the eternal, Boethius' "everlasting now" as applied to God has a strong similarity, if not identity, with Whitehead's conception of God as an everlasting concrescence.

551   Ford, Lewis S.   "Is Process Theism Compatible with Relativity Theory?" *Journal of Religion*, 48, 1968, 124–135.

Simultaneity; relativity, theory of; God: as actual entity, as living person; Cobb, John B., Jr.; Hartshorne, Charles; Wilcox, John T.; metaphysics.

The entitative view of God does not conflict with the theory of relativity on the issue of simultaneity. (Written in response to John T. Wilcox, "A Question from Physics for Certain Theists.")

552   Ford, Lewis S.   "Whitehead's Conception of Divine Spatiality." *Southern Journal of Philosophy*, 6, 1968, 1–23.

Space–time, and God; inclusion, regional; standpoint, extensive; unity, prehensive: God, as transspatial; perishing, perpetual; subjective aim; Boethius; Cobb, John B., Jr.; Christian, William A.

Just as God is both everlasting and eternal as well as transcending all time, so God is both omnipresent and transspatial, transcending all space by including it within the simplicity of divine subjectivity.

553   Ford, Lewis S.   "On Genetic Successiveness: A Third Alternative." *Southern Journal of Philosophy*, 7, 1969–1970, 421–425.

Concrescence, phases of; division, genetic; time, epochal theory of; Pols, Edward; Cobb, John B. Jr.

Concrescence may be understood as a series of sub–decisions constituting successive phases in the modification of the subjective aim.

554   Ford, Lewis S.   "Can Whitehead Provide for Real Subjective Agency?   A Reply to Edward Pols's Critique." *Modern Schoolman*, 47, 1970, 209–225.

Subjectivity; subjective aim: indivisibility of, genetic phases of; *causa sui*; creativity; Pols, Edward; metaphysics.

Edward Pols' argument against subjective agency in Whitehead is weakened by his questionable interpretation of genetic indivisibility, and by his failure to distinguish the shift in perspective occasioned by the correlation between temporality and the subject/object distinction.

555   Ford, Lewis S.   "On Some Difficulties with Whitehead's Definition of Abstractive Hierarchies." *Philosophy and Phenomenological Research*, 30, 1970, 453–454.

Eternal objects, as abstractive hierarchy; Roberts, George W.; Root, Vernon M.

Contrary to Roberts and Root, there is no inconsistency in Whitehead's distinction between finite and infinite abstractive hierarchies.   Whitehead's principle of connexity resolves the issue. (Written in response to G. W. Roberts, "A Problem in Whitehead's Doctrine of Abstractive Hierarchies," and V. M. Root, "Eternal Objects, Attributes, and Relations in Whitehead's Philosophy.")

556   Ford, Lewis S.   "Whitehead's Categoreal Derivation of Divine
         Existence." *Monist*, 54, 1970, 374–400.

         Interpretation: systematic, postsystematic; categoreal scheme;
         actual entity; prehensions: physical, conceptual; God: and
         categoreal scheme, subjective aim of, and creativity, as
         primordial; Neville, Robert C.; Christian, William.

         God's existence may be categoreally derived from Whitehead's
         first principles.   God fully exemplifies the principles, and is also
         their creator, insofar as such principles are capable of being
         created.   (Written in response to Robert C. Neville, *God the
         Creator.*)

557   Ford, Lewis S.   "The Viability of Whitehead's God for Christian
         Theology." *Proceedings of the American Catholic Philosophical
         Association*, 44, 1970, 141–151.

         God: and creativity, religious adequacy of, freedom of;
         philosophical theology.

         The process view of God and creativity meets and surmounts
         objections which opponents pose as fatal to such a view.

558   Ford, Lewis S.   "God as King: Benevolent Despot or
         Constitutional Monarch?" *Christian Scholar's Review*, 1, 1971,
         318–322.

         Symbol, religious; God: power of, primordial envisagement of,
         decision of, as persuasive power; evil; "On Thinking of God as
         King"; Westphal, Merold; theology.

         Process theology need not dispense with the biblical symbol of
         God as king; its metaphysics yields the model of a democracy
         with a constitutional monarch.

559   Ford, Lewis S.   "Genetic and Coordinate Division Correlated."
         Process Studies, 1, 1971, 109–209.

         Division: genetic, coordinate; becoming, epochal; phases,
         genetic; being, and appearance; Cobb, John B., Jr.; Neville,
         Robert.

         Coordinate division measures the being or the occurring of
         events, while genetic division measures the becoming of
         occasions.   Becoming is not instantaneous, but exhibits genetic
         successiveness.

560   Ford, Lewis S.   "Whitehead on Subjective Agency: A Response
         to Edward Pols." *The Modern Schoolman*, 49, 1972, 151–152.

         Indivisibility: genetic, coordinate; superject; agency; Pols,
         Edward.

         (This work is written in response to Edward Pols, "Whitehead
         on Subjective Agency: A Reply to Lewis S. Ford.")

561   Ford, Lewis S.   "Biblical Recital and Process Philosophy: Some
         Whiteheadian Suggestions for Old Testament Hermeneutics."
         Interpretation, 26, 1972, 198–209.

         Hermeneutics, Old Testament; God: as persuasive power, as

acting in history; creation; providence; authority, biblical; hermeneutics.

The logic of divine persuasion affirms and illuminates many biblical themes, notably creation, providence, and biblical authority.

562   Ford, Lewis S. "Neville on the One and the Many." *Southern Journal of Philosophy*, 10, 1972, 79–84.

Ultimate, category of; unity: cosmological, ontological; God: and creativity, primordial envisagement of; Neville, Robert C.

Contrary to Neville in "Whitehead on the One and the Many," Whitehead's category of the ultimate is sufficient to account for ontological unity when his account of creativity is considered in relation to the non–temporal primordial envisagement of God.

563   Ford, Lewis S. "The Incarnation as a Contingent Reality: A Reply to Dr. Pailin." *Religious Studies*, 8, 1972, 169–173.

Incarnation, contingency of; God, decision of; revelation: general, particular; Pailin, David A.; christology.

What is important in the incarnation is not what it tells us about God's constant character, but how that character is concretely embodied in a direct confrontation with the human situation. (Written in response to David A. Pailin, "The Incarnation as a Continuing Reality.")

564   Ford, Lewis S. "Reasons, Causes, and Decisions." *Southwestern Journal of Philosophy*, 3, 1972, 51–62.

Cause, efficient; rationality, principles of; decisions, existential; subjectivity; process, microscopic.

Whitehead's analysis of the actual entity clarifies the relation between reason, cause, and decision.

565   Ford, Lewis S. "Process Philosophy and Our Knowledge of God." *Traces of God in a Secular Culture*. Edited by George F. McLean. Staten Island, New York: Alba House, 1973, 85–115.

God: knowledge of, and categoreal scheme, as actual entity, as dipolar, and reversal of poles; Hartshorne, Charles.

Whereas Hartshorne approaches God through the logic of perfection, seeking to determine those properties appropriate to a being supremely worthy of worship, Whitehead uses a method of categoreal analysis, first determining those metaphysical properties that apply to all actualities, including God, and then showing that these properties entail a systematic contrast between God and the world.

566   Ford, Lewis S., editor. *Two Process Philosophers: Hartshorne's Encounter with Whitehead*. AAR Studies in Religion Number 5. Tallahassee, Florida: American Academy of Religion, 1973.

Whitehead, Alfred North: influence of, and other philosophers; Hartshorne, Charles.

(See individual entries under Griffin, Hartshorne, O'Mera, and Sessions.)

Reviews

Anonymous. *Journal of Religion*, 55, 1975, 125–137.

Anonymous. *Choice*, March 1974, 335.

Duclow, D. F. *Review of Metaphysics*, 28, 1974, 121.

Pailin, D. A. *Process Studies*, 4, 1974, 133–140.

567   Ford, Lewis S. "The Non–Temporality of Whitehead's God." *International Philosophical Quarterly*, 13, 1973, 347–376.

God: as non–temporal, decision of, primordial nature of, as becoming, and eternal objects, and temporality; eternal objects; Brown, Delwin.

The actuality of God is dependent upon a non–temporal decision which expresses God's self–functioning even in the temporality of divine concrescence.

568   Ford, Lewis S. "Can Whitehead Rescue Perishing?" *Personalist*, 54, 1973, 92–93.

Perpetual perishing; Simmons, James R.

Simmons' failure to distinguish between static unity and dynamic unification, and between the perishing of persons and the perishing of occasions, leads to misconceptions concerning Whitehead's doctrine of perpetual perishing. (Written in response to James R. Simmons, "An Antinomy of Perishing in Whitehead.")

569   Ford, Lewis S. "Response: Lionel S. Thornton and Process Christology." *Anglican Theological Review*, 55, 1973, 479–483.

Christology: high, evolutionary, docetic; trinity, social; Logos; Thornton, Lionel S.; Cooper, Robert M.; christology; dualism; theology.

Thornton's christology fails since it presupposes a self–sufficient Creator and depicts a docetic Christ wholly discontinuous with the on–going process of the world. (Written in response to Robert M. Cooper, "A Note on Lionel S. Thornton: An Early Process Theologian," *Anglican Theological Review*, 55. 1973, 182–188.)

570   Ford, Lewis S. "Whitehead's Ontology and Lango's Synonty: A Critical Study." *The Modern Schoolman*, 51, 1973–1974, 53–61.

Ontology, relational; synonty; subjective forms: interrelatedness of, mutual sensitivity of, symmetrical, asymmetrical; existence, categories of; nexūs; Lango, John W.; ontology; logic.

Lango's brilliant work of formalizing the categories of existence requires revision in his treatment of the relationship of subjective forms within an entity. (Written in response to John W. Lango, *Whitehead's Ontology*.)

571   Ford, Lewis S. "Process Philosophy," "Process Theology." *New*

Catholic Encyclopedia, 16, 1967–1974. Washington D. C.: Publishers Guild, 1974, 363–367.

Process philosophy: summary of, criticism of; process theology: summary of, and Catholicism; God; Hartshorne, Charles; Teilhard de Chardin.

572 Ford, Lewis S. "Kirkpatrick on Subjective Becoming." *Process Studies*, 4, 1974, 37–41.

Subject: as superject, unity of; concrescence, phases of; division, genetic; subjective aim; Kirkpatrick, Frank; Leclerc, Ivor.

The subject of an occasion of experience is to be defined as the total reciprocal activity of all the prehensions within the occasion as they are governed by the subjective aim.

573 Ford, Lewis S. "The Duration of the Present." *Philosophy and Phenomenological Research*, 35, 1974, 100–106.

Time; present: duration of, punctal, as coming into being, relation to past, relation to future; events; Zeno's paradox; Gale, Richard M.

While the durational present can be genetically subdivided into earlier and later phases, these phases cannot be construed as individual acts of becoming, since only the final phase terminates in being.

574 Ford, Lewis S. "The Possibilities for Process Christology." *Encounter*, 35, 1974, 281–294.

Christ aims, christological; Jesus: as special revelation, as unsurpassable, as totally obedient; universe, incarnational; Griffin, David R.; Williams, Ronald L.; christology.

Griffin's conclusion that Jesus expressed God's general aim for his entire creation is too abstract for theological purposes. A process christology must direct itself to the question of what God was trying to accomplish on behalf of mankind through Jesus.

575 Ford, Lewis S. "The Eternity of God and the Temporality of the World." *Encounter*, 36, 1975, 115–122.

God: as willing, as nontemporal, as temporal, activity of, in classical theism; knowledge: as timeless, as everlasting, as determinate; Hartshorne, Charles; Meynell, Hugo; theism: classical, process; theology.

Whitehead's integration of divine temporal experience within the nontemporality of God's primordial envisagement preserves classical theism's concern for the unalterability of divine will, while precluding the classical problem of divine foreknowledge.

576 Ford, Lewis S. "The Immutable God and Father Clarke." *The New Scholasticism*, 49, 1975, 189–199.

God: immutability of, of classical theism, and being, and contingency, infinity of; novelty; creativity: and esse, as principle of novelty; Clarke, W. Norris; Thomism.

While Father Clarke's "God Knowable and Unknowable" suggests a fruitful synthesis between Thomistic esse and Whitehead's cosmology, it is hampered by its adherence to a logic of delimitation which precludes the emergence of anything ultimately new.

577   Ford, Lewis S. "Process Trinitarianism." *Journal of the American Academy of Religion*, 43, 1975, 199–213.

Trinitarianism; Trinity: doctrine of, as process; God: as Logos, as Holy Spirit, and creativity, primordial nature, consequent nature of.

Whitehead's notion of God requires a trinity of principles within God to resolve the problem of how on the one hand God transcends and is immanent within the world and on the other hand how the world transcends and is immanent within God.

578   Ford, Lewis S. "The Power of God and the Christ." *Religious Experience and Process Theology*. Edited by Harry J. Cargas and Bernard Lee. New York: Paulist Press, 1976, 79–92.

God: power of, and world; evolution; process theology; christology.

Whitehead's understanding of how God is at work in the world helps explain how God acts in Jesus as the Christ.

579   Ford, Lewis S. "Our Prayers as God's Passions." Edited by Harry J. Cargas and Bernard Lee. *Religious Experience and Process Theology*. New York: Paulist Press, 1976.

Prayer; God, consequent nature of.

Prayer, as the feelings of creatures addressed to God, form the passions of God.

580   Forest, Ilse. "Creation versus Process: A Study of the Concept of God in the Philosophies of Thomas Aquinas and Alfred North Whitehead." Unpublished Ph.D. dissertation, Yale University, 1939.

God, as Being; monism; pluralism; Thomas Aquinas.

Because of its empirical basis and consistent intellectualism, Thomism is a more adequate system than that of Whitehead. It is questionable whether Whitehead's notion of God is necessary to his scheme of thought.

581   Fornasari, Archimedes, F. S. C. J. "Reality as a Solidarity of Creative Process: A Critical Interpretation of Whitehead's 'Category of the Ultimate'." Unpublished Ph.D. dissertation, Catholic University of America, 1969.

Creativity; ultimate: many: one; organism; value, and creativity; God, and creativity; unity, of universe; solidarity, of universe.

582   Forsyth, T. M. "The New Cosmology in its Historical Aspect: Plato, Newton, Whitehead." *Philosophy*, 7, 1932, 54–61.

Cosmology; space–time, absolute; matter; necessity; soul,

motion of; determinism, and indeterminism; Plato; Newton, Isaac; Platonism.

Whitehead's metaphysics is a return to Plato's fundamental thought through the progress of scientific inquiry brought about by Newton.

583   Forsyth, T. M.   "Creative Evolution in its Bearing on the Idea of God." *Philosophy*, 25, 1950, 195–208.

God, and the world; evolution: as creative, and God; Bergson, Henri; Alexander, Samuel.

Bergson, Alexander, and Whitehead develop theories based on creative evolution in which God is the eternal reality who acts only in and through nature, man, and history.

584   Fost, F. F.   "The Philosophical Theology of Charles Hartshorne: An Analysis and Critique of the Categories of Dipolar Theism." Unpublished Ph.D. dissertation, Claremont Graduate School, 1964.

God, as dipolar.

585   Foster, A. Durwood, Jr.   "The Resurrection of God." *Religion in Life*, 38, 1969, 131–147.

God, concept of; Jesus, and resurrection; theologians, death of God; theology.

The new vision of God's life in modern theology matches the consciousness of cosmic evolution and the positive secularity of the present.

586   Fowler, Dean.   "Relativity Physics and the Doctrine of God: A Comparative Study of Einstein and Whitehead." Unpublished Ph.D. dissertation, Claremont Graduate School, 1975.

Relativity: physics, general theory of, special theory of, Whitehead's theory of; God: and causation, and time, primordial nature of, consequent nature of; gravitation; strain–loci; impetus; duration; events; simultaneity; Whitehead, Alfred North: early theory of, relation of mathematics to physics and philosophy; Einstein, Albert; Ford, Lewis S.; Hartshorne, Charles; Wilcox, J. T.; science, and religion; epistemology; physics; mathematics.

By comparing the metaphysical, epistemological, and physical differences and similarities between Einstein and Whitehead's theories of relativity, and then showing how their respective doctrines of God may be correlated with their physics, it is argued that science and religion may be unified in their sharing a common metaphysical foundation.

587   Fowler, Dean.   "Disconfirmation of Whitehead's Relativity Theory—A Critical Reply." *Process Studies*, 4, 1974, 288–290.

Relativity, theory of; gravitation; mechanics, quantum; geometry; Ariel, Robert A.; Will, Clifford; Einstein, Albert; physics.

Contrary to the thesis of Robert A. Ariel, no empirical thesis can decide the adequacy of Whitehead's basic theory of relativity. The issue between Whitehead and Einstein must be settled on philosophical grounds.

588   Fowler, Dean. "Whitehead's Theory of Relativity." *Process Studies*, 5, 1975, 159–174.

Relativity, special theory of; gravitation; simultaneity; induction, ground of; deduction; causation.

Process philosophers have been too concerned with explicating aspects of process thought so as to make them conform to the demands of Einstein's theory of relativity. The dialogue between Whitehead and Einstein should be redirected toward the philosophical issues, with Whitehead's thought being construed as a viable alternative to the philosophical presuppositions which Einstein assumes.

589   Francovich, G. *Toynbee, Heidegger y Whitehead.* Buenos Aires: Editorial Raigal, 1951, 61–79.

Toynbee, Arnold; Heidegger, Martin.

590   Frankel, H. "Misadventure of Ideas: A Study of Whitehead's Philosophy." *Science and Society*, 26, 1962, 153–195.

Process philosophy, summary of; Marx, Karl; Marxism.

Faced in his philosophy with the irremovable dualism which is simply the contradiction between what is and what ought to be, and unable to point the way out of the contradictions because this would mean pointing the way out of capitalism, Whitehead took the last steps away from reality into the ivory tower of mysticism.

591   Frankena, W. K., editor. *Philosophy of Education.* New York: Macmillan and Company, 1965.

Philosophy, of education.

592   Frick, Ivan E. "A Study of the Objective and Subjective Aspects of Selfhood in the Thought of Alfred North Whitehead." Unpublished Ph.D. dissertation, Columbia University, 1959.

Self: and self–consciousness, and self–creativity, as series of experiences, unity of.

593   Frick, Ivan E. "Alfred North Whitehead and the 'Ordinary Language' Philosophers: A Study in Comparisons." *Indian Journal of Philosophy*, 4, 1964, 69–84.

Language: ordinary, and referent, Whitehead's use of; Wittgenstein, Ludwig; linguistic analysis.

Whitehead and Wittgenstein agree in their estimate of the limited value of the ideal language; they differ in Whitehead's insistence that the wider generalities themselves must be criticized, examined, and finally interpreted, and in the estimate of the referential element in language.

594   Fries, H. S. "The Functions of Whitehead's God." *Monist*, 46, 1936, 25–58.

God: function of, and creativity, as principle of limitation; Emmet, Dorothy M.

The metaphysical functions of God are served primarily by his primordial nature, whereas the merely religious functions are served primarily by his consequent and superject natures.

595   Fries, Horace S. "Ely on Whitehead." *Journal of Liberal Education*, 5, 1943, 96–97.

God: religious availability of, goodness of; immortality; Ely, Stephen L.

In *The Religious Availability of Whitehead's God*, Ely rightly argues that the Whiteheadian God cannot maintain, even within the context of its consequent nature, the value of the individual.

596   Frye, Robert E. "Pragmatism in Recent Non–Pragmatic Systems: Santayana, Bergson, Whitehead." Unpublished Ph.D. dissertation, Indiana University, 1956.

Reason, function of; philosophy, aim of; Santayana, George; Bergson, Henri; pragmatism.

597   Fuller, B. A. G. *A History of Philosophy*. New York: H. Holt and Company, 1938.

Actual occasion; eternal objects; God; relativity, principle of.

(The author provides a brief review of the general concepts of Whitehead's later philosophy.)

598   Fulton, Everett P. "A Critical Examination of Process Theology from the Perspective of the Doctrines of Sin and Salvation, with Special Reference to the Claim that it is a Natural Theology." Unpublished Ph.D. dissertation, The University of Iowa, 1966.

Salvation; evil; sin; God, and creativity; man; Hartshorne, Charles; Cobb, John B. Jr.; Meland, Bernard; Weiman, Henry Nelson; theology, process; theology, natural.

Process theologians have tended to identify God and creativity with the result that the relation between evil and God becomes problematic.

599   Fulton, James Street. "Whitehead's Footnote to Berkeley." *Rice University Studies*, 50, 1964, 13–22.

Sense perception, theory of; sense data; Berkeley, George.

Berkeley took presentational immediacy to be primary, and attempted to reduce the physical world to a display of sense ideas. Whitehead takes causal efficacy to be primary, and thus goes behind Berkeley to a more ancient realistic tradition.

600   Gale, Richard M. "Has the Present any Duration?" *Nous*, 5, 1971, 39–47.

Duration; time: as present, epochal theory of; Zeno.

The Zenonian paradoxes rest upon a conceptual absurdity involving an equivocal use of the present. The paradox may

be avoided by a doctrine of the punctual present. The epochal
theory does not suffice, since it continues the equivocation.

601   Gallagher, William J. "Whitehead's Psychological Physiology: A
        Third View." *Process Studies*, 4, 1974, 263–274.

        Physiology, psychological.

602   Gallagher, William J. "Intellectual Growth and the Teaching of
        Philosophy." *Metaphilosophy*, SUNY at Albany, Spring 1976.

        Philosophy, teaching of; learning; philosophy, of education.

603   Gambazzi, Paolo. "Note sulla Dialettica tra astratto e concreto."
        Aut Aut, 90, 1965, 68–78.

        Concrete; abstraction; concreteness, fallacy of misplaced; reason,
        speculative; Marx, Karl; philosophy, of science.

604   Gandhi, Ramchandra. "Whitehead on the Distrust of Speculative
        Philosophy." *International Philosophical Quarterly*, 12, 1972,
        389–414.

        Philosophy: speculative, aim of; reason: practical, speculative;
        perception, sensationalist doctrine of; language, ordinary;
        Function of Reason; *Process and Reality*; Bacon, Francis;
        Hume, David; Kant, Immanuel; Strawson, P. F.; Collingwood,
        R. G.; metaphysics; epistemology.

        Whitehead's defense of speculative philosophy, developed
        through *The Function of Reason* and *Process and Reality*,
        answers objections to metaphysics in the works of Bacon,
        Hume, Kant, Strawson, and Collingwood.

605   Gandillac, M. De. "Idealisme et realisme dans la pensée anglais
        contemporaine." *Revue D'Histoire Philosophie et Civilisation
        Francaise*, 46, 1944, 318–333.

        Idealism; realism.

606   Garcia Bacca, J. D. *Nueve grandes filósofos contemporaneos y
        sus temas.* Caracas: Imprenta Nacional, 1947, Volume 2,
        187–360.

        Whitehead, Alfred North: philosophical development of; process
        philosophy, summary of.

607   Garhart, John D. "Implications for Christian Moral Theory in
        Whitehead's Philosophy; a Study of Agape, Koinonia, and
        Organism." Unpublished Ph.D. dissertation, Yale University,
        1952.

        Ethics; morality, Christian; value; good; evil; love; theology.

        Whitehead's metaphysics provides a foundation in natural
        philosophy for the Christian concepts of love and fellowship.

608   Garland, William J. "Whitehead's Concept of Actuality."
        Unpublished Ph.D. dissertation, Johns Hopkins University,
        1966.

        Actuality, and time; past, as actual; decision, as meaning of
        actuality; definiteness; objective immortality; creativity;
        subjective immediacy; concrescence; possibility; eternal object;
        continuum, extensive.

'Decision' and 'definiteness of character' are two criteria by which an actual entity can be judged as 'actual'. Actuality is an inherently temporal concept which should be understood in terms of creative advance.

609   Garland, William J.   "The Ultimacy of Creativity."   *Southern Journal of Philosophy*, 7, 1969, 361–376.

Creativity: as ultimate, as substantial activity; creative advance; ontological principle; Christian, William A.; metaphysics.

Creativity can be used to explain or to account for the very features of the universe which it expresses, such as the unity of process and the ongoingness of time.   Thus, to eliminate creativity, as Christian suggests, would be to rob Whitehead's system of some of its explanatory richness.

610   Gentry, George.   "Prehension as an Explanatory Principle."   *Journal of Philosophy*, 35, 1938, 517–522.

Prehensions, theory of; subjectivist principle; emergence.

Whitehead's theory of the emergence of the subject and his theory of prehensions contradict each other, for prehensions presuppose the subject whose emergence they explain.

611   Gentry, George.   "The Subject in Whitehead's Philosophy."   *Philosophy of Science*, 11, 1944, 222–226.

Subject, as self–evolving historical unity; subjectivist principle, reformed; prehensions; metaphysics.

A subject conceived as the end result of a process of integrating feelings clearly cannot be conceived as a subject entertaining this end.   Whitehead is driven to ascribe the essential function of the subject to feelings as such.

612   Gentry, George.   "Eternal Objects and the Philosophy of Organism."   *Philosophy of Science*, 13, 1946, 252–260.

Eternal objects; objectification; feelings: physical, conceptual; novelty; metaphysics.

To eliminate the doctrine of eternal objects and at the same time retain the thesis that the actual entity is a novel emergent requires a complete revamping of the theory of causal objectification.

613   Geoghegan, William D.   "Varieties of Platonism in Contemporary Religious Thought."   Unpublished Ph.D. dissertation, Columbia University, 1950.

Eternal object; idea; Plato; Inge, W. R.; More, P. E.; Taylor, A. E.; Temple, William; Santayana, George; Platonism; religion.

614   Geoghegan, William D.   *Platonism in Recent Religious Thought.* New York: Columbia Univeristy Press, 1958, 110–139.

Eternal object: and Platonic forms, as universals; God: as principle of concretion, primordial nature of, as eros; idea; Christianity, Whitehead's attitude toward; religion: and reason, and science; prehension; sensa; experience, religious; Plato;

Inge, W. R.; More, P. E.; Taylor, A. E.; Temple, William; Santayana, George; Platonism; materialism; idealism.

While the Demiurge of Plato's *Timaeus* and the primordial nature of the Whiteheadian God have many similarities, Whitehead's doctrine of God as the foundation of the aesthetic order of the world is a distortion of Platonism. Whitehead merges the temporal with the eternal; Plato keeps them distinct.

615   Geran, J. "Alfred North Whitehead on the Ontological Principle: A Critique of Early Modern Epistemology in 'Process and Reality'." Unpublished Ph.D. dissertation, University of Chicago, 1975.

Ontological principle; epistemology; causal efficacy; presentational immediacy.

616   Gex, Maurice. "Quelques aspects du realisme contemporain." *Revue de Theologie et de Philosophie*, 23, 1935, 176–215. Also in *Varietes Philosophiques*, Rouge, 1948.

Organism; events, theory of; Leibniz, G. W.; Alexander, Samuel.

617   Gex, Maurice. "La philosophie d'inspiration scientifique." *Dialectica: Revue Internationale de Philosophie de la Connaissance*, 12, 1959, 160–183.

Whitehead, Alfred North: introduction to his thought.

618   Gibson, A. Boyce. "The Two Strands in Natural Theology." *Monist*, 47, 1963, 335–346. Reprinted in *Process and Divinity—The Hartshorne Festschrift*. Edited by William L. Reese and Eugene Freeman. Lasalle: Open Court, 1964.

Theology, natural; God: immutability of, activity of, as eternal, and time; Plato; Aristotle; Hartshorne, Charles; theology, natural.

Immobilism and activism are contradictory, but both are required for a doctrine of God. The strands may be combined by taking activity as the formula for the whole, supported by immobilist elements.

619   Gier, Nicholas. "Process Theology and the Death of God." *The Theology of Altizer: Critique and Response*. Edited by John B. Cobb, Jr. Philadelphia: Westminster Press, 1970, 164–193.

Theology, radical; God: transcendence of, primordial nature of, consequent nature of, immanence of; self; Altizer, Thomas J. J.; Cobb, John B. Jr.

620   Gilkey, Langdon B. "Maker of Heaven and Earth." Unpublished Ph.D. dissertation, Columbia University, 1954. Published as *Maker of Heaven and Earth: A Study of the Christian Doctrine of Creation*. New York: Doubleday & Company, 1959.

God, as creator; philosophical theology, method of; revelation;

ontology; metaphysics, speculative; monism; pluralism; faith; Bradley, F. H.; theology.

Whitehead's attempt to comprehend the totality of things in terms successfully applied to finite events breaks down when these same terms are univocally applied to the creator God of Christian theology. Theology rather than philosophy has primacy on questions concerning the creator God, although philosophy can be of help.

621   Gilkey, Langdon B. *Naming the Whirlwind: The Renewal of God–Language.* New York: The Bobbs–Merril Company, 1969.

Secularism; God: language about, and order, proofs of, and contingency; theology: natural, process, method of; Thomism; language analysis.

If metaphysics is to offer itself as a support for Biblical and Christian language, then a prolegomenon to metaphysical discourse is needed showing its possibility and meaningfulness. Theologians influenced by Whitehead must ask why it is justifiable both to believe in the objective rationality and coherence of process and in the power of speculative thought to reach beyond immediate experience.

622   Gilkey, Langdon. "Process Theology." *Vox Theologica*, 43, 1973, 5–29.

Process theology, summary of; metaphysics: and religious faith, and theology, and problem of God; Pelagianism; Christianity, liberal; theology; religion.

Insofar as theology needs ontological categories, process thought may be most adequate. The theological difficulties it entails are Pelagianism, and an inadequacy to cope with the uniqueness of God's activity, his mystery, and his grace.

623   Gillham, William R. B. "The God–World Relation in Whitehead, Hartshorne, and Wieman." Unpublished Ph.D. dissertation, Princeton University, 1964.

God: and world, primordial nature of, consequent nature of, superjective nature of, as principle of limitation, as eros, transcendence of; Hartshorne, Charles; Wieman, Henry Nelson; religion.

Whitehead, Hartshorne, and Wieman each conclude that the essence of the religious life is conscious participation in the divine creative process.

624   Gilmour, John C. "Analogical Generalization and Whitehead's Panpsychism." Unpublished Ph.D. dissertation, Emory University, 1966.

Panpsychism; nature, and subjectivity; analogy; generalization; metaphysics, and nature; philosophy, method of; adequacy; coherence; Hartshorne, Charles.

A Whiteheadian panpsychism can be defended on the basis of the criterion of adequacy.

625   Ginestier, P. *La pensée anglo–saxonne depuis 1900.* Paris: Presses Université de France, 1956.

Process philosophy, summary of.

626   Godsey, Raleigh K. "Relation and Substance in the Metaphysics of Alfred North Whitehead." Unpublished Ph.D. dissertation, Tulane University, 1969.

Substance; relations: internal, external; materialism; organism; location, fallacy of simple; creativity, as substantial activity; Aristotle, and substance; science.

627   Goheen, John. "Whitehead's Theory of Value." *The Philosophy of Alfred North Whitehead.* Edited by Paul A. Schilpp. La Salle, Illinois: Open Court Publishing Company, 1941.

Value: and eternal objects and feeling; unity, in experience; harmony; beauty; good; disorder; self–creativity; novelty; subjective aim; importance.

Whitehead's theory of value is divisible into a doctrine of pattern or form and into a doctrine of feeling.

628   Goldstein, Valerie S. "The Concept of Individuality in Whitehead's Metaphysics." Unpublished Ph.D. dissertation, University of Chicago, 1966.

Actual entities, individuality of; atomism; individuality, human; person; subjective aim, initial phase of; subjective form; philosophy, nature of.

629   Golightly, Cornelius L. "Inquiry and Whitehead's Schematic Method." *Philosophy and Phenomenological Research,* 11, 1951, 510–524.

Methodology; categoreal scheme; deduction, rationalistic; imagination; epistemology.

Whitehead's conception of the schematic method as the proper form of philosophical inquiry is an answer to the positivist position.

630   Goss, James. "Camus, God, and Process Thought." *Process Studies,* 4, 1974, 114–128.

God: and world, Whitehead without; beauty; adventure; Camus, Albert; Tillich, Paul; existentialism.

Camus' writings leave open the possibility of God as understood by Whitehead. Camus' thoughts on rebellion and its source in the beauty of nature are compatible with and made consistent by a process notion of God.

631   Gotshalk, D. W. *Structure and Reality: A Study of First Principles.* New York: Dial Press, 1937. New York: Greenwood Press, 1968.

Relations; time, and contemporaneity; universals; abstraction, extention.

(Although the work is not about Whitehead's philosophy, reference is made to some aspects of Whitehead's thought.)

632   Gould, Keith A.   "The Modern Wordsworth: A Comparative
        Study of William Wordsworth and Charles Hartshorne."
        Unpublished Ph.D. dissertation, Pennsylvania State University,
        1973.

        Poetry; Hartshorne, Charles; Wordsworth, William; literature.

        (Gould's dissertation is on Hartshorne and Wordsworth, but
        may be of interest to those who wish to explore the relation
        between Whitehead and Wordsworth.)

633   Gourlay, A. B.   *A History of Sherborne School.*   Dorset,
        England: Sawtells of Sherborne Limited, 1951, 1971, 44n, 120n,
        140.

        Whitehead, biography of.

        (This is a history of the school in Dorsetshire which
        Whitehead attended as a youth.)

634   Gragg, Alan.   *Charles Hartshorne.*   Waco, Texas: Word Books,
        1973, 25.

        Philosophy, speculative; Hartshorne, Charles; philosophical
        theology.

        (This work reviews the thought of Charles Hartshorne and
        concerns Whitehead only indirectly.)

635   Grange, Joseph.   "Tragic Value in the Thought of Alfred North
        Whitehead."   Unpublished Ph.D. dissertation, Fordham
        University, 1970.

        Value; tragedy; finitude; limitation; creativity, and value;
        beauty; human existence; civilization; actuality, and value;
        possibility, and value; peace.

        Whitehead's theory of value articulates the necessary
        relationship between creativity and finitude in human existence.

636   Grange, Joseph.   "Whitehead's Tragic Vision: Process, Progress
        and Existentialism."   *Bucknell Review,* 20, 1972, 144.

        Tragedy; value; beauty; finitude; ontological principle, and
        existentialism; Sartre, Jean Paul; Heidegger, Martin; Nietzsche,
        Friedrich; existentialism.

        Whitehead's metaphysics, value theory, and philosophy of
        civilization provide an approach to existence which sees tragedy
        as the lever of human process.   Such an approach complements
        several of the themes of existentialism.

637   Gray, Wallace.   "Whitehead and Ferré Discuss God."   *Hibbert
        Journal,* 56, 1957–1958, 262–272.

        God: nature of, and world; Jesus; Ferré, Nels; theology.

        In an imagined conversation between Whitehead and Ferré,
        key differences which might emerge would concern the degree
        of God's dependence on the world, and the nature of God's
        permanence.

638   Green, Thomas H. S. J.   "The Idea of Novelty in Peirce and

Whitehead." Unpublished Ph.D. dissertation, University of Notre Dame, 1968.

Novelty; evolution; organism; feeling, conceptual; purpose, physical; relation, internal; chance; Peirce, Charles S.; Darwin, Charles; Aristotle, and ousia; Leclerc, Ivor; Sherburne, Donald; biology; religion.

639   Greenfield, Stephen A.   "A Whiteheadian Perspective of the Problem of Evil: Whitehead's Understanding of Evil and Christian Theodicy." Unpublished Ph.D. dissertation, Fordham University, 1973.

Evil, as positive destruction; God, and evil; nature, and evil; human existence, and evil; theodicy; Augustine, and evil; theology.

Whitehead's understanding of evil as 'positive destruction' offers significant contributions to the consistency and adequacy of the Christian understanding of evil.

640   Greenman, Martin A.   "Whitehead's Theory of Meaning." Unpublished Ph.D. dissertation, University of Chicago, 1950.

Meaning, theory of; propositions: and facts, and statements, and meaning; experience; structure; fact: private, public.

641   Greenman, Martin A.   "A Whiteheadian Analysis of Propositions and Facts."   *Philosophy and Phenomenological Research*, 13, 1952–1953, 477–486.

Propositions: and eternal objects, and facts, ontological status of; contrasts, propositional; metaphysics; philosophy, analytic.

A proposition which is neither signified by a sentence nor realized in any actual world has the ontological status of a real possibility.   The relation between a proposition and a fact is the same as that between a real possibility and its actualization.

642   Greenman, Martin A.   "A Whiteheadian Theory of Meaning." *Philosophy of Science*, 20, 1953, 31–41.

Meaning: general theory of, special theory of, linguistic; language; feelings, propositional; philosophy, linguistic.

Whitehead's theory of propositional feelings constitutes a general theory of meaning.

643   Gregory, J. C.   "Three Clues to Whitehead's Philosophy of Organism." *Philosopher*, 3, 1951, 72–78.

Organism, philosophy of.

644   Grene, M.   *The Knower and the Known*.   Basic Books, 1966. Berkeley: University of California Press, 1974.

Event; panpsychism; time, as present; qualities: primary, secondary; Merleau–Ponty, Maurice; Bohm, David; Polanyi, Michael; Heidegger, Martin; existentialism; phenomenology; cosmology.

Out of the existential–phenomenological approach of Merleau–Ponty and the analogous approach of Michael Polanyi can emerge a process cosmology not unlike that of Whitehead's *Process and Reality.*

645   Griffin, David R. "Schubert Ogden's Christology and the Possibilities of Process Philosophy." *Christian Scholar,* 50, 1967, 290–303.

Jesus: as God's decisive act, as revelation; God: as acting in history, as love; aim, divine; Ogden, Schubert M.; christology; soteriology; subjective aim, initial phase of.

Ogden's christology does not adequately explain how one can speak of Jesus as God's decisive act. Further exploration of Whitehead's concept of the ideal aim can provide a corrective to Ogden's account.

646   Griffin, David R. "Jesus, Revelation, and Truth: A Whiteheadian Essay in Christology." Unpublished Ph.D. dissertation, Claremont Graduate School, 1970. (A revised version of this dissertation is published under the title *A Process Christology.)*

Jesus: as revelation, as God's decisive act; revelation; truth; Schleiermacher, Friedrich.

647   Griffin, David R. "Is Revelation Coherent?" *Theology Today,* 28, 1971, 278–294.

Revelation; God: as acting in history, and psyche/body analogy; Nielsen, Kai; Niebuhr, H. Richard; theology.

Revelation occurs when an event that is indeed a special act of God is appropriately received, so that God's basic character and essential purpose are communicated through the event to the believer. The believer thereby appropriates a vision of reality which provides a basis for making all reality intelligible.

648   Griffin, David R. "Whitehead's Contributions to a Theology of Nature." *Philosophy of Religion and Theology Section Papers, American Academy of Religion,* 1971, 137–147.

Nature: theology of, and value, order of, meaning of, and God; process philosophy, summary of; value: intrinsic, instrumental; ecology; religion, and science.

Aspects of Whitehead's philosophy are directly relevant for a theology of nature adequate for spiritual and practical needs, as well as for the need to reconcile science and religion.

649   Griffin, David R. "The Process Theology of Norman Pittenger: A Review Article." *Process Studies,* 1, 1971, 136–148.

Jesus, God's presence in; God, activity of; person, and personal immortality; Pittenger, Norman; christology; eschatology.

Pittenger's excellent contributions to process theology contain some imprecise use of Whitehead's conceptuality, which leads to certain difficulties particularly evident in his christology.

650   Griffin, David R. and Reeves, Gene. "Bibliography of Secondary Literature on Alfred North Whitehead." *Process Studies,* 1, 1971, 2–83.

Whitehead, Alfred North: bibliography of.

651   Griffin, David R.   "Whitehead's Contribution to a Theology of
       Nature."   *Bucknell Review*, 20, Winter 1972, 3–24.

       Nature, and human existence; panpsychism; God, and nature;
       theology, process.

652   Griffin, David R.   "The Essential Elements of a Contemporary
       Christology."   *Encounter*, 33, 1972, 170–184.

       Jesus: God's presence in, relation to nature, saving significance
       of, and christology, as revelation, as unique; God: nature of, as
       purposive, as actual being, and causation, presence of in Jesus;
       presuppositions: ontological,   anthropological,   theistic;
       christology, soteriology, ontology.

       Jesus is the decisive revelation to humanity of God's character
       and purpose.   An adequate contemporary christology which
       supports this statement must include nine elements concerning
       Jesus in his relation to God and nature.

653   Griffin, David R.   "Philosophical Theology and the Pastoral
       Ministry."   *Encounter*, 33, 1972, 230–244.

       Causality, divine; God: power of, as universal persuasive
       influence, goodness of, as creator, and creatio ex nihilo, as deus
       ex machina, and evil; revelation; church; Hartshorne, Charles;
       philosophical theology; ministry.

       Reflection upon issues of philosophical theology is essential to
       the   pastoral   ministry,   since   unclarified   and/or   unrealistic
       theological suppositions contribute to existential problems.

654   Griffin, David R.   "Hartshorne's Differences from Whitehead."
       Two   Process   Philosophers.   Edited   by   Lewis   S.   Ford.
       Missoula: University of Montana, 1973, 35–57.

       God: as dipolar, as living person, as a society; possibilities: as
       eternal objects, as metaphysical categories, as specific qualities,
       as universals; eternal objects: as objective, as subjective;
       contemporaries,   prehension   of;   objective   immortality: and
       subjective immediacy, and perishing, in God; metaphysics: and
       certainty, and method, as descriptive; Hartshorne, Charles;
       Ford, Lewis S.; Christian, William A.

       Major differences between Hartshorne and Whitehead fall
       under two categories: the nature of possibility, and the nature
       of actuality, particularly as both relate to God.

655   Griffin, David R.   *A Process Christology.*   Philadelphia:
       Westminster Press, 1973.

       Jesus: God's presence in, as disclosure of God, humanity of, as
       unique, as revelation; Christ: as Logos, and traditional
       christology; existence, structure of Christian; revelation;
       causation; Schleiermacher, Friedrich; Niebuhr, H. Richard;
       Tillich, Paul; christology.

       The Whiteheadian vision of reality resolves many of the
       traditional christological problems and allows the Christian to

affirm rationally and coherently that after the revelation in Christ, persons are capable of receiving aims which more directly express God's character and purpose.

Reviews

Brown, D. *Religious Education*, 19, 1974, 506–508.

Cobb, J. B. Jr. *Religion in Life*, 43, 1974, 505–506.

Empereur, J. *America*, 30, 1974.

Gaffney, P. *Review for Religious*, 33, 1974, 713–714.

Godsey, J. D. *Virginia Seminary Journal*, 17, November 1974.

Indinopulos, T. *Journal of the American Academy of Religion*, 43, 1975, 369–372.

Keegan, T. J. *Thomist*, 38, 1973, 657–661.

Kiwiet, J. J. *Southwestern Journal of Theology*, 17, 1975.

Meilach, M. *Cord*, 24, 1974, 550–561.

Pittenger, N. *Interpretation*, 29, 1975, 82–84.

Proudfoot, M. *Living Church*, 170, 1974.

Robinson, C. K. *Duke Divinity School Review*, 40, 1975, 62–63.

Swyhart, B. A. *Horizons*, 1, 1974, 108–109.

Treloar, J. L. *Modern Schoolman*, 52, 1974, 118–119.

Williamson, C. M. *Process Studies*, 4, 1974, 212–217.

Wing, E. *Christian Centenial*, 91, 1974, 620.

Zinger, D. H. *Lutheran Quarterly*, 26, 1974, 349–350.

656   Griffin, David R. "Whitehead and Niebuhr on God, Man, and the World." *Journal of Religion*, 53, 1973, 149–175.

Rationality: as internal consistency, as adequacy, and natural theology, and revelation; faith: and science, and reason; methodology; self: as partially self–determining, as organic unity; nature: and history, as organic unity, freedom and necessity in; God: as transcendent, as immanent, and psyche–body analogy, as persuasive; Niebuhr, Reinhold; theology.

Reinhold Niebuhr's basic presuppositions regarding God, man, and the world are compatible with the philosophical position of Alfred North Whitehead.

657   Griffin, David R. "Gordon Kaufman's Theology: Some Questions." *Journal of the American Academy of Religion*, 41, 1973, 554–572.

God: transcendence of, knowledge of, concept of, as agent, and world, experience of, power of; dualism, ontological; Kaufman, Gordon; philosophy: ordinary language, metaphysical.

Ordinary language analysis does not provide the precision needed to discuss issues involved in the problem of God; metaphysical philosophy is needed. (Written in response to Gordon Kaufman, *The Problem of God*.)

658   Griffin, David R. "Divine Causality, Evil, and Philosophical

Theology: A Critique of James Ross." *International Journal for Philosophy of Religion*, 4, 1973, 168–186.

Evil, problem of; God: in classical theism, power of; causality: divine, levels of; Ross, James; philosophical theology.

Classical theism must be abandoned, since it implicates God in evil. (Written in response to James F. Ross, *Philosophical Theology*.)

659   Griffin, David R. "A New Vision of Nature." *Proceedings for Earth Ethic Today and Tomorrow*. Edited by D. Scherer. Bowling Green: Bowling Green State University, 1973, 95–107.

Nature: ethic of, and value, and human existence; ecology.

Since attitudes toward nature reflect basic religious assumptions concerning value, these assumptions must be revised if environmental concerns are to be sustained on a long–term basis. Whitehead provides a theoretical framework in which the intrinsic value of nature is recognized.

660   Griffin, David R. "A Process Theology of Creation." *Mid–Stream*, 8, 1973–1974, 48–70.

Creation, doctrine of; ethic, ecological; value: intrinsic, instrumental; interdependence; complexity, hierarchy of; freedom; God: as immanent, as persuasive, as experiencing; Hartshorne, Charles; theology; ecology; ethics.

Whitehead and Hartshorne can provide a theology of creation which is consistent with Christian faith and science, and hence which supports an ecological ethic.

661   Griffin, David R. "Human Liberation and the Reverence for Nature." *Anticipation*, 16, 1974, 25–30.

Ecology; nature: value of, exploitation of, reverence for, continuity of, and human existence; God, and nature; value: intrinsic, hierarchy of; individuals: genuine, aggregates of; Derr, Thomas S.; anthropocentrism; dualism; ethics; ecology.

Nature is intrinsically valuable. Regarding it so through ecological action is consistent with Christianity, and corrects the excessive exploitation of nature hitherto associated with traditional western views. (Written in response to Thomas S. Derr, *Ecology and Human Liberation: A Theological Critique of the Use and Abuse of our Birthright*.)

662   Griffin, David R. "Faith, Reason, and Christology: A Response to Father Meilach." *Cord*, 24, 1974, 258–267.

Faith, and reason; Jesus: as Christ, and resurrection; person, and personal immortality; Meilach, Michael; christology; theology.

Father Meilach's criticisms of *A Process Christology* reflect basic differences regarding the normative nature of traditional beliefs, and the relationship between faith and reason. (Written in response to Michael Meilach's "Jesus and Process Philosophy," *Cord*, 24, 1974, 150–161.)

663   Griffin, David R. "Buddhist Thought and Whitehead's
         Philosophy." *International Philosophical Quarterly*, 14, 1974,
         261–284.

         Anatman; soul; co–production, conditioned; self–determination,
         limited; evenmindedness; peace; suffering; value: intrinsic,
         instrumental; Conze, Edward; Nagarjuna; Buddhism.

         Some inherent problems within Buddhism might be overcome
         through use of related Whiteheadian ideas.

664   Griffin, David R. "The Possibility of Subjective Immortality in
         the Philosophy of Whitehead." *The Modern Schoolman*, 53,
         1975, 39–57.

         Immortality: objective, subjective; death; psyche: and hybrid
         prehensions, as personally ordered society; mind–body problem;
         man, nature of; value.

         It is consistent with Whitehead's position to suggest that the
         important role now played by the body in providing
         experiences for the soul might be filled, after separation from
         the body, by a society of other souls.

665   Griffin, David R. "Relativism, Divine Causation, and Biblical
         Theology." *Encounter*, 36, 1975, 342–360.

         Causation: primary, secondary; revelation; God, as acting in
         history; subjective aim, in God; relativism; biblical studies.

         To avoid complete relativism in biblical theology, we need
         some means of speaking of some events as God's "special acts,"
         even though *all* events happen under the influence of a divine
         aim. The degree to which the aim given reflects God's own
         subjective aim and the degree to which that aim is conformed
         to are criteria for "special acts" and revelation.

666   Griffin, David R. "Holy Spirit: Compassion and Reverence for
         Being." *Religious Experience and Process Theology*. Edited
         by Harry James Cargas and Bernard Lee. New York: Paulist
         Press, 1976.

         Holy Spirit; Love; experience, religious; Taoism; Buddhism, and
         love; theology, process.

         Process theology can use Whitehead's categories to appropriate
         oriental emphases on compassion and reverence for being, and
         to reunderstand the Holy Spirit in light of the Tao of Taoism.

667   Griffin, David R. *God, Power, and Evil: A Process Theodicy.*
         Philadelphia: Westminster Press, 1976.

         God: power of (omnipotence), and evil, primordial nature,
         consequent nature, and world, and process, as creator,
         immutability of, and order, sovereignty of, and time,
         transcendence of; theodicy; good; theism, classical; biblical
         studies, and evil; Plato; Aristotle; Plotinus; Augustine; Thomas
         Aquinas; Luther, Martin; Calvin, John; Spinoza, B.;
         Hartshorne, Charles; Hick, John; Madden, Edward H.; Hare,

Peter H.; Flew, Anthony; Maritain, Jacques; Ross, James; metaphysics; neo–Thomism; philosophical theology.

The basic issue which has precipitated the problem of theodicy in classical theism has been that of divine omnipotence. This "omnipotence fallacy" can be overcome if one employs Whitehead's conception of divine persuasion along with a more adequate logical analysis of the nature of evil.

668   Gross, Mason W.   "Whitehead's Philosophy of Adventure." *American Scholar*, 9, 1940, 361–371.

Process philosophy, summary of; Hume, David; Descartes, Rene.

Whitehead's cosmology is a detailed attempt to describe the world in terms of three commonplace factors of human experience—absorption of energy from the past, awareness of present data, and creative intent toward the future.

669   Gross, Mason W.   "Whitehead's Answer to Hume: A Reply." *Journal of Philosophy*, 38, 1941, 95–102.

Induction, ground of; relations: external, internal; propositions; Robson, J. W.; Hume, David; Descartes, Rene; epistemology.

Whitehead's cosmology provides a ground for inductive inference which adequately interprets many fundamental aspects of our experience. (Written in response to J. W. Robson, "Whitehead's Answer to Hume.")

670   Gross, Mason W.   "Introductions and a Note on Whitehead's Terminology."   *Alfred North Whitehead: An Anthology.* Edited by F. S. C. Northrop and Mason W. Gross. New York: Macmillan Company, 1953.

Language, Whitehead's use of.

(In this anthology of selections from Whitehead's works the author supplies introductions and a note on Whitehead's terminology.)

671   Grünbaum, Adolf.   "Relativity and the Atomicity of Becoming." *Review of Metaphysics*, 4, 1950, 143–186.

Becoming, pulsational theory of; relativity, theory of; continuum, Cantorean; Zeno: dichotomy paradox of, flying arrow, paradox of; Reichenbach, H.; Weiss, Paul; James, William; physics.

The epistemological assumptions made by Whitehead and others in pulsational theories of becoming are at variance with those rightly held by Einstein. An intuitively grounded meaning of temporal order sacrifices the "nextness property" only on penalty of logical contradiction.

672   Grünbaum, Adolf.   "The Philosophy of Continuity: A Philosophical Interpretation of the Metrical Continuum of Physical Events in the Light of Contemporary Mathematical Conceptions." Unpublished Ph.D. dissertation, Yale University, 1951.

Abstraction, extensive; events, physical; time, epochal theory of; relativity, theory of; atomism; Zeno, and Zeno's paradox; Cantor, Georg; Leibniz, G. W.; Russell, Bertrand; James, William; Bergson, Henri; Weiss, Paul.

Despite Whitehead's contentions to the contrary, Zeno's dichotomy paradox can be solved without a theory of atomic becoming.

673   Grünbaum, Adolf. "Some Highlights of Modern Cosmology and Cosmogony." *Review of Metaphysics*, 5, 1952, 481–498.

Cosmology; cosmogony; universe: expanding, static, origin of; physics, relativity theory of; red shift; Milne, E. A.; Einstein, Albert; physics.

The question of the finitude of space has been brought into the sphere of the exact reasoning of natural science.

674   Grünbaum, Adolph. "Whitehead's Method of Extensive Abstraction." *British Journal for the Philosophy of Science*, 4, 1953, 215–226.

Abstraction, extensive; convergence; class, abstractive; extension; Zeno's paradox; region; philosophy, of science; Broad, C. D.; Ushenko, A. P.; Einstein, Albert; mathematics; science.

Whitehead's modification of his early doctrine of extensive abstraction in *Process and Reality* fails because, in the context of modern geometry, it requires the untenable notion of a nondenumerable infinity of perceivables. It also obviates the precision of meaning made possible in the statement of physical laws by the use of real variables, and its epistemological assumptions render gratuitous the postulate of the continuity of inclusion among the members of abstractive sets.

675   Grünbaum, Adolf. "Whitehead's Philosophy of Science." *Philosophical Review*, 71, 1962, 218–229.

Relativity, theories of; simultaneity, absolute; congruence, theories of; geometry, and physics; bifurcation; Palter, Robert M.; Einstein, Albert; Riemann, B.; philosophy, of science; physics.

Palter's defense of Whitehead in *Whitehead's Philosophy of Science* is unsuccessful, since it rests on the confusion of time's lack of the analogue of a distinctive metric geometry with its alleged lack of a congruence class.

676   Grünbaum, Adolf. "Geometry, Chronometry and Empiricism." *Minnesota Studies in the Philosophy of Science*, 3, 1962, 405–526.

Geometry; time; philosophy, of science; empiricism.

677   Grünbaum, Adolph. *Modern Science and Zeno's Paradoxes.* Middletown, Connecticut: Wesleyan University Press, 1967, 48–56, 65–66.

Zeno's paradox; time: epochal theory of, and continuity, and experience; mathematics, and time; James, William.

Whitehead's claim that the temporal order of physical events has a form similar to that of the 'nows' of human awareness is incorrect.   Physical events do not occur in a pulsational consecutive manner.

678   Gruenler, Royce Gordon.   *Jesus, Persons, and the Kingdom of God.* New York: Bethany Press, 1967.

Bible; God, Biblical view of; person, and personal immortality; Jesus Christ; Hartshorne, Charles.

679   Gunton, Colin.   "Process Theology's Concept of God: An Outline and Assessment." *Expository Times,* 84, 1973, 292–296.

God, Hartshorne's interpretation of; anthropomorphism; grace; Hartshorne, Charles.

Process theology is inadequate for doctrines of creation, incarnation, eschatology and grace, and has no real understanding of God's activity.

680   Gustafson, D. A.   "Christian on Causal Objectification in Whitehead."   *International Philosophical Quarterly,* 1, 1961, 683–696.

Objectification; perception; causal efficacy; God, and givenness of past; Christian, William A.

In *An Interpretation of Whitehead's Metaphysics,* Christian proposes an interpretation of causal objectification which is inconsistent with several of Whitehead's clearer statements of the doctrine, and which is not adequate to Whitehead's doctrines of nature and perception.

681   Gustafson, Donald F.   "The Structure of A. N. Whitehead's Speculative Philosophy."   Unpublished Ph.D. dissertation, University of Texas at Austin, 1961.

Philosophy; speculative, method of; language, and philosophy; Wittgenstein, Ludwig.

682   Guthrie, Shirley C. Jr.   "Theology and Metaphysics."   *The Future of Theology in America.*   Edited by William A. Beardslee. Philadelphia: Westminster Press, 1967, 127–135.

Philosophy, and theology; God, of classical theism; theology.

Without letting Whiteheadian categories be determinative or thematic, they might be used along with nonmetaphysical categories to clarify and contribute to the translation of Christian truth into political–ethical theology.

683   Guy, Fritz. "Comments on a Recent Whiteheadian Doctrine of God." *Andrews University Seminary Studies,* 4, 1966, 107–134.

God: as actual entity, Cobb's interpretation of; method, theological; Cobb, John B., Jr.; theology, natural.

Cobb's interpretation of God raises the question of the ground of God's personal unity; the problem might be solved by redefining God as a fourth ultimate.

684   Hall, David L.   "A Whiteheadian Theory of the Role of Religion in Culture."   Unpublished Ph.D. dissertation, Yale University, 1967.

Human existence; society; subjective aim; culture, and religion; civilization; value; experience: aim of, intensity of; aesthetics; harmony;   beauty;   adventure;   truth;   art,   and   nature; philosophy, analytic; idealism; realism; religion: and religious experience, and philosophy, and reason.

685   Hall, David L.   "The Autonomy of Religion in Whitehead's Philosophy."   *Philosophy Today*, 13, 1969, 271–283.

God: Whitehead without; religion: autonomy of, foundations of; morality; experience, religious; Sherburne, Donald W.

The deletion of the concept of "God" from Whiteheadian philosophy cannot in any valid manner lead to the interpretation of Whitehead's theory of religion in terms of ethical concepts.

686   Hall, David L.   "Whitehead's Theory of Cultural Interests." *Southern Journal of Philosophy*, 7, 1969, 457–472.

Culture; interests, cultural; abstraction: formal, selective; value.

Whiteheadian metaphysics provides a cultural interest theory which allows a synoptic vision of the viable connections of disciplines, and which insures a significant autonomy for each discipline vis–a–vis the others.

687   Hall, David L.   *The Civilization of Experience: A Whiteheadian Theory of Culture.*   New York: Fordham University Press, 1973.

Civilization;   aesthetics;   beauty;   transmutation;   intensity; appearance, and reality; harmony; adventure; peace; history; *Adventures of Ideas*; culture; art; religion.

Cultural aims, interests, problems, and development may be explained   with   Whitehead's   categories   of   transmutation, harmony, beauty, and artistic balance of appearance with reality, as used in his *Adventures of Ideas*.

688   Hall, Everett W.   "Of What Use are Whitehead's Eternal Objects?"   *Journal of Philosophy*, 27, 1930, 29–44.

Eternal   objects: as   universals,   functions   of;   ontological principle; God, and eternal objects; objectification.

By redefining occasions to incorporate both permanence and change, actual occasions can be made to account for all functions of eternal objects, thus eliminating them from Whitehead's philosophy.

689   Hallman, Joseph M.   "The Theological Relevance of Objective Immortality in the Philosophy of Alfred North Whitehead." Unpublished Ph.D. dissertation, Fordham University, 1970.

Person: and personal immortality, and personal identity; objective immortality; perishing; death; past, as objectively immortal; soteriology, Christian; redemption; Hartshorne, Charles; Cobb, John b., Jr.; theology, Christian.

690   Hallman, Joseph M. "Toward a Process Theology of the Church." *Religious Experience and Process Theology.* Edited by Harry James Cargas and Bernard Lee. New York: Paulist Press, 1976, 137–145.

Ecclesiology; church; adventure; authority; past, and present; experience, religious; theology, process.

Process theology can aid Catholics in reunderstanding the aim and authority of the Church. The prophetic aspects of religious experience would be highlighted through a prophetic, or self–critical, approach to the Church itself.

691   Hamilton, Peter N. "The Theological Importance of A. N. Whitehead." *Theology,* 68, 1965, 187–195.

Process philosophy, summary of; God, doctrine of; grace; Tillich, Paul; metaphysics, and religion: theology.

Whitehead's philosophy offers a positive contribution to many areas of theology, and can lead to an immense strengthening and revitalization of faith.

692   Hamilton, Peter N. *The Living God and the Modern World: Christian Theology Based on the Thought of A. N. Whitehead.* Boston: United Church Press, 1967.

Christianity; science; nature; evolution; God: transcendence of, immanence of, grace of, primordial nature of, and freedom of the world, as love, and Being, death of; Jesus Christ, as risen Lord; soul; person: and personal identity, and personal immortality; Bible; death; heaven; hell; Tillich, Paul; Hartshorne, Charles; Robinson, J. A. T.; Altizer, Thomas J. J.; theology; religion, and science.

In order to validate Christian theism it is necessary to consider it in relation to modern thought. Whitehead's philosophy can help Christians affirm the reality of God by showing how God is at work within the natural order as well as human existence.

693   Hamilton, Peter N. "Some Proposals for a Modern Christology." *Christ for Us Today.* Edited by Norman Pittenger. London: SCM Press Ltd., 1968.

Christology; Jesus Christ: ministry of, resurrection of; God: and Christology, and categoreal scheme; prehensions; Hartshorne, Charles; theology, process.

694   Hammerschmidt, William W. *Whitehead's Philosophy of Time.* New York: King's Crown Press, 1947.

Time: and transition, and temporality, and nature, and atomic events, passage of, and causality, in various stages of Whitehead's thought; space; extension; abstraction, extensive; duration; causal efficacy; presentational immediacy, and time.

For Whitehead, time is not a form nor is it derived from

forms, although, in its extensiveness and geometrical properties, it has a formal aspect.

Reviews

Lowe, Victor. *Philosophical Review*, 58, 1949, 171–177.

Mays, Wolfe. *Philosophy*, 25, 1950, 180–181.

695 Hammerschmidt, William W. "Alfred North Whitehead." *Scripta Mathematica*, 14, 1948, 17–25.

A. N. Whitehead, biography of.

696 Hamrick, William S. "Body, Space and Time in the Philosophies of Whitehead and Merleau–Ponty." Unpublished Ph.D. dissertation, Vanderbilt University, 1971.

Human existence; metaphysics, and phenomenology; body, human; psychology, physiological; mind–body problem; time, and human existence; space, and human existence; perception, and Gestalt psychology; intentionality; Merleau–Ponty, Maurice; phenomenology; existentialism.

Whitehead's conceptual categories enhance the phenomenological insights of Merleau–Ponty.

697 Hamrick, William S. "Whitehead and Merleau–Ponty: Some Moral Implications." *Process Studies*, 4, 1974, 235–251.

Identity, personal; *cogito ergo sum*; self; canalization; nexus; nonsocial; society: serially ordered, personally ordered, as structured; responsibility, moral; guilt; Merleau–Ponty, Maurice; psychology, physiological.

Whitehead's work on social and non–social nexūs, used within the context of psychological physiology, can yield a fruitful concept of personal identity based on behaviorial habits, a sense of moral responsibility, and a legitimate notion of guilt.

698 Hanna, Thomas. "The Living Body: Nexus of Process Philosophy and Existential Phenomenology." *Soundings*, 52, 1969, 465–473.

Body, living; nature, and human existence; evolution, biological; phenomenology; physiology; psychology, developmental.

Process philosophy and existential phenomenology can be unified and made consistent with each other through an appropriate understanding of the living human body.

699 Haring, Ellen S. "The Ontological Principle." *Review of Metaphysics*, 16, 1962, 3–12.

Ontological principle; causation; Aristotle; Plato; Weiss, Paul; metaphysics.

Philosophers such as Plato and Weiss who deny Whitehead's assertion that all causes are, or are integral to, concrete energetic beings claim to discern major causes, each of which is neither a divine subject nor an actuality nor a being integral to one of those.

700 Harrah, David. "The Influence of Logic and Mathematics on

Whitehead." *Journal of the History of Ideas*, 20, 1959, 420–430.

A. N. Whitehead, method of; mathematics, creative; ultimate, category of; *Principia Mathematica*; *Process and Reality*; metaphysics; mathematics; logic.

A comparison of Whitehead's mathematical and metaphysical works indicates that Whitehead's cast of mind was shaped in and through his procedures as a creative mathematician. These procedures were later sublimated into the basic principles of his cosmology.

701 Harrington, M. L. "Whitehead's Theory of Propositions." Unpublished Ph.D. dissertation, Emory University, 1972.

Propositions: and eternal objects, and facts, as lure for feeling, properties of.

702 Harris, Errol E. *Nature, Mind, and Modern Science*. New York: Macmillan Company, 1954.

Creativity; God, consequent nature of; process; mind; concrescence; prehension; pole, mental; eternal objects; potentiality; truth: correspondence theory of, coherence theory of; Hegel, G. W. F.; Bradley, F. H.; Bergson, Henri; idealism; realism.

A number of parallels exist between the philosophy of Hegel and that of Whitehead. Among them is the fact that, like the Absolute Mind in the philosophy of Hegel, the consequent nature of God in Whitehead's philosophy is the supreme reconciliation of the opposition between matter and mind.

703 Harris, Errol E. *The Foundations of Metaphysics in Science*. London: George Allen and Unwin Ltd., 1965.

Nature, as alive; eternal objects, as universals; relations, internal; concrescence, and nature; creativity, as substantial activity.

While Whitehead's thought offers much to the philosophy of nature, it leaves the status of mind uncertain and the nature of concrescence obscure.

704 Harris, Marjorie S. "Symbolic Logic and Esthetics." *Journal of Philosoophy*, 37, 1940, 533–540.

Beauty; art; poetry; logic; aesthetics.

In keeping with Whitehead's suggestion, mathematical logic can be used to produce a formula which expresses and exhibits that which is central in Whitehead's theory of beauty.

705 Harrison, R. K. "A. N. Whitehead on Good and Evil." *Philosophy*, 28, 1953, 239–245.

Good: as eternal object, as pattern, as dynamic, and God; evil: as eternal object, as triviality, as instability; God, and evil.

Whitehead's analysis of the eternal object of evil is penetrating and satisfactory; the same clarity of exposition has not been applied to a description of the eternal object of good.

706   Hart, Thomas N.   "Whitehead's Critique of Scientific
       Materialism." *New Scholasticism*, 43, 1969, 229–251.

       Concreteness, misplaced (fallacy of); materialism, scientific;
       qualities; bifurcation, of nature; Berkeley, George; philosophy,
       of science.

       Whitehead criticizes scientific materialism for ontologizing the
       conceptual instant, for absolutizing space and time, and for
       introducing the disastrous split between primary and secondary
       qualities.

707   Hartford, R. R.   "Whitehead's Irrationalism." *Hermathena*, 79,
       1945, 89–93.

       God: Whitehead's arguments for, as deus ex machina; evil;
       Hegel, G. W. F.; Wells, H. K.

       Whitehead's philosophy rests on a final irrationalism, for he
       holds that thought is inadequate to grasp the nature of
       ultimate reality.   A first-hand acquaintance with Hegel might
       have saved Whitehead from failure.

708   Hartford, R. R.   "Alfred North Whitehead (1861–1947)."
       Hermathena, 72, 1948, 71–79.

       Whitehead, Alfred North: obiturary notice.

709   Hartshorne, Charles.   "Redefining God." *New Humanist*, 7, 1934,
       8–15.

       God: infinity of, and time, power of, perfection of.

       Process thought allows theology a new theistic alternative.

710   Hartshorne, Charles.   "Ethics and the New Theology."
       International Journal of Ethics, 45, 1934, 90–101.

       Value: ethical, preservation of; God: as source of value,
       perfection of, as worthy of worship; ethics; theology.

       Ethical objections to theism are overcome through the
       temporalistic and ethical view of God which emerges from
       Whitehead's cosmology.

711   Hartshorne, Charles.   "On Some Criticisms of Whitehead's
       Philosophy." *Philosophical Review*, 44, 1935, 323–344.

       Panpsychism; qualities, secondary; nature, bifurcation of;
       relativism, objective; contemporaries, prehension of; eternal
       objects.

       Critics of Whitehead's solution to the bifurcation of nature fail
       to note the significance of panpsychism to the issue.

712   Hartshorne, Charles.   "The New Pantheism." *Christian Register*,
       115, 1936, 119–120, 141–143.

       God: as unity of universe, and world, and panentheism.

713   Hartshorne, Charles.   "The Compound Individual." *Philosophical
       Essays for Alfred North Whitehead*.   Edited by Otis H. Lee.
       New York: Longmans Green, 1936, 193–220.

       Substance: philosophies of, criticism of; individual: compound,
       composite; Gestalt; society, of actual entities; God, as a living

person; Leibniz, G. W.; Aristotle; Berkeley, George; atomism; monism; subjectivism; pluralism; dualism.

The process view of interrelationships and compound individuality answers problems insufficiently resolved by substance philosophies.

714   Hartshorne, Charles. *Beyond Humanism: Essays in the Philosophy of Nature.* Willett, Clark and Company, 1937. Lincoln, Nebraska: University of Nebraska Press, 1968, 1969.

Time: as aesthetic–ethical unity of memory and anticipation; memory: and preservation of the past, and causality; God, experience of; order; Russell, Bertrand; Heidegger, Martin; phenomenology.

715   Hartshorne, Charles. "The Interpretation of Whitehead." *Philosophical Review*, 48, 1939, 415–423.

Qualities: secondary, continuity of; feeling, of feelings; panpsychism; Blyth, John W.; epistemology.

Panpsychism is not a mere argument from analogy, since not just our own feelings are given to us in the mind–body relation. Insofar as these feelings are analogous, the force of the analogy is in the special sense that it exhibits generic traits which do not admit an alternative system of categories. (Written in response to John W. Blyth, "On Mr. Hartshorne's Understanding of Whitehead's Philosophy.")

716   Hartshorne, Charles. "Whitehead's Idea of God." *The Philosophy of Alfred North Whitehead.* Edited by Paul A. Schilpp. La Salle, Illinois: Open Court Publishing Company, 1941, 513–559.

God: Whitehead's arguments for, classical view of, primordial nature of, consequent nature of, perfection of, and the world, and eternal objects, as creator, and time, and evil, as principle of concretion.

In much of classical theism there have been two errors in conceiving God. One is to identify God with a sheer perfection to which nothing can be added; the other is to identify God with a sheer power which cannot be acted upon by the world. Whitehead's view of God points to the remedy of both these errors.

717   Hartshorne, Charles. *Man's Vision of God and the Logic of Theism.* New York: Harper and Row, Inc., 1941. Hamden, Connecticut: Archon Books, 1964.

God: panentheistic view of, proofs of, and temporality, perfection of, as unity of universe, objective immortality in, suffering of; reality, as social; materialism; panpsychism; philosophical theology.

(In the process of introducing new ideas and logical rigor into philosophical theology, the author finds much in common with Whitehead.)

Reviews

Bennett, J. C. *Christendom*, 7, 1942, 102–104.

Bixler, J. S. *Journal of Liberal Religion*, 5, 1943, 111–112.

Brightman, E. S. *Journal of Religion*, 22, 1942, 96–99.

Buchler, J. *Journal of Philosophy*, 39, 1942, 245–247.

Greene, T. M. *Philosophy and Phenomenological Research*, 3, 1942, 96–98.

Macintosh, D. C. *Review of Religion*, 6, 1942, 443–448.

Meland, B. E. *Christian Century*, 59, 1942, 1289–1290.

Niebuhr, R. *Christianity and Society*, 7, 1942, 43–44.

Nilson, S. *Philosophical Review*, 51, 1942, 520–522.

718   Hartshorne, Charles. "Organic and Inorganic Wholes." *Philosophy and Phenomenological Research*, 3, 1942, 127–136.

Monism; value; God: as purposive, as unity of universe, and world; Fechner, V. G. T.

All well–unified wholes are organic, and both involve and are involved in organic wholes. The universe has organic unity; God may be conceived to be the purposive integration of all its parts.

719   Hartshorne, Charles. "Is Whitehead's God the God of Religion?" *Ethics*, 53, 1942–1943, 219–227.

God: religious availability of, as love, power of, infinity of; immortality; Ely, Stephen Lee; theodicy.

Whitehead denies to God no infinity and no power which religion need claim for him. Whitehead's affirmation of God's love and his overcoming of evil are positive contributions to religion. (Written in response to Stephen Lee Ely, *The Religious Availability of Whitehead's God: A Critical Analysis.*)

720   Hartshorne, Charles. "Ely on Whitehead." *Journal of Liberal Religion*, 5, 1943, 97–100.

God: goodness of, religious availability of; objective immortality, in God; Ely, Stephen Lee; theodicy.

The inheritance of our experiences in God's consequent nature provides the preservation of us and our values which religion requires. (Written in response to Horace S. Fries, "Ely on Whitehead.")

721   Hartshorne, Charles. "A Mathematical Analysis of Theism." *Review of Religion*, 8, 1943–1944, 20–38.

God, perfection of, possibility of; logic: deductive, mathematical; mathematics; theology; astronomy; logic.

The perfection of God can be proved to as an exhaustive degree as mathematical possibility allows.

722   Hartshorne, Charles. "God and Man not Rivals." *Journal of Liberal Religion*, 6, 1944, 9–13.

God, concepts of; antheism, arguments for; humanism; Fries, Horace S.; Otto, M. C.

Some forms of belief in God are inferior to belief in no God (together with faith in man). The process concept of God is compatible with the values of humanism.

723   Hartshorne, Charles. "Efficient Causality in Aristotle and St. Thomas." *Journal of Religion*, 25, 1945, 25–32.

God: of classical theism, as cause, knowledge of; causality, efficient; Aristotle; Thomas Aquinas; Meehan, Francis X.; Thomism.

The Aristotelian–Thomistic concept of God results in a formal dilemma which may be resolved by admitting contingency, change, and reciprocal relations into the notion of God.

724   Hartshorne, Charles. *The Divine Relativity: A Social Conception of God*. New Haven, Connecticut: Yale University Press, 1948, 1964, 1974.

God: as relative, as persuasive power; society, as metaphysical category; universals; sympathy, as feeling of feeling.

725   Hartshorne, Charles. "Das metaphysische System Whiteheads." *Zeitschrift für philosophische Forschung*, 3, 1948–1949, 566–575.

God: as personal, as creator, power of, as eternal; future; subject; causality; rationalism; empiricism; realism; theism; pantheism.

Whitehead may not only be properly termed a "rationalist," but also an empiricist, a realist, and (when one compares his concept of God with pantheism) a theist.

726   Hartshorne, Charles. "Le priciple de relativité philosophique chez Whitehead." *Revue de Métaphysique et de Morale*, 55, 1950, 16–29.

Relativity, principle of; prehension, negative; substance, doctrine of; God: power of, as unity of the universe, as personal; creativity, principle of.

727   Hartshorne, Charles. "Whitehead's Metaphysics." *Whitehead and the Modern World: Science, Metaphysics, and Civilization, Three Essays on the Thought of Alfred North Whitehead*, by Victor Lowe, Charles Hartshorne, and A. H. Johnson. Boston: Beacon Press, 1950, 25–41. Also in *Whitehead's Philosophy*. Lincoln: University of Nebraska Press, 1972, 9–19.

A. N. Whitehead, method of; prehensions, theory of; God: as dipolar, as living person, religious adequacy of; rationalism; empiricism; idealism; metaphysics.

Whitehead gives the basic principles of our knowledge and experience an intellectual integration of incomparable worth.

728   Hartshorne, Charles. "Panpsychism." *A History of Philosophical Systems*. Edited by V. Ferm. Philosophical Library, 1950, 442–453.

Panpsychism; immanence, mutual; Plato; Leibniz, G. W.; Fechner, V. G. T.; Peirce, Charles S.

Panpsychism in its more significant form is the view that all things consist exclusively of units of experiencing, with their qualifications, relations, and groupings or communities.

729   Hartshorne, Charles. "The Divine Relativity and Absoluteness: A Reply." *Review of Metaphysics*, 4, 1950, 31–60.

God: as absolute, as relative, as related, as personal, as immutable, power of.

Instead of overestimating the independence or immutability of God, thereby limiting the possibility that God is love, we can speak of God as absolute and immutable in just those respects that love permits and requires. Likewise, we can speak of God as relative and mutable in just those other respects that love also permits and requires.

Reviews

Ferre, N. F. S. *Journal of Religion*, 29, 1949, 304–305.

Jessop, T. E. *Philosophy*, 24, 1949, 358–359.

Phenix, P. H. *Journal of Philosophy*, 46, 1949, 591–597.

Schilling, S. P. *Journal of Bible and Religion*, 17, 1949, 136–137.

Wieman, H. N. *Philosophical Review*, 58, 1949, 78–82.

Wild, J. *Review of Metaphysics*, 2, 1948, 65–77.

730   Hartshorne, Charles. "Philosophy of Religion in the United States." *Philosophy and Phenomenological Research*, 11, 1951, 406–410.

God: as absolute, as relative, as dipolar; Brightman, E. S.; Hocking, Richard; philosophy, of religion.

The great issue in the United States for philosophy of religion is to distinguish in a non–arbitrary and coherent way between the absolute–infinite–eternal and the relative–finite–temporal aspects of deity.

731   Hartshorne, Charles. "La philosophie de la religion aux Etats–Unis." *Les Etudes Philosophiques*, 11, 1951, 50–56.

God: doctrine of, primordial nature of, consequent nature of, proofs of, as absolute, as relative, and the world.

732   Hartshorne, Charles and Reese, William L. *Philosophers Speak of God*. Chicago: University of Chicago Press, 1953. Midway Reprint, 1976.

God: and classical theism, and panentheism, as eternal, as temporal, as conscious, and divine knowledge, as including the world, primordial nature of, consequent nature of, concrete nature of, and the world, and freedom, and order, perfection of, as a society, and tragedy, and objective immortality, and evil, and creativity; person: and personal identity, and memory; self, as series of experiences; Berdyaev, Nicholas; Aristotle; Plato; Augustine; Thomas Aquinas; philosophical theology.

(The authors classify Whitehead's view as pantheistic, comparing and contrasting it with classical and modern theistic views.)

Reviews

Evans, E. *Philosophical Quarterly*, 5, 1955, 89–90.

Parker, F. H. *Review of Metaphysics*, 14, 1960, 328–352.

Taubee, J. *Journal of Religion*, 34, 1954, 120–126.

733   Hartshorne, Charles.   *Reality as Social Process: Studies in Metaphysics and Religion.* New York: Free Press, 1953. New York: Hafner, 1971.

Reality, as social; interrelatedness; individual; metaphysics, and religion.

In viewing reality as social process it is contended that a number of the old dichotomies e.g., natural/supernatural, idealism/realism must be discarded in light of new options which alleviate the old problems.   Whitehead's metaphysics provides the basis for such an endeavor and the last chapter is specifically devoted to the religious availability of Whitehead's God, and the conception of immortality.

Review

Lawrence, N. M. *Philosophical Review*, 63, 1954, 449–451.

734   Hartshorne, Charles.   "The Immortality of the Past: Critique of a Prevalent Misinterpretation."   *Review of Metaphysics*, 7, 1953, 98–112.

Objective immortality; past, immortality of.

735   Hartshorne, Charles.   "Causal Necessities: An Alternative to Hume." *Philosophical Review*, 63, 1954, 479–499.

Relations, causal; relations, temporal; memory; Hume, David; epistemology.

Necessary causal connections are required not merely for our inductive knowledge of nature, but for its real existence as a succession of events.

736   Hartshorne, Charles. "Mind, Matter, and Freedom." *Scientific Monthly*, 78, 1954, 314–320.

Mind; matter; mind, and mind–body problem; freedom; panpsychism; physics; science.

Mind and matter are not two ultimately different sorts of entities, but two ways of describing a reality that has many levels of organization.

737   Hartshorne, Charles.   "Whitehead's Philosophy of Reality as Socially Structured Process."   *Chicago Review*, 7, 1954, 60–77.

Process philosophy, summary of; mind, and matter; psychology; metaphysics.

Whitehead's philosophy makes process and relativity the inclusive conceptions, and experience as such the universal form of reality.

738   Hartshorne, Charles.   "Whitehead and Berdyaev: Is There Tragedy in God?" *Journal of Religion*, 37, 1957, 71–83.

Berdyaev, similarities to Whitehead; God: as suffering, as

dipolar, as worthy of worship; tragedy, in God; Berdyaev, Nicolas; metaphysics.

For Whitehead and Berdyaev, God is supreme effect as well as supreme cause. His sympathy with creatures is participation in their sufferings as well as joys.

739   Hartshorne, Charles. "Whitehead on Process: A Reply to Professor Eslick." *Philosophy and Phenomenological Research*, 18, 1958, 314–320.

Substance: and subjectivity, and change, Aristotelian; causa sui; perishing; Hartshorne, Charles; Eslick, L. J.; Aristotle.

Whitehead's theory of the actual entity contains all the features of "substance" which common sense requires, providing a corrective to Aristotle's inadequate account of change. (Written in response to L. J. Eslick, "Substance, Change and Causality in Whitehead.")

740   Hartshorne, Charles. "The Logical Structure of Givenness." *Philosophical Quarterly*, 7, 1958, 307–316.

Perception, causal theory of; past, givenness of; relations: internal, external; Hume, David; epistemology.

The direct givenness of the past is the basic epistemic relation of givenness, providing a fundamental theory of perception.

741   Hartshorne, Charles. "The Philosophy of Creative Synthesis." *Journal of Philosophy*, 55, 1958, 944–953. Republished in *Americana*, 5, 1959, 80–90.

Creativity; synthesis, creative; process: social structure of, individualizing of; being, and becoming; metaphysics.

Creation can be viewed as a variable by identifying it with creative synthesis, whose data or constituents are prior acts of synthesis.

742   Hartshorne, Charles. "The Buddhist–Whiteheadian View of the Self and the Religious Traditions." *Proceedings of the Ninth International Congress for the History of Religions.* Tokyo: Maruzen, 1960, 298–302.

Self: oriental views of, as personal society, and personal immortality; self–identity; Buddhism; Hinduism.

The Indian religious tradition may aid the West to grasp the limitations of the idea of the soul; the Western tradition may help both Buddhism and Hinduism to accept the empirical plurality of selves in a more positive and consistent way than they have been able to do in the past.

743   Hartshorne, Charles. "Tillich and the Other Great Tradition." *Anglican Theological Review*, 43, 1961, 245–259.

God: as being–itself, as worthy of worship, as relative; language: symbolic, analogical; theology, negative; Tillich, Paul; Hartshorne, Charles; theology.

Tillich's definitions of God as being itself and as worthy of worship are also affirmed by process thought, which derives continuity with the past through a subordinate tradition of negative theology.

744   Hartshorne, Charles. "Whitehead, The Anglo–American Philosopher–Scientist." *Proceedings of the American Catholic Philosophical Association,* 35, 1961, 163–171.

Process philosophy, summary of; Whitehead, Alfred North, method of.

Whitehead's method and his philosophy demonstrate his generalizing from the thesis that nature is intelligible if, and only if, the specific traits which emerge are special cases of more general principles which do not emerge, but are found throughout reality.

745   Hartshorne, Charles. "Whitehead and Contemporary Philosophy." *The Relevance of Whitehead.* Edited by Ivor Leclerc. New York: Humanities Press Inc., 1961, 21–43.

Nature, and feeling; sense–perception; determinism; reason, sufficient; Leibniz, G. W.; Kant, Immanuel; positivism; materialism; realism, naive; Platonism; linguistic analysis.

Whitehead's revision of certain of Leibniz's doctrines has been ignored rather than refuted by contemporary philosophy.

746   Hartshorne, Charles. "Whitehead's Conception of God." *Actas Segundo Congreso Extraordinario Interamericano de Filosofia.* San Jose: Costa Rica, July 1961, 163–165.

God: as absolute, as relative, as primordial, as consequent, as personal, as a society.

God is a personally ordered society, the universally influential and universally influenced society, the supreme or universal Person.

747   Hartshorne, Charles. "Religion and Creative Experience." *Darshana International,* 2, 1962, 47–52.

Creativity, universality of; God: and order, as worthy of worship.

Creativity, as the experience of a free response to prior free responses, indicates God as the supreme instance of such experience.

748   Hartshorne, Charles. "The Modern World and a Modern View of God." *Crane Review,* 4, 1962, 73–85.

Theodicy; freedom; God: as persuasive power, objective immortality in.

The process theory of pervasive freedom explains evil, for freedom is always risk. The theory also explains good as a divine level of freedom, by whose influence all lesser freedom can be benignly guided and coordinated.

749   Hartshorne, Charles. "La creatividad participada." *Revista de Filosofia de la Universidad de Costa Rica,* 3, 1962, 237–244.

Creativity; freedom; novelty; God: freedom of, as creator, finitude of.

750   Hartshorne, Charles. *The Logic of Perfection.* La Salle, Illinois:
        Open Court Publishing Co., 1962.

        God: in process philosophy, perfection of; creativity, and
        indeterminism; causality; self, as society; mind–body problem;
        organism; philosophy, process.

        One is forced logically to decide that the proposition
        "perfection exists" is necessarily true or false, but not
        contingent. Anselm's insight in the ontological argument lay
        in this discovery. When coupled with the methods of modal
        logic the necessary falsity of the proposition also cannot be
        proved, thus reestablishing the credibility of the argument.

        Reviews

        Cobb, J. B. Jr. *Religion in Life,* 32, 1963, 294–304.

        Hartt, J. *Review of Metaphysics,* 16, 1963, 749–769.

        Hick, J. H. *Theology Today,* 20, 1963, 295–298.

        Johnstone, H. W. Jr. *Journal of Philosophy,* 60, 1963, 467–472.

        Reck, A. J. *Journal of Religious Thought,* 20, 1963–1964, 74–76.

751   Hartshorne, Charles. "Whitehead's Conception of God." *Actas
        Segundo Congreso Extraordinario Interamerica Filosofia.* San
        Jose, Costa Rica: Imprenta Nacional, 1963, 163–165.

        God: as relative, as absolute, as actual entity, superjective
        nature of, as a society.

        God is a personally ordered society of entities, a society which
        is universally influential and universally influenced.

752   Hartshorne, Charles. "Whitehead's Novel Intuition." *Alfred
        North Whitehead: Essays on His Philosophy.* Edited by
        George L. Kline. Englewood Cliffs, New Jersey, 1963.

        Ultimate, category of; one, and the many; indeterminism; God:
        consequent nature of, as love, as persuasive power; past;
        Buddhism.

753   Hartshorne, Charles. "Interrogation of Charles Hartshorne."
        Philosophical Interrogations. Edited by Sydney and Beatrice
        Rome. New York: Holt and Rinehart, 1964, 321–354.

        Dipolarity; contemporaries, prehension of; relations, temporal;
        monads; duration; becoming; Zeno's paradox; panpsychism;
        power; subjectivist principle, reformed; morality; responsibility;
        God: as actual entity, as creator, necessary existence of;
        panentheism; Ferré, Nels; Christian, William A.; Stallknecht;
        Čapek, Milič; Ducasse, Curtis J.; Bertocci, Peter A.; Wieman,
        Henry N.; Weiss, Paul; Hartshorne, Charles.

        (Hartshorne's position comes under the scrutiny of notable
        contemporaries in philosophy, and the result is printed as
        dialogue among peers.)

754   Hartshorne, Charles. "Introduction: The Development of Process
        Philosophy." *Philosophers of Process.* Edited by D. Browning.
        New York: Random House, 1965, v–xxii.

Process philosophy, summary of.

755   Hartshorne, Charles. *Anselm's Discovery: A Re-examination of the Ontological Argument for God's Existence.* La Salle, Illinois: Open Court Publishing Company, 1965.

God, and ontological proof; self, as series of experiences; Buddhism; Anselm; philosophical theology.

756   Hartshorne, Charles. "A New Look at the Problem of Evil." *Current Philosophical Issues: Essays in Honor of Curt John Ducasse.* Edited by F. C. Dommeyer. Springfield, Illinois: Charles C. Thomas, 1966, 201–212.

Evil, problem of; God: necessary existence of, perfection of, power of, decisions of, suffering of, freedom of; freedom, as absolute principle; truth, a priori; determinism; Anselm; Epicurus; Hume, David.

Since all creatures have some freedom, all evil can and should be viewed as involving unfortunate cases of creaturely decision.

757   Hartshorne, Charles. "The Idea of Creativity in American Philosophy." *Journal of Karnatak University—Social Sciences,* 2, 1966, 1–13.

Creativity; freedom, and determinism; theodicy; altruism; Peirce, Charles S.; Royce, Josiah; Dewey, John; Buddhism.

The essential creativity is self–creativity; this notion overcomes problems of theodicy raised by theological determinism.

758   Hartshorne, Charles. *A Natural Theology for Our Time.* La Salle, Illinois: Open Court Publishing Company, 1967.

God; creativity; soul, motion of; Platonism.

The basic questions of natural theology are addressed from the perspective which considers God to be the self–surpassing surpasser of all. This removes many of the traditional empirical and logical problems with natural theology.

Hudson, W. D. *Philosophical Quarterly,* 18, 1968, 380–381.

759   Hartshorne, Charles. "The Dipolar Conception of Deity." *Review of Metaphysics,* 21, 1967, 273–289.

God: as dipolar, of classical theism, objective immortality in; theodicy; Thomas Aquinas; Hartshorne, Charles; Westphal, Merold; Madden, Edward H.; Hare, Peter H., Thomism.

Critics of dipolar theism fail to reckon with the basic principles of dipolarity and universal creativity.

760   Hartshorne, Charles. "Process Philosophy as a Resource for Christian Thought." *Philosophical Resources for Christian Thought.* Edited by P. LeFevre. Nashville, Tennessee: Abingdon Press, 1968, 44–66.

Philosophy, right one for theology; God: as source of value, as persuasive power, consequent nature of, power of, objective immortality in; theodicy; Berdyaev, Nicolas; Buddhism.

In the final analysis all life is purely contributory. The

essential reward of virtue is intrinsic and present, not extrinsic and future.   Eventual future gains are for God, not for creatures.

761   Hartshorne, Charles.   "Whitehead in French Perspective: A Review Article."   *Thomist*, 33, 1969, 573–581.

Perishing, perpetual; immortality, subjective; God: Hartshorne's interpretation of, as love; Parmentier, Alix; Buddhism.

Parmentier's work is a brilliant study of Whitehead.   A conception of God as a society of entities, or a society of societies, answers some of the questions concerning the eminence of God which she raises.

762   Hartshorne, Charles.   "Divine Absoluteness and Divine Relativity."   *Transcendence.*   Edited by H. W. Richardson and D. R. Cutler.   Boston: Beacon Press, 1969, 164–171.

God: as worthy of worship, as absolute, as relative, and evil.

God is absolute and immutable in just those respects that love permits and requires, and he is relative and mutable in just those other respects that love also permits and requires.

763   Hartshorne, Charles.   "'Eternity', 'Absolute', 'God'."   *Prophetic Voices: Ideas and Words on Revolution.*   Edited by Ned O'Gorman.   New York: Random House, 1969.   New York: Vintage Books, 1970, 130–148.

God: as eternal, as absolute.

764   Hartshorne, Charles.   "Metaphysics in North America."   *Contemporary Philosophy: A Survey.*   Edited by Raymond Klibansky.   Firenze: La Nuova Italia Editrice, 1969, 36–49.

Weiss, Paul; Hartshorne, Charles; Tillich, Paul; metaphysics.

765   Hartshorne, Charles.   "Whitehead and Ordinary Language."   *Southern Journal of Philosophy*, 7, 1969, 437–445.

Language: Whitehead's use of, ordinary; philosophy, linguistic.

"Actual entity," "prehension," and "creativity" are the core of Whiteheadianism.   These three terms are consonant with ordinary usage, and hence are linguistically valid and good.

766   Hartshorne, Charles.   "The Development of My Philosophy."   *Contemporary American Philosophy: Second Series.*   Edited by J. E. Smith.   London: Allen & Unwin, 1970, 211–228.

Hartshorne, Charles, autobiography; experience, as social; freedom, and determinism; eternal objects.

767   Hartshorne, Charles.   "Ontological Primacy: A Reply to Buchler."   *Journal of Philosophy*, 67, 1970, 979–986.

Asymmetry; eternal objects, as universals; ontological principle; Buchler, Justus.

Buchler's critique of Whitehead in "On a Strain of Arbitrariness in Whitehead's System" overlooks the importance of asymmetry in process views.

768   Hartshorne, Charles.   "Charles Hartshorne's Recollections of

Editing the Peirce Papers." *Transactions of the Charles Peirce Society*, 6, 1970, 149–159.

Peirce, Charles S.; Hartshorne, Charles.

769   Hartshorne, Charles. *Creative Synthesis and Philosophic Method.* La Salle, Illinois: Open Court Publishing Co., 1970. London: SCM, 1970.

Creativity, and actuality; self–creativity; determinism, and indeterminism; potentiality, and actuality; prehensions; event; societies; self, as series of experiences; ontological principle; eternal objects; aesthetics, and value; God: and time, proofs of; Buddhism; process, philosophy; metaphysics, neo–classical; ethics.

(In developing his own views on a wide variety of metaphysical issues the author often compares his own position to that of Whitehead. With regard to eternal objects he finds Whitehead's doctrines of a multiplicity of discrete potentials problematic. As an alternative he suggests that the only eternal object in the universe is the simple, abstract, timeless aspect of deity.)

770   Hartshorne, Charles. "The Social Theory of Feelings." *Persons, Privacy and Feeling: Essays in the Philosophy of Mind.* Edited by Dwight Van de Vate, Jr. Memphis: Memphis State University Press, 1970, 39–51.

Feelings, theory of; prehensions.

771   Hartshorne, Charles. "Deity as the Inclusive Transcendence." *Evolution in Perspective: Commentaries in Honor of Pierre Lecomte du Novy.* Edited by George N. Shuster and Ralph E. Thorson. Notre Dame: University of Notre Dame Press, 1970, 155–160.

God: transcendence of, and panentheism.

772   Hartshorne, Charles. "Mind and Matter in Ryle, Ayer, and C. I. Lewis." *Idealistic Studies*, 1, 1971, 13–22.

Experience: of experience, as participatory, as extended; extension: as patterns of reactions, of mind, of matter, as social; mind, mind–body problem; mind; matter; Descartes, Rene; Ryle, Gilbert; Ayer, A. J.; Lewis, C. I.; Cartesianism; idealism; realism.

Participation is the basic epistemological phenomenon, applicable to all reality. Hence both mind and matter are social in nature; both are extended.

773   Hartshorne, Charles. "Could There Have Been Nothing? A Reply." *Process Studies*, 1, 1971, 25–28.

Existence; contingency; necessity; vacuity; judgments; Craighead, Houston; panpsychism; logic.

"There might have been nothing" is meaningless or contradictory, since it assumes that which it denies. (Written in response to Houston Craighead, "Non–Being and Hartshorne's Concept of God.")

774   Hartshorne, Charles. "Obligability and Determinism." *Journal of Social Philosophy*, 2, 1971, 1–2.

Freedom, and determinism; morality, and moral responsibility.

To have at least minimal ethical freedom we need no more exemption from determination by antecedent causes than we must have to be rational animals.

775   Hartshorne, Charles. "The Development of Process Philosophy." *Process Theology: Basic Writings.* Edited by Ewert H. Cousins. New York: Newman Press, 1971, 47–61.

Philosophy, process; Whitehead, Alfred North: philosophical development of.

776   Hartshorne, Charles. "Whitehead's Generalizing Power." *Whitehead's Philosophy: Selected Essays, 1935–1970.* Lincoln: University of Nebraska Press, 1972, 129–139.

Process philosophy, summary of; Whitehead, Alfred North, method of.

(This article is a slightly revised republication of "Whitehead, The Anglo–American Philosopher–Scientist" by the same author.)

777   Hartshorne, Charles. "Can There be Proofs for the Existence of God?" *Religious Language and Knowledge.* Edited by Robert H. Ayers and William t. Blackstone. Athens, Georgia: University of Georgia Press, 1972, 62–75.

God: proofs of.

778   Hartshorne, Charles. "Personal Identity from A to Z." *Process Studies*, 2, 1972, 209–215.

Identity: genetic, strict, personal; person: as series of experiences, and self–consciousness; Leibniz, G. W.; Buddhism.

Personal identity is a special form of genetic identity. A process view of identity is in some respects close to historical Buddhism.

779   Hartshorne, Charles. "Some Thoughts on Souls and Neighborly Love." *Anglican Theological Review*, 55, 1973, 144–147.

Altruism and egoism; person: as series of experiences, and identity, and immortality; sympathy; ethics; Buddhism.

In contradistinction to substance theories, a process view of the soul provides a philosophical basis for altruistic love.

780   Hartshorne, Charles. "Process and the Nature of God." *Traces of God in a Secular Culture.* Edited by George F. McLean. New York: Alba House, 1973, 117–141.

God: immutability of, consequent nature of, and change; perception, theory of; decision; Trinity; James, William; Royce, Josiah; Hocking, William E.

781   Hartshorne, Charles. "Creativity and the Deductive Method."
        Review of Metaphysics, 27, 1973, 62–74.

        Creativity; logic, deductive; causality; freedom and
        determinism; future, inherent in present; order, of nature;
        Hume, David; Popper, Karl; physics, logic.

        Partial though not complete predictability is an entailment of
        the view that becoming is both creative and cumulative.

782   Hartshorne, Charles. "Ideas and Theses of Process Philosophers."
        *Two Process Philosophers: Hartshorne's Encounter with
        Whitehead.* Edited by Lewis Ford. Tallahassee, Florida:
        American Academy of Religion: Studies in Religion, 1973,
        100–103.

        Philosophy, process.

783   Hartshorne, Charles. "Love and Dual Transcendence." *Union
        Seminary Quarterly Review*, 30, 1975, 94–100.

        God: transcendence of, immanence of, and categoreal scheme,
        as love; love; metaphysics; philosophical theology.

784   Hartshorne, Charles. "Whitehead's Differences from Buddhism."
        Philosophy East and West, 25, 1975, 407–413.

        Time: irreversibility of, symmetrical; value; experience;
        perception; Nagarjuna; Buddhism, Mahayana.

        Whitehead's asymmetrical view of time presents a marked
        difference to the Buddhist emphasis of the symmetry of past
        and future in the present.

785   Hartshorne, Charles. "Whitehead and Leibniz: A Comparison."
        Contemporary Studies in Philosophical Idealism. Edited by
        John Howie and Thomas O. Buford. Cape Cod,
        Massachusetts: Claude Starke and Co., 1975.

        Monads; being, and becoming; possibility, and incompossibles;
        truths: necessary, eternal; essence, and accident; contingency;
        pluralism; sense–data; sense perception; perception; occasion
        dominant; momentariness; God, as ground of order;
        individuality; relations: external, internal; value, as aesthetic;
        reason sufficient; space, as relational; time, as relational;
        continuity, as potential; a priori; Buddhism; Leibniz, G. W.;
        Peirce, Charles S.; idealism; empiricism; science, and
        philosophy.

        The substantial areas of overlap between the systems of
        Leibniz and Whitehead suggest truths which are neutral to the
        advances of knowledge and insight during the interval between
        the two men.

786   Harvey, Van A. *The Historian and the Believer.* New York:
        Macmillan Company, 1966, 253f.

        Religion in the Making; revelation, and history; religion, and
        history; Niebuhr, H. Richard.

        H. Richard Niebuhr and Whitehead were each struck by the
        insight that certain concrete events or experiences have the

capacity to bring about a new orientation in thought by means of their paradigmatic character. Whitehead, especially, made a distinction between the concrete image cast up by the event and the concepts abstracted by reason. The imagination is dominated by the image, but the image may be rationalized.

787   Hatchett, Marion J. "Charles Hartshorne's Critique of Christian Theology." *Anglican Theological Review*, 48, 1966, 264–275.

God: Hartshorne's interpretation of, immutability of, as love, and the world; Hartshorne, Charles; philosophical theology.

Hartshorne has reckoned seriously with the fundamental Christian assertion that God is love and has attempted to construct a metaphysics that avoids the deficiencies of inherited religions.

788   Hausman, Carl R. "Spontaneity: Its Arationality and Its Reality." *International Philosophical Quarterly*, 4, 1964, 20–47.

Spontaneity; creativity; novelty, origin of; Hartmann, Nicolai; poetry.

Theoretical approaches that assume the reality of spontaneity encounter an element of paradox inherent within the nature of spontaneity, for spontaneity eludes categories and principles which, in their capacity as being rational, insist upon unity and repeatability.

789   Hawkins, Robert B., Jr. "Change, Process and Democratic Theory: Some Urban Questions." Unpublished Ph.D. dissertation, University of Washington, 1970.

Philosophy, political; epistemology, and political philosophy; government; community; Boulding, Kenneth E.; Kuhn, Thomas S.; Peirce, Charles S.; Kaplan, Harold; political science; sociology; science, and political philosophy.

Whitehead's conceptual categories can be used to develop a set of primitive terms which reflect the dynamic and enduring characteristics of the political process.

790   Hayward, John F. "The Theology and Philosophy of Mythical Symbolism: A Study in the function and validity of non–cognitive symbols with special reference to the writings of Paul Tillich and Alfred North Whitehead." Unpublished Ph.D. dissertation, University of Chicago, 1949.

Myth; symbolism; art; causal efficacy, and myth; religion, and art; Tillich, Paul.

Whitehead's notion of the experiential depth revealed in causal efficacy is similar to Tillich's idea of the depth of the unconditional.

791   Hazelton, Roger. "The Relation Between Value and Existence in the Philosophies of Nicolai Hartmann and Alfred North Whitehead." Unpublished Ph.D. dissertation, Yale University, 1937.

Value: and existence, and potentiality, objectivity of; God, and
value; good; ethics; Hartmann, Nicolai.

792   Hazelton, Roger. "Time, Eternity, and History." *Journal of
Religion*, 30, 1950, 1–12.

Time: as continuum of existence, and eternity, and history;
history; God: and time, as eternal; existentialism; theology.

A philosophical and Christian understanding of history can be
reached through a perspective in which time and eternity are
conceived together, with history as the juncture of eternity and
time.

793   Heimsath, Star McDaniel. "Whitehead's Conception of God."
Unpublished Ph.D. dissertation, Yale University, 1941.

God: primordial nature of, consequent nature of.

794   Heimsath, Star McDaniel. "Whitehead's Idea of God." *Anglican
Theological Review*, 26, 1944, 129–135.

God: and evil, as creator, religious adequacy of; theodicy;
religion.

Inquiring Christians may find Whitehead's explanation of evil
and his conception of God religiously helpful.

795   Heipcke, Klaus. *Die Philosophie des Ereignissess bei Alfred
North Whitehead*. Würzburg: Julius–Maximilians Universität
zu Würzburg, 1964.

Events; actual entities; substance; extensive continuum;
space–time; fact; causality; coherence; God: immanence of,
consequent nature of, freedom of; eternal objects; Aristotle.

(This is the author's inaugural dissertation into the philosophy
faculty at the Julius–Maximilians Universität at Würzburg.)

796   Heise, H. R. "The Metaphysics of Alfred North Whitehead in
Relation to a Certain Experience of the Self." Unpublished
Ph.D. dissertation, University of Texas, 1960.

Self: unity of, and values; Whitehead, Alfred North:
introduction to his thought.

797   Hélal, Georges. "Le sens du development philosophique de
Whitehead." *Dialogue*, 2, 1963–1964, 398–423.

Whitehead, Alfred North, philosophical development of;
relativity, theory of; abstraction, extensive; dipolarity;
mathematics; physics; cosmology.

In order to understand Whitehead's thought, one must observe
the periods of development from the "earlier" to "later"
Whitehead very closely.

798   Hélal, Georges. "La structure et l'intentionnalité de la
philosophie de la nature de Alfred North Whitehead."
Unpublished dissertation, University of Montreal, 1966.

Intentionality; prehension.

799   Hélal, Georges. "La cosmologie: une nouvel examen de sa nature
et de sa raison d'etre." *Dialogue*, 8, 1969, 215–227.

Categoreal scheme; societies: of actual entities, structured, human; cosmology.

800   Helm, Bertrand P.   "Systemic Relations and Valuation: The Problem of Internal and External Relations." Unpublished Ph.D. dissertation, Tulane University, 1966.

Relation: internal, external, systemic; Mead, George H.; Bradley, F. H.; Royce, Josiah; Russell, Bertrand; Blanshard, Brand; Pepper, Stephen C.; Locke, John; Hume, David; Hegel, G. W. F.; Kant, Immanuel; idealism.

801   Hendel, Charles W. "The Subjective as a Problem: An Essay in Criticism of Naturalistic and Existential Philosophies." *Philosophical Review*, 62, 1953, 327–354.

Process philosophy; subject; subjectivist principle; existentialism.

The view and estimate of the subjective can provide a mutually corrective meeting point between existentialist and naturalistic philosophies.   In particular, existentialism can correct the human passivity entailed by Whitehead's doctrine of causal efficacy.

802   Henderson, Thomas G.   "For a Biographer of Whitehead." *Revue Internationale de Philosophie*, 21, 1967, 358–371.

Whitehead, Alfred North: biography of.

803   Henderson, Thomas G.   "Whitehead: Philosophy as Approximation." *Philosophy in the Mid–Century*.   Edited by R. Klibansky.   Florence: La Nuova Italia, 4, 1959, 205–209.

Dialogues of Alfred North Whitehead; philosophy, aim of.

In Whitehead's conception, the philosophic pursuit is a neverending attempt to clarify the mysterious.

804   Henry, Carl F. H.   "The Reality and Identity of God." *Christianity Today*, 13, 1969, 523–536, 580–584.

God: as living person, of classical theism; love; Williams, Daniel Day; Christianity, evangelical.

The process concept of God does not rest on evangelical and biblical motivations, but issues from attempts to fuse modern evolutionary theory with arbitrarily selected elements of the scriptural heritage.

805   Henry, Granville C., Jr.   "Aspects of the Influence of Mathematics on Contemporary Theology."   Unpublished Ph.D. dissertation, Claremont Graduate School, 1964.

Theology, and mathematics; mathematics; eternal objects.

806   Henry, Granville C., Jr.   "Aspects of the Influence of Mathematics on Contemporary Philosophy."   *Philosophia Mathematica*, 3, 1966, 17–38.

Mathematics: ground of, objects of, and logic; philosophy, of mathematics.

807   Henry, Granville C., Jr.   "Mathematics, Phenomenology, and

Language Analysis in Contemporary Theology." *Journal of the American Academy of Religion*, 35, 1967, 337–349.

Method, theological; Husserl, Edmund; Wittgenstein, Ludwig; phenomenology; linguistic analysis; mathematics; theology.

Phenomenology and language analysis originated as tools for the study of problems in the foundations of mathematics. Theologians, in their use of these tools, avoid reductionism only by restricting the tools to a function similar to that employed in the analysis of mathematics.

808   Henry, Granville C., Jr. "Whitehead's Philosophical Response to the New Mathematics." *Southern Journal of Philosophy*, 7, 1969, 341–349.

Eternal objects: mathematical basis of, as complex; mathematics: as formal, objects of, ground of; Husserl, Edmund; mathematics.

The concept of eternal objects was modeled primarily after Whitehead's understanding of mathematical existence, and his concept of actual entities was developed in large part to find a true ground for mathematics.

809   Henry, Granville C., Jr. "Mathematics and Theology." *Bucknell Review*, 20, 1972, 113–126.

Mathematics, and logic; relations, mathematical; soul; God: immutability of, language about; Euclid; Plato; geometry; philosophy, Greek.

Fundamental mathematical and logical structures have influenced and precipitated problems in the western conception of God.

810   Herbert, Gilbert. "The Organic Analogy in Town Planning." *American Institute of Planners Journal*, 29, 1963, 198–209.

Organism, philosophy of; growth, organic; one, and the many; environment; town planning; ecology.

Town planning theory and theorists have long used the language of organism and organic growth but have failed to implement the philosophical implications of the principle of organism, as it is developed in Whitehead's philosophy.

811   Hereford, Thomas G. "The Significance of 'Imaginative Contexts' in Analytical and Speculative Philosophy." Unpublished Ph.D. dissertation, University of Virginia, 1962.

Philosophy: analytic, speculative, method of, and imagination; imagination; Wittgenstein, Ludwig; Austin, J. L.; Wisdom, John; Warnock, G. C.

Language analysis and speculative philosophy can each be of value to the other, although ordinary language cannot be the paradigm ofr meaningfulness for all word usage.

812   Herrick, C. Judson. "Mechanism and Organism." *Journal of Philosophy*, 26, 1929, 589–597.

Mechanism; materialism.

In *Science and the Modern World*, Whitehead does scant justice to mechanism, for all mechanism has the quality of taking its character from its total situation. Mechanism and organism are not in conflict, and organism is still mechanism.

813 Herrick, C. Judson. "The Order of Nature." *Monist*, 40, 1930, 182–192.

Nature, orderliness of; laws, of nature; evolution.

Contrary to Whitehead's position in *Science and the Modern World*, faith in the order of nature is well–founded in experience. All happenings are knit into the Natural Order in law–abiding patterns.

814 Herrmann, Heinz. "Morphological and Functional Aspects of Living Matter and Whitehead's Category of Actual Entity." *Philosophy of Science*, 14, 1947, 254–260.

Actual entity: as final reality, and biology; metaphysics; biology.

Many aspects of the metaphysical concept of the actual entity, and the biological concept of the unification of structure and function, are of striking similarity. The philosophical correlate to the biological fact signifies development of a metaphysical system which relates the conceptual and physical realms.

815 Herzog, Frederick. *Understanding God: The Key Issue in Present–Day Protestant Thought.* New York: Charles Scribner's Sons, 1966, 31–33.

Theology, natural; God, and order; Cobb, John B., Jr.

In using Whitehead's notion of God in a theological perspective, John Cobb's position could have been strengthened if he had described how the question of God arises from within the Christian community. If philosophy is to aid theology, it must answer questions which theology, in its communal setting, asks.

816 Hill, Thomas E. *Contemporary Theories of Knowledge.* New York: The Ronald Press Company, 1961, 265–290.

Epistemology: in Whitehead's philosophy of nature, in Whitehead's metaphysics; event; duration; extension; cogredience; objects: of science, of perception; prehension; concrescence; presentational immediacy; causal efficacy; propositions; judgments; subject, and object; truth: nature of, function of; idealism; realism; Platonism; Aristotelianism.

Regarding the issue of the extent to which objects of knowledge are independent of experience, Whitehead is a realist. However, by virtue of the role he gives decision in the process of cognition, and by virtue of the role he gives to feeling in objects, his thought contains at least two suggestions indicating how a substantial part of what idealists have contended can be included in a plausible realism.

817   Hill, William J. "Does the World Make a Difference to God?" *The Thomist*, 38, 1974, 146–164.

God: of classical theism, as dipolar, as love, as personal; Thomas Aquinas; Thomism; theology.

Whitehead reduces the infinity of God to mere potentiality, the love of God to mere relationality, and the freedom of God to mere contingency. For this reason his view of God is less adequate to Christian theology than that of Thomas Aquinas.

818   Hiltner, Seward. "The Minister and Process Theology." *Theology Today*, 31, 1974, 99–103.

Ministry; theology, process.

819   Hintz, Howard W. "A. N. Whitehead and the Philosophical Synthesis." *Journal of Philosophy*, 52, 1955, 225–243.

God: as source of value, and order, and evil; religion: as solitariness, as societal, as universal; metaphysics.

Whitehead's philosophical synthesis is centered in his theory of religion and of God.

820   Hintz, Howard W. "Whitehead's Concept of Organism and the Mind–Body Problem." *Dimensions of Mind: A Symposium.* Edited by Sidney Hook. New York: New York University Press, 1960, 100–109.

Mind, mind–body problem; bifurcation, of nature.

As it is usually posed, the 'mind–body' problem implies that nature is bifurcated into the physical and mental. In its assertion that all reality, as process, partakes of both the physical and the mental, Whitehead's philosophy of organism permits of no such bifurcation.

821   Hobart, R. E. "Hume Without Scepticism." *Mind*, 39, 1930, 273–301, 409–425.

Causation; induction; causal efficacy; Hume, David; Kant, Immanuel.

Hume's doctrines respecting the nature of cause and of induction are analyses of fact without sceptical consequence. Whitehead's answer to Hume is unfounded, and is based on a misunderstanding of Hume's thought.

822   Hocking, Richard. "The Polarity of Dialectical History and Process Cosmology." *Christian Scholar*, 50, 1967, 177–183.

History: as dialectical, as aesthetic, and nature; cosmology, and history; existentialism.

Process cosmology and dialectical history are each based upon experience, and each is the polar opposite and complement of the other. Whitehead's philosophy might sustain both positions.

823   Hocking, William E. "Whitehead on Mind and Nature." *The Philosophy of Alfred North Whitehead.* Edited by Paul A. Schilpp. La Salle, Illinois: Open Court Publishing Company, 1941, 381–404.

Mind, and nature; being, and becoming; philosophy, method of; substance; bifurcation, of nature; perception; actual occasion; Hume, David; Bergson, Henri.

(The author compares and contrasts his view of the relation between mind and nature to that of Whitehead.)

824 Hocking, William E. *Science and the Idea of God.* North Carolina: University of North Carolina Press, 1944.

God, concept of; science, and religion.

825 Hocking, William E. "Whitehead As I Knew Him." *Journal of Philosophy*, 58, 1961, 505–516. Also in Alfred North Whitehead: Essays on His Philosophy. Edited by George Kline. Englewood Cliffs: Prentice Hall, Inc., 1963, 7–17.

A. N. Whitehead, biography of.

826 Hoernle, R. F. A. "The Revival of Idealism." *Contemporary Idealism in America.* Edited by Clifford Barrett. New York: The Macmillan Company, 1932, 301–326.

Idealism; Whitehead, Alfred North, as idealist; realism.

Whitehead's essay on speculative philosophy, his rejection of the principle of vacuous actuality, and his identification of existence with experience, align him with all Idealists and oppose him to all Realists.

827 Hoffert, Robert W. "A Political Vision for the Organic Model." *Process Studies*, 5, Fall 1975, 175–186.

Philosophy, political; civilization; love; justice; power; Roelofs, H. Mark; Deutsch, Karl W.; political science.

A new political vision based on Whitehead's philosophy would raise political questions from the perspective of involvement or participation, rather from that of isolation. It would include the affective as well as cognitive aspects of experience as data relevant to the analysis of political options.

828 Hoffmann, Charles G. "Whitehead's Philosophy of Nature and Romantic Poetry." *Journal of Aesthetics and Art Criticism*, 10, 1952, 258–263.

Poetry; science, and poetry; philosophy, and poetry; *Science and the Modern World*; Wordsworth, William; Shelley, Percy B.

Whitehead is right to say that a philosophy of nature should take into account a poetic view of nature, but he is wrong to suggest that poetic views of nature are the exclusive properties of particular eras.

829 Hogan, Donald J. "Whitehead's God: The Analogy of Actual Entity." *The New Scholasticism*, 46, 1972, 411–426.

God: as actual entity, functions of, as unity of universe, and the world; analogy, and God; identity; diversity; theology, natural.

Whitehead intended God to be construed as analogous to other actual entities; in terms of this construction Whitehead's God is consistent with his metaphysical principles.

830   Holling, J.   "Die Metafisik Whiteheads im Urteil der Sowjet-philosophie."   *Studies in Soviet Thought*, 5, 1965, 57–67.

Philosophy, Soviet.

831   Holmes, Henry W.   *The Educational Views of Whitehead.* Cambridge, Massachusetts: Harvard University Press, 1943.

Education; philosophy, of education.

(In a brief essay the author outlines Whitehead's general view of education. It is suggested that there are four emphases in Whitehead's view: an emphasis on education as a process of growth, on education as valuable in its utility, on education as involving a rhythmic process, and on education as having its final end in religion, aesthetic enjoyment, and adventure.)

832   Hook, Sidney.   "Whitehead's Final Views."   *Nation*, 1942, 401–403.

Whitehead, Alfred North, philosophical development of.

Whitehead's final writings, contained in P. A. Schilpp's *The Philosophy of Alfred North Whitehead*, are marred by misleading statements on the impossibility of adequate knowledge.   Written in review of *The Philosophy of Alfred North Whitehead*, edited by Paul Arthur Schilpp.

833   Hooper, Sydney E.   "Professor Whitehead's *Adventures of Ideas.*" *Philosophy*, 8, 1933, 326–344.

Adventures of Ideas, summary of.

834   Hooper, Sydney E.   "Discussion: Professor Whitehead's *Nature and Life.*"   *Philosophy*, 9, 1934, 465–472.

Nature and Life, summary of.

835   Hooper, Sydney E.   "Whitehead's Philosophy: Actual Entities." *Philosophy*, 16, 1941, 285–305.

Actual entities; creativity.

836   Hooper, Sydney E.   "Whitehead's Philosophy: Eternal Objects and God."   *Philosophy*, 17, 1942, 47–68.

Eternal objects; God, Whitehead's arguments for.

Organic philosophy asserts that in order to understand the temporal and spatial world it is necessary to take account of the realm of eternality: eternal objects and God.

837   Hooper, Sydney E.   "Whitehead's Philosophy: Space, Time and Things."   *Philosophy*, 18, 1943, 204–230.

Continuum, extensive; space–time; objects, enduring.

838   Hooper, Sydney E.   "Whitehead's Philosophy: Theory of Perception."   *Philosophy*, 19, 1944, 136–158.

Perception; causal efficacy; presentational immediacy; symbolic reference.

839   Hooper, Sydney E.   "Telepathy in the Light of Whitehead's Philosophy."   *Hibbert Journal*, 42, 1944, 248–253.

Telepathy; prehensions, hybrid.

Since the mental pole of an actual entity does not share in the spatial character of the physical pole, contiguity is not necessary for the transmission of mental feeling.   Telepathy may be explained through hybrid prehensions of non–contiguous conceptual feelings.

840   Hooper, Sydney E.   "Whitehead's Philosophy: Propositions and Consciousness."   *Philosophy*, 20, 1945, 59–75.

Propositions; feelings, propositional; consciousness.

841   Hooper, Sydney E.   "Whitehead's Philosophy: The Higher Phases of Experience."   *Philosophy*, 21, 1946, 57–78.

Feelings: intellectual, propostiional, comparative; judgment; purposes, physical.

842   Hooper, Sydney E.   "Whitehead's Philosophy: The World as Process."   *Philosophy*, 23, 1948, 140–160.

Process philosophy, summary of.

843   Hooper, Sydney E.   "A Reasonable Theory of Morality (Alexander and Whitehead)."   *Philosophy*, 25, 1950, 54–67.

Morality, as social; order: social, moral, God as source of; Alexander, Samuel; ethics.

Morality is one specialized exemplification of the metaphysical principle of order pervasive throughout the universe, whose function is the eliciting of value experience.

844   Hopper, Stanley R.   "Whitehead: Redevivus? or Absconditus?"   *The Future of Theology in America*.   Edited by William A. Beardslee.   Philadelphia: The Westminster Press, 1967, 112–126.

Aesthetics: and philosophy, primacy of; philosophy, and theology; cosmology, as aesthetic vision.

The aesthetic basis of Whitehead's philosophy has wrongfully been de–emphasized by his interpreters, including those who attempt to use his thought for theological purposes.

845   Horowitz, I. L.   *The Idea of War and Peace in Contemporary Philosophy*.   Paine–Whitman, 1957, 50–64.

War; peace; civilization.

846   Hoskyn, F. P.   "The Adjectival Theory of Matter."   *Journal of Philosophy*, 27, 1930, 655–668.

Relativity: special, general; motion, atomic; Einstein, Albert; Russell, Bertrand; physics, relativity; geometry.

The adjectival theory of matter advanced by Whitehead and Russell answers problems raised but not solved by the special and general theories of relativity: problems of kinetic atomic processes, and the realtion between metrical properties of the geometrical continuum and matter.

847   Hoβfeld, Paul.   "Das Christentum in der Religionsphilosophie von

Alfred North Whitehead." *Theologie und Glaube*, 59, 1969, 464–472.

Christianity; philosophy, of religion.

848   Hoβfeld, Paul. "Atom und Molekül der Seinslehren von N. Hartmann und A. N. Whitehead." *Philosophia Naturalis*, 12, 1970, 345–356.

Atom; molecule; God; Hartmann, Nicolai; ontology.

849   Howie, John. "Metaphysical Elements of Creativity in the Philosophy of W. E. Hocking: I." *Idealistic Studies*, 2, 1972, 249–264.

Creativity: definition of, as ultimate, elements of, and mind; mind: ingredients of, as self; self: as field of fields, as creativity; space, plural; Hocking, W. E.; idealism; empiricism: radical, widened.

To understand creativity by postulating an ultimate principle is to argue in a circle. Only an entity such as mind, with its inherent capacity to be what it is not, can be an appropriate referent as an explanation of creativity.

850   Hsieh, Yu–wei. "Huai–Hei–Te Lun Li–Hsing Ti Chi–Neng (Whitehead on the Function of Reason)." *Min–Chu P'ing–Lun (Democratic Critique)*, 11, 1959, Pt 1 #22, 9; Pt 2 #23, 10; Pt 3 #24, 12–16.

Reason: function of, speculative.

851   Hsieh, Yu–wei. "Huai–Hei–Te–Lun 'Li–Chich (Whitehead on Understanding)." *Min–Chu P'ing–Lun (Democratic Critique)*, 12, 1960, #20, 10–15.

Knowledge; truth, nature of.

852   Hsieh, Yu–wei. "Huai–He–Te Lun 'Yuan–Ching' (Whitehead on Foresight)." *Min–Chu P'ing–Lun (Democratic Critique)*, 13, 1961, #1, 10–15.

Foresight.

853   Hsieh, Yu–wei. "Huai–Hei–Te Lun Li Ch'eng Ti Hsing–Shih (Whitehead on the Forms of Process)." *Min–Chu P'ing–Lun (Democratic Critique)*, 13, 1961, #4, 6–10.

Process: principle of, microscopic and macroscopic, individualizing of.

854   Hsieh, Yu–wei. "Huai–Hei–Te Lun 'Wen–Ming Ti Yu–Chou' (Whitehead on the Universe of Civilization)." *Min–Chu P'ing–Lun (Democratic Critique)*, 13, 1961, #5, 7–12.

Civilization; value; society; history.

855   Hsieh, Yu–wei. "Huai–Hei–Te Ti Tsung–Chiao Kuan (Whitehead's Philosophy of Religion)." *Min–Chu P'ing–Lun (Democratic Critique)*, 13, 1961, #8, 2–8.

Philosophy, of religion.

856   Hsieh, Yu–wei. "Huai–Hei–Te Lun Chung–Yao (Whitehead on

Importance)." *Ta–Hsueh Sheng–Huo (University Life)*, 6, #21, 11–19.

Importance.

857 Hsieh, Yu–wei. "Huah–Hei–Te Lun Piao–Hsien (Whitehead on Manifestation)." *Ta–Hsueh Sheng–Huo*, 6, #23, 4–7, #24, 17–22.

Appearance; objective immortality.

858 Hsieh, Yu–wei. *Huai–hei–te te che–hsueh* (Whitehead's Philosophy). Taipei, Taiwan: Foresight Publishing House, 1974.

Whitehead, Alfred North: biography of, bibliography of, introduction to his thought; cosmology; actual occasions; events; prehensions: positive, negative; philosophy, of science; location, fallacy of simple; atomicity; religion; God: as principle of concretion, as principle of limitation, consequent nature of, primordial nature of; value, criteria for; mind; education.

(This is an introduction to Whitehead's thought by a Chinese student of Whitehead's from Harvard. It also contains a complete translation of *The Function of Reason*.)

859 Huang, T. "Huai–T'I–Hei Shih K'ung Kuan (Whitehead's Conception of Space and Time)." *Che–Hsueh P'ing–Lun (Philosophical Review)*, 6, 1936, #1, 46–57.

Space; time; extension.

860 Huckle, John J. "From Whitehead to Ogden: A Possibility in Contemporary Hermeneutic." *Dunwoodie Review*, 7, 1967, 177–198.

God: Hartshorne's interpretation of, and psyche–body analogy; method, theological; Hartshorne, Charles; Ogden, Shubert M.; Bultmann, Rudolf; hermeneutics; existentialism.

Ogden finds a complete theological method in the reconciliation of Bultmann's existentialism with Hartshorne's dipolar theism. This method gives significance to speech directly about God as well as humanity.

861 Huddart, Bonita J. "Time and Becoming in the Cosmology of *Process and Reality*." Unpublished Ph.D. dissertation, Yale University, 1962.

Time: epochal theory of, passage of; atomism; extension; division: coordinate, genetic; causation, final; Aristotle.

In Whitehead's philosophy it is actual occasions, rather than time itself, which is atomic.

862 Hudson, James. "The Doctrine of the Actual Occasion in Whitehead." Unpublished Ph.D. dissertation, Boston University Graduate School, 1946.

Actual occasion: as distinct from actual entity, and categories, and creativity, and space–time, and value; dipolarity; location, simple; relations: internal, external; substance.

(The purpose of the dissertation is to evaluate Whitehead's doctrine of the actual occasion. The author argues that the notion of actual occasion is generally adequate to a philosophy of nature, although problematic in a number of areas.)

863   Huescher, A. *Denker unserer Zeit, volume I.* Munich: Piper verlag, 1956, 327–330.

Whitehead, Alfred North, introduction to his thought.

864   Hughes, Percy. "The Technique of Philosophic Observation." *Journal of Philosophy,* 35, 1938, 295–302.

Categoreal scheme, as philosophic intuitions; method, philosophical; Aristotle.

Aristotle's observational scheme of the four causes is preferable to Whitehead's seven philosophical intuitions (categoreal scheme) derived from Plato. Whitehead's eighth intuition, Evil, must supplement the Aristotelian scheme.

865   Hughes, Percy. "Comments and Criticisms." *Journal of Philosophy,* 36, 1939, 103–105.

Language, Whitehead's use of; Urban, Wilbur M.

Obstacles to understanding Whitehead which are cited by Urban may be avoided by careful attention to Whitehead's clarifications and explanations of his terms. (Written in response to Wilbur M. Urban, "Elements of Unintelligibility in Whitehead's Metaphysics.")

866   Hughes, Percy. "'Elements of Unintelligibility in Whitehead's Metaphysics' Notes." *Journal of Philosophy,* 36, 1939, 103–105.

Whitehead, Alfred North, evaluation of.

867   Hughes, Percy. "Is Whitehead's Psychology Adequate?" *The Philosophy of Alfred North Whitehead.* Edited by P. A. Schilpp. New York: Tudor Publishing Co., 1941, 273–299.

Physiology, psychological; subjective form; life; person, and personal identity; perception; body, living; subjectivity; agent; psychology.

To reduce a person to a series of acts, as does Whitehead, is to make nonsense of personal identity. What Whitehead needs is a doctrine of the underlying agent. Nonetheless Whitehead's thought supplies various categories in which human psychology and psychological physiology might be developed.

868   Huntington, E. V. "New Set of Independent Postulates for the Algebra of Logic with Special Reference to Whitehead and Russell's 'Principia Mathematica'." *Proceedings of the National Academy of Science,* 18, 1932, 179–180.

Algebra; logic; *Principia Mathematica.*

869   Hutcheson, Richard E. J. "Whitehead's Theory of Causation." Unpublished Ph.D. dissertation, Harvard University, 1962.

Causation, and prehension; significance, doctrine of; concreteness, fallacy of misplaced; bifurcation, of nature; location, fallacy of simple.

870   Hutchins, Robert M. "A Reply to Professor Whitehead." *Atlantic Monthly,* 158, 1936, 582–588.

Education, purpose of; philosophy, of education.

Whitehead advocates a university education in which knowledge is suggestive of action. However, the present need is not an emphasis upon action, but upon theoretical studies which are the foundation of knowledge. (Written in response to A. N. Whitehead, "Harvard: The Future.")

871   Hutchison, John A. "The Philosophy of Religion: Retrospect and Prospect." *Journal of Bible and Religion*, 30, 1962, 12–17.

Positivism; existentialism; fideism; personalism; linguistic analysis; theology, and philosophy; philosophy, of religion.

The positivism of the first half of the twentieth century has given way to a renascent interest in philosophy of religion. Personalism and process theology are among the more promising trends.

872   Ichii, Saburô. "Alfred North Whitehead." *Tetsugaku Koza Chi Kuma Shobo*, 1, 1949, 239–242.

Whitehead, Alfred North: biography of, introduction to his thought, philosophical development of; process philosophy, summary of.

873   Ichii, Saburô. "Jissho Shugi E No Hanpatsu (The Rejection of Positivism)." *America Shisoshi Nippon Hydron–Sha*, 4, 1950, 271–298.

Positivism, logical.

874   Ichii, Saburô. "Whitehead." *Riso*, January 1950, 55–63.

Whitehead, Alfred North: introduction to his thought, biography of; process philosophy, summary of.

875   Ichii, Saburô. "Alexander Yori Whitehead E (From Alexander to Whitehead)." *Riso*, May 1954, 44–51.

Philosophy, in America; process philosophy, summary of; Alexander, Samuel; Whitehead, Alfred North: introduction to his thought.

876   Ichii, Saburô. "Whitehead's Theory of Significance and his 'Justification of Induction'." *Science of Thought*, 2, 1956, 50–68.

Induction; significance, theory of; perception: and causal efficacy, and presentational immediacy, and symbolic reference; possibility; Popper, Karl; logic; epistemology.

Whitehead attempted to justify his theory of induction through two means: his theory of significance and his metaphysical scheme. The theory of significance is important because it avoids the logical fallacy of question begging.

877   Ichii, Saburô. *Whitehead No Tetsugaku (The Philosophy of Whitehead)*. Tokyo: Kobundo, 1956.

Whitehead, Alfred North: introduction to his thought, philosophical development of; actual entities; eternal objects; God: primordial nature of, consequent nature of; perception.

878   Ichii, Saburô. "Whitehead No Senso Heiwa Shiso (The Views of Whitehead on War and Peace)." *Shiso*, 3, 1960, 13–22.

Civilization: prerequisites for, philosophy of; peace.

879   Iino, Norimoto. "Whitehead No Ingasetsu (Causality in Whitehead)." *Bun Seki Tetsugaku No Shomondai (Problems of Analytic Philosophy)*. Edited by Ueda Seiji. Tokyo: Waseda Daigaku Shuppan–Bu, 1957, 253–299.

Causality; causation: efficient, final.

880   Inada, Kenneth K. "Vijñanaváda and Whiteheadian Philosophy." *Journal of Indian and Buddhist Studies*, 7, 1959.

Perception; knowledge; Buddhism.

881   Inada, Kenneth K. "Whitehead's 'Actual Entity' and the Buddhist Anatman." *Philosophy East and West*, 21, 1971, 303–316.

Actual entity, comparison with anatman; immanence, mutual; process philosophy, comparison with Buddhism; Buddhism.

A comparative examination of the actual entity and anatman, central concepts of Whitehead and the Buddha respectively, reveals a remarkable similarity of basic insights.

882   Inada, Kenneth K. "The Metaphysics of Buddhist Experience and the Whiteheadian Encounter." *Philosophy East and West*, 25, 1975, 465–488.

Buddhist Metaphysics: as descriptive, principles of; being: Buddhist constituents of, genetic flow of; dependent coorigination, as Whiteheadian creativity; experience: dharmic analysis of, as relational, as nonvacuous; duhkha, as perpetual perishing; sūnyatā: as suchness, as emptiness, as perpetual perishing; nirvana, and Peace; God: as primordial, as consequent; Buddhism: God and Bodhisattva ideal, and correlates for God; Buddhism, Mahayana.

Construction of a consistent Buddhist metaphysics of experience indicates significant lines of convergence with Whiteheadian metaphysics.

883   Inbody, Tyron. "Process Theology and Personal Survival." *The Iliff Review*, 31, 1974, 31–42.

Immortality: objective, subjective, social, in memory of God; God: as dipolar, adequacy of; death: as perpetual perishing, as loss of value; panpsychism; theology.

Process views entail the survival of value through objective immortality in God, and offer possibilities for personal survival as well.

884   Inbody, Tyron. "Paul Tillich and Process Theology." *Theological Studies*, 36, 1975, 472–492.

Metaphysics, Tillichian; process, Tillichian critique of; Tillich, process critique of; Tillich, Paul; Hartshorne, Charles; metaphysics; theology; religion.

Despite agreements between Tillich and Hartshorne, they are

deeply separated by a fundamental divergence of religious perspective.

885   Jackson, Jerald H.   "An Investigation of the Implications of Process Philosophy for Christology with Special Attention to the Thought of Lionel Spencer Thornton and Charles Hartshorne."   Unpublished Ph.D. dissertation, Northwestern University, 1966.

Philosophy, process; soteriology; christology; redemption; atonement; revelation; evolution, and religion; Hartshorne, Charles; Thornton, Lionel Spencer; theology; religion.

The Christian claim of the significance of Christ can be elucidated by process philosophy.

886   Jacobson, Nolan P.   "Whitehead and Buddhism on the Art of Living."   *The Eastern Buddhist*, 8, 1975, 8–36.

Buddhism; process philosophy, and Buddhism; reason, and Buddhism; aesthetics, and Buddhism; relatedness; technology.

Process philosophy provides a channel through which Buddhism can promote its mode of living in the West.

887   James, Ralph E. Jr.   *The Concrete God: A New Beginning for Theology—The Thought of Charles Hartshorne.*   New York: Bobbs–Merrill Company, Inc., 1967, 43–55.

Hartshorne's theology, summary of; actual occasion; concreteness; aesthetics; harmony; contrast; freedom; metaphysics, descriptive; memory; eternal objects; God; concreteness, fallacy of misplaced; Hartshorne, Charles; Heidegger, Martin; Husserl, Edmund; phenomenology; existentialism; theology.

Hartshorne and Whitehead are both committed to concrete actuality, constitutive memory, aesthetic evaluation, descriptive metaphysics, real creativity, the reality of change, freedom and social becoming. Their disagreement on the question of eternal objects is, in Hartshorne's view, secondary. Perhaps their greatest disagreement will be found in Hartshorne's development of Whiteheadian theology. (This is the author's Ph.D. dissertation at Drew University in 1965.)

888   James, Ralph E. Jr.   "Process Cosmology and Theological Particularity."   *Process Philosophy and Christian Thought.* Edited by D. Brown, R. E. James and G. Reeves, 399–407.

Cosmos; history; hope; evolution; Moltmann, Jürgen; Pannenberg, Wolfhart; anthropology; eschatology; cosmology.

Hope, based on the continuing process of reality towards its potentialities in God, raises human horizons above traditional divisions based on the particulars of history and orients individuals toward the openness of the future.

889   Janzen, J. Gerald.   "Modes of Prescence and the Communion of Saints."   *Religious Experience and Process Theology.*   Edited by Harry J. Cargas and Bernard Lee.   New York: Paulist Press, 1976, 147–172.

Church; contemporaries, prehension of; organism; causal efficacy; presentational immediacy; Lee, Bernard; ecclesiology. Whitehead's philosophical metaphor of "organism" converges with the biblical metaphor of the Church as the body of Christ.

890   Jentz, Arthur H. Jr.   "Ethics in the Making: The Genesis of Ethical Theory in the Philosophy of Alfred North Whitehead." Unpublished Ph.D. dissertation, Columbia University, 1965.

Human existence, and morality; good; morality; value; judgment, moral; feeling, intellectual; ethics.

From a Whiteheadian perspective the nature of ethical theory is traceable to the rise of intellectual feelings and the contrast between actuality and possibility.   By virtue of the creative process of existence, a single pattern of good cannot be defined, although primary moral values can be outlined.

891   Joad, C. E. M. *Guide to Philosophy*. London: Victor Gollancz Ltd., 1936.

Bifurcation; dualism; mind, and matter; causation, and induction; substance; subjective aim; prehension; God, as principle of limitation; science, and value; Locke, John; Hume, David.

An essential part of Whitehead's indictment of the scientific picture of the world as an abstraction is that, while science gives an account of the entities which are prehended into the unity of a thing, it leaves out of account the prehending activity which is informed by the thing's subjective aim.   In the case of a human being, this prehending activity constitutes the personality.

892   Joad, C. E. M. "Whitehead." *New Statesman and Nation*, 35, 1948, 26.

Whitehead, Alfred North, evaluation of; *Science and the Modern World*.

The best of Whitehead's critical work is contained in the first half of *Science and the Modern World*, which should be ranked as a classic.   Whitehead's constructive work is obscurely expressed, and of more dubious value.

893   Joad, C. E. M. "Whitehead, A Rejoinder." *New Statesman and Nation*, 35, 1948, 96.

Whitehead, Alfred North, method of.

Philosophical writing may be obscure for either of two reasons: the nature of the subject matter, or the insufficiencies of the philosopher.

894   John, Helen James.   "A Philosopher's Philosopher." *Commonweal*, 75, 1961, 312–314.

Whitehead, Alfred North, biography of.

895   Johnson, Allison H. *Actual Entities, A Study of Alfred North*

Whitehead's Theory of Reality.   Toronto: University of Toronto, 1937.

Actual entities; eternal objects; causal efficacy; presentational immediacy; civilization; process philosophy, summary of.

(This is the author's Ph.D. dissertation in published form.)

896   Johnson, Allison H.   "A Criticism of D. Bidney's 'Spinoza and Whitehead'."   *Philosophical Review,* 47, 1938, 410–414.

Creativity; Bidney, D.; Spinoza, B.

Contrary to Bidney's interpretation, Whitehead does not attempt to derive the actual from the potential, nor does he try to combine a monistic metaphysics with a pluralistic theory of physics and biology.

897   Johnson, Allison H.   "Some Notes on: The Psychology of Alfred North Whitehead."   *Bulletin of the Canadian Psychological Association,* 3, 1943, 53–55.

Psychology.

Whitehead's analysis of the subject involves primarily affective and purposive terms, with a constant stress on inter–relatedness.

898   Johnson, Allison H.   "The Intelligibility of Whitehead's Philosophy."   *Philosophy of Science,* 10, 1943, 47–55.

Language, Whitehead's use of; subject; value; Urban, Wilbur M.; metaphysics.

A careful reading of *Process and Reality* reveals the inaccuracy of many of Urban's criticisms of Whitehead.   (Written in response to W. M. Urban, "Elements of Unintelligibility in Whitehead's Metaphysics.")

899   Johnson, Allison H.   "The Social Philosophy of Alfred North Whitehead."   *Journal of Philosophy,* 40, 1943, 261–271.

Democracy; tolerance; philosophy, social; political science.

The theory of reality formulated by Whitehead provides a philosophical basis for democracy.

900   Johnson, Allison H.   "'Truth, Beauty and Goodness' in the Philosophy of A. N. Whitehead."   *Philosophy of Science,* 11, 1944, 9–29.

Value, theory of; good: as eternal object, as pattern; beauty; truth; evil; Goheen, John; Schilpp, P. A.; Morris, B.; ethics.

Whitehead's total philosophy yields a positive and adequate theory of value.   Misunderstandings of Whitehead's theory of value have arisen chiefly because only some phases of Whitehead's complete treatment have been taken into consideration.

901   Johnson, Allison H.   "The Psychology of Alfred North Whitehead."   *Journal of General Psychology,* 32, 1945, 175–212.

Subject: as psychical, as self–evolving historical unity, as thinking; perception; consciousness; intuition; psychology.

Whitehead's discussion of psychological topics is based upon his analysis of the subject in primarily affective and purposive terms.

902 Johnson, Allison H. "Whitehead's Theory of Actual Entities: Defence and Criticism." *Philosophy of Science*, 12, 1945, 237–295.

Process philosophy: summary of, criticisms of; Whitehead, Alfred North, method of; Emmet, Dorothy; Hooper, Sydney E.; Lintz, E. J.

Many criticisms of Whitehead arise from misunderstanding of some aspect of his philosophy. Appropriate criticisms may be directed toward his anthropomorphism, his insufficient attention to endurance of the self in human experience, and his exceptional treatment of God as differing from other actual entities.

903 Johnson, Allison H. "Whitehead and the Making of Tomorrow." *Philosophy and Phenomenological Research*, 5, 1945, 398–406.

Society, problems of; freedom, and social systems; education; sociology.

Whitehead is keenly aware of economic and political problems, and offers specific practical suggestions to overcome them.

904 Johnson, Allison H. "Whitehead's Discussion of Education." *Education*, 66, 1946, 653–671.

Education: purpose of, as self–development, stages of; philosophy, of education; *Aims of Education*.

The most valuable contribution which Whitehead makes to the cause of education is his vigorous and enduring devotion to the ideal that education shall provide the means and the stimulus to a good life in a civilized society.

905 Johnson, Allison H. "The Wit and Wisdom of Whitehead." *Philosophy of Science*, 13, 1946, 223–251.

Whitehead, Alfred North, biography of.

(This article takes the form of a series of quotations from Whitehead's books and writings designed to indicate and locate representative samples of Whitehead's wit and wisdom.)

906 Johnson, Allison H. "Alfred North Whitehead." *University of Toronto Quarterly*, 15, 1946, 373–383.

Whitehead, Alfred North, evaluation of.

Whitehead's great and ever increasing influence flows through two channels: his numerous books and articles, and his direct personal associations.

907 Johnson, Allison H. "Whitehead's Philosophy of History." *Journal of the History of Ideas*, 7, 1946, 234–249. Also in *Philosophia*, 4, 1947, 128–139.

Philosophy, of history; history: dimensions of, and values; God, as acting in history; history.

Whitehead offers a philosophy of history which recognizes the function of great thinkers and their ideas, the pressure of economic forces, and the effect of the physical environment. The practical outcome of this philosophy is that the stream of history can be directed by human efforts.

908 Johnson, Allison H. *The Wit and Wisdom of A. N. Whitehead.* Boston: The Beacon Press, 1947.

Philosophy, task of; Whitehead, Alfred North: introduction to his thought, biography of; science; morality; philosophy, social; religion; education; history.

(The work consists of a series of quotations from Whitehead's books and articles designed to sample the philosopher's wit and aphorismic wisdom. The introduction includes a biography of Whitehead's life and a brief exposition of aspects of his thought.)

909 Johnson, Allison H. "A. N. Whitehead's Theory of Intuition." *Journal of General Psychology,* 37, 1947, 61–66.

Intuition: religious, moral, as non–sensuous perception; Bergson, Henri; Santayana, George; psychology.

Whitehead's theory of intuition claims that there exist immediate experiences of data which many other analyses of experience disregard, and that these experiences are verifiable.

910 Johnson, Allison H. "Recent Discussions of A. N. Whitehead." *Review of Metaphysics,* 5, 1951–1952, 293–308.

Beer, S. H.; Lowe, Victor; Hartshorne, Charles; Johnson, A. H.; Shahan, E. P.; Wells, H. K.; King, H. R.; Christian, William A.; Lawrence, Nathaniel; Malik, C.; McCreary, J. K.; Page, F. H.; Weiss, Paul.

As of 1951, there was no adequate comprehensive discussion of Whitehead's metaphysics.

911 Johnson, Allison H. "Hartshorne and the Interpretation of Whitehead." *Review of Metaphysics,* 7, 1954, 495–498.

Perishing, perpetual; objective immortality, in God; prehensions: negative, and God; Hartshorne, Charles.

The position that some available data are eliminated from God's nature is supported not only by passages in *Process and Reality,* but by Whitehead's personal comments. (Written in response to Charles Hartshorne, "The Immortality of the Past: Critique of a Prevalent Misinterpretation.")

912 Johnson, Allison H. "Whitehead's Philosophy of Civilization." *Whitehead and the Modern World.* Edited by Victor Lowe, Charles Hartshorne and Allison H. Johnson. Boston: Beacon Press, 42–54. London: Mayflower Press, 1958. New York: Dover Publications, 1962. Gloucester, Massachusetts: Peter Smith, 1962. Plainview, New York: Books for Libraries, 1972.

Civilization; adventure; peace; harmony; zest.

Reviews

Boas, G. *Journal of the History of Ideas*, 19, 1958, 591.

Burnett, J. R. *Harvard Educational Review*, 28, 1958, 359–361.

Hirschberger, J. *Philosophischer Literatureanzuger*, 17, 1964, 296–303.

Lawrence, N. *Philosophy and Phenomenological Research*, 20, 1959–1960, 130–131.

Schrag, C. O. *Journal of Philosophy*, 56, 1959, 464–468.

Shalom, A. *Etudes Philosophiques*, 18, 1963, 361–362.

913   Johnson, Allison H. *Whitehead's Philosophy of Civilization.* Toronto, Canada: University of Western Ontario, 1958. New York: Dover Publications, Inc., 1962.

Falsafat Whitehead Fil Hadarat. Trans. Abdul Rahman Yaghi. Beirut: Al–Maktabah Al–Asriyah, 1970.

Whitehead, Alfred North: introduction to his thought; civilization: prerequisites for, definition of, and metaphysics, and tolerance, importance of individuals in; philosophy: of history, social, of education; God: and order, tenderness of, religious availability of, and history; value; adventure; peace; beauty; art; economics; religion; Christianity, and Buddhism; democracy; communism; geography; minority groups; liberty, civil; international relations.

Whitehead's theory of reality provides support for his theory of civilization and for the ideals and techniques of western democracy. In arguing for the value of freedom, tolerance, persuasion, and wisdom as prerequisites for civilization, and in defining truth, beauty, adventure, and peace as the ideals of civilization, Whitehead provides a framework through which the inadequacies of uncivilized perspectives can be exposed.

914   Johnson, Allison H. "A Philosophical Foundation for Democracy." *Ethics*, 68, 1958, 281–285.

Democracy, political; philosophy, political.

Whitehead's analysis of the actual entity exemplifies qualities of freedom, equality, and fraternity, thus providing a philosophical foundation for the democratic way of life.

915   Johnson, Allison H. "Leibniz and Whitehead." *Philosophy and Phenomenological Research*, 19, 1959, 285–305.

Actual entity, and Leibnitian monads; harmony; God, function of; Leibniz, G. W.; metaphysics.

Examination of agreements and differences between Leibniz and Whitehead constitutes the basis for an adequate evaluation of their common mentalistic position.

916   Johnson, Allison H. "Editor's Introduction." *Whitehead's American Essays in Social Philosophy.* Edited by A. H. Johnson. Harper & Bros., 1959.

Whitehead, Alfred North, introduction to his thought.

917   Johnson, Allison H. "Editor's Introduction." *Whitehead: The*

Interpretation of Science. Edited by A. H. Johnson. Bobbs–Merrill, 1961, XI–XLI.

Science: method of, and objectivity, and religion; philosophy, of science; bifurcation, of nature; space–time: absolute, relative; matter; event; objects: of perception, of science; sense–data; relativity, theory of; abstraction, extensive; points; simultaneity; education; religion; Einstein, Albert.

Whitehead contends that natural science is incapable of providing an adequate understanding of the complexities of the universe because it tends toward excessive abstraction, but that nonetheless its methods and data cannot be ignored by the philosopher.

Review

Malhorta, M. K. *Philosophischer Literatureanzuger,* 16, 1963, 265–268.

918   Johnson, Allison H. "Whitehead on the Uses of Language." *The Relevance of Whitehead.* Edited by Ivor Leclerc. New York: Humanities Press Inc., 1961, 125–141.

Language: uses of, and meaning; symbolism; linguistic analysis.

Whitehead outlines three uses of language: to refer to data, to express emotions, and to influence behavior.

919   Johnson, Allison H. "Alfred North Whitehead." *Architects of Modern Thought.* Toronto: Canadian Broadcasting Corporation, 1962, 41–50.

Whitehead, Alfred North, biography of.

920   Johnson, Allison H. *Whitehead's Theory of Reality.* Boston: Beacon Press. New York: Dover Publications. Gloucester, Massachusetts: Peter Smith, 1962.

Organism, philosophy of; prehensions, theory of; events; actual occasions; God; Whitehead, Alfred North, introduction to his thought.

Reviews

Shalom, A. *Etudes Philosophiques,* 18, 1963, 361–363.

Vasa, A. *Rivista Critica di Storia della Filosofia,* 10, 1955, 303.

921   Johnson, Allison H. "Some Aspects of Whitehead's Social Philosophy." *Philosophy and Phenomenological Research,* 24, 1963, 61–72.

Aims, societal; philosophy: aim of, social.

Whitehead based his metaphysics not only on data of the natural sciences, but also on the social life of human beings. He strongly advocated the responsibility of the philosopher to influence social change for the good.

922   Johnson, Allison H. "Alfred North Whitehead." *Encyclopedia Britannica,* 23, 1967, 486.

Whitehead, Alfred North: biography of, philosophical development of; process philosophy, summary of.

923   Johnson, Allison H.   "Whitehead as Teacher and Philosopher."
        Philosophy and Phenomenological Research, 29, 1969, 351–376.

        Eternal objects; objectification; God: primordial nature of,
        consequent nature of, as actual entity; creativity; Johnson, A.
        H.

        (Johnson's notes from graduate study with Whitehead indicate
        Whitehead's answers to specific questions raised concerning
        central points in his philosophy.)

924   Johnson, Allison H.   *Experiential Realism*.   New York:
        Humanities Press, Inc., 1973.

        Experience: ordinary, and value, and insight; objects, physical;
        causality; space; time; qualities: primary, secondary; deduction;
        induction; nature, and subjectivity; language, ordinary; God;
        Ayer, A. J.; Hume, David; Wittgenstein, Ludwig; realism;
        phenomenology; science.

        (In outlining aspects of his own philosophical scheme the
        author finds himself in agreement with several of the empirical
        insights of Whitehead, although he disparages Whitehead's
        emphasis on speculation.   Among the many topics discussed
        are words, meaning, mind, physical objects, knowledge, and
        values.)

925   Johnson, J. A. Jr.   "A Comparative Study of the Ideas of God in
        the Philosophy of Alfred North Whitehead and Henry Nelson
        Wieman."   *Center*, 2, 1961, 16–37.

        God: concept of, nature of; creativity; Wieman, Henry N.

926   Jonas, H.   "Note on Whitehead's Philosophy of Organism."   *The
        Phenomenon of Life*.   New York: Dell Publishing Co., Inc.,
        1966, 95–96.

        Dualism, metaphysical; death; life; philosophy, of biology;
        Leibniz, Gottfried.

        Whitehead follows Leibniz in reducing the difference between
        life and nonlife to one of degree rather than kind.   As a result
        Whitehead, like Leibniz, loses the important distinction
        between being and nonbeing, and hence has no place for death
        in his system.

927   Jones, W. T.   *A History of Western Philosophy*.   New York:
        Harcourt, Brace and World, 1952, 965–979; 4, 1969, 308–330.

        Whitehead, Alfred North, introduction to his thought.

928   Jordan, J. A.   "A Concept of Self and Value from Whitehead
        and Its Implications for Education."   Unpublished Ph.D.
        dissertation, Emory University, 1959.

        Self, and values; value; philosophy, of education.

929   Jordan, Martin.   *New Shapes of Reality: Aspects of A. N.
        Whitehead's Philosophy*.   London: George Allen and Unwin
        Ltd., 1968.

        Whitehead, Alfred North: introduction to his thought;
        interrelatedness; occasions, of experience; relations, organic;

space–time; God; explanation, and generalization; subject–object; presentational immediacy; causal efficacy; bifurcation, of nature; location, simple; feeling, and process; consciousness; propositions; eternal objects; truth; religion, and solitariness.

(This book, presented as a literary essay without footnotes, is an introduction to more technical studies. Divided into two parts, the first part expounds prominent features of Whitehead's philosophy, the second part deals with Whitehead's particular approach to metaphysics.)

Review

Ford, L. S. *Process Studies*, 1, 1971, 152–153.

930   Jung, Walter. "Über Whiteheads Atomistik der Ereignisse." *Philosophia Naturalis*, 7, 1961–1962, 406–441.

Atomism; events; extensive continuum.

931   Jung, Walter. "Zur Entwicklung von Whiteheads Gottesbegriff." *Zeitschrift für philosophische Forschung*, 19, 1965, 601–636.

God: as principle of limitation, primordial nature of, consequent nature of, and the future, as a society, and the world; *Science and the Modern World*; *Religion in the Making*; *Process and Reality*; metaphysics, and theology; philosophical theology.

932   Kaiser, C. Hillis. "The Continuity of Change." *Journal of Philosophy*, 33, 1936, 628–639, 645–656.

Process philosophy, summary of; perception, theory of; epistemology.

Process philosophy is self–consistent as a cosmology, and demonstrates power and adequacy in solution of certain traditional problems such as causal laws, chance, and aesthetic phenomena.

933   Kambartel, F. "The Universe is More Various, More Hegelian (Zum Weltverständnis bei Hegel und Whitehead)." *Collegium Philosophicum, Studien Joachim Ritter zum 60. Geburtstag*. Basel, Stuttgart: Schwabe, 1965, 72–89.

World; cosmos; God, and world; Hegel, G. W. F.

934   Kao, M. "Huai–T' I–Hei Chih Hsin Hsing–Erh–Shang–Hsueh (The Metaphysics of Whitehead)." *Che–Hsueh P'ing–Lun (Philosophical Review)*, 5, 1933, 12–34.

Whitehead, Alfred North: introduction to his thought.

935   Karlin, Eli. "The Nature of the Individual." *Review of Metaphysics*, 1, 1947, 61–88.

Individual; soul; body; Weiss, Paul; metaphysics.

An adaptation of Weiss' vectoral theory of the individual explains the otherwise insufficient Whiteheadian account of the relation between body and soul.

936   Kattsoff, L. O. *A Philosophy of Mathematics*. Iowa: Iowa State College Press, 1948.

Mathematics: objects of, and logic; logic; philosophy, of mathematics.

937   Kauffman, Alvin H.   "Elan Vital, Nisus, and Creativity as Treated in the Thought of H. Bergson, S. Alexander, and A. N. Whitehead." Unpublished Ph.D. dissertation, Boston University Graduate School, 1952.

Creativity: as principle of novelty, and Bergson's Elan Vital, and Alexander's Nisus, and time, as ultimate; novelty: subjective, objective; Bergson, Henri; Alexander, Samuel; Plato; Aristotle; Plotinus; Thomas Aquinas.

The element of mystery which surrounds both the elan vital of Bergson and the nisus of Alexander is absent in the Whiteheadian analogue to those notions, creativity. However, Whitehead fails to clarify the relation of creativity to actual entities.

938   Kaufman, Maynard.   "Post–Christian Aspects of the Radical Theology." Toward a New Christianity. Edited by Thomas J. J. Altizer. New York: Harcourt, Brace and World, 1967.

Theology: radical, post–liberal; God: transcendence of, death of, as dipolar; Altizer, Thomas J. J.; Robinson, John A. T.

939   Keating, Jerome F.   "Personal Identity in Jonathon Edwards, Ralph Waldo Emerson, and Alfred North Whitehead." Unpublished Ph.D. dissertation, Syracuse University, 1972.

Person, and personal identity; Edwards, Jonathon; Emerson, Ralph Waldo; transcendentalism, American; literature; religion.

940   Kecskemeti, P.   "Whitehead and the Revolt Against Metaphysics." Modern Review, 2, 1948, 247–260. Also in Amerikanishe Rundschall, 4, 1948, 40–50.

Metaphysics: method of, nature of, verification of.

941   Kelly, Anthony J.   "God: How Near a Relation?" Thomist, 34, 1970, 191–229.

God: immutability of, of classical theism, and world; Thomas Aquinas; Ogden, Schubert M.; Hartshorne, Charles; Thomism.

Process philosophy induces Thomists to explicate more fully the real relatedness between God and the world which is implicit within Thomistic categories.

942   Kelly, Anthony J.   "Trinity and Process: Relevance of the Basic Christian Confession of God." Theological Studies, 31, 1970, 393–414.

Trinity: concepts of, as psychological image, as process; Rahner, Karl; Macquarrie, John; theology: Thomism.

The revealed mystery of the Trinity is the process par excellence, and as such is the beginning and end, explanation and support, of the integral human process.

943   Kennard, Kenneth C.   "Whitehead's Contribution to Contemporary Discussion of the Nature of Metaphysics." Unpublished Ph.D. dissertation, Northwestern University, 1966.

Philosophy: and metaphysics, and metaphor, method of; adequacy; coherence; imagination; reason; intuition; Collingwood, R. G.; Kierkegaard, Soren; Lazerowitz; Wittgenstein, Ludwig; Waismann, F.; philosophy, analytic; positivism, logical; existentialism; empiricism.

944   Kennick, William E.   "A Methodological Approach to Metaphysics with Special Reference to the Philosophies of Aristotle, Hume, Dewey, and Whitehead." Unpublished Ph.D. dissertation, Cornell University, 1952.

Metaphysics: nature of, method of; categoreal scheme; God; Aristotle; Hume, David; Dewey, John.

A critical examination of the philosophical methods of Aristotle, Hume, Dewey, and Whitehead can aid in defining the aim and nature of metaphysics.

945   Kerby–Miller, S.   "Causality."   *Philosophical Essays for Alfred North Whitehead*. Edited by F. S. C. Northrop et. al. New York: Russell & Russell, 1936, 67, 174–192.

Causation: efficient, final, as real influence; present, in relation to past; memory; perception, and causal efficacy.

According to the 'regularity theory' of causation a universal correlation between two identifiable events constitutes complete causal explanation.   According to the 'intrinsic connection' theory, there must be a perceived connection between events in order for causation to be affirmed.   Purpose and memory provide kinds of experiences in which the latter type of causal theory is supported.   (The author mentions Whitehead only briefly, suggesting that Whitehead attempts to integrate these two theories of causation.)

946   Kerlin, Michael J.   "'Where God Comes In' for Alfred North Whitehead."   *The Thomist*, 36, 1972, 98–116.

Religion: and religious experience, and intuition of permanence, as aesthetic harmony; philosophy: task of, method of; God: as ground of possibility, as source of value, as principle of aesthetic harmony, as eros; religion.

God comes into Whitehead's philosophy because Whitehead is preoccupied with the religious and aesthetic reading of experience from beginning to end.

947   Keyser, C. J.   *Human Worth of Rigorous Thinking*. New York: Columbia University Press, 1923, 215–227.

Reason: function of, and rationality.

948   King, Hugh R.   "A. N. Whitehead and the Concept of Metaphysics."   *Philosophy of Science*, 14, 1947, 132–151.

Relations, internal; immanence, doctrine of; philosophy, task of; metaphysics; cosmology; epistemology.

Whitehead's notion of internal relations is the metaphysical basis from which may be constructed the philosophy of science, cosmology, and epistemology.

949   King, Hugh R.   "Whitehead's Doctrine of Causal Efficacy."
        Journal of Philosophy, 46, 1949, 85–100.

        Causal efficacy; induction; togetherness; immediacy; Hume,
        David; epistemology: metaphysics.

        Causal efficacy is fundamental in the sense that it is the
        organism's awareness of its own derivation, sustenance, and
        mutual becoming with the other events of its environment.
        But the element of causal feeling within immediate experience
        cannot   itself   be   disclosed   apart   from   metaphysical
        generalizations.

950   Kirkpatrick, Frank G.   "Process or Agent: Models for Self and
        God."   *Thought*, 18, 1973, 33–60.

        Self: unity of, process model of, inadequacy of process model
        of, agent model of; God: satisfaction of, as agent, Cobb's
        interpretation of; prehensions, contemporary in God; language,
        Whitehead's use of; Cobb, John B., Jr.

        The agent model of the human self does more than the
        process model to sustain adequately the notion of God as a
        relating, acting, personal other.

951   Kirkpatrick, Frank G.   "Process or Agent: Two Models for Self
        and God."   Philosophy of Religion and Theology Section
        Papers, American Academy of Religion, 1971, 74–94.

        Self: as series of experiences, and self–transcendence, and
        creativity; self–creativity; agent; freedom: and agency and
        person.

952   Klausner, N. W. and Kuntz, Paul G.   *Philosophy: The Study of
        Alternative Beliefs.*   New York: Macmillan Company, 1961.

        Mind, and matter; concreteness, fallacy of misplaced; duration;
        events; interrelatedness; eternal objects; self–creativity; God, as
        principle of concretion.

        In attempting to relate the order of nature to the nature of
        mind   Whitehead   exemplifies   one   of   the   chief   aims   of
        metaphysics.   The success of his endeavor can be judged by
        the extent to which it does justice to every aspect of
        experience.

953   Klausner, S. Z.   "The Relation between A. N. Whitehead and
        Kurt Lewin (In Hebrew)."   *Iyyun*, 6, 1955, 142–155.

        Personality, theory of; ego; self; concrescence; psychology;
        social sciences.

954   Kliever, Lonnie D.   "A New Natural Theology."   *Philosophy of
        Religion and Theology: 1972; American Academy of Religion
        Section Papers.*   Missoula, Montana: Scholars Press, 1972,
        82–103.

        Faith, and reason; revelation; Cobb, John B., Jr.; Gilkey,
        Langdon; metaphysics; theology, natural.

        Secularism   and   mythopoeic   consciousness   challenge
        metaphysical systems.   Christian natural theology, as an

immanent metaphysics, offers one mode of retaining the significance of religious symbols for contemporary humanity.

955   Kline, George L., editor. "Whitehead Centennial Issue." *Journal of Philosophy*, 58, 1961, 505–576.

Whitehead, Alfred North, biography of; becoming, theory of; strains; past; beauty; God, and time; algebra; logic; deduction; extension; mathematics.

(George Kline was the special editor of this commemorative issue. See the individual entries under Chappell, Chiaraviglio, Christian, Hocking, Lawrence, Leblanc, Leclerc, and Palter.)

956   Kline, George L., editor. *Alfred North Whitehead: Essays on His Philosophy*. Englewood Cliffs, New Jersey: Prentice–Hall, 1963.

Whitehead, Alfred North, biography of; ethics; aesthetics; epistemology; metaphysics; cosmology; philosophical theology.

(These essays clarify and criticize the theoretical development of Whitehead's central philosophical ideas. See entries under Chappell, Chiaraviglio, Christian, Gross, Hall, Hartshorne, Hocking, Lawrence, Leblanc, Leclerc, Lowe, Norman, Palter, Robson, Rorty, Sherburne, and Vlastos.)

957   Kline, George L. "Whitehead in the Non–English–Speaking World." *Process and Divinity*. Edited by W. L. Reese and E. Freeman. La Salle, Illinois: Open Court Publishing Co., 1964, 235–268.

Philosophy, of science; epistemology; metaphysics; experience; perception; Husserl, Edmund; Heidegger, Martin; Wahl, Jean; Russell, Bertrand.

New publications show that the prospects for an increase of study and interest in Whitehead's philosophy in the non–English speaking world continue to grow.

958   Kline, George L. "Bibliography of Writings By and About Alfred North Whitehead in Languages Other Than English." *Process and Divinity*. Edited by W. L. Reese and E. Freeman. La Salle, Illinois: Open Court Publishing Co., 1964, 593–609.

Whitehead, Alfred North, bibliography of.

959   Kline, George L. "Form, Concrescence, and Concretum: A Neo–Whiteheadian Analysis." *Southern Journal of Philosophy*, 7, 1969, 351–360.

Agency; causal efficacy; concrescence; transition; prehensions, contiguous; metaphysics.

Whitehead makes contradictory and ambiguous statements concerning completed and concrescing actualities. A consistent neo–Whiteheadian analysis makes a sharp distinction between the two actualities, positing all agency in the concrescing entity, and restricting prehensions to contiguous occasions.

960   Kogan, Jacob. "Arte y metafísica en Whitehead." *Cuadernos Americanos*, 22, 1963, 75–119.

Aesthetics; language: uses of, limitations of; appearance, and reality; beauty; truth; harmony; contrasts; intensity; adventure; logic.

Whitehead's theory of art may be explicated through his understanding of the relations between language and reality, reality and appearance, and truth and beauty.

961 Koort, A. *Kaasaegset Filosoofist (Contemporary Philosophy).* Estonia: Akdeemline Kooperativ, 1938.

Philosophy; process philosophy, summary of; Whitehead, Alfred North: philosophical development of.

962 Kosaka, Masaaki. *Gendai Tetsugaku.* Tokyo: Kobundo, 1952, 63–80.

Whitehead, Alfred North: and American philosophy; concreteness, fallacy of misplaced; consciousness; subject; ego; James, William.

963 Kraus, E. M. "Individual and Society: A Whiteheadian Critique." *Persons and Community.* Edited by R. J. Roth. New York: Fordham University Press, 1975, 103–132.

Individual; self; society; culture.

964 Kremer, R. "La evolution du neo–realisme en Angleterre." *Revue Neo–Scholastique de Philosophie*, 30, 1928, 5–17.

Whitehead, Alfred North: introduction to his thought; neo–realism.

965 Krikorian, Y. H. "The Philosophy of Alfred North Whitehead." *Recent Perspectives in American Philosophy.* The Hague: Martinus Nijhoff, 1973, 63–70.

Whitehead, Alfred North: and American philosophy, introduction to his thought.

966 Kruse, Cornelius. "A filosofia norteamericana contemporania." *Revista Brasileira de Filosofia*, 7, 1957, 173–186.

Philosophy, and science; naturalism; Santayana, George; Dewey, John.

(The author compares the naturalistic philosophy of Whitehead with those of Dewey and Santayana.)

967 Kuhń, Helmut. "Die Philosophie in den Vereinigten Staaten." *Studium Generale*, 1, 1948, 426–434.

Process philosophy, summary of; nature, bifurcation of; science, philosophy of; mathematics.

968 Kultgen, J. H. "The 'Future of Metaphysics' of Peirce and Whitehead." Kant–Studien, 51, 1959–1966, 285–293.

Metaphysics; reason: practical, speculative; Kant, Immanuel; Peirce, Charles S.

(This paper contrasts the thought of Whitehead and Peirce with that of Kant in order to suggest the direction metaphysics might take in light of Kant's critiques.)

969 Kultgen, J. H. "Whitehead's Epistemology 1915–1917." *Journal of the History of Philosophy*, 4, 1966, 43–61.

Epistemology, in Whitehead's early writings.

970   Kultgen, J. H.   "Intentionality and the Publicity of the
       Perceptual   World."   *Philosophy   and   Phenomenological
       Research*, 23, 1973, 503–513.

       Intentionality; perception; phenomenology.

971   Kuntz, Paul G.   "Whitehead on Order."   *Nous*, 8, 1961, 1–12.

       Order: teleological, and nature.

972   Kuntz, Paul G.   "Religion of Order or Religion of Chaos?"
       Religion in Life, 35, 1966, 433–449.

       Order: and chaos, faith in; chaos: and mysticism, and freedom;
       Berdyaev, Nicolas; Hartshorne, Charles; religion.

       The truth of the religion of order and the truth of the religion
       of chaos may only be grasped coherently together in synthesis.

973   Kuntz, Paul G.   "Omnipotence: Tradition and Revolt in
       Philosophical Theology."   *New Scholasticism*, 42, 1968, 270–279.

       God: power of, as persuasive power, religious availability of;
       Aquinas, Thomas; philosophical theology.

       The Thomistic development of God's power continues to raise
       questions concerning what God can and cannot be said to do.
       Human beings are confronted with the need to defend, destroy,
       or revise the Thomistic tradition.

974   Kuntz, Paul G., editor.   *The Concept of Order.*   Seattle,
       Washington: University of Washington Press, 1968.

       Order: causal, teleological and nature, and novelty, and chaos;
       society; ethics; science, history of.

975 . Kuntz, Paul G.   "What Do You Mean by 'God'?"   *Personalist*,
       50, 1969, 393–397.

       God: concepts of, proofs for, as worthy of worship; theology,
       and philosophy; Richardson, Herbert W.; Hartshorne, Charles;
       theology.

       The contrasts and agreements in the works of Hartshorne and
       Richardson present grounds for a fruitful dialogue on the issue
       of God.

976   Kuntz,   Paul   G.   "The   Dialectic   of   Historicism   and
       Anti–Historicism."   *Monist*, 53, 1969, 656–669.

       Method: historical, philosophical; philosophy, history of;
       Wittgenstein, Ludwig; Gilson, Etienne; Mill, John Stuart;
       Russell, Bertrand; philosophy; history.

       Whitehead's *Science and the Modern World* illustrates the
       harmonious utilization of both history and philosophy.

977   Kuntz, Paul G.   "God and the World Order: The Present
       Situation."   *Philosophy Forum*, 8, 1970, 33–57.

       God, as source of order; nature, order of; theodicy; Hume,
       David; existentialism; religion, and science.

       In his answer to Hume, Whitehead develops more adequate

notions of God and of order, bridging the contemporary gulf between religion and science.

978   Kuntz, Paul G. "Introduction." *Lotze's System of Philosophy.* George Santayana, with an introduction and Lotze bibliography by Paul G. Kuntz. Bloomington, Indiana: Indiana University Press, 1971, 69–83.

Process; event; pluralism; self, as series of experiences; teleology; language, and subject–predicate mode of expression; Lotze, Rudolph H.; idealism; process philosophy.

Significant parallels exist between Whitehead's philosophy and that of Rudolph Lotze. The dominating philosophic problem in both Lotze and Whitehead is that of the many and the one, the relations between the parts that make them wholes, and the problem of order. Lotze, like Whitehead, understands the basic units of the universe to be events that require one another. The real relation between such events, for Lotze as for Whitehead, is causal efficacy.

979   Kurtz, P., editor. *American Philosophy in the XXth Century: A Sourcebook from Pragmatism to Philosophical Analysis.* New York: Macmillan Company, 1966, 263–305.

Philosophy, American; pragmatism; realism; Whitehead, Alfred North: introduction to his thought.

980   Kuspit, Donald B. "Whitehead on Divinity." *Archiv Fuer Philosophie* (Stuttgart), 11, 1961, 64–171.

God: and categoreal scheme, and world, as primordial, as consequent; Hegel, G. W. F.; metaphysics.

Critics of Whitehead's concept of God generally view the concept as systematic or as organic, but never as systematically organic. Considered as systematically organic, God exemplifies the categories, and illustrates the active reciprocity between God and the World.

981   Kuspit, Donald B. "Whitehead's Cosmology." *Archiv Fuer Philosophie* (Stuttgart), 12, 1962, 110–122.

Philosophy: aim of, and science; cosmology.

Cosmos in Whitehead is an extension of his idea of environment, which in turn is an extension of his idea of communication.

982   Kuspit, Donald B. "Whitehead's God and Metaphysics." *Essays in Philosophy.* University Park, Pennsylvania: Pennsylvania State University Press, 1962, 183–219.

God: and categoreal scheme, function of, primordial nature of, consequent nature of.

983   Lachs, J. "God's Actions and Nature's Ways." *Idealistic Studies,* 3, 1973, 223–228.

God: and world, as cause; Cobb, John B. Jr.

(The author criticizes John Cobb's article "Natural Causality and Divine Action" on the grounds that it fails to provide an alternative to the Newtonian–Humean theory of causation and that it fails to show what kind of explanation results from claiming the presence of divine agency in the world. Cobb's argument that the ways of nature can be explained in part by reference to divine action is invalid.)

984   Lackey, Douglas P. "The Whitehead Correspondence." *Journal of the Bertrand Russell Archives*, 5, 1972, 14–16.

Whitehead: biography of.

985   Lackner, Vincent F. "Alfred North Whitehead's Conception of Scientific Method." Unpublished dissertation, University of Toronto, 1962.

Science: method of, and philosophy; objects, of science; induction; laws, of nature; theory; explanation; hypothesis; mathematics, and science; congruence; measure; logic.

986   Ladriére, Jean. "Langage scientifique et langage spéculatif." *Revue Philosophique de Louvain*, 69, 1971, 250–282.

Significance, doctrine of; field theory; language; interpretation; propositions; reason, speculative; imagination; Kant, Immanuel; epistemology; philosophy, speculative; semantics.

987   Lafleur, L. J. "If God Were Eternal." *Journal of Religion*, 20, 1940, 382–389.

God: as eternal, and time.

988   Lamont, Corliss. "Equivocation on Religious Issues." *Journal of Religion*, 14, 1934, 412–427.

God: concepts of, religious adequacy of; immortality, personal; Wieman, Henry Nelson; religion.

"God" and "immortality" are perennial philosophical issues. Whitehead and Wieman equivocate on these issues by redefining both terms beyond practical usefulness.

989   Lamprecht, Sterling P. "Sense Qualities and Material Things." *Philosophical Review*, 38, 1929, 23–41.

Dualism: methodological, metaphysical; substance; qualities, sense; Dewey, John; Locke, John; Descartes, Rene; metaphysics; epistemology; realism.

The fusion of methodological dualism with medieval notions of substance has been a largely uncriticized supposition of much modern philosophy. Such dualism must be replaced with a concept of the relational event as the ultimate unit of reality.

990   Lamprecht, Sterling P. *Our Philosophical Traditions*. New York: Appleton–Century–Crofts, 1955, 476–486.

Whitehead, Alfred North: philosophical development of, evaluation of; process philosophy: summary of.

991   Langbauer, Delmar. "Sanatana Dharma and Modern Philosophy: A Study of Indian and Whiteheadian Thought." Unpublished Ph.D. dissertation, Claremont Graduate School, 1970.

God: consequent nature of, primordial nature of; creativity, and Nirguna Brahman; theism, Indian; Isvara; Ramanuja; Madhva;

Shankara; Bhagavadgita; Vedas; Upanishads; yoga, disciplines of; philosophy, Indian; metaphysics.

The relation between the transcendent absolute (Nirguna Brahman) and the creator god (Isvara) is a central problem in Indian philosophy, and a central issue for the Indian theist, Ramanuja. A creative dialog between Whitehead and Ramanuja shows that Whitehead's distinction between Creativity and God can be of aid in interpreting the above relation.

992   Langbauer, Delmar. "Indian Theism and Process Philosophy." *Process Studies*, 2, 1972, 5–28.

God: consequent nature of, primordial nature of; Indian philosophy, and God; creativity, and Nirguna Brahman; theism, Indian; Isvara; Upanishads; Ramanuja, Shankara; philosophy: Indian, comparative; theology.

In making a distinction between creativity and God, Whitehead allows for resolution of the traditional Indian problem of the relation of Brahman and Isvara.

993   Langer, Susanne K. *Philosophy in a New Key: A Study in the Symbolism of Reason, Rite, and Art.* Cambridge: Harvard University Press, 1942.

Symbolism: and feeling, and freedom; aesthetics.

994   Langeveld, M. J. "Some Considerations on Whitehead's 'Aims of Education'." *Algeheen Nederlands Tijdschrift Voor Wijsbegeerte En Psychologie*, 58, 1966, 95–105.

Aims of Education; education, purpose of; culture, philosophy of; education.

Whitehead's essay on the aims of education is a call to teachers to teach for understanding. However, as an essay on the aims of education, it lacks consequence, clarity and unity.

995   Lango, John W. "The Logic of Simultaneity." *Journal of Philosophy*, 66, 1969, 340–350.

Relativity, special theory of; simultaneity: pre–relativistic, relativistic; duration; Putnam, Hilary; Carnap, Rudolf; Stein, Howard; philosophy, of science; physics, relativity.

Despite its nontransitivity, relativistic topological simultaneity is a relation by means of which space–time is decomposable into what may aptly be characterized as "instantaneous cross sections."

996   Lango, John W. "Towards Clarifying Whitehead's Theory of Concrescence." *Transactions of the Charles Peirce Society*, 7, 1971, 150–167.

Concrescence; prehensions: concrescence of, asymmetry of; subjective forms: mutual sensitivity of, symmetry of; metaphysics.

The use of logic clarifies the relations between prehensions and subjective forms in the concrescence of an actual entity.

997   Lango, John W.   "The Relatedness of Eternal Objects in
         Whitehead's *Process and Reality."   Process Studies, 1, 1971,*
         124–128.

         Eternal objects: as relational, relational essence of, universal
         relativity of, ingression of, and patterning, and God; *Process*
         and Reality.

         Eternal objects in *Process and Reality* are interrelated by
         patterning or diversity.

998   Lango, John W.   *Whitehead's Ontology.*   Albany, New York:
         State University of New York Press, 1972.

         Categories of Existence; logic; language, formal; relativity,
         principle of; synonty; entities, types of; actual entities;
         concrescence; prehensions; subjective form; synthesis; contrast;
         eternal   objects,   relational   essence   of;   propositions;
         presentational immediacy.

         In Whitehead's ontology 'being' is a 'relation between entities'
         which can be termed 'synonty'. The various types of entity in
         Whitehead's thought can be defined in terms of the formal
         properties of synonty.   What emerges is a logic of relations.
         (This is the author's Ph.D. dissertation at Yale University in
         1969.)

999   Laszlo, Ervin.   *Essential Society: An Ontological Reconstruction.*
         The Hague, Netherlands: Martinus Nijhoff, 1963, 3, 36, 45,
         152.

         The Function of Reason;   value; society, human; politics;
         sociology.

         Whitehead defines the basic premise of human existence as a
         three–fold urge: to live, to live well, to live better.   A scheme
         of political axiology can be based on this definition.   'To live'
         and 'to live well' are related to the existing conditions of social
         organization.   'To live better' corresponds to the optimum
         fulfillment of all needs toward which society aims.

1000   Laszlo, Ervin.   *Beyond Scepticism and Realism: A Constructive*
         Exploration of Husserlian and Whiteheadian Methods of
         Inquiry.   The Hague, Netherlands: Martinus Nijhoff, 1966.

         Philosophy, method of; epistemology; knowledge; experience;
         realism;   being;   world,   physical;   process;   sense–data;   eternal
         objects;   relatedness;   skepticism;   consciousness;   mind;
         intentionality; Husserl, Edmund; Plato; Descartes, Rene; Ayer,
         A. J.; phenomenology; linguistic analysis.

         By comparing and contrasting Whitehead's objectivist realism
         with   Husserl's   subjectivist   skepticism,   the   problem   of
         consistently accounting for the world of physical objects and
         that of subjective sensation can be illumined.   The root–axiom
         in Whitehead's philosophy is 'being', and the heuristic principle
         is   'process'.   The   root–axiom   of   Husserl's   philosophy   is
         'consciousness', and the heuristic principle is 'intentionality'.
         Whitehead emphasizes the manner in which   the experiencing

agent is in the world; Husserl emphasizes the fact that the world is in the experiencing agent.

1001   Laszlo, Ervin. "Idealista Es Tudomanyos Komponensek Jelentoessege Whitehead Metafizikajaban (The Significance of Idealistic and Scientific Elements in Whitehead's Metaphysics)." *Magyar Filozofiai Szemle*, 10, 1966, 285–294.

Whitehead, Alfred North: philosophy of science; idealism.

1002   Laszlo, Ervin. *La métaphysique de Whitehead: recherche sur les Prolongements anthropologiques.* Translated by Christiane Harzic. The Hague: Martinus Nijhoff, 1970.

Experience, human; prehension; concrescence; feedback: homeostatic, sensory, meta–sensory; structures: biological, cognitive, anthropological; adaption; order; anthropology; biology.

1003   Laszlo, Ervin. *Introduction to Systems Philosophy: Toward a New Paradigm of Contemporary Thought.* New York: Gordon and Breach, 1972.

Systems, theory of; consciousness; value; philosophy, social.

1004   Latour, Jean–Jacques. "La nature dans la pensée de Whitehead." *Idée de monde et philosophie de la nature. Recherches de philosophie, VII.* Edited by Régis Jolivet, Maurice Nédpncelle, Stanislas Breton, Jean Châtillon, Dominique Dubarle, and Jean–Jacques Latour. Bruges, Belgium: Presses Saint–Augustine for Desclée de Brouwer, 1966.

The Concept of Nature; nature: bifurcation of, diversification of; time; events; relations; space–time; abstraction, extensive; Bergson, Henri; Einstein, Albert.

Approached metaphysically, the definition of the concept of nature raises the question of the intelligibility of relations in their different modalities.

1005   Lavelle, Louis. "Le réalisme de Whitehead." *Panorama des doctrines philosophiques*, paris: Albin Michel, 1967, 140–149.

Process philosophy, summary of; prehension; objects; events; subject; realism; materialism.

1006   Lawrence, John S. "A. N. Whitehead's Panpsychical Theory of the Individual Existent." Unpublished Ph.D. dissertation, University of Texas at Austin, 1964.

Panpsychism; subjectivism; subjectivist principle, reformed; experience; substance.

Whitehead's 'panpsychism' lacks philosophical credibility.

1007   Lawrence, John S. "Whitehead's Failure." *Southern Journal of Philosophy*, 7, 1969–1970, 427–435.

Prehensions; time, epochal theory of; phases, genetic; metaphysics.

The key to Whitehead's system of intrinsically relative existents, the prehension, proves to be incoherent.

1008   Lawrence, Nathaniel M. "The Development of Whitehead's

Epistemology." Unpublished Ph.D. dissertation, Harvard University, 1949.

Epistemology; truth; causality; perception; extensive abstraction.

1009 Lawrence, Nathaniel. "Whitehead's Method of Extensive Abstraction." *Philosophy of Science*, 17, 1950, 142–163.

Abstraction, extensive; pole: physical, mental; methodology; *Concept of Nature; Enquiry Concerning the Principles of Natural Knowledge; Process and Reality*; philosophy, of science.

The incompatibilities between conceptualistic and realistic strands implied in Whitehead's early method of extensive abstraction are resolved in *Process and Reality*.

1010 Lawrence, Nathaniel. "Locke and Whitehead on Individual Entities." *Review of Metaphysics*, 4, 1950, 215–238.

Bifurcation, of nature; perception, theory of; individuals; Locke, John.

While Whitehead is able to avoid the qualitative difficulties of Locke on the problem of individuals, he gets into an analogous problem with regard to the quantitative delineation of an individual. This leads him to a bifurcation remarkably similar to Locke's.

1011 Lawrence, Nathaniel M. "Single Location, Simple Location, and Misplaced Concreteness." *Review of Metaphysics*, 7, 1953, 225–247.

Location: fallacy of simple, single; ingression; concreteness, misplaced (fallacy of); immanence, mutual; Alston, William.

The denial of simple location is the assertion of neither multiple nor complex location; it is the assertion of complex ingression, of which location is one single feature.

1012 Lawrence, Nathaniel. *Whitehead's Philosophical Development: A Critical History of the Background of Process and Reality.* Berkeley: University of California Press, 1956. New York: Greenwood Press, 1968.

Whitehead: philosophical development of, introduction to his thought, early works of, philosophy of science; *An Enquiry Concerning the Principles of Natural Knowledge; The Concept of Nature; The Principle of Relativity; Science and the Modern World; Religion in the Making; Symbolism, its Meaning and Effect; Adventures of Ideas; Modes of Thought*; perception, and relation between mind and nature; objects, of science; events; abstraction, extensive; mind, and nature; relativity, theory of; causality; order; law; philosophy: aim of, method of; actual occasions; location, simple; interconnectedness; truth; freedom; value; God; realism; idealism.

Whitehead's philosophical development can be divided into three periods: the early philosophy of science from 1919 to 1922, the transition to cosmology from 1925 to 1927, and the mature cosmology from 1929 to 1938. Whitehead's thought develops from an attempted isolation of the problems of the philosophy of natural science to an inclusion of these problems in the larger field of cosmology. Within the realm of cosmology, Whitehead focuses his attention on the notion of value.

Reviews

Leclerc, I. *Review of Metaphysics*, 11, 1957, 68–93.

Murphy, A. E. *Philosophical Review*, 67, 1958, 261–264.

1013   Lawrence, Nathaniel. "Time, Value, and the Self." *The Relevance of Whitehead*. Edited by Ivor Leclerc. New York: Humanities Press Inc., 1961, 145–166.

Value, intrinsic; self, and value; time, and value; past, as alterable.

(By elaborating Whitehead's thesis that the primary type of experience involves value, the author discusses the manner in which past events are alterable.)

1014   Lawrence, Nathaniel. "The Vision of Beauty and the Temporality of Deity in Whitehead's Philosophy." *Alfred North Whitehead: Essays on His Philosophy*. Edited by George L. Kline. Englewood Cliffs, New Jersey: Prentice–Hall, Inc., 1963, 168–178.

God: religious availability of; experience, religious; aesthetics; beauty; language, religious; Ely, Stephen; Plato.

1015   Lawrence, Nathaniel. "Whitehead's Educational Philosophy and Mechanized Teaching." *Philosophy of Education Proceedings*, 23, 1967, 199–215.

Education: stages of, as self–development, mechanized; education; philosophy, of education.

Teaching machines are appropriate only during the second stage of educational development, that of precision. To use such machines at other stages undercuts the basically social nature of education.

1016   Lawrence, Nathaniel. *Alfred North Whitehead: A Primer of his Philosophy*. New York: Twayne Publishers Inc., 1974.

Organism, philosophy of; actual occasion; concrescence, phases of; eternal objects; existence, categories of; obligation, categories of; nature: order of, bifurcation of; novelty; value, and valuation; life; society; mind, mind–body problem; perception; causation; presentational immediacy; causal efficacy; symbolic reference; consciousness; propositions; judgements; transmutation; feeling: physical, mental; aesthetics; harmony; intensity; division: coordinate, genetic; time: epochal theory of, passage of; *Process and Reality*; *Symbolism*; *Religion in the Making*; Whitehead, Alfred North: introduction to his thought, biography of; God, primordial nature of, consequent nature of; philosophy, method of; Kant, Immanuel.

(The first three chapters of the work include a biography, a general statement of the principal aspects of Whitehead's philosophy, and a presentation of how these principles are embodied in the coming into existence of an actual occasion. The remaining six chapters treat principal topics of *Process and Reality*.)

1017   Leblanc, Hugues. "The Algebra of Logic and the Theory of Deduction." *Alfred North Whitehead: Essays on His Philosophy*. Edited by George L. Kline. Englewood Cliffs, New Jersey: Prentice–Hall, Inc., 1963, 27–32.

Logic, symbolic; mathematics.

(The author explains two ways of converting postulates for the Boolian class calculus into postulates for propositional calculus.)

1018   Leclerc, Ivor. "Internal Relatedness in Whitehead: A Rejoinder." *Review of Metaphysics*, 6, 1952, 297–299.

Immanence, mutual; relatedness, internal; Alston, William P.

If one actual entity be internally related to another, it does not follow that the latter must be internally related to the former. Thus Whitehead's principle of internal relatedness does not reduce to a monistic all–embracing totality of process. (Written in response to William P. Alston, "Internal Relatedness and Pluralism in Whitehead.")

1019   Leclerc, Ivor. "Whitehead's Transformation of the Concept of Substance." *Philosophical Quarterly*, 3, 1953, 225–243.

Substance; creativity; ultimate, category of; actual entity: as activity, as substance, as epochal; Aristotle; Locke, John.

The insight that the nature of actuality is to be understood in terms of its activity and not of spatio–temporal adventures is realized in Whitehead's theory of the actual entity.

"Whitehead: La transformación del concepto de substancia." *Convivium*, 1, 1956, 181–208.

1020   Leclerc, Ivor. "Whitehead's Philosophy." *Review of Metaphysics*, 11, 1957, 68–93.

Whitehead, Alfred North: introduction to his thought, early theory of; mind, and nature; dualism; Lawrence, Nathaniel.

Contrary to Mr. Lawrence, Whitehead's basic problems during the early period were not epistemological, but rather cosmological. Whitehead's thought presents an increasing realization of the crucial relevance of metaphysics for both science and the philosophy of science. (Written in response to Nathaniel Lawrence, *Whitehead's Philosophical Development: A Critical History of the Background of "Process and Reality."*)

1021   Leclerc, Ivor. *Whitehead's Metaphysics: An Introductory Exposition*. London: George Allen & Unwin, Ltd., 1958, 1965.

Philosophy: method of, aim of; metaphysics; ontology; ontological principle; actual entity; being; act, and Aristotle; becoming; substance; process; atomicity; actuality, epochal theory of; creativity, as ultimate; concrescence; eternal objects:

178 WHITEHEAD BIBLIOGRAPHY

as forms of definiteness, as potential; giveness; relativity, category of; potentiality: as abstract, as real; objectification; objective immortality; experience; subjectivist principle, reformed; relations: internal, external; presentational immediacy; causal efficacy; prehension; subject, as superject; feelings: physical, conceptual; valuation, conceptual; prehensions: pure, hybrid; subjective aim; causation, self; analysis, genetic; God: primordial nature of, consequent nature of; value; order; society; Aristotle: and form, and ousia, and being, and substance; Plato; Zeno; Descartes, Rene; Leibniz, G. W.; Locke, John; Hume, David.

In seeking 'to conceive a complete fact' Whitehead aligns himself with the classical metaphysical tradition. The original nature of his thought can thus be understood through a comparison with and contrast to the questions and answers of the major thinkers of western thought.

Reviews

Anonymous. *Revue de Metaphysique et de Morale*, 65, 1960, 363.

Burnheim, J. *Philosophical Studies*, 8, 1958, 188–191.

Chappell, V. C. *Review of Metaphysics*, 13, 1959–1960, 278–304.

Copleston, F. C. *Gregorianum*, 40, 1959, 785–786.

Deledale, G. *Etudes Philosophiques*, 13, 1958, 553.

Hartman, K. *Kant–Studien*, 51, 1959–1960, 219–225.

Hepburn, R. W. *Philosophy*, 35, 1960, 80–81.

Johnson, A. H. *Philosophy and Phenomenological Research*, 20, 1959–1960, 124–126.

Jung, W. *Philologische Rundschau eine Verte Jahreschrift für Philosophische Kritik*, 6, 1958, 182–214.

Lawrence, N. *Philosophical Review*, 68, 1959, 540–542.

Lowe, V. *Philosophy of Science*, 27, 1960, 410–414.

Mays, W. *Philosophical Quarterly*, 10, 1960, 284–285.

Ramsey, I. T. *Church Quarterly Review*, 160, 1959, 399–401.

Schiavone, M. *Giornale Di Metafisica*, 15, 1960, 188–189.

Simmons, J. R. *Journal of Philosophy*, 56, 1959, 550–552.

Stokes, W. E., S. J. *Modern Schoolman*, 36, 1958–1959, 289–290.

1022 Leclerc, Ivor. "Being and Becoming in Whitehead's Philosophy." *Kant–Studien*, 51, 1959–1960, 427–437.

Being, and becoming; actuality, and potentiality; creativity, and actuality; ousia; eternal objects; actual entities; Parmenides; Plato; Aristotle; Leibniz, Gottfried; Spinoza, Benedict.

In his mature metaphysics Whitehead deals with the traditional metaphysical problem of 'being' as such. Whitehead is in agreement with Aristotle, Spinoza, and Leibniz in holding that the primary sense of being is act, action, and agency.

1023   Leclerc, Ivor.   "Form and Actuality."   *The Relevance of Whitehead*, New York: Humanities Press Inc., 1961, 169–189.

Form; eternal object; actuality; creativity; matter, as prime; substance; objective immortality; Aristotle; Plato.

Whereas Aristotle ascribes act to form, Whitehead holds that form as such cannot act.

1024   Leclerc, Ivor.   "The Structure of Form."   *Revue Internationale de Philosophie*, 15, 1961, 185–203.

Eternal objects: structure of, relational essence of, generic, continuity of; Christian, William A.

Structural relatedness is involved in the very nature of forms, and hence cannot be derivative from God's primordial envisagement. The relatedness is both general and complete, involving generic as well as particular possibilities.

1025   Leclerc, Ivor, editor.   *The Relevance of Whitehead, Philosophical Essays in Commemoration of the Centenary of the Birth of Alfred North Whitehead.*   London: George Allen & Unwin, Ltd., 1961. New York: Humanities Press Inc., 1961.

Reason; philosophy, method of; judgments; language, Whitehead's use of; time; value; form; actuality; "On Mathematical Concepts of the Material World"; aesthetics; objective immortality; empiricism; humanism; theology.

(See individual entries under Christian, Fitch, Hartshorne, Johnson, Lawrence, Leclerc, Lowe, Martin (Gottfried), Mays, Schaper, Wein, Weiss, Wightman, Williams.)

Reviews

Bell, D. R.   *Mind*, 71, 1962, 422–424.

Emmet, D. M.   *Philosophical Review*, 72, 1963, 120–122.

Harris, E. E.   *Philosophy*, 40, 1965, 60–67.

Heinemann, F. H.   *Hibbert Journal*, 59, 1969, 364.

Kline, G. L.   *Journal of Philosophy*, 58, 1961, 823–827.

Nowell–Smith, P. H.   *Spectator*, April 7, 1961.

Perez, B. O.   *Convivium*, 1962, 199–200.

Roberts, G. W.   *Month*, 26, 1961, 172–175.

Ruytinx, J.   *Revue Internationale de Philosophie*, 56–57, 1961, 289–293.

1026   Leclerc, Ivor.   "Whitehead and the Problem of Extension."   *Alfred North Whitehead: Essays on His Philosophy.* Edited by George L. Kline. Englewood Cliffs, New Jersey: Prentice–Hall, Inc., 1963, 117–123.

Extension; continuity; space–time; actuality, and potentiality; Descartes, Rene; Leibniz, Gottfried.

1027   Leclerc, Ivor.   "Whitehead and the Theory of Form."   *Process and Divinity: Philosophical Essays Presented to Charles Hartshorne.* Edited by W. L. Reese and E. Freeman. La Salle, Illinois: Open Court Publishing Co., 1964, 127–137.

Actuality, and potentiality; eternal objects: as potential, relations between, as data of conceptual feeling; prehension, conceptual; continuity; form; decision; Aristotle.

Whitehead construes form as that aspect in the nature of things whereby there is potentiality in contrast to actuality. Form qua form can be apprehended only in thought, not in experience.

1028   Leclerc, Ivor.   "Kant's Second Antinomy, Leibniz and Whitehead." *Review of Metaphysics*, 20, 1966, 25–41.

Actuality, as discrete; possibility, as continuum; continuum, extensive; Zeno; Leibniz, G. W.; Kant, Immanuel.

Whitehead's theory of the metaphysical roles of actuality and possibility in unitary actuality leads to his solution to the problem of the "composition of the continuum," which in Kant's view led inevitably to an antinomy.

1029   Leclerc, Ivor.   "Kants Antinomie der Teilung und die Metaphysik von Whitehead." *Kant Studien*, 56, 1966, 289–391.

Actuality; possibility: as continuous, ontological status of; continuum, extensive; division; monads; Kant, Immanuel; Leibniz, G. W.

With the help of a special theory of the metaphysical role of actuality and possibility (in his notions of extensive continuum with infinite divisibility) Whitehead sought to resolve the problem of continuity which for Kant only lead to an antinomy, to an "unavoidable contradiction of reason."

1030   Leclerc, Ivor.   "The Problem of the Physical Existent." *International Philosophical Quarterly*, 9, 1969, 40–62.

Existence, physical; object, physical; society: corporeal, as compound; philosophy, of science; Aristotle; Leibniz, Gottfried.

Although both Whitehead and Leibniz see the necessity of interpreting a body or society as something more than an aggregate of individual components, neither succeed in doing so.

1031   Leclerc, Ivor.   "Whitehead and the Problem of God." *Southern Journal of Philosophy*, 7, 1969, 447–455.

God: concept of, as creator, transcendence of, and world; Eriugena, John Scotus; theology, medieval.

Whitehead's conception of God and the many beings constituting one total process of necessary interrelatedness is close, in many respects, to the theology of John Scotus Eriugena.

1032   Leclerc, Ivor.   "Whitehead and Physical Existence: A Rejoinder." *International Philosophical Quarterly*, 10, 1970, 126–128.

Existence, physical; society: and social organization, corporeal; Treash, Gordon.

(This article is written in response to one written by Gordon Treash. The author argues that Treash inadvertently supports his own claim that Whitehead could not adequately account for the nature of corporeal bodies.)

1033 Leclerc, Ivor. "A Rejoinder to Justus Buchler." *Process Studies*, 1, 1971, 55–59.

Existence, categories of; ontological principle; actuality; potentiality; Buchler, Justus; Aristotle.

Justus Buchler's criticism of Whitehead's move from the delineation of types of existence to the assignment of priorities among the types is invalid. Actual entities should be assigned priority over other types of existence because they alone have agency.

1034 Leclerc, Ivor. *The Nature of Physical Existence.* London: George Allen & Unwin, Ltd., 1972. New York: Humanities Press Inc., 1972.

Reviews

Anonymous. *Choice*, 9, 1973, 1603.

Anonymous. *Times Literary Supplement*, Feb. 23, 1973, 218.

Bargeliotes, L. *Platon*, 26, 1975, 51–52.

Dubois, P. *Revue Philosophique*, 163, 1973, 363–364.

Jouhnson, A. H. *Dialog*, 12, 1973, 714–717.

Mays, W. *Mind*, 83, 1974, 305–307.

Mercier, A. *Erasmus*, 25, 1973, 716–721.

North, J. D. *Philosophical Quarterly (Scotland)*, 23, 1973, 362–363.

Turck, D. *Studia Leibniziana*, 5, 1973, 294–297.

Turck, D. *Philosophia Naturalis*, 15, 1974, 152–154.

Wagner, Hans. *Studi Internazionali di Filosofia*, 1974; *Archiv für Geschichte der Philosophie*, Spring, 1975.

Wilshire, B. *International Philosophy Quarterly*, 13, 1973, 435–441.

Nature; philosophy, of nature; matter; body, physical; prehension, physical; substance; relation; activity; actuality; society; creativity: as principle of novelty, as Aristotle's prime matter, potentiality of, and eternal objects; extension; continuity, and potentiality; potentiality; prehension; event; space; God, and order; Aristotle; Leibniz, G. W.; Newton, Isaac; Kant, Immanuel; science; physics.

Relations, in Whitehead as in Leibniz, exist as a feature within each of the monads or actual entities constituting a physical body or society. Although Whitehead claims that such relations bring actual entities into special kinds of unity constitutive of 'societies', his specific doctrines do not render actual entities any less existentially separate than are Leibniz' monads. As a consequence, physical bodies are, for Whitehead, as for Leibniz, aggregates whose overall unity is not sufficiently explained.

1035   Leclerc, Ivor. "The Necessity Today of the Philosophy of
          Nature." *Process Studies*, 3, 1973, 158–168.

          Nature; Newton, Isaac; Descartes, Rene; Leibniz, G. W.; Kant,
          Immanuel; Einstein, Albert; von Weizsäcker, C. F.; nature,
          philosophy of; science, philosophy of; physics.

          The concept of nature originating in the seventeenth century
          has been destroyed; a new concept is indispensable to science
          and to humanity.

1036   Lee, Bernard. "Towards a Process Theology of the Eucharist."
          Worship, 48, 1974, 194–205.

          Eucharist; symbols, religious; world, actual; theology,
          sacramental.

          Process philosophy offers a revitalized understanding of the
          eucharist through its explication of the real presence of one
          event in the constitution of another.

1037   Lee, Bernard. *The Becoming of the Church: A Process Theology
          of the Structures of Christian Experience.* New York: Paulist
          Press, 1974.

          Christianity; Church; sacrament; Catholicism; Christology; God:
          and classical theism, Biblical view of, as persuasive power,
          tenderness of, religious availability of; language, religious;
          symbolism; society; emotion, and religion; adventure; actual
          entities, as present in others; Jesus as Christ; Teilhard de
          Chardin; Cobb, John B. Jr.; Thomas Aquinas; Dewey, John;
          Tyrell, George; theology: process, Catholic; religion.

          Whitehead's philosophy provides categories which illuminate the
          Christian notions of Church and Sacrament, and which suggest
          ways in which Christ can be understood. The Church can be
          understood as the process in which human beings interact with
          each other and the 'Jesus event'. The Sacraments are related
          to 'how' the Church evolves. The Church and Sacraments
          together help to establish the place of human emotion in
          religion.

1038   Lee, Bernard. "The Lord's Supper." *Religious Experience and
          Process Theology.* Edited by Harry James Cargas and Bernard
          Lee. New York: Paulist Press, 1976, 369–384.

          Eucharist; symbolism; actual entity, as present in others;
          experience, religious; theology, process.

          In interpreting the eucharistic notion of 'real presence',
          Whitehead's notions of event, interrelatedness, and symbolism
          can be illuminating. The deepest meaning of 'presence' should
          not be the nearness of substance, but rather the efficaciousness
          of what shapes one's reality.

1039   Lee, Bernard. "The Appetite of God." *Religious Experience and
          Process Theology.* Edited by Harry James Cargas and Bernard
          Lee. New York: Paulist Press, 1976, 369–384.

God: as dipolar, as eros; eros; experience, religious; appetition; Hartshorne, Charles; theology, process.

Using the natural theology of Hartshorne and Whitehead, the experiences of intimacy, sexual attraction, and eating can be explored for their spiritual implications.

1040   Lee, Harold N. "Causal Efficacy and Continuity in Whitehead's Philosophy." *Tulane Studies in Philosophy*, 10, 1961, 59–70.

Atomism; perception: and causal efficacy, and presentational immediacy; empiricism.

If actual entities are discrete, Whitehead's cosmology breaks down, for it is based on a primary ontological continuity. Since perception in the mode of causal efficacy is the experience of a full continuity, a greater emphasis on this doctrine would resolve the problem.

1041   Lee, R. T. "Whitehead's Theory of the Self." Unpublished Ph.D. dissertation, Yale University, 1962.

Self; ego; consciousness; society, personally–ordered; relations; anthropology; psychology.

1042   Lehman, Merle D. "'A Still More Excellent Way': An Introduction of Whiteheadian Theology To Lay People." Unpublished D.Min. dissertation, School of Theology at Claremont, 1975.

God, as love; Williams, Daniel D.; Lee, Bernard; Cobb, John B. Jr.; theology, process.

(The author develops a course in Christian adult education designed to present the thought of Whitehead and show its religious relevance.)

1043   Lenzen, V. F. "Scientific Ideas and Experience." *University of California Publication in Philosophy*, 8, 1926, 175–189.

Abstraction, extensive; duration; reason, and experience; physics, mathematical.

Contrary to Whitehead's view, mathematical physics is not logically derivable from experience, but is essentially a rational construction. This is necessitated by the fundamental dualism between reason and experience.

1044   Lenzen, Victor F. *The Nature of Physical Theory: A Study in Theory of Knowledge.* New York: Wiley & Sons, Inc., 1931.

Epistemology; abstraction, extensive; relations, mathematical.

1045   Lenzen, Victor F. "La philosophie de la science en Amérique." *L'Activité philosophique contemporaine en France et aux États–Unis.* Edited by Marvin Farber. Paris: Presses Universitaires de France, 1950, 171–196.

Philosophy, of science; abstraction, extensive; organism; biology.

After the first world war, Whitehead brought a metaphysical basis to the American discussion of the philosophy of science.

1046   Leonard, H. S. "Logical Positivism and Speculative Philosophy."

Philosophical Essays for Alfred North Whitehead. Edited by
F. S. C. Northrop, et al. New York: Russell & Russell, 1936,
125–152.

Positivism, logical; philosophy, speculative.

1047   Leonard, H. S. "The Mental and the Physical." *Centennial
Review,* 8, 1964, 337–352.

Mind, and matter; panpsychism.

1048   Leroy, Andre–Louis. "Science et Philosophie Chez Alfred North
Whitehead." *Revue de Synthese,* 3, 1961, 22–24, 43–66.

Science, and philosophy; Plato; Descartes, Rene; ideas, as clear
and distinct; actual occasion, relation to others; philosophy, of
nature; concreteness, fallacy of misplaced; dictionary, fallacy of
perfect; simple location, fallacy of; philosophy, and experience;
language; feeling, and satisfaction.

1049   Leroy, Andre–Louis. "Introduction á la philosophie
contemporaine d'expression anglaise." *Revue Philosophique de
la France et de l'Etranger,* 87, 1962, 433–466.

Process philosophy, summary of; Leplace, equations of; space,
as infinite, as divisible; Sellars, Roy Wood; Capek, Milic;
physics.

(A brief section entitled "Retour á Whitehead" traces the
renewed interest in Whitehead in the United States.)

1050   Leue, William. "Metaphysical Foundations for a Theory of Value
in the Philosophy of A. N. Whitehead." Unpublished Ph.D.
dissertation, Harvard University, 1952.

Value: relative, absolute; importance; activity; evil; ethics.

1051   Leue, William H. "Process and Essence." *Philosophy and
Phenomenological Research,* 21, 1960, 62–79.

Eternal objects: individual essence of, relational essence of,
functions of.

"Actual occasions" and "eternal objects" are the two poles of
Whitehead's thought; each is incomplete and unintelligible
without the other; both are needed for an adequate process
philosophy.

1052   Levi, Albert W. "The Problem of Higher Education: Whitehead
and Hutchins." *Harvard Educational Review,* 7, 1937, 451–465.

Philosophy, of education; education, and society; Hutchins,
Robert M.; metaphysics; sociology.

The controversy between Whitehead and Hutchins regarding
the aims and methods of education stems from divergent views
on metaphysics and social theory.

1053   Levi, Albert W. "Substance, Process, Being: A
Whiteheadian–Bergsonian View." *Journal of Philosophy,* 55,
1958, 749–761.

Substance; time, epochal theory of; Aristotle; Bergson, Henri;
metaphysics.

Differences between cosmologies of substance and cosmologies of process can be attributed to alternative renderings of temporality.

1054   Levi, Albert W.   *Philosophy and the Modern World.* Bloomington, Indiana: Indiana University Press, 1959.

Civilization; philosophy, aim of; wisdom; experience; feeling; relatedness; value; God; creativity; process; prehension; eternal objects; Bergson, Henri; Spengler, Oswald; Toynbee, Arnold; Freud, Sigmund; Lenin, V. I.; Thorstein, Veblin; Marx, Karl; Einstein, Albert; Planck, Max; Dewey, John; Russell, Bertrand; Carnap, Rudolph; Jaspers, Karl; Sartre, Jean–Paul; Moore, G. E.; Wittgenstein, Ludwig; logical positivism; existentialism; analytic philosophy; religion; science.

Whitehead's philosophy synthesizes the insights of experience and science into a vision of the whole which unifies the diverse intellectual traditions of the West.

1055   Levi, Albert W.   "Bergson or Whitehead?"   *Process and Divinity.* Edited by W. L. Reese and E. Freeman.   La Salle, Illinois: Open Court Publishing Co., 1964, 139–159.

Matter; life; coherence; eternal objects; actual occasion; Bergson, Henri; Platonism.

For Whitehead, the Platonic realist, the analysis of reality requires both actual entities and eternal objects. For Bergson, using the concepts of biology, it is sufficient that there is matter and life.

1056   Levinson, J. D.   "Philosophy and Philosophy Teaching: A Whiteheadian View."   Unpublished Ph.D. dissertation, Harvard University, 1965.

Education; philosophy: speculative, of education, teaching of; romance; precision; generalization; Dewey, John; Jaspers, Karl; Ayer, A. J.; Wittgenstein, Ludwig.

Whitehead's conceptions of philosophy and education have relevance for the teaching of philosophy by functioning as normative criteria by which to evaluate the aims, content, and methods of teaching philosophy.

1057   Lewis, C. I.   "The Categories of Natural Knowledge."   *The Philosophy of Alfred North Whitehead.*   Edited by Paul A. Schilpp.   La Salle, Illinois: Open Court Publishing Co., 1941, 701–744.

Objects: physical, scientific, perceptual; bifurcation, of nature; perception, and knowledge; *The Principles of Natural Knowledge; The Concept of Nature; The Principle of Relativity*; Bergson, Henri; Kant, Immanuel; Einstein, Albert.

In the 'middle period' of his career Whitehead shows that the world of sense experience and common knowledge is the same as that world of which science gives account. The fundamental notions which Whitehead develops in this period are not abandoned in his later writings.

1058   Lewis, Donald F. "The Notion of Time in the Cosmology of A. N. Whitehead." Unpublished Ph.D. dissertation, Southern Illinois University, 1970.

Time: and human experience, as physical, epochal theory of; concrescence, and human experience; being, in Heidegger; Heidegger, Martin; ontology; phenomenology; existentialism.

Significant affinities exist between Whitehead and Heidegger on the nature of time and its relation to human existence. Heidegger better articulates the relation between time and Being.

1059   Lewis, William C. "Structural Aspects of the Psychoanalytic Theory of Instinctual Drives, Affects, and Time." *Psychoanalysis and Current Biological Thought.* Edited by Norman S. Greenfield and William C. Lewis. Madison, Wisconsin: University of Wisconsin Press, 1965.

Psychoanalysis; unconscious; causal efficacy: and instinct, and psychoanalysis; Freud, Sigmund; psychology.

Whitehead's notion of causal efficacy gives clarity to the nature of instinctual drive structure in the human psyche and can therefore be of aid in psychoanalytic theory.

1060   Lewis, William C. *Why People Change: The Psychology of Influence.* New York: Holt, Rinehart and Winston, Inc., 1972.

Causal efficacy, examples of in psychology; symbolic reference; sense–perception, and psychology; psychotherapy; instinct; psychology.

Psychological experiments with human babies confirm Whitehead's analyses of perception. Whitehead's distinction between causal efficacy and sense–perception is useful in understanding aspects of psychotherapy.

1061   Lichtigfeld, Abraham. "Jaspers and Whitehead" (In Hebrew). *Iyun,* 13, 1962, 30–35.

God: primordial nature of, consequent nature of; connectedness; interrelatedness.

1062   Lichtigfeld, Abraham. "Jaspers und Whitehead: Eine vergleichende Untersuchung ihrer philosophischen Grundbegriffe." *Philosophia Naturalis,* 8, 1964, 301–306.

God: as creator, consequent nature of; aim, subjective; freedom; Jaspers, Karl; Leclerc, Ivor; existentialism.

Whitehead and Jaspers are in agreement that one's existence is open and that not even God can pre–determine it.

1063   Lichtigfeld, Abraham. "Leibniz und Whitehead: Eine vergleichende Untersuchung ihrer metaphysicher Grundbegriffe und deren Weiterentwicklung durch Jaspers." Akten des Internationalen Leibniz Kongresses, Hannover, 14–19, November, 1966. Band V: Geschichte der Philosophie (Studia Leibnitiana, Suppl. Volume 5), Wiesbaden: F. Steiner, 1971.

Metaphysics, principles of; Leibniz, G. W.; Jaspers, Karl.

1064   Lidgett, J. S. "Contrasted Cosmologies." *Centennial Review*, 144, 1933, 550–558.

Cosmology; Whitehead, Alfred North: introduction to his thought.

1065   Liewellyn, Robert R. "Alfred North Whitehead's Analysis of Metric Structure in *Process and Reality*." Unpublished Ph.D. dissertation, Vanderbilt University, 1971.

Extension; relativity: general theory of, Whitehead's theory of; time; space; continuum, extensive; geometry, as physical science; metrics; perception, and science; Einstein, Albert; Newton, Isaac; Palter, Robert M.; Grunbaum, Adolph; science; mathematics.

Although Whitehead's endorsement of a uniform metric structure is defensible in theory, it may be inconsistent with his commitment to the ontological primacy of process. The practical import of Whitehead's endorsement is problematic.

1066   Lillie, Ralph S. *General Biology and Philosophy of Organism*. Chicago: University of Chicago Press, 1945.

Evolution, and novelty; mind: and novelty, and matter in nature; teleology; subjective aim, in nature; creativity; biology, theoretical.

Biology must go beyond the physical to the psychical if it seeks to know and explain all organisms, including the human organism. Living beings are psychophysical systems in which a directive and synthesizing activity, essentially psychical in nature, exercises a fundamental control over physical processes.

1067   Lillie, Ralph S. "Biological Directiveness and the Psychical." *Philosophy of Science*, 14, 1947, 226–268.

Nature, and subjectivity; panpsychism; philosophy, of biology; biology.

1068   Lindqvist, Martti. *Economic Growth and the Quality of Life: An Analysis of the Debate within the World Council of Churches 1966–1974*. Helsinki: The Finnish Society for Missiology and Ecumenics, 1975.

World Council of Churches; ethics; economics; nature, and *history*; God; Cobb, John B. Jr.; Birch, Charles; theology, process.

1069   Lindsey, J. E. "An Interpretation of Whitehead's Epistemology." Unpublished dissertation, Union Theological Seminary (Virginia), 1970.

Epistemology; causal efficacy; presentational immediacy; perception.

1070   Lingswiler, Robert D. *The Concept of Subjective Aim in the Philosophy of Alfred North Whitehead*. Unpublished Th.D. dissertation, Iliff School of Theology, 1965.

Subjective aim; eternal objects, as pure possibilities; God, primordial nature of; teleology; purpose; evolution; novelty;

causation: mechanical, final; concrescence; feelings, intellectual; propositions; determinism; Nagel, Ernest; Toulmin, Stephen; Goodfield, June; science; biology.

The notion of 'pure potentiality' does not necessarily imply the eternal existence of all potentiality, nor does the 'ordering' of potentiality necessarily imply a deity with a primordial nature. Whitehead's notion of subjective aim can be understood without reference to eternal objects and the primordial nature of God.

1071   Lintz, Edward J.   "The Unity of the Universe According to Alfred North Whitehead."   Unpublished Ph.D. dissertation, University of Fribourg, 1939.

Unity: of universe, of finality, individual, prehensive; causation: efficient, final; God: as creator, as primordial, as consequent, as principle of concretion, as unity of universe.

Whitehead reintroduces the importance of the final unity of the world, but is mistaken in denying this finality to the primordial nature of God and in ascribing the power of prehensive unification to *all* entities in the world.

1072   Lintz, Edward J.   *The Unity in the Universe, According to Alfred N. Whitehead.*   Fribourg: University of Fribourg Press, 1939.   Revised and reprinted in *Thomist*, 6, 1943, 135–179, 318–366.

Process philosophy: summary of, criticism of.

Whitehead is to be admired because he dared to re–introduce finality into the world. However, his idea of creation is not in conformity with the true doctrine, for to create means to produce from absolutely nothing.

1073   Livingston, J. C.   *Modern Christian Thought from the Enlightenment to Vatican II.*   New York: MacMillan Company, 1971.   London: Collier MacMillan, 1971, 484–491.

Whitehead, Alfred North: introduction to his thought; theology, process; God: primordial nature of, consequent nature of, as source of initial aim; christology; Jesus, as Christ; Hartshorne, Charles; Cobb, John B. Jr.

(Process theology is introduced in the context of surveying major thinkers and movements in Christian thought from the enlightenment to Vatican II.)

1074   Long, Marcus.   "Whitehead and Definition."   *University of Toronto Quarterly*, 23, 1954, 208–210.

Language, Whitehead's use of; Johnson, A. H.

Johnson defends and explains Whitehead's terminology as well as possible, but the definitions leave many controversies unsettled. (Written in review of A. H. Johnson, *Whitehead's Theory of Reality.*)

1075   Loomer, Bernard M.   "Ely on Whitehead's God."   *Journal of Religion*, 24, 1944, 162–179.   Also in *Process Philosophy and*

Christian Thought. Edited by Delwin Brown, Ralph E. James, and Gene Reeves. Indianapolis, Indiana: Bobbs–Merrill Co., Inc., 1971, 264–286.

God: religious adequacy of, consequent nature of, goodness of, and value, and evil; Ely, Stephen Lee; philosophical theology.

In many instances Ely's interpretation and criticism of Whitehead's theology arise from ambiguities in Whitehead's concept of God, thus indicating the need for a fuller development of coherently interrelated religious categories in process theology.

1076   Loomer, Bernard M. "Theological Significance of the Method of Empirical Analysis in the Philosophy of A. N. Whitehead." Unpublished Ph.D. dissertation, University of Chicago, 1942.

Analysis, empirical; philosophy: aim of, method of; generalization, descriptive; God, and order; logic; necessity; knowledge, limits of; language; epistemology: in Whitehead's early philosophy, in Whitehead's later philosophy; empiricism, and theology, theology, and empiricism.

Whitehead's method is one of speculative empiricism. Although some of his statements can be interpreted as being logical arguments for the existence of God, Whitehead's analysis of God aims at being descriptive. The fact of order in experience points to the divine element.

1077   Loomer, Bernard M. "Neo–Naturalism and Neo–Orthodoxy." *Journal of Religion,* 28, 1948, 79–91.

Revelation; Jesus, as revelation; God, in human experience; process philosophy, summary of; Brunner, Emil; Niebuhr, H. Richard; theology, neo–orthodox.

Brunner and Niebuhr give accounts of revelation as a personal encounter and as internal history which correspond to process principles, notably those involving causal efficacy.

1078   Loomer, Bernard M. "Christian Faith and Process Philosophy." *Journal of Religion,* 29, 1949, 181–203.

Theology, and philosophy; history, and nature; revelation; nature: discontinuity of, and human existence; Niebuhr, Reinhold; theology, neo–orthodox.

Criticisms raised against process philosophy from the standpoint of neo–orthodoxy involve the relation of philosophy to theology, and the inadequacy of either history or nature to provide norms for Christian faith. These criticisms can be answered, thus proving the adequacy of process philosophy as an intellectual framework for Christian faith.

1079   Loomer, Bernard M. "Empirical Theology Within Process Thought." *The Future of Empirical Theology.* Edited by B. E. Meland. Chicago, Illinois: University of Chicago Press, 1969, 149–173.

Relativity, principle of; God, concrete nature of; self, as society; ontological principle; God, knowledge of; christology;

experience, appeal to; Niebuhr, Reinhold; Wieman, Henry N.;
Hartshorne, Charles; rationalism; empiricism; theology:
empirical, process.

Whitehead's ontological principle, principle of relativity, and
notion of self have direct relevance to empirical theology in
that they stem from observations derived from experience.

1080   Loomer, Bernard M. "Dimensions of Freedom." *Religious
Experience and Process Theology.* Edited by Harry James
Cargas and Bernard Lee. New York: Paulist Press, 1976,
323–339.

Freedom: and human existence, and society; solitariness;
interdependence; self–creativity; self–transcendence; power;
theology, process.

Freedom can best be understood in terms of the interplay
between relatedness and solitariness. The reason that it is
difficult to account for human decision lies in the fact that the
self and its decisions cannot be separated.

1081   Lovejoy, A. O. *The Revolt Against Dualism.* La Salle, Illinois:
Open Court Publishing Co., 1930.

Dualism: revolt against, ontological, metaphysical.

1082   Lowe, Victor A. "Conceptions of Nature in the Philosophical
Systems of Whitehead, Russell, and Alexander." Unpublished
Ph.D. dissertation, Harvard University, 1935.

Nature; · perception; sense data; space–time; prehension;
Alexander, Samuel; Russell, Bertrand; realism; idealism.

1083   Lowe, Victor. "Mr. Miller's Interpretation of Whitehead."
Philosophy of Science, 5, 1938, 217–229.

Whitehead, Alfred North, method of; mind, and nature; Miller,
David L.; philosophy of science.

Critics who claim Whitehead repudiated his earlier works in his
fully developed system fail to note Whitehead's stated
restriction of the earlier works to formulation of specific
principles of science. (Written in response to David L. Miller,
"Purpose, Design, and Physical Relativity.")

1084   Lowe, Victor. *Bibliography of the Writings of Alfred North
Whitehead to November 1941.* Cambridge, Massachusetts:
Harvard University Press, 1941.

Whitehead, Alfred North, bibliography of.

1085   Lowe, Victor. "William James and Whitehead's Doctrine of
Prehensions." *Journal of Philosophy,* 38, 1941, 113–126.

Prehensions: theory of, asymmetry of; immanence; empiricism,
radical; James, William.

James' account of the experience of transition in *Psychology* is
an early description of the experience later developed by
Whitehead in the doctrine of prehensions.

1086   Lowe, Victor. "The Development of Whitehead's Philosophy."
The Philosophy of Alfred North Whitehead. Edited by Paul

A. Schilpp.   La Salle, Illinois: Open   Court   Publishing
Company, 1941, 1951, 1971, 15–124.

Whitehead,   Alfred   North: introduction   to   his   thought,
philosophical   development   of;   *Universal   Algebra*,   "On
Mathematical Concepts of the Material World;" epistemology,
pre–speculative; metaphysics; philosophy: of science, aim of,
method of; idealism; experience, as datum for philosophy.

The unity of Whitehead's thought can only be grasped by
tracing its development through the mathematical and logical
investigations to the philosophy of science to the metaphysics
and philosophy of history.   In tracing this development one
discovers, not so much that the conclusions of one period form
the premises of the next, but rather that at each period
Whitehead is constantly touching on all the conditions involved
in human existence.

1087   Lowe, Victor.   "Empirical Method in Metaphysics."   *Journal of
Philosophy*, 44, 1947, 225–233.

Philosophy: method of, and experience, and imagination, and
language; empiricism, radical; metaphysics.

In metaphysics, the method which thinks of existences as
analogous to occasions of experience deserves an empiricist's
preference.   An obstacle to the empiricist is the limitations of
language   which   restrict   the   expression   of   experience   to
previously established ideas.

1088   Lowe, Victor.   "The Philosophy of Whitehead."   *Antioch Review*,
8, 1948, 223–239.

Whitehead, Alfred North, biography of; process philosophy,
summary of.

1089   Lowe, Victor.   "The Influence of Bergson, James and Alexander
on Whitehead."   *Journal of the History of Ideas*, 10, 1949,
267–296.

Whitehead, Alfred North, method of; abstraction, extensive;
duration; Bergson, Henri; James, William; Alexander, Samuel;
metaphysics.

Whitehead worked the metaphysical intuitions of Plato and the
more modern emphases on experience and process into a new
metaphysical design.   Alleged influences from Bergson are
highly   overstated,   and   in   many   instances   erroneous.
Whitehead's similarities to James and Alexander are primarily
due to sympathy rather than influence.

1090   Lowe, Victor.   "Whitehead's Philosophy of Science."
*Whitehead and the Modern World: Science, Metaphysics, and
Civilization, Three Essays on the Thought of Alfred North
Whitehead*.   Victor Lowe, Charles Hartshorne and Allison H.
Johnson.   Boston: Beacon Press, 1950.   Reprinted by Books for
Libraries Press, 1972, 3–24.

Philosophy, of science.

1091   Lowe, Victor; Hartshorne, Charles and Johnson,

Allison H. *Whitehead and the Modern World: Science, Metaphysics, and Civilization, Three Essays on the Thought of Alfred North Whitehead.* Boston: Beacon Press, 1950. Reprinted by Books for Libraries Press, 1972.

Philosophy, of science; civilization, philosophy of; metaphysics.

Reviews

Krikorian, Y. H. *New Republic*, 125, August 6, 1951, 17–19.

Leclerc, I. *Philosophical Quarterly*, 2, 1952, 82–84.

1092   Lowe, Victor. "Alfred North Whitehead: Introduction." *Classic American Philosophers.* Edited by Max H. Fisch. New York: Appleton–Century–Crofts, 1951, 395–417.

Whitehead, Alfred North: introduction to his thought, life of; Experience: occasion of, as model for philosophy; creativity; actual entities; God; concrescence; eternal objects; possibility; value; feelings; societies; causal efficacy; presentational immediacy; propositions; perishing.

(A general introduction to Whitehead's life and philosophy.)

1093   Lowe, Victor. "The Approach to Metaphysics." *The Relevance of Whitehead.* Edited by Ivor Leclerc. New York: Humanities Press Inc., 1961.

Metaphysics: nature of, and religion, and intuition, and language; particulars; universals.

1094   Lowe, Victor. "What Philosophers May Learn From Whitehead." *Revue Internationale de Philosophie*, 15, 1961, 251–266.

Whitehead, Alfred North, introduction to his thought.

1095   Lowe, Victor. *Understanding Whitehead.* Baltimore, Maryland: Johns Hopkins University Press, 1962, 1966.

Whitehead, Alfred North: philosophical development of, early works of, philosophy of science.

Reviews

Johnson, A. H. *Philosophy and Phenomenological Research*, 24, 1964, 286–287.

Lawrence, N. M. *Philosophical Review*, 73, 1964, 116–118.

Leclerc, I. *Philosophical Quarterly*, 15, 1965, 71–72.

Rorty, R. *Journal of Philosophy*, 60, 1963, 246–251.

Stokes, W. E. *New Scholasticism*, 38, 1964, 532–533.

1096   Lowe, Victor. "The Concept of Experience in Whitehead's Metaphysics." *Alfred North Whitehead: Essays on His Philosophy.* Edited by G. L. Kline. Englewood Cliffs, New Jersey: Prentice–Hall, Inc., 1963, 124–133.

Experience: as model for philosophy, as datum for philosophy, and nature, appeal to; actual occasions; togetherness.

Whereas in his early philosophy Whitehead was concerned with the space–time structure of observed nature, and thus construed experience in terms of sense–perception, Whitehead turned his attention to experience as immediate value–enjoyment in his later thought.   The chief concern of Whitehead's later thought is to depict the synthetic and dynamic character of such experience.

1097   Lowe, Victor.   "Peirce and Whitehead as Metaphysicians." *Studies in the Philosophy of Charles Sanders Peirce.*   Edited by E. C. Moore and R. S. Robin.   Amherst: University of Massachusetts Press, 1964, 430–454.

Metaphysics: as descriptive, and logic; method, philosophical; Peirce, Charles Sanders; metaphysics.

A basic difference between Peirce and Whitehead lies in the conception of metaphysics.   For Peirce, metaphysical concepts mirror logical concepts; for Whitehead, logic is but one tool in the larger task of metaphysics, the imaginative generalization of experience.

1098   Lowe, Victor.   "Whitehead's Gifford Lectures."   *Southern Journal of Philosophy*, 7, 1969, 329–338.

Whitehead, Alfred North: and Gifford Lectures, biography of; *Process and Reality*, writing of.

(The article gives a personal account of events in Whitehead's life connected with presentation of the Gifford Lectures and preparation of *Process and Reality* for publication.)

1099   Lowe, Victor. "Whitehead, Alfred North."   *Collier's Encyclopedia*, 23, 1969, 467–469.

Whitehead, Alfred North: biography of, works of.

1100   Lowe, Victor.   "Whitehead, Alfred North."   *Encyclopedia of Education*, 9, 1969, 549–557.

Whitehead, Alfred North: biography of, educational philosophy of.

1101   Lowe, Victor.   "Whitehead, Alfred North."   *Encyclopedia Brittanica*, 19, 1974, 816–818.

Whitehead, Alfred North, biography of.

1102   Lowe, Victor.   "A. N. Whitehead on his Mathematical Goals: A Letter of 1912."   *Annals of Science*, 32, 1975, 85–101.

Whitehead, Alfred North: mathematical goals, collaboration with Russell, relation of mathematics to physics and philosophy; Russell, Bertrand; Maxwell, J. C.; mathematics; logic.

A letter of 1912 indicates that the period of Whitehead's career which he devoted to physics is closely allied with his mathematical goals.

1103   Lowry, Ann P.   "The Ontological Status of the Mathematicals." Unpublished Ph.D. dissertation, Emory University, 1968.

Mathematics; number; eternal objects: as forms of definiteness, as pure possibilities, as data for conceptual prehensions; extension; abstraction; geometry; Pythagorus; Plato; Aristotle; Plotinus; Augustine; Scotus, Duns; Aquinas, Thomas; William of Ockham; Descartes, Rene; Leibniz, Gottfried; Gauss, C. F.;

Kronecker, Leopold; Dedekind, Richard; Poincare, Henri; Hilbert, David; Russell, Bertrand.

From Whitehead's perspective mathematics explores the relations between eternal objects. Whitehead's view counters that of Kant, in which mathematicals are the outcome of mental activity, and represents a return to the 'objective' standpoint of Greek thought.

1104   Lowry, Ann P. "Whitehead on the Nature of Mathematical Truth." *Process Studies*, 1, 1971, 114–123.

Truth, mathematical; forms, Platonic; eternal objects: as abstractions, as mathematical forms, relational essence of; Plato; Kant, Immanuel; mathematics.

The view of mathematical truths as process rather than as analytic more adequately accounts for the fundamental characteristics of mathematical truths: universality and applicability to the world.

1105   Luce, Robert E. "A Comparative Study of Certain Basic Categories in the Philosophies of Leibniz and Whitehead." Unpublished Ph.D. dissertation, Harvard University, 1940.

Monads, and actual occasions; ontological principle, and principle of sufficient reason; eternal objects, as pure possibilities; God, and the world; Leibniz, Gottfried.

(This work is an endeavour to show similarities in the metaphysics of Leibniz and Whitehead. It argues that certain problems in the thought of Leibniz are better dealt with in Whitehead's thought.)

1106   Lundeen, Lyman T. "Language About God: Some Implications of Whitehead's Philosophy For Religious Language." Unpublished Th.D. dissertation, Union Theological Seminary, 1969.

Language: religious, analogical, descriptive, emotional tone of, and logic, and meaning; God, language about.

1107   Lundeen, Lyman, T. *Risk and Rhetoric in Religion: Whitehead's Theory of Language and the Discourse of Faith.* Philadelphia: Fortress Press, 1972.

Language: religious, spoken, written, cognitive, affective, and Whorfian hypothesis, and perception; faith, and language; God, language about; fact, and value; interpretation; analogy; decision, symbolism; symbolic reference; belief; experience; metaphor; myth; experience, and language; causal efficacy; presentational immediacy; Wittgenstein, Ludwig; theology; religion: and language, and science.

In dealing with experience human beings must make value judgments which are closely tied to the ultimate concerns expressed in religious language. Whitehead's thesis that all knowledge is value–laden, together with his theory of language, provides a way of understanding religious language and relating it to other aspects of culture.

Reviews

Crosby, D. *Process Studies*, 3, 1973, 55–64.

Gill, J. *Theology Today*, 29, 1973, 442–444.

Hallman, J. M. *Theological Studies*, 34, 1973, 179–181.

Holbrook, C. A. *Journal of the American Academy of Religion*, September, 1974.

Norlin, D. A. *Dialog*, 3, 1972, 230–231.

Ogden, S. *Perkins Journal*, Winter, 1973.

Peden, W. C. *Interpretation*, 29, 1973, 244–245.

Sontag, F. *Review of Books and Religion*, February, 1973.

1108   Lyman, E. W. *The Meaning and Truth of Religion*. New York: Charles Scribner's Sons, 1933, 272–283.

Cosmology; panpsychism; purpose; mechanism.

The new cosmology of organism surpasses in adequacy a philosophy of mechanism, but does not yet give sufficient attention to purposefulness. A new theism is required which can integrate the insights of organism with the experience of purposefulness.

1109   Lynch, J. A. "Time–Systems as Perspectives." *Journal of Philosophy*, 26, 1929, 657–662.

Relations, relativity of; qualities, emergence of; time, relativity view of.

The argument from the relativity of relations to the relativity of qualities discredits the conception of activity as an underlying substrate, as well as the event as a kind of Absolute of which qualities are aspects or modes.

1110   Lyon, Q. M. "El espiritu y la filosofia del organismo." *Actas del Segundo Congreso Extraordinario Interamericano de Filosofia, San Jose*, 1961.

Whitehead, Alfred North: introduction to his thought; process philosophy, summary of.

1111   MacCormac, Earl R. "Indeterminacy and Theology." *Religion in Life*, 36, 1967, 355–370.

Science, and religion; freedom, and determinism; quantum mechanics; Heisenberg, Werner; theology.

Indeterminacy provides a context in which a concept of human freedom can be developed. Corresponding doctrines of providence must admit paradox, or be developed upon the basis of immanence.

1112   MacCormac, Earl R. "Whitehead's God: Categoreally Derived or Reformulated as a 'Person', or Neither?" *International Journal for Philosophy of Religion*, 3, 1972, 66–82.

God: Cobb's interpretation of, Hartshorne's interpretation of, and categoreal scheme; satisfaction; Cobb, John B., Jr.; Hartshorne, Charles; Ford, Lewis S.; Christian, William A.; metaphysics.

Because God does not perish upon attaining satisfaction, he is an exception to the categoreal scheme. The reformulations of Cobb and Hartshorne avoid the problem, but encounter enormous difficulties with relativity theory. An alternative is to view God as a hypothetical theoretical entity in a metaphysical scheme.

1113   Mace, C. A., ed. *British Philosophy in the Mid–Century*. London: Allen & Unwin, 1957.

Whitehead, Alfred North: introduction to his thought.

1114   Mack, Robert D. *The Appeal to Immediate Experience: Philosophic Method in Bradley, Whitehead, and Dewey*. Freeport, New York: Books for Libraries Press, 1945.

Experience, as datum for philosophy; philosophy: method of, of nature; sense–perception; awareness; presentational immediacy; causal efficacy; mind: as spectator, and nature; abstraction; Bradley, Francis H.; Dewey, John.

In his early philosophy of nature Whitehead is concerned with the 'ultimate data' of experience and treats the human mind as a spectator of those data. In his mature metaphysics Whitehead gives a more active role to the mind and treats its 'awareness' as an important philosophical datum. Whitehead's mature thought differs from that of Bradley and Dewey in that it considers immediate experience to be inherently cognitive.

1115   MacKenzie, W. Leslie. "What does Dr. Whitehead Mean by an 'Event'?" *Proceedings of the Aristotelian Society*, 23, 1923, 229–244.

Event: as spatio–temporal, as event–particle, as relational; *Enquiry Concerning the Principles of Natural Knowledge; Concept of Nature*; "Space, Time, and Relativity."

Although it is clear that Whitehead uses the word 'event' with reference to physical facts to stress their temporal as well as spatial nature, his doctrine of event becomes ambiguous when he attempts to explain the relation between events as perceived and events as they exist in nature.

1116   Madden, Edward H. and Hare, Peter H. "Evil and Unlimited Power." *Review of Metaphysics*, 20, 1966, 278–289. Also in *Evil and the Concept of God*. Springfield, Illinois: Charles C. Thomas, 1968, 115–125.

Evil; value; God: power of, primordial nature of, consequent nature of; Hartshorne, Charles; theodicy.

The quasi–theism of Whitehead and Hartshorne fails on three counts: it fails to make the distinction between a limited and a relative God meaningful; it does not produce a concept of God that guarantees the triumph of good in this world; and it characterizes the concepts of evil and value in a way that is not only incompatible with theism, but odd on any view.

1117   Madden, Edward H. *The Structure of Scientific Thought: An*

Introduction to the Philosophy of Science. Houghton Mifflin, 1960.

Philosophy, of science.

1118 Maitra, S. K. *The Meeting of the East and West in Sri Aurobindo's Philosophy.* Pondicherry, India: Sri Aurobindo Ashram Press, 1968, 399–439.

God: primordial nature of, consequent nature of, superjective nature of; prehension; eternal objects; creativity; metaphysics; Aurobindo.

Whitehead is to be praised for his organismic and processive approach, but ultimately his system falls short of adequacy due to his rejection of all forms of substance. Aurobindo's system lacks a prejudice against substance and is thus superior to Whitehead's.

1119 Malecek, Francisco. *An Application of Alfred North Whitehead's Principles of Metaphysics as a Possible Theory of Civil Society.* Rome: Pontificia Universitas Gregoriana, 1966.

Society, civil; ethics; good; value; morality; feelings; nexus; causation, final; duty.

(This work shows the manner in which a civil society might be understood from a Whiteheadian perspective. It argues that, given Whitehead's theory of society, there can exist no ultimate conflict between the individual and the common good, since the substantial person is substantial only as related to the function of the total society.)

1120 Malik, Charles. "The Metaphysics of Time in the Philosophies of A. N. Whitehead and Martin Heidegger." Unpublished Ph.D. dissertation, Harvard University, 1937.

Cosmology, and phenomenology; time, and human experience; subjective form; concrescence; one, and many; human existence, finitude of; Heidegger, Martin; existentialism; phenomenology.

Most of the major concepts in Whitehead's philosophy become unambiguous only when related to personal experience. When so related, they oftentimes parallel the phenomenological insights of Heidegger. Both philosophers find the nature of existence to be essentially temporal.

1121 Malik, Charles. "An Appreciation of Professor Whitehead With Special Reference to his Metaphysics and to his Ethical and Educational Significance." *Journal of Philosophy*, 45, 1948, 572–582.

Whitehead, Alfred North; ethics; education.

The ethical and educational significance of a great teacher is his life and example.

1122 Manchester, Peter P. "Time in Whitehead and Heidegger: A Response." *Process Studies*, 5, 1975, 106–113.

Time, and human existence; Heidegger, Martin; Dasein.

(This article is a response to David R. Mason's "Time in

Whitehead and Heidegger: Some Comparisons", *Process Studies*, 5, 1975, 83–105.)

1123   Manferdini, Tina. *Ontologismo critico e filosofie dell' esperoenza concreta.* Reggio Calabrid: Edizioni Historica, 1954.

Nature; romanticism; God.

1124   Mangrum, Franklin M. "An Interpretation of Revelation within the Context of A. N. Whitehead's Philosophical System." Unpublished Ph.D. dissertation, University of Chicago, 1957.

Christianity, and revelation; faith, and reason; Christ; Calvin, John; Niebuhr, H. Richard; Tillich, Paul; theology.

1125   Marshall, K. K. "Wieman's Philosophy of Art." *The Empirical Theology of Henry Nelson Wieman.* Edited by R. W. Bretall. New York: MacMillan Company, 1963, 222–235.

Experience: religious, aesthetic; aesthetics, and religion.

Wieman accepts Whitehead's claim that religious experience is of the aesthetic order rather than of the moral or conceptual orders, but he goes beyond Whitehead in claiming that mystical experience is richer than purely aesthetic experience.

1126   Martin, F. David. "Unrealized Possibility in the Aesthetic Experience." *Journal of Philosophy*, 52, 1955, 393–400.

Possibility, unrealized; music; experience, aesthetic; prehensions: conceptual, physical; aesthetics.

Unrealized possibility is immanent in the "given" of works of art; therefore the awareness of unrealized possibility is necessary for the most complete and intense aesthetic experience. Whitehead's theory of the relationship between physical and conceptual feelings is replete with insights about unrealized possibility.

1127   Martin, F. David. "The Power of Music and Whitehead's Theory of Perception." *Journal of Aesthetics and Art Criticism*, 25, 1967, 313–322.

Music; emotion; perception, and causal efficacy; Meyer, Leonard B.; aesthetics.

The aesthetic experience of music is dominated by perception in the mode of causal efficacy—the feeling of process, of "on–goingness", of the immanence of past and future in the present.

1128   Martin, F. David. "The Persistent Presence of Abstract Painting." *Journal of Aesthetics and Art Criticism*, 28, 1969, 23–31.

Art; music; perception: and causal efficacy, and presentational immediacy; aesthetics.

Abstract painting, more than any other art, is perceived mainly in the mode of presentational immediacy.

1129   Martin, F. David. "Heidegger's Thinking Being and Whitehead's Theory of Perception." *Bucknell Review*, 27, 1969, 79–102.

Perception; being; beauty; Heidegger, Martin; existentialism; metaphysics.

Whitehead's theory of perception, especially with respect to the insights it suggests about the conformation of human experience to things, provides a remarkable clarification of Heidegger's crucial claim that in the experience of Being, "the thing thinks in me."

1130   Martin, F. David. *Art and the Religious Experience: The 'Language' of the Sacred.* Lewisburg, Pennsylvania: Bucknell University Press, 1972.

Aesthetics, and religion; religion: and art, and religious experience; Being: and art, participation in; perception; music, and process; painting, and presentational immediacy; literature; architecture; beauty; Heidegger, Martin.

Heidegger's ontology and Whitehead's theory of perception illuminate the 'participative' aesthetic experience and show their relation to religious experience. Whitehead's notion of causal efficacy provides clarification to Heidegger's claim that in the experience of Being 'the thing thinks in me.'

1131   Martin, Gottfried. "Neuzeit und Gegenwart in der Entwicklung des mathematischen Denkens." *Kant–Studien,* 45, 1953–1954, 155–165. Also in *Gesammelte Abhandl,* Koln: Kölner Universitäts–Verlag, 1961, 138–150.

Philosophy, of mathematics; mathematics.

1132   Martin, Gottfried. German translation: "Metaphysik als 'Scientia Universalis' und als 'Ontologia Generalis'." *Kant–Studien,* 81, 1961, 212–232.

"Metaphysics as 'Scientia Universalis' and as 'Ontologia Generalis'." *The Relevance of Whitehead.* Edited by Ivor Leclerc. New York: Humanities Press Inc., 1961, 219–231.

Metaphysics: and being, as theory of principles; ontology; Plato; Aristotle; Leibniz, Gottfried; Kant, Immanuel.

Whitehead's metaphysics combines a theory of principles with a theory of being.

1133   Martin, Oliver. "Whitehead's Naturalism and God." *Review of Religion,* 3, 1939, 149–160.

God, and creativity; naturalism; supernaturalism.

Whitehead's philosophy is essentially naturalistic, having much in common with dialectical materialism. There is no significant sense in which this philosophy can be of service to those who are attempting to reconstruct Christian philosophy.

1134   Martin, Richard M. "On Whitehead's Concept of Abstractive Hierarchies." *Philosophy and Phenomenological Research,* 20, 1960, 374–382.

Science and the Modern World; eternal objects: as abstractive hierarchy, and type theory; logic; metaphysics.

The main features of the doctrine of abstractive hierarchies set forth in "Abstractions" are consonant with type theory. This logic then underlies the later cosmology.

1135   Martin, Richard M. "On Hartshorne's 'Creative Synthesis' and Event Logic." *Southern Journal of Philosophy*, 9, 1971, 399–410.

Synthesis, creative; logic.

1136   Martin, Richard M. *Whitehead's Categoreal Scheme and Other Papers.* The Hague, Netherlands: Martinus Nijhoff, 1974.

Categoreal scheme, logical structure of; God, logical structure of; division, coordinate; connection, extensive; hierarchies, abstractive; abstraction; geometry; Hartshorne, Charles; logic, symbolic.

(The author reconstructs several of Whitehead's doctrines from a logical point of view in order to show the logical structure of the categoreal scheme.)

1137   Martin, Richard M. "On the Whiteheadian God." *God and Contemporary Philosophy.* Edited by S. Matschak. Louvain: Navrwelaerts, forthcoming.

God: nature of, concept of, and world.

1138   Martin, William Oliver. "Whitehead's Philosophy as the Ideology of Consensus Theory." *Educational Theory*, 8, 1958, 1–7, 64.

Ideology; purpose, social.

Whitehead's philosophy is not insight into metaphysical truth, but is ideological in nature, and is determined by social and educational theory.

1139   Martland, T. R. "Is a Theology of Dialogue (of Process) Permissible?" *Christian Scholar*, 50, 1967, 197–209.

Language: religious, uses of; God, experience of; Cappadocian Fathers; theology.

A theology of dialogue, involving man–God relations, is logically and theologically permissible, and is fruitful in enabling the religious person to see coherent patterns of relationship.

1140   Marx, Lucy A. "The Use of Whiteheadian Principles in University Adult Education." Unpublished Ph.D. dissertation, University of Chicago, 1949.

Education: and concrescence, university adult; value; rhythm; learning.

Whitehead's notion of concrescence can be used to design a curriculum for university adult education.

1141   Mascall, E. L. "Three Modern Approaches to God." *Theology*, 30, 1935, 18–35, 70–86.

God: of classical theism, proofs of; Tennant, F. R.; Taylor, A. E.; theology.

The root defect in Whitehead's theology is that the presence of the created world adds something to God which he did not previously possess.

1142   Mascall, E. L. *He Who Is.* London: Longmans, Green, 1943, 150–160.

God, of classical theism; theology.

Whitehead's doctrine of God is inadequate from the point of view of Christian theology. The inadequacy stems from two grave defects: Whitehead has never apprehended the radical contingency of finite beings, nor has he any conception of the doctrine of *analogia entis.*

1143   Mason, David R. "An Examination of 'Worship' as a Key for Reexamining the God Problem." *Journal of Religion,* 55, january, 1975, 76–94.

Worship; God, problem of.

1144   Mason, David R. "Time in Whitehead and Heidegger: Some Comparisons." *Process Studies,* 5, 1975, 83–105.

Time: and present experience, Heidegger's theory of, and causality; perishing, perpetual; Dasein; relations, internal; present, as specious; subjectivist principle, reformed; Heidegger, Martin.

1145   Mattingly, Susan S. "Whitehead's Theory of Eternal Objects." Unpublished Ph.D. dissertation, The University of Texas at Austin, 1968.

Eternal object: individual essence of, relational essence of, subjective species of, objective species of, functioning of, as datum of conceptual feeling, ingression of, as potential, and God, as relational, in objectification.

For a given actual entity, eternal objects function in how other entities are objectified for it, in how it becomes subjectively, and in how it is a superject for others.

1146   Maurer, A. A. *Recent Philosophy.* Edited by E. Gilson, T. Langan and A. A. Maurer. New York: Random House, 1962, 507–519.

Whitehead, Alfred North: introduction to his thought; process philosophy, summary of.

1147   Mays, Wolfe. "Whitehead's Account of Speculative Philosophy in *Process and Reality.*" *Proceedings of the Aristotelian Society,* 46, 1945, 17–46.

Whitehead, Alfred North, method of; philosophy: speculative, task of; verifiability; metaphysics.

Whitehead's philosophy is modelled on the method of postulates with a purely hypothetical character. The resultant metaphysical scheme has only a tentative character, and depends for its truth upon its empirical verification, and not merely upon logical criteria.

1148   Mays, W. "Whitehead's Theory of Abstraction." *Proceedings of the Aristotelian Society,* 52, 1951, 95–118.

Eternal objects; abstraction, extensive; *Science and the Modern World.*

Whitehead was not putting forth a Platonic realism in his concept of eternal objects, but was rather applying certain techniques derivative from symbolic logic to elucidate the structure of experience.

1149   Mays, Wolfe. "Determinism and Free Will in Whitehead." *Philosophy and Phenomenological Research*, 15, 1955, 523–534.

Freedom, and determinism; mind: mind–body problem, and nature; physics, field theory of.

Whitehead's attempt to bridge the gap between matter and mind seems to have failed, for if one set of patterns in the system follows physical laws and the other set are purely self–determinative, there can be no action or re–action between them without each obtaining some of the properties of the other, thus losing their essential characteristics.

1150   Mays, Wolfe. *The Philosophy of Whitehead*. New York: The Macmillan Company, 1959.

Philosophy: method of, and symbolic logic; God, logical nature of; eternal objects, as logical forms of events; abstraction, extensive; feelings: theory of, simple physical, intellectual; perception: authentic, illusory; judgment; freedom, and determinism; societies: theory of, structured; systems; time; probability; extensive continuum; language; teleology; consciousness; "On Mathematical Concepts of the Material World"; belief; Aristotle; mathematics; logic, symbolic; psychology, Gestalt; biology; physics; cybernetics.

In Whitehead's philosophy two kinds of entities are postulated: those making up the general scheme of order (or God) underlying the universe, and which guarantee induction, and the physical events (or the World) related within this structure. In analyzing these types of entities, Whitehead's method bears close resemblance to the axiomatic method used by modern logic.

Reviews

Barth, L. A. *Modern Schoolman*, 38, 1960–1961, 77–78.

Burnell, J. *Philosophical Studies*, 9, 1959, 256–258.

Chappell, V. C. *Ethics*, 70, 1959–1960, 181.

Collins, J. *Cross Currents*, 10, 1960, 157–158.

Grensted, L. W. *Church Quarterly Review*, 161, 1960, 105–106.

Johnson, A. H. *Philosophy and Phenomenological Research*, 21, 1961, 428.

Kennick, W. E. *Philosophical Review*, 70, 1961, 116–119.

Leclerc, I. *New Scholasticism*, 34, 1960, 387–390.

McClure, G. *Philosophy of Science*, 27, 1960, 220–222.

Selvaggi, F. *Gregorianum*, 42, 1961, 124–125.

Shalom, A. *Etudes Philosophiques*, 15, 1960, 118.

Tapp, R. B. *Hibbert Journal*, 58, 1960, 315.

Tucker, J. *Philosophy*, 35, 1960, 276–277.

1151   Mays, Wolfe. "Whitehead and the Idea of Equivalence." *Revue Internationale de Philosophie*, 15, 1961, 167–184.

Equivalence: quantitative, qualitative; identity; symbols, mathematical; Quine, Willard Van Orman; De Morgan, Augustus; mathematics; logic.

Whitehead's views on equality and identity as developed in *Universal Algebra* and *The Principle of Relativity* have a direct bearing on central features of his philosophical thinking. What emerges from both accounts is that the notion of equality is always relative to a context or purpose.

1152   Mays, Wolfe. "The Relevance of 'On Mathematical Concepts of the Material World' to Whitehead's Philosophy." *The Relevance of Whitehead*. Edited by Ivor Leclerc. New York: Humanities Press Inc., 1961.

"On Mathematical Concepts of the Material World"; concepts: linear, punctual; points, and interpoints; logic, symbolic; geometry.

Whitehead's metaphysics may be said in some ways to be a return to the position of "On Mathematical Concepts of the Material World," published in 1906.

1153   Mays, Wolfe. "Whitehead and the Philosophy of Time." *Studium Generale*, 23, 1970, 509–524.

Time: and human experience, philosophy of; abstraction, extensive; simultaneity; Merleau–Ponty, M.; Husserl, Edmund; Grünbaum, A.; Northrop, F. S. C.

Whitehead bridges the gap between the time of human experience and that of science through his method of extensive abstraction. His views on simultaneity and congruence are concerned with immediate sense experience, and are epistemological rather than causal in nature.

1154   Mazzantini, C. "La filosofia di Alfred North Whitehead." *Quaderni di Roma*, 2, 1948, 175–193.

Whitehead, Alfred North: introduction to his thought; process philosophy, summary of.

1155   Mazzueca, John Louis. "Reflections on the Divine Tragedy in the Universe of Alfred North Whitehead." *Encounter*, 33, 1972, 185–202.

Evil; tragedy; Peace; perpetual perishing; God: as source of initial aim, and tragedy; harmony; discord; theodicy.

Whitehead's God embodies eternally the quality of tragic consummation, encountering and experiencing the evil exemplified in actual occasions. Despite evil, the aim at the ideal persists; yielding Peace.

1156   McClendon, James William, Jr. "Can There Be Talk About God–And–The–World?" *Harvard Theological Review*, 62, 1969, 33–49.

Language: about God, uses of; God: as acting in history, doctrines of; mind, doctrines of; Ryle, Gilbert; Wittgenstein, Ludwig; linguistic analysis.

Doctrines of God are paralleled by doctrines of mind; talk about God may be clarified by investigating talk about human acts.

1157   McCreary, John K.   "Recent Developments in the Philosophy of Religion."   Unpublished dissertation, University of Toronto, 1939.

Philosophy, of religion.

1158   McCreary, John K.   "A. N. Whitehead's Theory of Feeling." *Journal of General Psychology*, 41, 1949, 67–78.

Prehensions, theory of; self; psychology.

Whitehead's philosophy of organism can provide underlying generalities for psychological theory.

1159   McDaniel, Jay and Cobb, John B., Jr.   "Introduction: Conference on Mahayana Buddhism and Whitehead."   *Philosophy East and West*, 25, 1975, 393–405.

Experience: becoming, relational; perception; self: as series of experiences, and Buddhism; sūnyatā: and creativity, and concrescence, and immediacy; perishing: perpetual, and samsāra; Peace, and nonattachment; time: irreversibility of, symmetrical; atomism; dualism, and God; Abe, Masao; Altizer, Thomas J. J.; Dilworth, David; Hartshorne, Charles; Inada, Kenneth; King, Winston; Noda, Matao; Olson, Robert; Ramanan, K. Venkata; Streng, Frederick; Suchocki, Marjorie; Tanaka, Takao; Yu, David; Buddhism, Mahayana.

The conference explored methodological and epistemological problems in the Buddhism/Whitehead dialogue, areas of agreement in the understanding of human experience, metaphysical diversities, and creative possibilities for future interchange.

1160   McElroy, Elliott W.   "The Nature of Experience and the Role of God: Whitehead's Response to Hume."   Unpublished Ph.D. dissertation, University of Georgia, 1972.

God: Whitehead's arguments for, function of, Whitehead without; experience; causation; self; epistemology; Hume, David.

Working within a Humean framework, Whitehead applies certain of Hume's principles more consistently than Hume himself, and arrives at a conception of God.

1161   McEwen, William Peter.   "Whitehead's View of Personal Growth."   *Personalist*, 24, 1943, 46–56.

Personality, theory of; self–consciousness; self–identity; self–creativity; psychology.

Whitehead's metaphysical explanation of human experience is unintelligible apart from the concept of an enduring self–realization of a self–conscious, relatively self–determined, and self–identical temporal process of teleological growth.

1162 McFarlane, William H. "Philosophy and Common–Sense: A Neo–Scholastic Appraisal of a Conflict in Contemporary Philosophy." Unpublished Ph.D. dissertation, University of Virginia, 1957.

Epistemology; common sense; conceptual feelings; Aquinas, Thomas; Descartes, Rene; Gilson, Etienne; Maritain, Jacques; Ayer, A. J.; realism; nominalism; Neo–Scholasticism.

Whitehead's doctrine of conceptual prehensions implies a theoretical nominalism. In contrast to Whitehead, Neo–Scholasticism affirms a position more analogous to that of classical and medieval realism. The Neo–Scholastic position is more suitable to the logical certainty philosophy seeks.

1163 McGilvary, Evander B. "Space–Time, Simple Location, and Prehension." *The Philosophy of Alfred North Whitehead.* Edited by Paul A. Schilpp. New York: Tudor Publishing Co., 1951, 209–239.

Space–time; location, fallacy of simple; prehension; relativity, theory of; simultaneity; extensive continuum; perspective; presentational immediacy; philosophy, of nature; Russell, Bertrand.

Whitehead's doctrine of the denial of simple location can only be understood in relation to his doctrine of prehension, which itself is intimately connected with his view of perspective.

1164 McGilvary, Evander B. *Toward a Perspective Realism.* Edited by Albert G. Ramsperger. La Salle, Illinois: Open Court Publishing Company, 1956.

Relativity, theory of; perspective: spatial, temporal, perceptual; space; time; simultaneity; location, simple; event; prehension; actual occasion; extensive continuum; sense–perception; nature, Whitehead's early definition of; Einstein, Albert; Leibniz, Gottfried W.; Russell, Bertrand; science; physics; mathematics.

Whitehead's arguments against simple location do not find verification in immediate experience.

1165 McLeod, A. N. "A Treatment of Some of the Difficulties Raised by Zeno's Paradoxes of Motion." *Journal of Philosophy,* 33, 1936, 656–659.

Zeno, paradoxes of; time, epochal theory of; James, William.

The epochal theory of time is not necessary to a resolution of Zeno's paradoxes.

1166 McWilliams, James A. "Professor Whitehead's Conception of an Event." *Proceedings of the American Catholic Philosophical Association,* 3, 1927, 40–53.

Philosophy, and mathematics; event; language, Whitehead's use of.

Whitehead is a great mathematician, but when he turned

philosopher he tried to mathematize philosophy. His unusual views give rise to an obscure and bizarre diction which by too many readers is mistaken for the garb of profound truth.

1167 Mead, George H. *The Philosophy of the Present.* La Salle, Illinois: Open Court Publishing Co., 1932.

Education; Dewey, John.

1168 Mead, George H. *The Philosophy of the Act.* Edited with introduction by Charles W. Morris. Chicago: University of Chicago Press, 1938.

Relativity, theory of; time, systems of; simultaneity; space; perspective; sense–perception; motion; permanence; nature, laws of; extensive abstraction; science.

(This volume consists primarily of unpublished papers which Mead left at his death. It includes a section titled 'Fragments on Whitehead', pages 523–528.)

1169 Meilach, O. F. M., Michael D. "Religious Encounter and the Philosophy of Organism: Suggestions for a Whiteheadian Ontology." Unpublished Ph.D. dissertation, Fordham University, 1971.

God: transcendence of, immanence of, Whitehead's arguments for, as actual entity; soul; person, as series of experiences; experience, religious; Plotinus; religion; theology.

In order to render Whitehead's thought adequate to religious experience, his doctrine that the soul is a series of actual entities must be replaced by the view that the soul is a single enduring entity without a physical pole, and his suggestion that God is a determinate actual entity must be replaced by the view that God is an indeterminate creative unity.

1170 Meilach, Michael D. "Jesus and Process Philosophy." *Cord,* 24, 1974, 150–161.

Christology; Jesus, as Christ; theology.

1171 Meland, Bernard E. "The Mystic Returns." *Journal of Religion,* 17, 1937, 961–963.

Mysticism.

1172 Meland, Bernard E. *Seeds of Redemption.* New York: MacMillan Company, 1947.

God: as principle of concretion, as source of value, and creativity; religion, nature of; Wieman, Henry N.

According to Whitehead God is the redemptive influence on the creativity of the universe. Because of God's operations every event of existence is connected with every other event, rather than being merely solitary. It is by virtue of this metaphysical situation that Whitehead can define religion as individuality in community.

1173 Meland, Bernard Eugene. "The Genius of Protestantism." *Journal of Religion,* 27, 1947, 273–292.

Protestantism: analysis of, critique of, history of.

. Whitehead opens the way for giving cognitive structure to what Protestant thinkers have been impelled to defend either on grounds of sentiment or on a basis that compels desperate decision in the face of an implied skepticism.

1174   Meland, Bernard E. *The Reawakening of Christian Faith.* New York: Macmillan, 1949; paperback, New York: Books for Libraries, 1972.

Christianity; faith; order, as aesthetic; perception, and emotion; ethics, and aesthetics; theology.

1175   Meland, Bernard E. *Faith and Culture.* New York: Oxford University Press, 1953; London: George Allen and Unwin, 1955; paperback, Carbondale: Southern Illinois University Press, 1970.

Faith, and culture; religion; Christianity; God, tenderness of; theology.

(This is a discussion of the relation between religious faith and culture from a liberal Christian perspective.)

1176   Meland, Bernard E. "Interpreting the Christian Faith Within a Philosophical Framework." *Journal of Religion,* 33, 1953, 87–102.

Process philosophy, summary of; theology, and philosophy; Kant, Immanuel.

Process philosophy can move theological thinking beyond the impasse of the Kantian *Critiques* without blurring the distinction between man and God.

1177   Meland, Bernard E. *Higher Education and the Human Spirit.* Chicago: University of Chicago Press, 1953; paperback, Chicago: Seminary Cooperative Bookstore, 1965.

Education; consciousness; nature of, depth of experience behind; poetry: and metaphysics, and depth of feeling, and analytic discourse, function of in human culture; imagination; James, William; Wordsworth, William; Shelley, Percy B.; religion, and culture.

Whitehead's analysis of consciousness has marked similarities to that of William James. Whitehead's use of poetry in carrying on metaphysical discussion is an example of how imagination and emotion can bear relation to analytic thought.

1178   Meland, Bernard Eugene. "From Darwin to Whitehead: A Study in the Shift in Ethos and Perspective Underlying Religious Thought." *Journal of Religion,* 40, 1960, 229–245.

Evolution: Darwinian, emergent; method, theological; freedom; personalism; Darwin, Charles; Bergson, Henri; Lotze, Hermann; theology.

The theological significance of Whitehead's reorientation of evolutionary thinking is considerable, for it provides radically different views of freedom, of individuality, and of human fulfillment.

1179   Meland, Bernard Eugene. "Analogy and Myth in Postliberal

Theology." *Perkins School of Theology Journal*, 15, 1962, 19–27. Also in *Process Philosophy and Christian Thought*. Edited by Delwin Brown, Ralph E. James and Gene Reeves. Indianapolis, Indiana: Bobbs–Merrill Co., Inc., 1971, 116–127.

Christ; faith, and culture; myth, and mythology; analogy; Ogden, Schubert M.; Bultmann, Rudolf; theology.

Through process metaphysics, Ogden replaces mythological knowledge of the universal love of God with analogical knowledge about such love. However, ogden does not take sufficient account of the sense in which the myths of a culture inform all knowledge within the culture.

1180   Meland, Bernard E.   *The Realities of Faith: The Revolution in Cultural Forms.*   New York: Oxford University Press, 1962; paperback, Chicago: Seminary Cooperative Bookstore, 1970.

Evolution, and religion; self: communal character of, and relations; religion: and science, and community, and metaphysics; prehension, and internal relations; relations, as experienced; God: tenderness of, and Christ; *Religion in the Making*, impact on theological community; Darwin, Charles; Wieman, Henry Nelson; Bergson, Henri; empiricism; religious; theology; physics, and religion; biology, and religion.

The mechanization of nature gave rise to an idealization of human existence and its powers. New visions of the relation between human existence and nature, such as that of Whitehead, can serve in correcting this idealization.

1181   Meland, Bernard E. ·   "The Root and Form of Wieman's Thought." *The Empirical Theology of Henry Nelson Wieman.* Edited by R. W. Brctall.   New York: MacMillan Company, 1963, 44–68.

Religion, nature of; perception, and the external world; Wieman, Henry N.; theology, empirical.

(The author traces the effect of Whitehead's notion of religion in the development of Wieman's thought and suggests differences in the theories of knowledge which Wieman and Whitehead respectively hold. Whereas Wieman tends to view perception as a psychological act alone, Whitehead understands perception in a cosmological context.)

1182   Meland, Bernard Eugene.   "How is Culture a Source for Theology?"   *Criterion*, 3, 1964, 10–21.

Method, theological; culture; myth, and culture; God, as acting in history; empiricism, radical; theology.

The realities of faith are living, vital energies in the immediacies of experience, existing through but not restricted to the cultural forms and institutions we create.

1183   Meland, Bernard E.   "Can Empirical Theology Learn Something From Phenomenology?"   *The Future of Empirical Theology.* Edited by Bernard E. Meland.   Chicago, Illinois: University of Chicago Press, 1969, 283–305.

Phenomenology; theology, empirical.

1184   Meland, Bernard Eugene.   "The New Realism in Religious
        Inquiry." *Encounter*, 31, 1970, 311–324.

        Faith, and culture; encounter; otherness; Tillich, Paul; Barth,
        Karl; Niebuhr, Reinhold; Wieman, Henry Nelson; theology:
        liberal, neo–orthodox.

        A line of protest and inquiry, extending from Barth to
        Whitehead, forms a new frontier of realism, breaking free of
        the enclosure of mentalism which was imposed upon Christian
        thinking for more than three hundred years and which had
        shaped the imagery of theological liberalism since the time of
        Kant.

1185   Meland, Bernard E.   "The Christian Legacy and Our Cultural
        Identity." *Philosophy of Religion and Theology*, 1972 (Section
        Papers, American Academy of Religion) David Griffin, editor.
        22–42.

        Culture;   myth;   causal   efficacy;   tradition;   civilization;
        Christianity.

        Our Christian religious legacy is still present to us and
        influential for us through the causal efficacy of its past
        expressions.

1186   Mellert, Robert B.   "The Relationship of God to Man and
        Nature in the Philosophy of Alfred North Whitehead."
        Unpublished Ph.D. dissertation, Fordham University, 1972.

        Nature, and value; God; man; ecology.

        Whitehead's cosmology provides a basis through which human
        self–understanding can develop with reverence and restraint
        toward nature.

1187   Mellert, Robert B.   *What is Process Theology?*   new York:
        Paulist Press, 1975.

        Whitehead, Alfred North: introduction to his thought; God:
        nature of, primordial nature of, consequent nature of, as source
        of initial aim, as superject, as creator; grace, of God; kingdom
        of God; religion: nature of, and religious experience; human
        existence; self: as series of experiences, and self–identity;
        church; sacraments; eucharist; morality; beauty; person, and
        personal immortality; Jesus, as Christ; theology, process.

        (This is a concise introduction to process theology for clergy,
        educators, and lay persons who have no prior knowledge of
        Whitehead or process thought.)

1188   Mellert, Robert B.   "A Pastoral on Death and Immortality."
        Religious Experience and Process Theology.   Edited by Harry
        J. Cargas and Bernard Meland.   New York: Paulist Press,
        1976, 399–408.

        Immortality, subjective; objective immortality; God: primordial
        nature of, consequent nature of; grief; counseling.

        Whitehead's doctrine of objective immortality can be used

satisfactorily in counseling the bereaved who are not concerned about a personal after–life while the theory of subjective immortality derivable from his system satisfies those who are.

1189   Menge, Edward J. v.K.   "Professor Whitehead's Philosophy." *Catholic World*, 134, 1932, 420–428.

Whitehead, Alfred North, method of; process philosophy, summary of; science.

Whitehead has taken all of the controversial points appearing in contemporary scientific philosophy and has tried to unify them in terms of energy.

1190   Merrill, Kenneth R.   "Whitehead's Theory of Givenness." Unpublished Ph.D. dissertation, Northwestern University, 1963.

Perception; causality; subjectivist principle, reformed; sensationalist principle; solipsism; Hume, David; Santayana, George; phenomenology.

Although Whitehead's causal theory of perception is vitiated by an excessive reliance on physiology and physical theory, it has the virtue of being sensitive to the less distinct elements of experience, of being consonant with the human experience of the world, and of being articulated from a metaphysical perspective.

1191   Merrill, Kenneth R.   "Whitehead on Order and Freedom: A Reply." *Personalist*, 50, 1969, 148–154.

Freedom: and determinism, and order; Al–Azm, Sadik.

Al–Azm's charge that Whitehead vacillates between indeterminism and determinism is based on an erroneous interpretation of Whitehead's doctrine of freedom. Written in response to Sadik Al–Azm, "Whitehead's Notions of Order and Freedom."

1192   Metz, R. *Die Philosophischen Stroemungen der Gegenwart in Gross Britannien.*   Leipzig: F. Meiner, 1935, Volume 2, 136–169.

Process philosophy, summary of; Whitehead, Alfred North: introduction to his thought.

1193   Metz, R.   "The New Realism."   *A Hundred Years of British Philosophy.* London: Allen & Unwin, 1938, 589–662.

Whitehead, Alfred North, method of; process philosophy, summary of.

1194   Meynell, Hugo.   "The Theology of Hartshorne."   *Journal of Theological Studies*, 24, 1973, 143–157.

Hartshorne's theology, summary of; God: Hartshorne's interpretation of, relations of, of classical theism; paradox; Hartshorne, Charles; Aquinas, Thomas; theology.

Hartshorne's theism is impressive and worthy of serious attention, but his metaphysical and moral objections to a Thomistic doctrine of God cannot be sustained.

1195   Michalson, Carl. *The Hinge of History: An Existential Approach to the Christian Faith.*   New York: Charles Scribner's Sons, 1959.

Christianity, and existentialism; history, and nature; nature, and order; science: method of, and religion; God, and classical theism, death of; theology, existential.

Whitehead's philosophy is deficient in its account of history and human existence, because it fails to acknowledge the sinister and disorderly aspect of the universe and because it substitutes mathematical syntax for concrete existential relation.

1196   Mickey, Paul A.   "Toward a Theology of Individuality: A Theological Inquiry based on the Work of Alfred North Whitehead and David Rapaport."   Unpublished Th.D. dissertation, Princeton Theological Seminary, 1970.

Human existence; ego; psychology; consciousness; feeling; subjectivity; subjective aim; time, as perpetual perishing; Rapaport, David; Freud, Sigmund; Langer, Susanne; theology, and psychology.

The psychological dynamics of human individuality are illuminated by Whitehead's understanding of experience, although Whitehead himself must be psychologically interpreted.   For Christian theology the result of such an interpretation can bridge the gap between practical and theoretical concerns.

1197   Millard, Richard M.   "The Place of Value in Whitehead's Thought."   Unpublished Ph.D. dissertation, Boston University Graduate School, 1950.

Value: nature of, criteria of, intrinsic, secondary, and fact; concrescence, as realization of value; aesthetics, and value; God, and value.

Whitehead's thought about value follows a clear line of development and change from his first methodological restriction of value considerations from philosophy through his last important philosophical writings.   In this development Whitehead tends to move from a conception of intrinsic value to an emphasis on objective, eternal, and unchanging Platonic values, the latter being evidenced in "Mathematics and the Good" and "Immortality."

1198   Millard, Richard M.   "The Ghost of Eternalism in Whitehead's Theory of Value."   *Philosophical Forum*, 9, 1951, 16–22.

Value: theory of, preservation of; eternalism; immortality; Plato.

Despite Whitehead's fundamental emphasis on process, he also shows a propensity for eternalism.   This tendency triumphs in his later writings, with the result that value was transferred from actuality to a timeless and immortal status.

1199   Millard, Richard M.   "Whitehead's Aesthetic Perspective."   *Educational Theory*, 11, 1961, 255–268.

Aesthetics, and metaphysics; values: criteria for, intrinsic, aesthetic; beauty; aesthetics.

Whitehead's metaphysical synthesis of reality is thoroughly and, for Whitehead, self–consciously aesthetic in character.

1200   Miller, D.   "Value and Some Key But Unfinished Doctrines in Whitehead's Philosophy."   Unpublished Ph.D. dissertation, Southern Illinois University, 1969.

Value.

1201   Miller, David L.   "Purpose, Design and Physical Relativity." *Philosophy of Science*, 3, 1936, 267–285.

Relativity, special theory of; purpose, physical; Einstein, Albert; Moore, Merritt H.; teleology.

The innovation of the physical theory of relativity has made it more difficult to separate either design and mind or design and teleology.   Whitehead therefore holds that design and teleology are organically related, and that design is an objective fact.

1202   Miller, David L. and Gentry, George V.   *The Philosophy of A. N. Whitehead*.   Minneapolis, Minnesota: Burgess Publishing Company, 1938.

Philosophy, of nature; abstraction, extensive; space–time, and time systems; eternal objects; perception, and causation; extension; motion; points; cogredience; duration; causality; novelty; concrescence.

(In this commentary on Whitehead's philosophy, the authors pose detailed criticisms of Whitehead's doctrines of extensive abstraction and space–time.   They also criticize Whitehead's attempt to synthesize the notion of efficient cause with that of physical perception.   The authors endorse the view that eternal objects are necessary to Whitehead's scheme.)

1203   Miller, David L.   "Whitehead's Extensive Continuum." *Philosophy of Science*, 13, 1946, 144–149.

Extensive continuum, atomization of; potentiality; teleology; Leibniz, G. W.

The problem concerning the extensive continuum is to show that the divisions into past, present, and future are connected; that there is a real continuity with no absolute break between them lest we be forced to accept the mechanistic, atomistic world of disconnection, the parts of which are complete in themselves and similar to Hume's impressions.

1204   Miller, David L.   *George Herbert Mead: Self, Language and the World*.   Austin, Texas: University of Texas Press, 1973.

Self; language; world; ethics; aesthetics; logic; epistemology; Mead, George Herbert.

(In the process of outlining Mead's thought the author compares and contrasts Mead's theories of emergence, process, and creativity with aspects of Whitehead's thought.   There are about twenty entries in the index to Whitehead, although the discussion of Whitehead is not specific enough to require any textual citation.)

Review

Allan, G. *Process Studies*, 4, 1974, 42–51.

1205   Miller, E. V. "The Emergence of Relativity in A. N. Whitehead's Philosophy." *Australian Journal of Psychology and Philosophy*, 1, 1923, 256–267.

Relativity, special theory of; physics; philosophy, of science.

By appeal to reasoning based on universal experience, Whitehead's philosophy demolishes the presupposition that for all observers there is only one space and one time, which are independent and incommensurable.

1206   Miller, Hugh. *An Historical Introduction to Modern Philosophy.* New York: Macmillan Company, 1949, 471–476.

Eternal objects, as essences; realism; Leibniz, Gottfried; Russell, Bertrand.

Whitehead proffers a philosophical realism by holding that eternal objects make possible an understanding of particular fact.

1207   Miller, Randolph C. "Semi-Theism: The Quest for a Position Between Humanism and Theism." Unpublished Ph.D. dissertation, Yale University, 1936.

Religion: and theism, and humanism; God, and value; Dewey, John; Mathews, Shailer; Wieman, Henry N.; theology.

1208   Miller, Randolph C. *The American Spirit in Theology.* Philadelphia: United Church Press, 1974.

Theology: American, process; religion: and religious experience, and empiricism; process; God: as dipolar, as persuasive, power of, religious availability of; James, William; Temple, William; Wieman, Henry Nelson; Hartshorne, Charles; Ogden, Scubert; Northrop, F. S. C.

Reviews

Cousins, E. H. *Review of Books and Religion*, 4, 1975.

Meland, B. *Religious Education*, 70, 1975, 82–90.

Nicholas, (Brother OHC). *New Life*, May, 1975, 40.

1209   Miller, Randolph C. "Process Thinking and Religious Education." *Anglican Theological Review*, 57, 1975, 271–288.

Process theology, summary of; theodicy; worship; liberation; christology; education, religious.

Process theology's broad interpretation of existence allows clarification of many problems in contemporary society.

1210   Miller, Randolph C. "Whitehead and Religious Education." *Religious Education*, 68, 1973, 315–322.

Education, religious.

1211   Miller, Veronica A. "The Paradox of the Reformed Subjectivist

Principle in Whitehead's Philosophy." Unpublished Ph.D. dissertation, Tulane University, 1970.

Subjectivity; objectivity; subjectivist principle, reformed; epistemology; metaphysics; Husserl, Edmund; Heidegger, Martin; Sartre, J. P.; phenomenology.

As is evidenced by his reformed subjectivist principle, there is a basic phenomenological trend in Whitehead's thought. Many of Whitehead's metaphysical concepts, in consistency with the reformed subjectivist principle, may be developed to explicate lived subjectivity and the lived world. However as an objectivist metaphysics, Whitehead's philosophy is inconsistent in that it violates his epistemological commitment to the reformed subjectivist principle.

1212   Miller, Veronica. "Whitehead's God, Analogy, and Consistency of his Metaphysics." *The New Scholasticism*, 46, 1972, 339–349.

God: and categoreal scheme, experience of, analogy; infinity, mathematical; subjectivist principle, reformed; Hogan, Donald J.

Whitehead's God cannot be understood as analogous to occasions. The notion of the actual entity is inconsistent in that an attempt is made to erect the actual entity as object into a reality equal with the actual entity as subject. (Written in response to Donald J. Hogan, "Whitehead's God: The Analogy of Actual Entity.")

1213   Milligan, Charles. "A Critique of the Doctrine of Divine Eros in the Philosophy of Alfred North Whitehead." Unpublished Ph.D. dissertation, Harvard University, 1951.

Eros: actuality of, as immanent, as persuasive urge towards perfection, as dynamic, and primordial nature of God; God: primordial nature of, as Eros, and creativity, and creatio ex nihilo, power of, and order; evil; beauty; value; theodicy; *Adventures of Ideas*; Alexander, Samuel; pantheism; Platonism.

Whitehead's doctrine of Eros as unchanging violates the principle of relativity and does not escape involvement with the problem of evil. Eros should not be equated with the primordial nature of God.

1214   Milligan, Charles S. "Religious Values of Whitehead's God Concept." *Iliff Review*, 9, 1952, 117–128.

God: as Eros, religious adequacy of, religious availability of; morality; religion.

Whitehead's concept of God as Eros, as developed in *Adventures of Ideas*, can provide ethical motivation as a technique carrying religious as well as ethical significance. This answers those critics of Whitehead who claim that his concept of God is neither adequate nor available for religious purposes.

1215   Milligan, Charles S. "A Rejoinder to Professor Wieman." *Iliff Review*, 18, 1961, 55–57.

Creativity: structure of, human; Wieman, Henry Nelson; God, and creativity.

Wieman does not give adequate attention to the enduring structure of reality.

1216   Milligan, Charles S. "Broader than the Measure of Man's Mind, But...." *Iliff Review*, 19, 1962, 43–47.

God: knowledge of, activity of; Wieman, Henry Nelson; epistemology; metaphysics.

Wieman's construct of God is limited, for while he holds God to be more than a human construct, this God nevertheless seems to work and operate only in the human realm. We must relate our concept of God to the hetero–human aspects of existence.

1217   Miro Quesada, Francisco. "Hartmann y Whitehead." *Mercurio Peruano: Revista Mensual de Ciencias Sociales y Letras*, 22, 1947, 449–466.

Science: method of, and metaphysics; substance, defense of; rationalism; eternal objects, as essences; ontology.

The scientific rigor and innovativeness of Whitehead's thought are laudable. However, Whitehead does not logically justify the elimination of the traditional notion of substance by simply positing dynamism. He fails to consider that the end result of the process of concrescence is substance.

1218   Mohanty, Jitendra N. "Whitehead's Philosophy of 'Process'." *Philosophical Quarterly* (India), 24, 1951, 89–104.

Whitehead, Alfred North: introduction to his thought; process philosophy, summary of.

1219   Mohanty, Jitendra N. *Nicolai Hartmann and Alfred North Whitehead: A Study in Recent Platonism.* Calcutta: Progressive Publishers, 1957.

Eternal objects: Whitehead's arguments for, as abstractions, as ideal continuum, as potential, as individuals, relational essence of, individual essence of, and universals, as abstractive hierarchy, subjective species of, objective species of, and ingression; ontological principle; propositions; objectification, and eternal objects; objective immortality; potentiality: as real, as ideal; Hartmann, Nicolai; Husserl, Edmund; Plato; Hartshorne, Charles; realism; idealism; Platonism; phenomenology; logic, ontological status of.

Although external affinities exist between the distinctions Whitehead and Hartmann each make between real and ideal being, the two thinkers differ. Hartmann seeks to lay the foundation of a 'Realontologie,' whereas Whitehead grants more philosophical status to the ideal.

Reviews

Hedman, C. *Journal of Philosophy*, 55, 1958, 255–258.

Johnson, A. H. *Philosophy and Phenomenological Research*, 19, 1958–1959, 115–117.

Schlaretzki, W. E. *Philosophical Review*, 68, 1959, 132–134.

1220 Molina, Fernando R. "Whitehead's Realism in Relation to the Problem of Perception." Unpublished Ph.D. dissertation, Yale University, 1959.

Epistemology; perception: Whitehead's early theory of, and sense data, and strain feelings, and projection; causality; sensationalist principle; realism; physiology.

Whitehead's attempt to establish a realistic epistemology that circumvents both the bifurcation of nature and the doctrine of private psychological fields does not succeed.

1221 Mollenhauer, B. "Whitehead and the Adventure of Philosophy." *Philosophical Quarterly* (India), 24, 1951, 51–55.

Philosophy: aim of, method of, speculative.

1222 Montgomery, W. R. "A Critical Study of Alfred North Whitehead's Philosophy of Education in the Light of its Historical, Biographical and Metaphysical Backgrounds." Unpublished dissertation, University of Toronto, 1961.

Education: aims of, stages of, and society, organic theory of; philosophy, of education.

1223 Moore, Harold; Neville, Robert; and Sullivan, William. "The Contours of Responsibility: A New Model." *Man and World*, 5, 1972, 392–421.

Responsibility; ecosystem; cultures and ecology; action theory; agent; agency; ethics, models of; ethics; ecology; sociology.

Traditional western ethical theories are based on abstractions of agents from environment, and are not adequate for contemporary culture. A model of ecosystems redefines the contours of responsibility by considering dependency relationships in fields of existents.

1224 Moore, Merritt Hadden. "Mr. Whitehead's Philosophy." *Philosophical Review*, 40, 1931, 265–275.

Process philosophy: summary of, criticisms of.

Whitehead's later work dwarfs, if it does not destroy, its foundations in his earlier work. Whitehead errs in emphasizing feeling, for while feeling and value are real aspects of our experience, they cannot serve as the criteria of all reality.

1225 Moore, Robert L. "Process Philosophy and General Systems Theory: A Review Article." *Process Studies*, 4, 1974, 291–299.

Systems, theory of; consciousness; nature; value.

(This is a critical study of Laszlo's *Introduction to Systems Philosophy: Toward a New Paradigm of Contemporary Thought*.)

1226 More, Paul E. *The Demon of the Absolute*. Princeton, New Jersey: Princeton University Press, 1928.

Science, and metaphysics; absolutes; religion, and science.

By introducing the hypothetical method of science into the study of religion, Whitehead fails to realize the difference in kind between the subject matter of science and that of religion.

1227   Morgan, C. Lloyd.   "The Bifurcation of Nature."   *Monist*, 40, 1930, 161–181.

Bifurcation, of nature; relations: internal, external; *Concept of Nature*; dualism.

Whitehead's organic thesis is founded on the doctrine that all relations are internal.   However, there is a sense in which nature is closed to mind, so that relations between nature and mind would seem to be external.   This raises the question of bifurcation.

1228   Morgan, C. Lloyd.   "Subjective Aim in Professor Whitehead's Philosophy."   *Philosophy*, 6, 1931, 281–294.

Subjective aim; language, Whitehead's use of; Morgan, C. Lloyd; psychology.

Subjective aim, as psychologically defined, may unhesitatingly be imputed to humans who have reached a high status of concrescent mentality; it is questionably attributed to all forms of creativity.   Whitehead's terminology requires clarification regarding its psychological meaning.

1229   Morgan, George, Jr.   "Whitehead's Theory of Value." *International Journal of Ethics*, 49, 1936, 309–316.

Value: theory of, criteria for; beauty; evil; ethics; aesthetics.

Whitehead's theory of value is part of a general reconstruction of categories; value is an intrinsic aspect of actuality.

1230   Morgan, William.   "The Organization of a Story and a Tale." *Journal of American Folklore*, 58, 1945, 169–194.

Story, organization of; experience, primitive human; Navaho; anthropology: mythology.

Whitehead's terminology and categories are used to define and describe some of the physical and subjective processes, in individuals and in groups, which are involved in the formation of a story and a folktale.   Introduction by Alfred North Whitehead.

1231   Morgret, Frank.   "Whitehead et. al. vs. Human Death (A Puzzled Quiry by a Concerned Counsellor)."   *Springfielder*, 38, 1974, 185–192.

Death: normal, abnormal; life; society: personally ordered, living; immortality; Cobb, John B., Jr.; Pittenger, Norman; Hartshorne, Charles; psychology; counseling.

Cobb, Pittenger, and Hartshorne have been unsuccessful in defining death as anything but the mere last link in a chain of experiences.   This makes death seem trite in its normality, whereas for the person experiencing it, it is never trite nor merely the last of a series of experiences.

1232   Morkovsky, M. C.   "The Elastic Instant in Aristotle's Becoming and Perishing."   Modern Schoolman, 46, 1968–1969, 191–217.

Becoming, epochal; time, epochal theory of; present; Aristotle.

1233   Morra, G.   "Religione e sociologia nel pensiero di Whitehead." Filosofia e Sociologia.   Edited by F. Battaglia and Nicolai Hartmann.   Bologna: Il Mulino, 1954.

Adventures of Ideas; civilization; sociology.

Inconsistencies in Adventures of Ideas, together with Whitehead's relativism, undermine his religious vision.

1234   Morris, Bertram.   "The Art–Process and the Aesthetic Fact in Whitehead's Philosophy."   The Philosophy of Alfred North Whitehead.   Edited by Paul A. Schilpp.   La Salle, Illinois: Open Court Publishing Company, 1941, 461–486.

Art: and coordinate analysis, and genetic analysis, and creativity; aesthetics; beauty; symbolism; contrast; triviality; vagueness; massiveness; subjective form; harmony.

Of signal importance to aesthetics is the historical process through which the aesthetic fact comes into being.   The analysis of this historical process corresponds to what Whitehead calls genetic division.   The categories which Whitehead develops to analyze the genetic process can be useful in aesthetic analysis, although further clarification is necessary.

1235   Morris, Charles W.   "Mind in Process and Reality."   Journal of Philosophy, 28, 1931, 113–127.

Mind: theory of, as emergent; relativism, objective; Dewey, John; epistemology; psychology.

An admission of the importance of emergence and relativity need not require such a divergence from the earlier new realism as is found in Whitehead.   Whitehead's generalization of mind to all entities limits his functional usefulness in psychology.

1236   Morris, Charles W.   Six Theories of Mind.   Chicago: University of Chicago Press, 1932.

Mind: as prehension of eternal objects, as intentional act; Husserl, Edmund; realism; idealism.

Whitehead's introduction of the concepts of relativity and emergence into the realistic world–view open the possibility of creating a neo–realistic doctrine of mind.   However his account is rendered ambiguous by its retention of a theory of direct knowledge of eternal objects.   The latter gives an idealistic turn to his philosophy which is at variance with the dominant attitude of realism.

1237   Morrison, Charles Clayton.   "Thomism and the Re–Birth of Protestant Philosophy."   Christendom, 2, 1937, 110–125.

Philosophy: history of, and religion; Thomas Aquinas; Compte, Auguste; Dewey, John; Wieman, Henry Nelson; Thomism.

The new phase of philosophy represented by Henry Nelson Wieman provides for protestant philosophy an alternative to Thomism which preserves the values of Thomism.

1238   Moxley, D. J. "The Conception of God in the Philosophy of Whitehead." *Proceedings of the Aristotelian Society*, 34, 1933–1934, 157–186.

God: and evil, and creativity, consequent nature of, primordial nature of; creativity: as substantial activity, and God, and value, as principle of novelty; ontological principle; relations, internal; Hume, David; Platonism.

Whitehead's conceptions of Creativity, God, and the self–creation of actual entities are intended both to avoid the skepticism inherent in Hume's view of causation and to provide an explanation and solution to the problem of evil.

1239   Müller, G. E. "North American Philosophy." *Actas del Primero Congreso Nacional de Filosofía*, 1, 1949, 456–479.

Philosophy, in America; Whitehead, Alfred North: introduction to his thought.

1240   Müller, G. E. *Amerikanische Philosophie.* Stuttgart: F. Frommann, 1950, 183–185.

Philosophy, in America; Whitehead, Alfred North: introduction to his thought.

1241   Mullen, Wilbur H. "A Comparison of the Value Theories of E. S. Brightman and A. N. Whitehead." Unpublished Ph.D. dissertation, Boston University Graduate School, 1955.

Value: theory of, criteria for; person, and value; God, and value; religion, and value; evil; Brightman, E. S.

Brightman's personalism and Whitehead's panpsychism each provide ground for the development of a theory of value. A fruitful synthesis of the thought of the two might begin by placing more emphasis on organic relatedness in Brightman's personalism, and by altering Whitehead's concept of God in the direction of Brightman's clear–cut theism.

1242   Murphree, Wallace A. "The Status of the Mental: A Whiteheadian Response to Armstrong's Materialism." Unpublished Ph.D. dissertation, Vanderbilt University, 1972.

Mind, mind–body problem; Armstrong, D. M.; Descartes, Rene; Sellars, Wilfrid; materialism; science.

Whereas Armstrong's materialistic philosophy of mind distorts certain common sense ideas concerning mental phenomena, Whitehead's philosophy takes such ideas into account. For this reason Whitehead's philosophy is to be preferred over Armstrong's.

1243   Murphy, Arthur E. "Ideas and Nature." *University of California Publication in Philosophy*, 8, 1926, 193–213.

Nature, and ideas; bifurcation, of nature; qualities: primary, secondary; events.

(Although the author refers to several of Whitehead's ideas in his discussion of the relation between ideas and nature, there is no extended discussion of Whitehead's thought.)

1244   Murphy, Arthur E.   "Objective Relativism in Dewey and Whitehead." *Philosophical Review*, 36, 1927, 121–144. Also in *Reason and the Common Good: Selected Essays*. Edited by W. H. Hay and M. G. Singer. Englewood Cliffs, New Jersey: Prentice–Hall, Inc., 1963, 163–167.

Relativism, objective; bifurcation; Dewey, John.

The objective relativism of Dewey and Whitehead respectively shows great promise as a contemporary effort to build upon the insights of relativity theory and overcome the errors of dualism.   Taken in his own terms, Whitehead in particular offers a theory of great coherence; the major difficulty for critics of the theory is their inability to leave a substantive position.

1245   Murphy, Arthur E.   "What is an Event?" *Philosophical Review*, 37, 1928, 574–586.

Events: theory of, geometry of; abstraction, extensive; concreteness, misplaced (fallacy of); relativity, theory of.

Absolute space–time is not involved in the theory of events and is in fact in conflict with it.   Whitehead's ambiguity on this point results in philosophical confusion.

1246   Murphy, Arthur E.   "The Anti–Copernican Revolution." *Journal of Philosophy*, 26, 1929, 281–299.

Bifurcation, of nature; dualism, revolt against; nature, and subjectivity; philosophy, of science.

Whitehead goes too far in his revolt against the Copernican induced dualism.   There is no basis for the generalization of percipience, volition, and mentality from human experience to the whole of nature.

1247   Murphy, Arthur E.   "The Development of Whitehead's Philosophy."   *New World Monthly*, 1, 1930, 81–100.   *Reason and the Common Good: Selected Essays of Arthur E. Murphy.* Edited by William H. Hay, Marcus G. Singer, and Arthur E. Murphy.   Englewood Cliffs, New Jersey: Prentice–Hall, Inc., 1963, 126–141.

Whitehead: philosophical development of; relativity, principle of; freedom, and God; process, principle of; Wilson, Woodrow.

In asserting that all conceptual feelings are reproductive, Whitehead adopts the view that all novel feelings are derived from God.   Such a view does not adequately account for freedom.

1248   Murphy, Arthur E.   "Whitehead and the Method of Speculative Philosophy."   *The Philosophy of Alfred North Whitehead.*

Edited by Paul A. Schilpp. *Reason and the Common Good: Selected Essays of Arthur E. Murphy.* Edited by William H. Hay, Marcus G. Singer, and Arthur E. Murphy. Englewood Cliffs, New Jersey: Prentice–Hall, Inc., 1963, 142–162.

Philosophy: method of, speculative; aesthetics, and metaphysics; ontological principle; verifiability.

Whitehead's rehabilitation of speculative philosophy does not succeed because its methods are problematic and because the 'ultimates' it posits do not pass the test of experiential verification.

1249   Murphy, Arthur E. "Whitehead's Objective Immortality." *Reason and the Common Good: Selected Essays of Arthur E. Murphy.* Edited by William H. Hay, Marcus G. Singer, and Arthur E. Murphy. Englewood Cliffs, New Jersey: Prentice–Hall, Inc., 1963, 163–172.

Philosophy: and system, method of, aim of; Whitehead, Alfred North: influence of.

(This essay is concerned, not with Whitehead's doctrine of objective immortality, but with the 'objective immortality' of Whitehead's thought in its role of contributing to philosophy after it. The author suggests that there are two aspects to Whitehead's thought, the system–building aspect and the exploratory aspect, and that the latter aspect is most relevant to later philosophy.)

1250   Murphy, Frances. "The Place of Moral Responsibility in the Philosophies of Whitehead and Peirce." Unpublished Ph.D. dissertation, Brown University, 1940.

Morality, and moral responsibility; justice: educative, retributive; determinism, and indeterminism; utilitarianism; libertarianism; Peirce, Charles S.

Whitehead and Peirce each believed that an indeterministic theory accounted for moral responsibility better than a deterministic theory. It may be surmised that by 'responsibility' each had in mind retributive as well as educative punishment and reward.

1251   Nagel, Ernest. "Alfred North Whitehead." *Sovereign Reason, and Other Studies in the Philosophy of Science,* New York: The Free Press, 1954, Chapter 9. Also in *Nation,* 166, 1948, 187–188.

Whitehead, Alfred North, obituary notice.

1252   Nagel, Ernest. *The Structure of Science: Problems in the Logic of Scientific Explanation.* New York: Harcourt, Brace and World, Inc., 1961, 271–274.

Relativity, theory of; space–time, uniformity of; geometry; Einstein, Albert; physics.

Whitehead's criticisms of Einstein raise two questions. The first is whether a system can be constructed within a framework of non–uniform geometry which adequately expresses the facts of nature. The second concerns the manner in which the differences between diverse theories of relativity, each employing different geometrical systems, can be measured.

1253   Nagley, W. "Alfred North Whitehead's Analysis of the Cognitive Function of Religious Intuition." Unpublished Ph.D. dissertation, University of Southern California, 1947.

Intuition; experience, religious; religion: and intuition of permanence, and reason.

1254   Nedoncelle, M. *La philosophie religieuse en Grande Bretagne 1950 a nos jours.* Paris: Blout et Gay, 1934, 109–142.

Whitehead, Alfred North: introduction to his thought; philosophy, of religion.

1255   Needham, J. "A Biologist's View of Alfred North Whitehead's Philosophy." *The Philosophy of Alfred North Whitehead.* Edited by Paul A. Schilpp. New York: Tudor Publishing Co., 1951, 241–271. Also in *Time: The Refreshing River.* By J. Needham. New York: MacMillan Company, 1943, 178–206.

Dualism; materialism; panpsychism; organism, philosophy of; evolution: as biological; determinism, and indeterminism; nature; Marx, Karl; Aristotle; biology; philosophy, of biology.

While dialectical materialism and emergent evolutionism have much to teach the biologist, Whitehead's philosophy of organism provides a world view which is particularly suited to integrating the insights of the two perspectives. It can be criticized only because it fails to carry out the analysis of the social and political directions to which it points.

1256   Neidorf, Robert A. "Bifurcation and Events: A Study in Einstein, Russell, and Whitehead." Unpublished Ph.D. dissertation, Yale University, 1959.

Bifurcation, of nature; philosophy, of science; relativity: general theory of, special theory of; Einstein, Albert; Russell, Bertrand.

A dualistic epistemology, in which nature–as–perceived is explained in terms of nature unperceived, is inherent in all deductive sciences. Whitehead's and Russell's attempts to avoid such dualism do not succeed.

1257   Nemesszeghy, E. Z. and Nemesszeghy, E. A. "Is $(p \supset q) = (-p \lor q)$Df. A Proper Definition in the System of *Principia Mathematica?*" *Mind*, 80, 1971, 282–283.

Axioms; definitions; Lesniewski, S.; mathematics; logic.

From the proof that $(-p \lor q)$ cannot be deduced from the axioms of *Principia* without the definition $(p \supset q) = (-p \lor q)$Df., it may be concluded that as the axioms are written in the system of *Principia* $(p \supset q) = (-p \lor q)$Df. is not a proper definition.

1258   Neville, Robert C. "A Theory of Divine Creation." Unpublished Ph.D. dissertation, Yale University, 1963.

God, as creator.

1259 Neville, Robert C. "Reply." *Christian Scholar*, 59, 1967, 324–325.

Theology, and philosophy; Christian, William A.

Answers to theological questions often turn critically on answers to metaphysical questions. The relationship between the two disciplines is dialectic rather than dianoetic. (Written in response to William A. Christian, "The New Metaphysics and Theology.")

1260 Neville, Robert C. *God the Creator: On the Transcendence and Presence of God.* Chicago: University of Chicago Press, 1968.

Cosmology, versus ontology; God: as Being, as creator, and creatio ex nihilo; novelty; eternal objects; religion, nature of; Hartshorne, Charles; Plato; Aristotle; Platonism; Aristotelianism.

Whitehead blends Platonism and Aristotelianism. His Platonism allows him to say that the natural process of events has novel elements in it but only because those novel events are eternal elsewhere. His Aristotelianism requires him to say that what is novel in the world of process must be the actualization of what is potential in God. Whitehead's cosmological approach to the transcendence of God inhibits his account of God's nature. An ontological approach to God, construing God as Being itself, is more adequate.

1261 Neville, Robert C. "Neoclassical Metaphysics and Christianity: A Critical Study of Ogden's *Reality of God.*" *International Philosophical Quarterly*, 9, 1969, 605–624.

God: concept of, religious adequacy of; faith; secularism; Ogden, Schubert M.

The neoclassical concept of God fails on both philosophical and theological grounds. Philosophically, it wrongly implies that the concrete reality of God is inclusive of abstractions, and that God unifies the world without including the world's subjectivity. Theologically, it wrongly implies that the divine love does not actually touch human subjectivity.

1262 Neville, Robert C. "Whitehead on the One and the Many." *Southern Journal of Philosophy*, 7, 1969, 387–393.

Many, and the one; creativity; ontological principle; unity; metaphysics.

Whitehead's distinctive contribution to the discussion of the one and the many was to assign the unifying function traditionally ascribed to God to two different factors: actual entities and creativity. However, creativity is not sufficient to account for ontological unity.

1263 Neville, Robert C. "The Impossibility of Whitehead's God in Christian Theology." *Proceedings of the American Catholic Philosophical Association*, 44, 1970, 130–140.

God: and creativity, and categoreal scheme, and evil, as worthy of worship; freedom; Ford, Lewis S.; philosophical theology.

Many of the virtues of Whitehead's conception of God are also possessed, sometimes more satisfactorily, by the alternative conception of a God who creates every novel value or pattern by which an event is constituted.

1264   Neville, Robert C. "Genetic Succession, Time, and Becoming." *Process Studies*, 1, 1971, 104–108.

Division: coordinate, genetic; concrescence, phases of; prehensions; actual entity: becoming of, being of; time: physical, genetic; Ford, Lewis S.

Ford's attribution of genetic time to the phases of concrescence misconstrues genetic division as an analysis of phases rather than of prehensions, and neglects the distinction between becoming and being.

1265   Neville, Robert C. "Experience and Philosophy: A Review of Hartshorne's *Creative Synthesis and Philosophic Method*." *Process Studies*, 2, 1972, 49–67.

Metaphysics, Hartshorne's; creativity; causation; perishing, perpetual; subjective immediacy; freedom and determinism; person, continuity of; universals, status of; dipolarity; God: as dipolar, Hartshorne's interpretation of; asymmetry; knowledge, a priori; Hartshorne, Charles; Weiss, Paul; metaphysics; philosophical theology; theology, natural.

Hartshorne's book deals carefully with nearly all the philosophic questions its theories require. However, on issues such as personal continuity and the problem of God and evil, Hartshorne's philosophy does not capture the living waters of experience.

1266   Neville, Robert C. "The Limits of Freedom and the Technologies of Behavior Control." *Human Context*, 4, 1972, 433–445.

Freedom: and society, and value; technology.

1267   Neville, Robert C. *The Cosmology of Freedom*. New Haven, Connecticut: Yale University Press, 1974.

Freedom: and human existence, and person, and society, and value, and determinism, and human existence; coordinate division; genetic division; duration; concrescence; prehension; action, intentional; Dewey, John.

The thought of Whitehead and Dewey can aid in the understanding of human freedom, although, with respect to Whitehead, greater emphasis should be placed on events of a human scale, and, with respect to Dewey, greater emphasis should be placed on the role of conflict in a pluralistic society.

Reviews

Anonymous. *Choice*, October, 1974.

Anonymous. *Book Review Digest*, 13, 1975.

Bourke, V. J. *Review for Religions*, 33, 1974, 1540.

Duclow, D. F. *Review of Metaphysics*, 28, 1975, 762.

Meilach, M. D. *Cord*, 24, 1974, 371.

Shideler, E. W. *Review of Books and Religion*, February, 1975.

1268   Nicod, J. *Foundations of Geometry and Induction*. London: Routledge and Kegen Paul, 1950, 40–43.

Induction; geometry; mathematics.

1269   Niebuhr, H. Richard. *The Meaning of Revelation*. New York: Macmillan Company, 1941, 93.

Revelation; theology.

(This work contains only passing mention of Whitehead.)

1270   Nobo, J. L. "Whitehead's Principle of Process." *Process Studies*, 4, 1974, 275–284.

Process, principle of; becoming; categoreal scheme; subject, as superject; actuality.

In regard to its complete history, an actual entity is both process and product, both becoming and being, both subject and superject. The superjective aspect of the actual occasion is as actual as the subjective aspect.

1271   Noda, Matao. "Yukiteki Shizen—Whitehead No Tetsugaku (An Organic View of Nature: The Philosophy of Whitehead)." *Kindai Seishin Sobyo (Portraits of the Modern Mind)*, Tokyo: Chikuma Shobo, 1947, 252–283.

Whitehead, Alfred North: introduction to his thought; philosophy, of nature.

1272   Norlin, Dennis A. "The Construction and Testability of Whitehead's Metaphysical Conception of God." Unpublished Ph.D. dissertation, The University of Iowa, 1972.

God: functions of, Whitehead's arguments for, Whitehead without, and creativity, and ontological principle; creativity; eternal objects; quantum mechanics; Everett, Hugh; Graham, Neill; Wheeler, J. A.; Cobb, John B. Jr.; Sherburne, Donald; Reeves, Gene; Christian, William; Pols, Edward; Ford, Lewis; science.

If, as is the case, a metaphysical doctrine of God based on an interpretation of quantum theory that is foreign to Whitehead can be established, then there is no satisfactory means of choosing between this view of God and that of Whitehead.

1273   Norman, Ralph V. "Theodicy and the Form of Redemption: An Essay in the Christian Understanding of Evil with an Examination of the Notion of Redemptive Order in Josiah Royce and Alfred North Whitehead." Unpublished Ph.D. dissertation, Yale University, 1961.

Evil; God, and evil; theodicy; redemption; Royce, Josiah.

1274   Norman, Ralph. "Whitehead and 'Mathematicism'." *Alfred North Whitehead: Essays on His Philosophy*. Edited by

George E. Kline. Englewood Cliffs, New Jersey: Prentice–Hall, Inc., 1963, 33–40.

Philosophy, and mathematics; aesthetics; skepticism.

Whitehead suggests two uses of mathematics for philosophy. One is the 'skeptical' use, which rests upon mathematics as a means which tries, and oftentimes fails, to build certainty. The other is the 'aesthetic' use, which rests upon mathematics as a means of discovering and exhibiting types and models of coherence.

1275   Norman, Ralph. "Steam, Barbarism, and Dialectic: Notations on Proof and Sensibility." *Christian Scholar*, 50, 1967, 184–196.

Judgment, ethical; relativity, cultural; Plato; Kierkegaard, Soren; Hampshire, Stuart; ethics; aesthetics.

Problems of ethical sensibility and judgment are compounded in the anomie of contemporary society. Whitehead and Hampshire, with support from Plato, offer a viable ethical thesis in which the divorce of fact and value is not allowed to become ultimate, and in which the aesthetic definition of order has become ultimate instead.

1276   Norris, Donald C. "A Critique of Whitehead's Theory of Consciousness." Unpublished Ph.D. dissertation, Boston University Graduate School, 1972.

Consciousness; imagination; propositions; feelings, physical; contrast; subjectivist principle, reformed.

An analysis of conscious imagination shows that Whitehead's theory of consciousness should be revised so that it does not require physical feelings.

1277   Northrop, F. S. C. "The Unitary Field Theory of Einstein and its Bearing on the Macroscopic Atomic Theory." *Monist*, 40, 1930, 325–338.

Relativity: general theory of, special theory of; measurement; geometry: Euclidian, Riemannian; Einstein, Albert; physics.

Whitehead rejected the general theory of relativity on the grounds that it described a universe in which the measurement of astronomical distances should be impossible. He reconceived the metrical structure of space as a relatedness between events, which entails the independence of matter from space–time structure. An alternative solution is the author's macroscopic atomic theory.

1278   Northrop, F. S. C. *Science and First Principles*. New York: The Macmillan Company, 1931.

Relativity, theory of; measurement; simultaneity; matter; space–time; qualities: secondary, tertiary; science, and philosophy; Einstein, Albert.

Whitehead believes that the passage of nature is too ambiguous to insure that the simultaneity which is intuitively given for the whole of nature is the same for one person as for another. It is because of this that Whitehead derives a meaning for relativity which does not depend upon physical reference frames and light rays.

Review

Adams, G. P. *Philosophical Review*, 46, 1937, 672–674.

1279   Northrop, F. S. C. "Whitehead's Philosophy of Science." *The Philosophy of Alfred North Whitehead.* Edited by Paul A. Schilpp. La Salle, Illinois: Open Court Publishing Company, 1941, 1951, 1971, 125–163.

Nature, bifurcation of; philosophy, of science; sense–perception; objects, of science; relativity, theory of; simultaneity; time, public; *The Concept of Nature; The Principle of Relativity*; Galilei, Galileo; Newton, Isaac; Locke, John; Leibniz, Gottfried; Kant, Immanuel; Bergson, Henri; Einstein, Albert; science.

Whitehead's philosophy of science has been produced by three factors: (1) Bergson's emphasis upon the all–sufficiency of immediate intuition and the primacy of process, (2) the epistemological difficulties into which the scientist's bifurcation of nature led modern philosophers, and (3) the reconstruction in the fundamental concepts of contemporary science necessitated especially by Einstein's theory of relativity. It has both the strengths and weaknesses of these influences.

1280   Northrop, F. S. C. *The Meeting of East and West.* New York: The Macmillan Company, 1946.

Philosophy, of culture; continuum, aesthetic; sense–perception, and aesthetic continuum.

1281   Northrop, F. S. C. *The Logic of the Sciences and the Humanities.* New York: Macmillan Company, 1947; New York: World Publishing Company, 1959.

Eternal objects: and Aristotle's forms, and Plato's ideas; concepts: of postulation, of intuition; abstraction, extensive; sense–perception, and nature; *Concept of Nature*; Plato; Aristotle.

Whitehead's eternal objects and Aristotle's forms are quite different from Plato's 'ideas'. An Aristotelian form, like a Whiteheadian eternal object, is a Platonic 'sensible' given an immortal persistence by postulation. A Platonic idea, on the other hand, is not even in part a sensible.

1282   Northrop, F. S. C. "Whitehead, Alfred North." *Science*, 107, 1948, 262–263.

Whitehead, Alfred North, obituary notice.

1283   Northrop, F. S. C. and Gross, M. W. *Alfred North Whitehead: An Anthology.* New York: Macmillan Company, 1953, 1961.

Language, Whitehead's use of; Whitehead, Alfred North: introduction to his thought.

1284   Northrop, F. S. C. *The Complexity of Legal and Ethical*

Experience. Boston: Little, Brown, and Company, 1959, 161–164.

Needham, Joseph; philosophy, Chinese.

(Although the work does not contain a sustained discussion of Whitehead's philosophy, there is brief mention of Joseph Needham's comparisons of Chinese philosophy and Whitehead's thought.)

1285   Northrop, F. S. C. "Foreword." *A Whiteheadian Aesthetic.* By Donald Sherburne. New Haven, Connecticut: Yale University Press, Inc., 1961. Reprinted Hamden, Connecticut: Archon Press, 1970. XIII–XXIX. Also as "Whitehead's Prose and Concrete Experience." *Man, Nature and God.* By F. S. C. Northrop.

Aesthetics; art; sense–perception; language: Whitehead's use of, and subject–predicate mode of expression; concreteness, fallacy of misplaced.

In response to the fact that ordinary language distorts the facts of experience, a philosopher may (a) use the language of symbolic logic and mathematics instead of ordinary language, or (b) supplement ordinary language by introducing technical terms and unordinary word usages. Whitehead used both methods to illuminate the aesthetic nature of immediate experience.

1286   Northrop, F. S. C. "From Kindergarten Onward." *Main Currents,* 25, 1969, 122–125.

Language: limitations of, and subject–predicate mode of expression, and reality; substance, criticism of; education: and learning, and curriculum.

Aryan prose corrupts our thinking and education from the kindergarten level upward by its substantialist language. (The author cites three pieces of advice which Whitehead personally gave to him—1) "Spend your days and nights with David Hume," 2) "You can't be too suspicious of ordinary language," and 3) "the two greatest achievements of the western mind were the ideas of the entity–variable and the general theory of proportion.")

1287   Novak, P. "Studien zur Kohärenz des Whiteheadischen Denkens." Unpublished dissertation, Heidelberg University, 1968.

Coherence; adequacy; categoreal scheme; Whitehead, Alfred North, method of.

1288   O'Brien, John. "The Place and Notion of God in the Philosophy of Alfred North Whitehead." Unpublished dissertation, National University of Ireland, 1954.

God: function of, Whitehead's arguments for, as dipolar, consequent nature of, primordial nature of, superjective nature of.

1289   O'Brien, John A. "'God' in Whitehead's Philosophy: A Strange

New 'Deity'." *American Ecclesiastical Review*, 110, 1944, 444–450, and 111, 1944, 124–130.

God: concept of, religious adequacy of.

Whitehead's concepts of the deity are probably as strange, bizarre and grotesque as can be found in the philosophic or theological literature of modern times.

1290   Odagaki, Mayaya. "An Attempt at Anthropological Theology: Schubert Ogden and the Philosophy of Kitaro Nishida." *Drew Gateway*, 44, Spring, 1974, 120–131.

Buddhism; Nishida, Kitaro.

1291   Ogden, Schubert M. "Bultmann's Project of Demythologization and the Problem of Theology and Philosophy." *Journal of Religion*, 37, 1957, 156–173.

Theology, and philosophy; kerygma; Jesus, as God's decisive act; Bultmann, Rudolf; existentialism.

Bultmann's distinction between theology and philosophy is inconsistent. The alternative position which is involved in a consistent acceptance of his demythologization project is theology's acknowledgement of its ultimate identity with the "right philosophy."

1292   Ogden, Schubert. *Christ Without Myth*. New York: Harper and Row, 1961.

Demythologizing; language, analogical; Jesus: as Christ, as unique, as special revelation; existence; God: as acting in history, language about, presence in Jesus; analogy; revelation; myth; possibility; Bible, and history; Bultmann, Rudolf; Barth, Karl; Hartshorne, Charles; Heidegger, Martin; anthropology; christology.

In speaking of Jesus of Nazareth as the decisive manifestation of God's love and as a "possibility in fact" for authentic human existence, a process philosophical analysis of Bultmann's Heideggerian categories shows that it is possible to speak of God analogously without simultaneously speaking mythologically.

1293   Ogden, Schubert M. *The Reality of God and Other Essays*. New York: Harper and Row, 1963, 1965, 1966.

Metaphysics, neoclassical; subjectivist principle, reformed; God: classical view of, and temporality, and categoreal scheme; death, as perpetual perishing; Hartshorne, Charles; theology.

With the help of neoclassical metaphysics such as that of Whitehead and Hartshorne, Christian theology can affirm God's temporality in its relation to human existence. The starting point for such a metaphysical position must be what Whitehead calls the 'reformed subjectivist principle'.

Reviews

Flew, A. *Journal of Religion*, 58, 1968, 150–161.

Gilkey, L. B. *Interpretation*, 21, 1967, 447–459.

Hudson, W. D. *Philosophical Quarterly*, 18, 1968, 380–381.

Neville, R. C. *Philosophical Quarterly*, 19, 1969, 605–624.

1294   Ogden, Schubert M. "What Sense Does It Make To Say, 'God Acts in History'?" *Journal of Religion*, 43, 1963, 1–19.

God: as acting in history, Hartshorne's interpretation of; Jesus, as God's decisive act; Bultmann, Rudolf; Hartshorne, Charles; theology.

Wherever or insofar as an event in history reveals or expresses God's characteristic action as Creator and Redeemer, it actually is God's act in a sense in which other historical events are not. Jesus is the decisive act of God.

1295   Ogden, Schubert M. "Beyond Supernaturalism." *Religion in Life*, 33, 1963, 7–18.

God, language about; supernaturalism; secularism; Robinson, John A. T.; Hartshorne, Charles; Tillich, Paul; theology.

The constructive conception of God to which Robinson wants to point in *Honest to God* can be fully brought into its own only when it is seen to be, in some respects, as much an alternative to the Tillichian model as to the other alternatives.

1296   Ogden, Schubert M. "Zur Frage der "richtigen" Philosophie." *Zeitschrift Fuer Theologie und Kirche*, 61, 1964, 103–124.

Philosophy, right one for theology; analysis, existential; existence: Heidegger's understanding of, human, divine; dipolarity; God, as dipolar; Heidegger, Martin; Hartshorne, Charles.

The "right" philosophy for Christian theology is not Heidegger's analysis of Dasein alone, but that analysis in connection with Hartshorne's dipolar doctrine of God.

1297   Ogden, Schubert M. "Theology and Philosophy: A New Phase of the Discussion." *Journal of Religion*, 44, 1964, 1–16.

The Logic of Perfection and Other Essays in Neoclassical Metaphysics; theology, and philosophy; God, proofs of; Hartshorne, Charles; Kant, Immanuel; philosophical theology.

Hartshorne's neoclassical version of the ontological argument implies that much of what has been written by theologians concerning the possibilities and limits of arguments for God is no longer relevant. Hartshorne's work offers unique resources to his theological colleagues, since his philosophy has such deep and determining affinities with the scriptural revelation.

1298   Ogden, Schubert M. "A Christian Natural Theology?" *Christian Advocate*, 9, 1965, 11–12. Also in *Process Philosophy and Christian Thought*. Edited by Delwin Brown, Ralph E. James and Gene Reeves. Indianapolis, indiana: Bobbs–Merrill Company Inc., 1971, 111–115.

Theology, natural; God, doctrine of; Cobb, John B., Jr.; anthropology.

(This is a response to Cobb's *A Christian Natural Theology*.)

1299   Ogden, Schubert M. "Faith and Truth." *The Christian Century,*
        1965, 1057–1060. .

        Faith: truth of, experience of; truth: and faith, verification of;
        procedure, theological; theism: classical, neoclassical; Bultmann,
        Rudolf; Tillich, Paul; Hartshorne, Charles; theology; religion.

        Responsibility to the Christian faith requires that faith be
        understood in terms of the experience and reason by which
        human beings live.

1300   Ogden, Schubert M.   "Theology and Objectivity."   *Journal of
        Religion,* 45, 1965, 175–195.

        Language: uses of, theological, about God; faith; objectivity;
        van Buren, Paul; Hartshorne, Charles; theology.

        Theology is in its own way scientific; its statements in their
        most proper part are assertions about God and divine action;
        justification of these assertions can only be a metaphysical
        justification.   Process philosophy in its most mature and fully
        developed forms provides an adequate metaphysics for this
        task.

1301   Ogden, Schubert M.   "Love Unbounded: The Doctrine of God."
        Perkins School of Theology Journal, 19, 1966, 5–17.

        God: doctrine of, as love, language about; theism, process;
        Wesley, John; theology.

        Process metaphysics offers full philosophical generalization of
        the ancient insight that the very nature of being is love.
        Thus it provides terms and categories in which we may
        formulate theologically what has always been the burden of the
        church's preaching, that God is pure unbounded love.

1302   Ogden, Schubert M.   "The Christian Proclamation of God to
        Men of the So–Called 'Atheistic Age'."   *Is God Dead?*
        Concilium, 16. Edited by J. B. Metz. Paramus, N. J.: Paulist
        Press, 1966, 89–98.

        Faith; God, language about; theism, process; atheism.

        Classical theism is neither the only nor the most appropriate
        form in which Christian faith in God can now be expressed.
        The nature of faith and proclamation, both as existential and
        as   theoretical,   demands   more   adequate   contemporary
        expression.

1303   Ogden, Schubert M. "How Does God Function in Human Life?"
        Christianity and Crisis, 27, 1967, 105–108.

        God: language about, function of; religion.

        The function of God is to make the whole venture of human
        life worthwhile and to evoke in human beings an abiding
        confidence in life's worth.

1304   Ogden, Schubert M.   "God and Philosophy: A Discussion with
        Antony Flew." *Journal of Religion,* 48, 1968, 161–181.

        Metaphysics, method of; God: proofs of, power of; Flew,
        Antony; Hartshorne, Charles; philosophical theology.

The theism Antony Flew refutes is not the only theism a
Christian today may affirm. The underlying assumption of
Flew's refutation of theism is the rule of empirical falsifiability.
Since his own atheism cannot comply with this rule, the
assumption is inappropriate to the sense of metaphysical
statements, whether theistic or atheistic.

1305   Ogden, Schubert M. "Present Prospects for Empirical Theology."
The Future of Empirical Theology. Edited by Bernard E.
Meland. Chicago, Illinois: University of Chicago Press, 1968,
65–88.

Theology, empirical.

1306   Ogden, Schubert M. "Toward a New Theism." *Process
Philosophy and Christian Thought.* Edited by Delwin Brown,
Ralph E. James and Gene Reeves. Indianapolis, Indiana:
Bobbs–Merrill Company Inc., 1971, 173–187.

God: as absolute, as relative, relations of; theism, classical;
Hartshorne, Charles.

Although the classical metaphysics and its conception of divine
attributes contains some element of truth, it neglects the social,
temporal, and therefore truly personal aspects of God.

1307   Ogden, Schubert M. "Lonergan and the Subjectivist Principle."
Journal of Religion, 51, 1971, 155–172.

Subjectivist principle; philosophy: method of, task of;
Lonergan, Bernard; Thomism.

There are difficulties in Lonergan's work which lie in the fact
that regardless of 'his expressed method of working from
self–understanding, he continues to use philosophical categories
derived from point of view other than the subjectivist principle.

1308   Ogden, Schubert M. "The Task of Philosophical Theology." *The
Future of Philosophical Theology.* Edited by R. Evans.
Philadelphia, Pennsylvania: Westminster Press, 1971, 55–84.

Theology: philosophical, method of.

1309   Ogletree, Thomas W. "A Christological Assessment of Dipolar
Theism." *Journal of Religion*, 47, 1967, 87–99. Also in *Process
Philosophy and Christian Thought.* Edited by Delwin Brown,
Ralph E. James and Gene Reeves. Indianapolis, Indiana:
Bobbs–Merrill Company, Inc., 1971, 331–346.

God, Hartshorne's interpretation of; incarnation; Jesus;
theology, and philosophy; Hartshorne, Charles; Altizer, Thomas
J. J.; christology.

A critical explication of the central Christian motif of the
incarnation confirms in general Hartshorne's doctrine of God.

1310   O'Keefe, Thomas. *The Actual Entity and the Concept of
Substance in the Philosophy of Alfred North Whitehead.*
Rome: Pontificia Universitas Gregoriana, 1952.

Substance: Whitehead's reasons for rejecting, and physical
substance, and scientific matter, and Aristotle; actual entity,

unity of; subject, as superject; knowledge; metaphysics; abstraction, extensive; Aristotle; empiricism.

The concept of 'substance' which Whitehead rejects is that of an imperceptible substratum to that which is disclosed in sense–awareness. Whitehead errs in identifying all other concepts of substance with this one. Aristotle's concept of substance avoids the problems which Whitehead seeks to avoid, and is more intelligible than Whitehead's doctrine of actual entity. (This is the author's dissertation at Pontificia Universitas Gregoriana, 1950.)

1311   O'Keefe, Thomas. "Empiricism and Applied Mathematics in the Natural Philosophy of Whitehead." *Modern Schoolman*, 28, 1951, 267–289.

Mathematics, as applied; abstraction, extensive; *Concept of Nature*; empiricism; metaphysics.

Whitehead attempts to set up a correspondence between exact mathematical entities, which do not exist in nature, and essentially inexact natural entities. Only by using the word "is" instead of "corresponds to" is he enabled to assert that the exact mathematical entities are in nature.

1312   Olewiler, B. T. "Whitehead's Philosophy of Language and the Whorf Hypothesis." Unpublished Ph.D. dissertation, Johns Hopkins University, 1971.

Language: and subject–predicate mode of expression, and Whorfian hypothesis; philosophy, of language; Whorf, Benjamin.

1313   Olive, D. D. "The Relation of Faith and History in Selected Works of Karl Barth, G. Ernest Wright, and Alfred North Whitehead." Unpublished dissertation, South Western Baptist Theological Seminary, 1966.

Faith; history; Barth, Karl; Wright, G. Ernest.

1314   Olson, Robert F. "Whitehead, Madhyamika, and the Prajnaparamita." *Philosophy East and West*, 25, 1975, 450–464.

Truth: Buddhism's two kinds of, as dependent origination; perception: as presentational immediacy, as causal efficacy, as symbolic reference; nondualism; Nagarjuna; Buddhism: Madhyamika, Prajnaparamita.

Prajnaparamita Buddhism is characterized by a thoroughgoing program of invalidating conceptual thought; Whitehead's program is premised on its inherent validity. Nevertheless, process philosophy provides a coherent possible ontological explanation for the modes of knowing and the two–truths doctrine of Prajna Buddhism.

1315   O'Mahony, T. J. "'Essential Relevance' in Whitehead." *Proceedings of the American Catholic Philosophical Association*, 22, 1947, 104–112.

Process philosophy: summary of, criticisms of; substance.

Relevance entails a real fusion between Whitehead's world of eternal values and world of fact in order to account for the substantial aspect of things. Perennial metaphysics gives a more adequate answer to the problem through the notion of substance.

1316 O'Meara, William M. "Speculative Reason and Religious Experience in Whitehead." Unpublished Ph.D. dissertation, Loyola University, 1969.

Experience, religious; reason: and experience, speculative, function of; religion: and reason, and intuition of permanence.

1317 O'Meara, William M. "Whitehead's Description of Religious Intuition." *Encounter*, 34, Spring, 1973, 101–113.

Intuition; religion: and intuition of permanence, and value; experience, religious.

1318 Orsi, C. *La filosofia dell' organismo di Alfred North Whitehead.* Napoli: Libreria Scientifica, 1956.

Whitehead, Alfred North: introduction to his thought; actual entities; eternal objects; God, nature of.

Reviews

Arata, C. *Metafisica*, 12, 1957, 767–769.

Basciani, D. *Humanitas*, 14, 1959, 236–239.

Bertolini, P. *Revista Rosminiana di Filosofia e di Cultura*, 50, 1956, 238–239.

Decloux, S. *Revue Philosophique de Lourain*, 55, 1957, 133–134.

Echari, J. *Pensamiento*, 13, 1957, 236–237.

1319 Otto, M. C. "Alfred North Whitehead and Science." *New Humanist*, 7, 1934, 1–7.

Philosophy, and science; science, and metaphysics.

1320 Overholser, James A. *A Contemporary Christian Philosophy of Religion.* Chicago: Henry Regnery Company, 1964.

Christianity, and Christ; concrescence, and Christ; religion, and science; Jesus Christ; Kierkegaard, Soren; Bergson, Henri; Jaspers, Karl; Heidegger, Martin; theology.

(This work is an existential interpretation of the personal being of Jesus Christ as understood in reference to several philosophical perspectives, Whitehead's among them. The author attempts an interpretive synthesis of Whitehead's thought with that of Heidegger.)

1321 Overman, Richard H. "Evolutionary Theory and the Christian Doctrine of Creation: A Whiteheadian Interpretation." Unpublished Ph.D. dissertation, Claremont Graduate School, 1966.

God: as creator, Biblical view of, of classical theism, and order, as source of initial aim; evolution: as biological, and embryonic development, and genetics, as organic, and natural selection; causation: efficient, final; genetics; teleology; panpsychism;

Darwin, Charles; Macquarrie, John; Teilhard de Chardin; Gilkey, Langdon; Lamarck, J. B.; biology; theology, process.

1322 Overman, Richard H. *Evolution and the Christian Doctrine of Creation.* Philadelphia, Pennsylvania: Westminster Press, 1967.

God: as creator, Biblical view of, of classical theism, and order, primordial nature of, as source of initial aim; evolution: as biological, and embryonic development, and genetics, as organic, and natural selection, and human existence; causation: efficient, final; genetics; teleology; panpsychism; Darwin, Charles; Lamarck, J. B.; Macquarrie, John; Teilhard de Chardin; Gilkey, Langdon; biology; theology, process.

Whitehead's philosophy provides a framework for understanding evolution which gives proper expression to both scientific and Biblical experience, allowing for the belief that God is literally the creator of the world.

Reviews

Allshouse, M. F. *Christian Century,* 85, 1968, 1340.

Johnson, S. *Library Journal,* 92, 1967, 3044.

1323 Overman, Richard H. "A Christological View of Nature." *Religious Education,* January–February, 1971.

Nature, and human existence; christology; theology.

1324 Overman, Richard H. "Hat die Theologie die Natur vergessen?" *Radius,* September, 1973.

Nature, and God; theology, process.

1325 Overman, Richard H. "What We Need is Indoor Plumbing or, Whiteheadian Style and the Search for a New Scientific Order." *Religious Experience and Process Theology.* Edited by Harry James Cargas and Bernard Lee. New York: Paulist Press, 1976, 53–67.

Whitehead, Alfred North: evaluation of; experience, religious; psychology.

(The author talks about his own life and his encounter with process thought as a way of discoursing about history and the evolution of human consciousness.)

1326 Owen, William A. "Whitehead's Philosophy of Science and the Concept of Substance." Unpublished Ph.D. dissertation, Georgetown University, 1964.

Substance; philosophy, of science; objects: of science, external, material; event; sense–perception.

1327 Owen, William A. "The Philosophy of Science, According to Whitehead." *Atenea* (Puerto Rico), 3, 1966, 9–26.

Sciences, relation between; nature, analysis of; philosophy, of science.

Exactness, neatness, and trimness are abstractions which cannot specify the basic raw material of the sciences. Whitehead's rejection of these abstractions is the key to characteristic features in his philosophy of science.

1328   Paci, Enzo. "Presentazione di Whitehead." *Aut Aut*, 12, 1952, 507–517.

Whitehead, biography of.

Whitehead's self–understanding of being a teacher and philosopher emerge from his autobiographical notes.

1329   Paci, Enzo. "Prospettive empiristiche e relazionistiche nel Whitehead pre–speculativo." *Aut Aut*, 16, 1953, 279–297.

Whitehead, early theory of; empiricism; organicism; Russell, Bertrand; logic; mathematics; physics.

In Whitehead's early philosophy of science there are many aspects which point to his later theory of experience and lead beyond classical empiricism.

1330   Paci, Enzo. "Definizione e funzione della filosofia speculativa." *Giornale Critico della filosofia italiana*, 32, 1953, 304–334.

Philosophy: speculative, aim of, task of, of civilization; Plato; Dewey, John.

Whitehead's conception of speculative philosophy may be reappraised against neo–positivistic and reductionistic trends of thought.

1331   Paci, Enzo. "Sul primo periodo della filosofia di Whitehead." *Revista di filosofia*, 44, 1953, 397–415.

Whitehead, early theory of.

1332   Paci, Enzo. "Whitehead e Russell." *Revista di filosofia*, 45, 1954, 14–25.

Philosophy, of organism; Russell, Bertrand; Jorgensen, J.; logic; neo–positivism.

(Whitehead and Russell's early philosophies are compared.)

1333   Paci, Enzo. *Tempo e relazione.* Turin: Taylor, 1954.

Relations, temporal; time, as relational.

1334   Paci, Enzo. *Dall' esistenzialismo al relazionasmo.* D'Anna: Messine–Florence, 1957.

Existence; relations; Kierkegaard, Soren; Jaspers, Karl; Heidegger, Martin; Dewey, John; Santayana, George; Woodbridge, Frederick, G. E.; Russell, Bertrand; Merleau–Ponty, Maurice; cybernetics; existentialism; naturalism; phenomenology; neo–positivism.

Whitehead's philosophy, as related to Paci's "relationalism", shows its speculative importance for the major issues confronting contemporary philosophy.

1335   Paci, Enzo. "Introdduzione." *La scienza e il mondo moderno.* Second edition. Milano: bompiani, 1959.

Whitehead, introduction to his thought.

1336   Paci, Enzo. "Über einige Verwandschaften zwischen der Philosophie Whiteheads und der Phenomenologie Husserls." *Revue Internationale Philosophie*, 15, 1961, 237–250.

Life–world; concreteness, fallacy of misplaced; time; relatedness; philosophy, and science; mathematics; logic.

Both Whitehead's philosophy and Husserl's phenomenology are philosophies of time and relatedness.

1337   Paci, Enzo. "Alfred North Whitehead." *Les grands courants de la pensée mondial contemporaine.* Edited by M. F. Sciacca. Paris: Fishbacher, 1964.

Process philosophy, summary of.

1338   Paci, Enzo. "Whitehead e Husserl." *Aut Aut,* 1964, 7–18.

Husserl, Edmund; phenomenology.

1339   Paci, Enzo. "Sull' orizzonte di verita della scienza." *Aut Aut,* 90, 1965, 7–16.

Concreteness, fallacy of misplaced.

1340   Paci, Enzo. "Il senso delle parole." *Aut Aut,* 90, 1965, 79–84.

Language, and meaning.

1341   Paci, Enzo. *Relazioni e significati,* Volume I. Milano: Nigri, 1965.

Relation: internal, external; meaning, general theory of.

1342   Paci, Enzo. "Sulla struttura della scienza." *Aut Aut,* 86, 1965, 27–36.

Time; Husserl; philosophy, of science.

1343   Paci, Enzo. *La filosofia de Whitehead e i problemi del tempo e della struttura.* Milano: Goliardica, 1965.

Time: epochal theory of, relativity view of, as past, as present, as future, classical view of.

1344   Page, F. H. "Whitehead's Philosophy." *Dalhousie Review,* 28, 1948, 133–144.

Language, Whitehead's use of; process philosophy, summary of.

Whitehead's obscurity of language resulted both from his mathematical habits of thought, and from his rejection of traditional categories for an organic analysis of experience. His philosophy itself is the statement of the mutual creation of the world and God by the participation of Form in Fact through the mediation of God.

1345   Page, F. H. "A. N. Whitehead: A Pupil's Tribute." *Dalhousie Review,* 28, 1948, 71–80.

Whitehead, Alfred North, biography of.

1346   Pai, Young. "The Free Will–Determinism Controversy and its Educational Implications." Unpublished Ph.D. dissertation, Rutgers University, 1959.

Freedom; causality; philosophy, of education.

1347   Pailin, David A. "The Incarnation as a Continuing Reality." *Religious Studies,* 6, 1970, 303–327.

Incarnation: purpose of, verification of, as revelation; Jesus, as revelation; God, and Christology; Christology.

The revelation seen in Jesus is a valid insight into the active actuality of God, who is the ground and goal of being. This insight is true of all processes of being at all times; thus the incarnation is a continuing reality.

1348   Pailin, David A.   "Process Theology—Why and What?"   *Faith and Thought*, 100, 1972–1973, 45–66.

Process theology, summary of.

1349   Palter, Robert.   "Philosophic Principles and Scientific Theory." *Philosophy of Science*, 23, 1956, 111–135.

Relativity: general theory of, special theory of; method, scientific; Einstein, Albert; physics; philosophy, of science.

Einstein's and Whitehead's diverse theories of relativity are initially neutral with respect to empirical content. Extrapolation of each leads to new theories which are no longer neutral, even with respect to empirical content. This demonstrates the pluralism of science, its dependence upon and reflection of philosophy, and the necessity of continued attention to scientific diversity.

1350   Palter, Robert M.   *Whitehead's Philosophy of Science*.   Chicago: University of Chicago Press, 1960, 1970.

Nature, philosophy of; nature: atomicity of; events: infinite, indeterminate; extension; abstraction, extensive; duration; time, systems of; space; simultaneity; relativity: theory of, special theory of, and Minkowski's space–time geometry; measurement; motion; force: centrifugal, conservative, gravitational, inertial, relativistic; energy; geometry: projective, metrical; points; lines; regions; congruence; flatness; field: electromagnetic, inertial; gravity; tensors; vectors; objects: material, of science; *The Principles of Natural Knowledge; The Concept of Nature*; science; physics.

Whitehead's doctrine of event and his relational theory of space and time enable him to avoid the difficulties which result from the classical concept of the material world. His aim is to show how the high–level abstractions of theoretical science can be systematically derived from certain aspects of sense–experience.

Reviews

Chappell, V. C.   *Ethics*, 71, 1960–1961, 72.

Diamadoupoupolos, P.   *Revue Internationale de Philosophie*, 15, 1961, 436–440.

Gruenbaum, A.   *Philosophical Review*, 71, 1962, 218–229.

Hutten, E. H.   *Philosophy*, 38, 1963, 185–186.

Leclerc, I.   *New Scholasticism*, 37, 1963, 102–104.

Mays, W.   *Philosophical Quarterly*, 12, 1962, 188–189.

McMullin, E.   *Philosophical Studies* (Ireland), 12, 1963, 216–220.

1351   Palter, Robert.   "Whitehead's Theory of Relativity: Its Scientific and Philosophic Implications." *Journal of Philosophy*, 58, 1961, 691–692.

Relativity: special theory of, general theory of; Einstein, Albert; physics; philosophy of science.

Accepting the spatiotemporal framework of special relativity, Whitehead constructs a law of gravitation which is in a sense the simplest possible relativistic counterpart of Newton's law of universal gravitation.

1352   Palter, Robert M. "The Place of Mathematics in Whitehead's Philosophy." *Journal of Philosophy*, 58, 1961, 565–576. Slightly revised in *Alfred North Whitehead: Essays on His Philosophy*. Edited by George L. Kline. Englewood Cliffs, New Jersey: Prentice–Hall, Inc., 1963, 41–52.

Eternal objects; actual occasions; deduction; generalization, descriptive; societies, corpuscular; mathematics, as eternal objects; geometry; logic.

In logic, Whitehead understands the subject matter of mathematics to be eternal objects. Such mathematics deals with necessary truths and its method of validation is deductive. In natural knowledge, Whitehead understands the subject matter of mathematics to be physical objects or corpuscular societies. Such mathematics deals with empirical truths and its method of validation is through sense perception. In cosmology, Whitehead understands the subject matter of mathematics to be actual occasions. Such mathematics deals with metaphysical truths and its method of validation is descriptive generalization.

1353   Palter, Robert M. "Science and Its History in the Philosophy of Whitehead." *Process and Divinity*. Edited by William L. Reese and Eugene Freeman. La Salle, Illinois: Open Court Publishing Company, 1964, 51–78.

Relativity, theory of; science, and philosophy; geometry; mathematics.

1354   Pardington, G. Palmer III. "Transcendence and Models of God." *Anglican Theological Review*, 54, 1972, 82–93.

Transcendence; God: concept of, language about; theology, radical; Altizer, Thomas J. J.; Hartshorne, Charles; theology.

Panentheism provides a model of God which expresses the contemporary experience of transcendence as a power immanent in reality contributing to human self–transcendence.

1355   Pardington, G. Palmer. "The Holy Ghost is Dead—The Holy Spirit Lives." *Religious Experience and Process Thought*. Edited by Harry James Cargas and Bernard Lee. New York: Paulist Press, 1976, 121–132.

God: as love, and panentheism; Holy Spirit; nature, and God; theology, process.

From a Whiteheadian perspective the Holy Spirit can be interpreted as the immanent presence of God as creative–transforming love.   This Spirit finds expression in nature as well as human history.

1356 Parker, DeWitt H. *Experience and Substance: An Essay in Metaphysics.* Ann Arbor, Michigan: University of Michigan Press, 1941; Westport, Connecticut: Greenwood Press, 1968.

Experience; substance; relations; person, and personal identity; self: as personal society, and eternal objects; eternal objects, as universals; Platonism; empiricism.

(Although the work is not explicitly on Whitehead's philosophy, the author argues for a view of personal identity which he says resembles that of Whitehead and William James.   However he finds a fundamental difference between his view of the relation between experience and universals, and Whitehead's view of the relation between the self, as a series of experiences, and eternal objects.)

1357 Parker, Francis M.   "Head, Heart, and God."   *Review of Metaphysics*, 14, 1960, 328–352.

Panentheism; emotion, and knowledge; Hartshorne, Charles; Reese, William L.; Skutch, Alexander F.; philosophical theology.

The basic presupposition of the philosophico–religious speculation of panentheism appears to be that whatever is true of human emotional and intellectual experience is true of objective reality and of God.   Written in response to Charles Hartshorne and William L. Reese, *Philosophers Speak of God*, and Alexander F. Skutch, *The Quest of the Divine.*

1358 Parker, Franklin H.   "Alfred North Whitehead (1861–1947): A Partial Bibliography."   *Bulletin of Bibliography*, 23, 1961, 90–93.

Whitehead, Alfred North, bibliography of.

1359 Parmentier, Alix. *La philosophie de Whitehead et le problème de Dieu.*   Paris: Beauchesne, 1968.

Philosophy: and mathematics, of nature, speculative; actual entities; prehensions, theory of; creativity; eternal objects; God: primordial nature of, consequent nature of, superjective nature of, as eros, immanence of, and evil, as personal, objective immortality in; evil; Whitehead, Alfred North: bibliography of, introduction to his thought, philosophical development of; Aristotle; Plato; mathematics; epistemology.

(This work, the author's dissertation at the Universite de Paris–Nanterre, contains important primary and secondary bibliographies on Whitehead, including one of secondary works in French.)

Reviews

Antoniotti, L.–M.   *Revue Thomiste*, 70, 1970, 330–334.

Hartshorne, C.   *Thomist*, 33, 1969; *Archives de Philosophie*, 33, 1970, 661–667.

Philippe, M. D.   *Renovatio* (Genova), 4, 1969, 158–159.

1360   Parmentier, Alix. "A. N. Whitehead: Esquisse d'une biographie."
         Bulletin du Cercle Thomiste, 45, 1968, 23–32 and 46, 1969,
         21–28.

         Whitehead, Alfred North, biography of.

1361   Parmentier, Alix. "Actualité de Whitehead." *Revue de Theologie
         et de Philosophie*, 4, 1969, 225–234.

         Dualism, cartesian; esse, est percipere; perception; subject, as
         superject; mover, prime; God, as principle of limitation;
         subjectivism; Aristotle.

1362   Parmentier, Alix. "Whitehead et la découverte de l'existence de
         Dieu." *Revue Theologie et de Philosophie*, 5, 1969, 307–317.

         God: existence of, discovery of, as transcendent, as principle of
         concretion, as personal, as primordial; a priori; *Science and the
         Modern World; Religion in the Making; Process and Reality.*

1363   Parsons, Barbara A. "The Importance of Man in Whitehead's
         Philosophy." Unpublished Ph.D. dissertation, Tulane
         University, 1970.

         Man; nature; bifurcation; humanism; self; language; value;
         existentialism.

         There is reason to think, despite the understandable attention
         given by Whiteheadian scholars to *Process and Reality*, that
         Whitehead himself did not in the end consider system–building
         to be the philosopher's principle means of promoting that 'art
         of life' which is civilization.

1364   Parsons, Howard L. "God and Man's Achievement of Identity:
         Religion in the Thought of Alfred North Whitehead."
         Educational Theory, 11, 1961, 228–254.

         Process philosophy, summary of; reverence; education;
         curriculum; philosophy: of religion, of education.

         Whitehead's philosophy of religion has direct relevance to
         educational philosophy, methodology, and curricula.

1365   Parsons, Howard L. "Religious Naturalism and the Philosophy of
         Charles Hartshorne." *Process and Divinity*. Edited by
         William L. Reese and Eugene Freeman. La Salle, Illinois:
         Open Court Publishing Company, 1964, 533–560.

         Nature; value; God, knowledge of; Hartshorne, Charles.

1366   Parsons, Howard L. "History as Viewed by Marx and
         Whitehead." *Christian Scholar*, 50, 1967, 273–289.

         Philosophy, of history; history: as conflict, as dialectical, as
         teleological; Marx, Karl; philosophy, of history.

         The philosophies of history of Marx and Whitehead
         complement one another in a dialectical tension. Each is
         inadequate for theory and practice without the other;
         consequently, there is need for a more adequate philosophy of
         history and nature which in using both will supersede both.

1367   Passmore, John. *A Hundred Years of Philosophy*. London:
         Duckworth, 1957, 337–344.

Process philosophy, summary of.

A recurrent theme in Whitehead's philosophy is his insistence that an adequate account of the relation between material objects and space must make use of polyadic relations.

1368　　Pastore, Annibale. "Whitehead e Heidegger contro Kant circa la natura emotova del tempo." *Revista di Filosofia*, 38, 1947, 181–190.

Time: emotional character of, Heidegger's theory of, and feeling; temporality; Heidegger, Martin; Kant, Immanuel; Wahl, Jean.

Whitehead and Heidegger share a common emphasis on the emotional character of time.

1369　　Paul, L. *Persons and Perception*. London: Faber & Faber, 1961.

Perception; person, and consciousness; causal efficacy; presentational immediacy.

1370　　Peden, W. Creighton. "The Structure of Whitehead's Method of Philosophy." *Radford Review*, 21, 1967, 169–184.

Philosophy, method of.

1371　　Peden, W. Creighton. "Whitehead's Doctrine of God." *Radford Review*, 23, 1969, 59–71.

God: concept of, primordial nature of, consequent nature of.

1372　　Peden, W. Creighton. "Wieman's Non–Theistic Process–God." *Journal of Religious Thought*, 27, 1970, 29–36.

God: creativity of, transcendence of, immanence of, and good; Wieman, Henry Nelson; theology.

The theism rejected by Wieman is Hellenistic; his own theology is essentially compatible with the biblical tradition.

1373　　Pemberton, Harrison J. "The Problem of Personal Identity with Special Reference to Whitehead and Bergson." Unpublished Ph.D. dissertation, Yale University, 1953.

Person, and personal identity; enduring object; physical purpose; receptacle, of Plato; substance; time, and transition; Bergson Henri.

Whitehead's account of personal identity is inadequate, but can be reformulated through an elaboration of his own suggestion that there exists a relation between personal identity and the Platonic notion of receptacle.

1374　　Pepe, G. R. *Il pensiero educativo di Whitehead*. Firenze: La Nouva Italia, 1972.

Education: aims of, and society, stages of; philosophy, of education.

1375　　Pepper, Stephen C. *World Hypotheses: A Study in Evidence*. Berkeley, California: University of California Press, 1942, 112–113.

Philosophy, and root–metaphors.

Whitehead's metaphysics results in confusion because it tries to fuse different kinds of cosmologies.

1376   Pepper, Stephen C.   "Whitehead's 'Actual Occasion'."   *Tulane Studies in Philosophy*, 10, 1961, 71–88.

Actual occasion: as purposive act, and time; metaphor.

The actual occasion, as a purposive act, is a new root metaphor which could be the source of a new philosophical school.

1377   Pepper, Stephen C.   "A Proposal for a World Hypothesis."   *Monist*, 47, 1963, 267–286.

Act, purposive; metaphor; bifurcation; metaphysics.

A purposive act allows a qualitative description and a conceptual description, each referring to exactly the same actual process.   By giving rise to both types of knowledge, the act is also an instrument for a comprehensive unification of knowledge.   It thus qualifies as a root metaphor for a new world hypothesis.

1378   Pérez Navarro, F.   "Los díalogos postumos del filósofo Whitehead."   *Cuadernos Hispanoamericanos*, 26, 1956, 386–387.

Whitehead, Alfred North: biography of.

1379   Permartín, José.   "Sobre el pensamiento de Alfred North Whitehead."   *Revista de Filosofia*, 7, 1948, 591–604.

Process philosophy, summary of; realism; idealism.

1380   Peters, Eugene H.   *The Creative Advance: An Introduction to Process Philosophy as a Context for Christian Faith*.   St. Louis, Missouri: Bethany Press, 1966.

God: and divine knowledge, primordial nature of, consequent nature of, superjective nature of; Christianity; philosophy, process; dualism, of mind and matter; panpsychism; occasion, of experience; societies; metaphysics, and religion; religion, and science; incarnation; sin; Whitehead, Alfred North: biography of; Jesus Christ; Hartshorne, Charles; Aristotle; Descartes, Rene; Newton, Isaac; theology, process.

Process philosophy is a 'spiritual' philosophy and is in alignment with the attitude and outlook of religion.   Its categories provide new starting points for understanding the relation between human existence and God.   In this way they provide a framework for understanding the Christian faith.

1381   Peters, Eugene H.   "A Framework for Christian Thought."   *Journal of Religion*, 46, 1966, 374–385.

God: Hartshorne's interpretation of, as acting in history, objective immortality in; Jesus, as God's decisive act; Hartshorne, Charles; Ogden, Schubert M.; theology.

Process themes have special relevance for Christian theology, particularly with reference to God's action in Christ, his immanence in the world, and the immanence of the world in God.

1382   Peters, Eugene H.   *Hartshorne and Neoclassical Metaphysics: An*
         Interpretation.   Lincoln, Nebraska: University of Nebraska
         Press, 1970.

         Hartshorne's theology, summary of; panpsychism; metaphysics;
         neoclassical, and aesthetics; prehension, and objectification;
         contemporaneity, and causal independence of contemporaries;
         Hartshorne, Charles: biography of, philosophical relation to
         Whitehead, personal relation to Whitehead.

         (This is an interpretation of Hartshorne's metaphysics with
         various references to Hartshorne's relation to Whitehead.)

         Review

         Reeves, G.   *Process Studies*, 1, 1971, 149–151.

1383   Phenix, Philip H.   *Intelligible Religion.*   New York: Harper and
         Brothers, 1954.

         Change, as religious problem.

         (This work aims to present an intelligible view of religion on
         the basis of five fundamental aspects of religious experience:
         change, dependence, order, value, and imperfection.   Reference
         to Whitehead's philosophy is quite minimal.)

1384   Phillips, B.   "Being and Process: A Study in Two Philosophies."
         Unpublished Ph.D. dissertation, Yale University, 1940.

         Being; process.

1385   Pichl, K.   "Überwindung des Geschichtspositivismus.   Der
         englische Beitrag: Whitehead, Russell und Toynbee."   *Wort*
         und Wahrheit, 4, 1949, 748–763.

         Positivism; Russell, Bertrand; Toynbee, Arnold.

1386   Pinottini, M.   "Il problema della storia come Adventura di Idee
         in Whitehead."   *Filosofia*, 20, 1969, 441–472.

         Civilization; history; *Adventures of Ideas*; Husserl, Edmund;
         Russell, Bertrand; Lowith, Karl.

         (This is an expository commentary on the first three parts of
         Adventures of Ideas.)

1387   Pinottini, Marzio.   "La civilta e i suoi valori in Whitehead."
         Filosofia, 20, 1969, 607–624.

         Civilization; harmony; truth; beauty; adventure; peace; *The*
         Adventure of Ideas.

1388   Pinottini, M.   "Bibliographia Whiteheadiana."   *Filosofia*, 20, 1969,
         614–624.

         Whitehead, Alfred North: bibliography of.

1389   Pittenger, W. Norman.   *Theology and Reality: Essays in*
         Restatement.   Greenwich, Connecticut: The Seabury Press,
         1955.

         Theology, and philosophy; Christianity; religion, and science.

1390   Pittenger, Norman W.   *The Word Incarnate: A Study of the*
         Doctrine of the Person of Christ.   New York: Harper and
         Brothers, 1959.

Christology; philosophy, process; Hartshorne, Charles; Berdyaev, Nicholas; theology, process; Christology; Christianity; philosophy, process; Christ; Hartshorne, Charles; Berdyaev, Nicholas; theology, process.

(In discussing the nature of Christ and Christ's role in Christianity the author suggests ways in which process philosophy can aid in Christological understanding.)

1391   Pittenger, W. Norman. "A Contemporary Trend in North American Theology: Process–Thought and Christian Faith." *Expository Times*, 76, 1965, 268–273. Also in *Religion in Life*, 34, 1965, 500–510.

God: as love, and christology; theology, process.

Emergent evolution, existentialist analysis of subjective human experience, history, and depth psychology converge in process thought to provide a context of faith with strong affinities to biblical perspectives.

1392   Pittenger, Norman. *God in Process.* London: SCM Press Ltd., 1967.

God; Jesus Christ; Holy Spirit; Trinity; man; person: and personal immortality, and society; sacraments; church; theology, process.

(This work consists of a series of lectures presented by the author to audiences in the United States and England.)

1393   Pittenger, W. Norman. "Toward a More Christian Theology." *Religion in Life*, 36, 1967, 498–505.

Love, cosmic ground of; God, as love; Jesus, as revelation; theology: radical, process.

Process thought offers a metaphysical setting into which assurances of Christian faith about the centrality of the love of God which was in Christ Jesus can be fitted without serious distortion.

1394   Pittenger, W. Norman. "Bernard E. Meland, Process Thought, and the Significance of Christ." *Religion in Life*, 37, 1968, 540–550.

Love; Jesus: humanity of, as God's decisive act; redemption; Meland, Bernard E.; christology.

Process thought allows a christology in which Jesus is the coincidence of God's agency and human responsive action. As such, Jesus is the actualization of genuine human possibilities, understood as the fullness of love.

1395   Pittenger, Norman. *Process–Thought and Christian Faith.* New York: Macmillan Company, 1968.

Christianity; theology, process; God: Biblical view of, and the world, and time, and categoreal scheme, and eternal objects, primordial nature of, consequent nature of, objective immortality in, and evil; person, and personal immortality; morality; sexuality; Hartshorne, Charles; Teilhard de Chardin.

(The author introduces process theology to the general reader, devoting specific attention to Whitehead, Charles Hartshorne, and Teilhard de Chardin.)

1396   Pittenger, Norman. *Alfred North Whitehead.* Richmond, Virginia: John Knox Press, 1969.

Christianity; theology, process; Whitehead, Alfred North: biography of, introduction to his thought, attitude toward Christianity; God: and the world, and classical theism; human existence; nature; creativity; Hartshorne, Charles.

(This work is designed to introduce Whitehead's thought and process theology to laypersons in the Christian church. Its first section gives an account of Whitehead's life and writing; the second considers the chief emphases of his philosophy; and the third discusses process theology.)

1397   Pittenger, Norman. *The Christian Situation Today.* London: Epworth Press, 1969.

Christianity, in the Twentieth century; love; theology, process.

1398   Pittenger, Norman. *God's Way with Men: A Study of the Relationship Between God and Man in Providence, Miracle, and Prayer.* Valley Forge, Pennsylvania: Judson Press, 1969.

God: as creator, providence of, and novelty, of classical theism, as persuasive power: Jesus, God's presence in; miracle; prayer; theology, process.

1399   Pittenger, W. Norman. "Process Theology Revisited." *Theology Today,* 27, 1970, 212–220.

God: as love, as persuasive power, and evil; theology.

Process thought may properly be styled a metaphysics of love precisely because it takes with such utter seriousness the fact of relationship.

1400   Pittenger, W. Norman. *Christology Reconsidered.* London: SCM, 1970.

Christology; God: tenderness of, of classical theism, as divine despot; importance; love; Jesus, as Christ; theology, process.

The Whiteheadian notion of importance defines an event as important when it occurs within a continuing process of events, provides illumination of what has gone before, speaks with special impressiveness, and offers new ways of understanding in consequent history. Given such a definition, the Christian can understand the decisive importance of Jesus Christ.

1401   Pittenger, W. Norman. *'The Last Things' in a Process Perspective.* London: Epworth, 1970.

Heaven; hell; kingdom of God; eschatology; God: as love; eschatology; theology, process; existentialism.

The insights of process thought and existentialism can illuminate the reality of death, judgment, heaven, and hell in ways which are both modern and true to the ultimate intent of traditional understandings. Death is the revelation of finitude; judgment is the recognition of the extent to which one contributes to the good; hell signifies loss of meaning and frustration; and heaven is the fulfillment and realization of love.

1402 Pittenger, W. Norman. "The Doctrine of Christ in a Process Theology." *Expository Times*, 82, 1970, 7–10.

Jesus: as Christ, as man, as God's decisive act, uniqueness of; christology.

We can most satisfactorily understand Jesus Christ as the direct and intimate union of the activity of love which is God and the activity of man which is becoming responsive to that love and hence on the way to becoming creatively love in action in society.

1403 Pittenger, Norman. "The Attributes of God in the Light of Process-Thought." *Canterbury Occasional Papers*, January 1970, 15–17.

God: nature of, as love; theology, process.

(The author gives a brief summary of the Whiteheadian view of God in non-technical language.)

1404 Pittenger, W. Norman. *Making Sexuality Human*. Philadelphia: Pilgrim Press, 1970.

Sexuality; love; theology, process.

1405 Pittenger, W. Norman. *Goodness Distorted*. Bath, England: A. R. Mowbray and Co. Ltd., 1970.

Evil; love; God: and process, as persuasive lure, and evil, as creator; Hartshorne, Charles; theology, process.

1406 Pittenger, W. Norman. "Theological Table-Talk." *Theology Today*, 28, 1971, 78–82.

Theology, twentieth-century; institutions, Christian: secularism.

The second half of the twentieth century is a period of constructive theology, particularly with regard to the re-discovering of God as love, yet it is also a period of decline in the institutional church.

1407 Pittenger, W. Norman. *The Promise of Whitehead*. New York: J. P. Lippincott, 1971.

Whitehead, Alfred North: introduction to his thought.

1408 Pittenger, Norman. *The Christian Church as Social Process*. Philadelphia: Westminster Press, 1971.

Church: and society, and ministry; society, human; ethics, Christian; God, and social change; Jesus Christ; theology, process.

(The relationship between the Christian God, the church, and the ministry is discussed in light of process theology.)

1409 Pittenger, W. Norman. "Process Theology and Its Implications." *Learning for Living*, March and May, 1971.

Theology, process; Whitehead, Alfred North: introduction to his thought.

1410   Pittenger, W. Norman. "Trinity and Process: Some Comments in Reply." *Theological Studies*, 32, 1971, 290–296.

God: as dipolar, as love, as worthy of worship; redemption; Kelly, Anthony J.; theology.

While process thought provides for the truth of God's transcendent supremacy, it has insisted that the priority in theology must be on God's actual nature as related to creation. (Written in response to Anthony J. Kelly, "Trinity and Process.")

1411   Pittenger, W. Norman. "A Strictly Personal Account." *Process Studies*, 1, 1971, 129–135.

God, as suffering; Pittenger, W. Norman; theology, process.

The tragedies of World War II set the stage for the personal realization that God is involved in, suffers with, receives from, and shares with human anguish. Process thought provides categories for articulating this realization.

1412   Pittenger, W. Norman. "Whitehead and 'Catholicism'." *Theological Studies*, 32, 1971, 659–670.

Whitehead, Alfred North: religion of; God, religious availability of; worship, as sacramental; Matthews, W. R.; Catholicism.

Whitehead's religious attitudes toward worship clarify his comment to Dean Matthews that "nearly all the things Catholics do are right, and nearly all the reasons they give are wrong."

1413   Pittenger, W. Norman. "The Doctrine of God and its Implications in Process Theology." *Religion in Life*, 60, 1971, 73–77.

God: nature of; theology, process.

1414   Pittenger, W. Norman. "Process Theology and the Fact of Evil." *Expository Times*, 83, 1971, 73–77.

God: and evil, as love, as suffering; evil; theodicy.

Process theology does not come too easily to the conception of God as love, nor does it overlook or minimize the fact of evil. Rather, the event of Jesus Christ discloses God as love–in–act against all contradiction. (Written in response to H. Cunliffe–Jones, *Christian Theology Since 1600*.)

1415   Pittenger, W. Norman. "The Fact of Evil and the Concept of God." *Modern Free Churchman*, 1971, 2–8.

God: as love, as suffering; freedom; theodicy.

The process view of God working in the world in love safeguards human freedom and answers the basic difficulty of evil.

1416   Pittenger, W. Norman. "Secular Faith in Christ, Without Belief in God: Alistair Kee's Proposal." *The Modern Churchman*, 15, 1971–1972, 111–115.

Cosmic lover, God as; secularism; Kee, Alistair; Ogden, Schubert M.; panentheism.

Kee's rejection of Ogden's concept of God is based on a misinterpretation. Kee in no way demonstrates that a process conception of deity is illogical or impossible.

1417 Pittenger, W. Norman. "What is 'Process Thinking'?" *Modern Churchman*, 15 1971–1972, 159–169.

Existence, significance of; decisions, importance of; man, as organic; religion.

The process vision can restore some awareness of unity and significance to human existence in the world.

1418 Pittenger, W. Norman. "The Nature of Human Nature." *Princeton Seminary Bulletin*, 64, 1971.

Human existence, nature of; theology, process.

1419 Pittenger, W. Norman. "Return to 'Spirituality'?" *Religion in Life*, 41, 1972, 311–316.

Spirituality: active, contemplative; discipleship; religion.

The need in twentieth century thought is for a new, yet traditionally grounded, approach to spirituality.

1420 Pittenger, W. Norman. "The Question of 'Personal Survival' after Death." *Christian Renewal*, 1972, 2–4.

Immortality, as personal; God, as love; Jesus, and resurrection.

Anyone who has begun to live in love has also begun to live in God, and by that token, shares in love's immortality.

1421 Pittenger, W. Norman. "Whitehead and Christian Theism." *Theological Digest*, 19–20, 1972–1973, 306–318.

Process theism, summary of; Jesus: as disclosure of God, as revelation; love; sin; justice; theology.

The position of process thought about the reality and nature of deity aids in living the Christian life.

1422 Pittenger, W. Norman. "Christian Faith and a World in Process." *Modern Free Churchman*, 1973.

Christianity: and culture, in the twentieth century.

1423 Pittenger, W. Norman. "Suffering and Love." *The Expository Times*, 85, 1973–1974, 19–22.

Suffering: reality of, positive aspects of; love; God, as Cosmic Lover, consequent nature of; theodicy.

Suffering can enrich our relationship to others, and enable us to grasp more profoundly the nature of the God who suffers with the world.

1424 Pittenger, W. Norman. "Process Thought and Christian Faith." *Christian Renewal*, 1973, 16–18.

Process philosophy, summary of; God, as love.

Process thought is particularly applicable to Christian faith in its interpretation of God as persuasion, which is love.

1425   Pittenger, W. Norman. "Prayer in Process Terms." *Modern Free Churchman*, Spring 1973, 2–6.

Prayer: as active passivity, as passive activity; God: consequent nature of, as love; relatedness; mutuality; creative advance.

Prayer in process terms means the adventure of 1) raising the mind to God in dedication and 2) willing to be influenced by God's aims and purposes for the world.

1426   Pittenger, W. Norman. "The Incarnation in Process Theology." *Review and Expositor*, Winter 1973–1974.

Incarnation; christology.

1427   Pittenger, W. Norman. *Life as Eucharist*. Grand Rapids, Michigan: Eerdmans, 1973.

Eucharist; sacraments.

1428   Pittenger, W. Norman. *Christian Faith and the Question of History*. Philadelphia: Fortress Press, 1973.

Christianity, as historical religion; Bible, as history; faith; miracle; eschatology; value, and fact; Jesus Christ: ministry of, resurrection of; God: and history, objective immortality in; myth; theology, process.

(Disallowing a sharp dichotomy between natural processes and historical developments, the author discusses the historical nature of the Christian faith from the perspective of process theology.)

1429   Pittenger, W. Norman. "Process Theology and Christian Education." *Religious Education*, 68, 1973, 307–314.

Education: purpose of, religious; love; theology, process.

The particular value which process theology contributes to religious education is to be found in the process recognition that stress on dynamism, growth, life, community, and love is not simply humanly valuable, but is also tied in with the way God is and works in his creation.

1430   Pittenger, W. Norman. "Theology and the Future." *Modern Churchman*, 1974, 211–214.

Theology, process; future.

1431   Pittenger, W. Norman. *Love and Control in Sexuality*. Philadelphia: Pilgrim Press, 1974.

Love; sexuality; morality; value.

1432   Pittenger, W. Norman. *Praying Today*. Grand Rapids, Michigan: Eerdmans, 1974.

Prayer.

1433   Pittenger, W. Norman. *The Holy Spirit*. Philadelphia: United Church Press, 1974.

Holy Spirit; God: and Holy Spirit, as creator, as source of initial aim, as object of worship; Jesus Christ; theology, process.

An inclusive view of God and the world must take account of

the operation of the Holy Spirit in nature, human history, personal experience, and social experience. Process theology provides categories of thought which illumine that operation.

1434 Pittenger, W. Norman. "Towards a Christian Theology of Sexuality." *Union Seminary Quarterly Review*, 30, 1975, 121–129.

Sexuality, theology of; love; mutuality; self, as psychosomatic unity.

Loving depends upon the total psychosomatic reality of human beings; sexuality is the basis and ground for many forms of mutuality.

1435 Pittenger, W. Norman. "An Interpretation of Sin." *Religion in Life*, Winter 1975, 428–431.

God, as divine despot; sin; theology, process.

The image of God as moral dictator must be purged from the Christian consciousness.

1436 Pittenger, W. Norman. "Towards an Understanding of the Self." *Contemporary Studies in Philosophical Idealism.* Edited by John Howie and Thomas O. Buford. Cape Cod, Massachusetts: Claude Starke and Company, 1975.

Self: as personal society, and love, as evolutionary emergent, and self–identity, as relational; person; decision; love; Bertocci, Peter; theology, process.

The human self is always in relationship with other selves, with the created order, and with God who is the agency towards love.

1437 Pittenger, W. Norman. "Process Theology: A Whiteheadian Version." *Religious Experience and Process Theology.* Edited by Harry J. Cargas and Bernard Lee. New York: Paulist Press, 1976, 3–21.

Event; actual entities; Cosmic Lover, God as; freedom; responsibility; sexuality; prehension; persuasion; love; philosophical theology; sacrament; ecclesiology.

The basic concepts of process thought and their significance for human nature, human sexuality, Christian community, and Eucharistic life become unified through the efficacy of God as Cosmic Lover.

1438 Pittenger, W. Norman. *Unbounded Love: God and Man in Process.* New York: Seabury Press, 1976.

Process theology; God: as love, and christology; Holy Spirit; church; sacraments; anthropology; eschatology; christology.

1439 Pixley, Jorge V. "La filosofia de Whitehead como recurso para la teología cristiana." *Cuadernos Teologicos*, 15, 1966, 170–182.

Theology, process; theism, classical.

1440 Pixley, Jorge V. "Whitehead y Marx sobre la dinámica de la historia." *Dialogos*, 7, 1970, 83–107.

Civilization; society: human, subhuman; history, periodization of; capitalism; epoch, cosmic; eternal objects; God: as principle of limitation, doctrine of; history, interpretation of; Marx, Karl.

1441 Pixley, Jorge V. "Justice and Class Struggle: A Challenge for Process Theology." *Process Studies*, 4, 1974, 159–175.

Ethics; justice; history: as conflict; value; theology, process.

While a revolutionary process theology is possible, it must also be admitted that Whitehead's own philosophical investigations of culture and civilization are open to appropriation for counterrevolutionary purposes. In order to undercut these latent counterrevolutionary tendencies, any Christian process theology must include justice among its fundamental cultural aims.

1442 Pizante, William A. "The Concept of Value in Whitehead's Philosophy." Unpublished Ph.D. dissertation, Johns Hopkins University, 1961.

Value: and knowledge, and becoming, and causality, and evil, intrinsic, instrumental; evil; experience, intensity of; ethics, and value.

Value is measured in terms of the intensity of experience. Experiential intensity increases as the number of elements positively felt increases. If a method of analyzing experience so as to reveal the number of elements and the general conditions regulating the compatibility of elements for synthesis is developed, it might be possible to create adequate standards for the judgment of good and evil.

1443 Platt, David. "Some Perplexities Concerning God's Existence." *Journal of Bible and Religion*, 34, 1966, 244–252.

God: proofs of, religious adequacy of; Hartshorne, Charles.

While God may appear in metaphysical contexts, he must be regarded primarily as a concrete entity, whose existence cannot be proved. Religious consciousness, not metaphysical thought, is our main source of data for theistic belief.

1444 Platt, David. "Transcendence of Subjectivity in Peirce and Whitehead." *Personalist*, 49, 1968, 238–255.

Subjectivism, transcendence of; Peirce, Charles S.: synechism of, similarities with Whitehead; causal efficacy; epistemology.

Whitehead gives a direct epistemological realism of process, alternating between subjectivity and objectivity, wherein subjectivity is constantly transcended and reasserted, only to be transcended again.

1445 Platt, David. "Is Empirical Theology Adequate?" *International Journal for Philosophy of Religion*, 2, 1971, 28–42.

God: proofs of, experience of, and evil, as dipolar; James, William; Hartshorne, Charles; theology, empirical.

Empirical theism may help begin the process of religious exploration, and serves as the foundation for later theological explication. Hartshorne's dipolar theism takes experience into account in the metaphysical explication of the divine nature.

1446 Platt, David. "Does Whitehead's God Possess a Moral Will?" *Process Studies*, 5, 1975, 114–122.

God, and value; value, maximization of; morality; ethics; Kant, Immanuel.

The Whiteheadian God would seem to be implicated in evil in that God seeks the maximization of value in *every* occasion, even those which are evil. However, because God enters emphathetically into the experience of all creatures, does not mean that God would not prefer and indeed entice those creatures to enjoy richer experiences.

1447 Pokharana, Lata. "Organismic Philosophy: A Comparative Study." *Darshana International*, 14, 1975, 49–54.

Vedas; God; theism, Indian; Shastri, Motilal.

A study of the Indian philosopher Motilal Shastri shows that the dynamic philosophy of the Vedas is close to the organic philosophy of Whitehead.

1448 Pols, Edward. "The Idea of Freedom in the Metaphysics of Whitehead." Unpublished Ph.D. dissertation, Harvard University, 1949.

Freedom; determinism; causality; causa sui; metaphysics.

1449 Pols, Edward. *Whitehead's Metaphysics: A Critical Examination of Process and Reality.* Carbondale, Illinois: Southern Illinois University Press, 1967.

Whitehead, Alfred North: introduction to his thought; actual entity; ontological principle; freedom; agency; self–creation; subject, as superject; subjective aim; subjective form; concrescence, phases of; feeling, types of; intensity; contrast; proposition; novelty; pole: physical, mental; power; eternal object: and Platonic forms, ingression of, objective species of, subjective species of, as form of definiteness, relations between, ontological status of, and potentiality, and power; God; primordial nature of, experience of, and initial subjective aim, and eternal objects; time, epochal theory of; society, man as; togetherness; unity; creativity: as ultimate, as conditioned, and creative advance; Spinoza, B.; Platonism.

Whitehead's emphasis on the subject as superject renders his doctrine of freedom contradictory since it allows no active or substantial agents. In fact Whitehead endows eternal objects, or Platonic forms, with more marks of concreteness than actual entities. As a consequence his philosophy is highly deficient.

1450 Pols, Edward. "Whitehead's Metaphysics: A Reply to A. H. Johnson." *Dialogue*, 7, 1968, 476–479.

Subject–superject; actual entities, examples of; eternal objects, and power; Johnson, A. H.

In his review of *Whitehead's Metaphysics*, Johnson mistakenly

reads criticisms against Whitehead's doctrines as
mis–statements of those doctrines. He fails to note that the
burden of the book was to show that the internal logic of the
doctrines often produces a different emphasis from the one
Whitehead intended. (Written in response to A. H. Johnson.)

Reviews

Ford, L. S. *Modern Schoolman*, 47, 1970, 209–225.

Lowe, V. *Journal of Philosophy*, 65, 1968, 515–519.

Schmidt, P. F. *Journal of the History of Philosophy*, 7, 1969,
99–101.

1451   Pols, Edward. "Freedom and Agency: A Reply." *Southern
Journal of Philosophy*, 7, 1969, 415–419.

Freedom, and agency; subjective aim: modification of,
indivisibility of; Cobb, John B., Jr.; Ford, Lewis S.;
metaphysics.

If Whitehead requires any type of temporality in the phases of
concrescence, then he cannot avoid radical mechanism; if
temporality be denied through the indivisibility of the mental
pole and the subjective aim, then he cannot avoid radical
finalism. Whitehead does not provide a coherent account of
freedom. (Written in response to John B. Cobb, Jr., "Freedom
in Whitehead's Philosophy: A Response to Edward Pols," and
Lewis S. Ford, "Can Whitehead Provide for Real Subjective
Agency? A Reply to Edward Pols' Critique.")

1452   Pols, Edward. "Power and Agency." *International Philosophical
Quarterly*, 11, 1971, 293–313.

Agency, and power; causality; time, epochal theory of; mind,
and mind–body problem; metaphysics.

The most fundamental and concrete sense of power accessible
to intelligence is power in the sense of agency. Development
of this thesis bears analogies to Whitehead's epochal theory of
time, but differs in that the units of action are not restricted
to microscopic occasions.

1453   Pols, Edward. "Whitehead on Subjective Agency: A Reply To
Lewis S. Ford." *The Modern Schoolman*, 49, 1971–1972,
144–150.

Subjective aim, modification of; indivisibility: genetic,
coordinate; agency; Ford, Lewis S.

The subjective aim must undergo genetic modification during
concrescence. Whitehead underemphasizes the subjective aspect
of actual occasions. By developing further the notion of
subjecthood, process thinkers might give a better philosophical
account of the human agent. (Written in response to Lewis S.
Ford, "Can Whitehead Provide for Real Subjective Agency? A
Reply to Edward Pols's Critique.")

1454   Pols, Edward. *Meditation on a Prisoner: Towards Understanding*

Action and Mind. Carbondale, Illinois: Southern Illinois University Press, 1975.

Time: epochal theory of; James, William.

William James furnished much of the original impetus for Whitehead's epochal theory of time.

1455   Potthoff, Harvey H.   "God and the Newer Views of the Universe." *Iliff Review*, 15, 1959, 41–52.

God: concept of, experience of; cosmology; theology, empirical.

Newer views of the universe—its vastness, its dynamic character, its directional tendencies, and implications for causality—require a reinterpretation of the traditional concept of God.

1456   Potthoff, Harvey H.   "Theology and the Vision of Greatness." *Iliff Review*, 16, 1959, 1–13.

Method, theological; theology, twentieth century.

Whitehead's statement that the expression of religious principles requires continual development epitomizes the task and purpose of liberal theology.

1457   Power, W. L.   "The Imago Dei and Man Come of Age." *Iliff Review*, 27, 1970, 35–41.

Imago dei; God, and the world; anthropology.

1458   Power, William L.   "Philosophic Logic and Process Theory in the Work of Richard M. Martin: A Review Article." *Process Studies*, 5, 1975, 204–213.

Semantics; logic, symbolic; theology: process, and mathematics; Martin, Richard; Hartshorne, Charles.

(The author outlines the general character of Richard Martin's application of symbolic logic to the concepts of process theology.)

1459   Prager, H. R.   "A Comparative Study of the Concept of God in Alfred North Whitehead and Charles Hartshorne." Unpublished M.A. Thesis, University of Southern California, 1952.

God: Hartshorne's interpretation, Whitehead's arguments for, primordial nature, consequent nature of, superjective nature of, as dipolar, as absolute, as relative; Hartshorne, Charles.

1460   Press, Howard E.   "The Aesthetic Basis of Whitehead's Philosophy."   Unpublished Ph.D. dissertation, Columbia University, 1967.

Aesthetics; beauty; art; value; contrast; intensity; enjoyment; morality; peace; Plato; Spinoza, B.

The final cause of existence for Whitehead is aesthetic value. From this it follows that 'taste' is the norm for morality.

1461   Press, Howard.   "Whitehead's Ethic of Feeling." *Ethics*, 81, 1971, 161–168.

Value: aesthetic, ethic; morality, and moral responsibility;

altruism; ethics.

At the root of Whitehead's metaphysics is a moral philosophy grounded in an aestheticism.

1462   Price, Lucien. *Dialogues of Alfred North Whitehead.* Boston: Little, Brown and Company, 1954. New York: New American Library, 1956.

Whitehead, Alfred North: biography of; bibliography of.

Translation

Huai–hai–te tuei–hua lu. Trans. Den–sing Lee. Taipei, Taiwan: Chih Wen Publishing House, 1974.

This is a complete translation of Lucien Price's *Dialogues of Alfred North Whitehead.*

1463   Price, Lucien. "Alfred North Whitehead." *The Saturday Club: A Century Completed, 1920–1956.* Edited by Edward W. Forbes and John H. Finley, Jr. Boston: Houghton Mifflin Company, 1958.

Whitehead: biography of.

(This biographical sketch is excerpted from Price's *Dialogues of Alfred North Whitehead.*)

1464   Prins, D. H., Jr. "De natuurfilosofische Denkbeelden van A. N. Whitehead." *Physica,* 7, 1927, 122–142.

Nature, philosophy of; *The Concept of Nature; An Enquiry Concerning the Principles of Natural Knowledge*; physics, classical; time; space.

(This survey article exposits Whitehead's criticism of the foundation of classical physics, his theory of events and objects, and his abstraction of the concepts of time and space from the relations between events and various time systems.)

1465   Prins, D. H., Jr. "De kritische Snelheid der Relativiteits–theorie." *Physica,* 7, 1927, 156–162.

Physics, relativity theory of; symmetry, kinematic; velocity; Galilie, Galileo.

(A discussion of Whitehead's principle of kinematic symmetry and his method of deducing the existence of a maximum velocity.)

1466   Proctor, George L. "Propositions, Facts, and Immediate Experience." Unpublished Ph.D. dissertation, University of Virginia, 1957.

Language; propositions; Wittgenstein, Ludwig; Ayer, A. J.; Carnap, Rudolf; philosophy, analytic.

1467   Proudfoot, Wayne. "Conceptions of God and the Self." *Journal of Religion,* 55, 1975, 57–75.

God, as related; self, process model of.

1468   Pruitt, Sylvia. "An Inquiry into the Ethical Implications of Whitehead's Metaphysics." Unpublished Ph.D. dissertation, Emory University, 1970.

Ethics; morality: and moral judgment, and moral behavior, and moral obligation, and responsibility; value: moral, general; person: and consciousness, and personal identity; freedom, and determinism; Aristotle; Neoplatonism; Leibniz, G. W.

Although Whitehead's thought deals successfully with several problems in ethics, its account of self–identity is insufficient for an account of moral responsibility.

1469   Prusak, B. P.   "Changing Concepts of God and Their Repercussions in Christology." *Does Jesus Make a Difference?* Edited by T. M. McFadden.   Proceedings of the American College Theological Society.   New York: Seabury, 1974, 56–78.

God, concept of; christology.

1470   Purtill, R. L.   "Hartshorne's Modal Proof."   *Journal of Philosophy*, 43, 1966, 397–409.

God, proofs of; argument, ontological; necessity: senses of, and existence; Hartshorne, Charles; logic, modal; metaphysics.

There is no sense of necessity that can be legitimately connected with existence for which the ontological argument is valid and for which its premises can be shown to be true.

1471   Pustilnik, Jack.   "Process and Causality: Whitehead's Reply to Hume."   Unpublished Ph.D. dissertation, Columbia University, 1958.

Causality; necessity; substance; Aristotle; Hume, David; empiricism; realism.

Whitehead seeks causal connectedness in the dimension of time rather than space.   In so doing he suggests an alternative to Hume's view of causality.

1472   Quine, Willard V. O.   "The Logic of Sequences: A Generalization of Principia Mathematica."   Unpublished Ph.D. dissertation, Harvard University, 1932.

Relations: dyadic, and relational degree; *Principia Mathematica*; mathematics; logic, symbolic.

(Showing that the treatment of relations in the *Principia Mathematica* is confined to dyadic relations, the author introduces a system of logic which exhibits an additional dimension of geometry, that of 'relational degree.' To achieve this end he adopts a new array of primitive ideas and postulates in lieu of those of the Principia.)

1473   Quine, Willard V.   "Whitehead and the Rise of Modern Logic." *The Philosophy of Alfred North Whitehead.*   Edited by Paul A. Schilpp.   La Salle, Illinois: Open Court Publishing Company, 1941, 1951, 1971, 125–163.

Logic: modern, mathematical, symbolic; algebra; arithmetic; equivalence; quantification, theory of; *Universal Algebra*; *Principia Mathematica*; Peano, Guiseppe; Russell, Bertrand.

1474   Radhakrishnan, Sarvepalli.   *History of Philosophy: Eastern and*

Western. London: Allen & Unwin, 1952, Chapter 44B. New York: Barnes and Noble, Inc., 1952.

Location, fallacy of simple; bifurcation, of nature; philosophy, and science.

(Process philosophy is considered from the standpoint of Whitehead's basic denials of simple location and of the bifurcation of nature.)

1475   Rainer, J. *Intelligence in the Modern World: John Dewey's Philosophy.* New York: Random House, 1939.

Philosophy, of education; Dewey, John.

1476   Rajagopal, L. V. *The Philosophy of A. N. Whitehead: The Concept of Reality and Organism.* Mysore, India: University of Mysore Press, 1966.

Process philosophy, summary of; philosophy: speculative, method of; categoreal scheme; actual occasion; space; time; causality; prehensions; values; God; perishing, perpetual; dualism: epistemological, psycho–physical; coherence; relations: internal, external; idealism; realism; epistemology; cosmology.

1477   Rapp, Richard J. "The Concept of God in the Philosophy of A. N. Whitehead, Dealing Specifically with the Problem of the Superjective Nature." Unpublished Ph.D. dissertation, Duquesne University, 1969.

God: superjective nature of, and categorical scheme, as actual entity, primordial nature of, consequent nature of, functions of; subject, as superject; perishing; Christian, William A.; Hartshorne, Charles.

1478   Rapport, S. and Wright, H., editors. *Science: Method and Meaning.* New York: New York University Press, 1963.

Method, scientific; meaning.

1479   Rather, L. J. "Existential Experience in Whitehead and Heidegger." *Review of Existential Psychology and Psychiatry,* 1, 1961, 113–119.

Subject, as experiencing itself; value; Heidegger, Martin; existentialism; psychology, existential.

Heidegger's *Sorge* is Whitehead's "immanent inter–relatedness involving emotion, purpose and valuation."

1480   Rattigan, C. S. J., Mary T. "Christology and Process Thought: Decisiveness of Jesus Christ in the Thought of Bernard E. Meland, W. Norman Pittenger, Daniel Day Williams." Unpublished Ph.D. dissertation, Fordham University, 1973.

Christology; God, and Christ; redemption; Meland, Bernard E.; Pittenger, Norman; Williams, Daniel Day; theology, process.

1481   Rawlins, F. I. G. "Alfred North Whitehead." *Nature,* 161, 1948, 267–268.

Whitehead, Alfred North: introduction to his thought.

1482   Rayner, C. B. "Foundations and Applications of Whitehead's

Theory of Relativity." Unpublished Ph.D. dissertation, University of London, 1953.

Relativity, theory of; gravity; space; time; light; Synge, J. L.; Temple, G.; Miller, D. C.; Einstein, Albert; science; physics.

1483 Rayner, C. B. "The Application of the Whitehead Theory of Relativity to Nonstatic, Spherically Symmetrical Systems." *Proceedings of the Royal Society of London*, 222, 1954, 509–526.

Relativity, theory of; motion; gravitation; space–time; physics.

(This paper develops the application of Whitehead's theory of flat space–time to a static, spherical system. The purpose of the application is to establish the age of the expanding universe.)

1484 Rayner, C. B. "The Effects of Rotation in the Central Body on Its Planetary Orbits, after the Whitehead Theory of Gravitation." *Proceedings of the Royal Society of London*, 232, 1955, 135–148.

Relativity, theory of; gravitation; motion; acceleration; Einstein, Albert; physics.

Einstein's and Whitehead's theories predict the same deviations from the Newtonian orbits of planets moving in the gravitational field of a uniformly rotating sphere.

1485 Rayner, C. B. "Whitehead's Law of Gravitation in a Space–Time of Constant Curvature." *Proceedings of the Physics Society of London*, section B, 68, 1955, 944–950.

Cosmology; space–time; gravitation; events.

(Whitehead's theory written in flat space–time is rewritten to make it applicable in a uniformly curved space–time, which is crucial in establishing the age of the universe.)

1486 Reck, Andrew J. "Substance, Process, and Nature." *Journal of Philosophy*, 55, 1958, 762–772.

Substance: defense of, and change; Russell, Bertrand.

To press the claim that substance in the Aristotelian sense of unitary, continuant, and independent individuals is obsolete, is to undo the possibility of process, since our awareness of process as well as its reality would be thereby impugned. The notion of event as a center of activity can never satisfactorily supplant substance.

1487 Reck, Andrew J. "The Philosophy of Charles Hartshorne." *Tulane Studies in Philosophy*, 10, 1961, 89–108.

Continuum, affective; panpsychism; realism, social; panentheism; Hartshorne, Charles.

Hartshorne's creative assimilation of Whitehead's thought leads to a theory of panpsychism with implications for psychological theory and for science.

1488 Reck, Andrew J. "The Fox Alone is Death: Whitehead and Speculative Philosophy." *American Philosophy and the Future.*

Edited by Michael Novak. New York: Charles Scribner's Sons, 1968, 138–172.

Process philosophy, summary of; Northrop, F. S. C.; Hartshorne, Charles; Weiss, Paul.

Whitehead's philosophy exemplifies his own demand that reason be more than practical, that it must supply a theoretical understanding of life and the world.

1489 Reck, Andrew J. *Speculative Philosophy: A Study of its Nature Types and Uses.* Albuquerque, New Mexico: University of New Mexico Press, 1972.

Process philosophy; philosophy: speculative, method of, aim of; generalization: descriptive, imaginative; coherence; adequacy; actual entity; prehension; ontological principle; nexus; God; creativity; eternal object; Pepper, Stephen; empiricism; rationalism; science, and philosophy.

Whitehead's definition of speculative philosophy combines the virtues of rationalism and empiricism. His specific kind of process philosophy differs from other types in that it differentiates various kinds of process and emphasizes the significance of permanence as well as flux.

1490 Redding, Earl W. "Aesthetic, Religious, and Moral Intuition in the Philosophy of Alfred North Whitehead." Unpublished Ph.D. dissertation, University of Miami, 1969.

Intuition; aesthetics; religion; morality; value; experience; language; sensationalist principle; Hume, David; Dewey, John; philosophy, analytical; empiricism.

Whitehead's treatment of aesthetic, religious, and moral intuition corrects the tendency among analytic philosophers to exclude such subjects from philosophical enquiry.

1491 Reese, William L. "Philosophic Realism: A Study of the Modality of Being in Peirce and Whitehead." Unpublished Ph.D. dissertation, Harvard University, 1952.

Being; Peirce, Charles S.; realism.

1492 Reese, William L. "Philosophical Realism: A Study of the Modality of Being in Peirce and Whitehead." *Studies in the Philosophy of Charles Sanders Peirce.* Edited by P. P. Wiener and F. H. Young, 225–237.

Being; Peirce, Charles S.

Reviews

Cobb, J. B. Jr. *Journal of Religion,* 45, 1965, 335–337.

Johnson, A. H. *Dialogue,* 4, 1965–1966, 389–391.

Robinson, D. S. *Philosophy and Phenomenological Research,* 26, 1965, 461–462.

Scharlemann, R. P. *Personalist,* 47, 1966, 265.

Zaslawsky, D. *Revue de Theologie et de Philosophie,* 98, 1965, 185–186.

1493   Reese, William L. and Freeman, Eugene, editors. *Process and Divinity: Philosophical Essays Presented to Charles Hartshorne.* La Salle, Illinois: Open Court Publishing Company, 1964.

Science, and philosophy; location, fallacy of simple; biology; eternal object; God, and world; extension; abstraction; language; Bergson, Henri.

(See articles by Milic Capek, Lucio Chiaraviglio, William Christian, Bowman Clarke, George Kline, Ivor Leclerc, Albert Levi, Robert Palter, Daniel Day Williams, and Sewall Wright for studies in Whiteheadian philosophy which are included in this festschrift for Charles Hartshorne.)

1494   Reese, William L. "Process Philosophy and Metaphysics." *The Future of Metaphysics.* Edited by R. E. Wood. New York: Quadrangle Books, 1970.

Process philosophy; metaphysics.

1495   Reeves, Gene. "God and Creativity." *Southern Journal of Philosophy,* 7, 1969, 377–385.

Creativity: as ultimate, as substantial activity; God: as creator, and creativity; standpoints; Cobb, John B., Jr.; philosophical theology.

Cobb has not succeeded in attributing to God the decisive role in the creation of the actual occasion: the four formative elements are equally necessary, with the past itself being most influential. (Written in response to John B. Cobb, Jr., *A Christian Natural Theology,* esp. 203–214.)

1496   Reeves, Gene and Brown, Delwin. "The Development of Process Theology." *Process Philosophy and Christian Thought.* Edited by Delwin Brown, Ralph E. James, and Gene Reeves. Indianapolis, Indiana: Bobbs–Merrill Company, Inc., 1971, 21–64.

Process theology, summary of.

1497   Reeves, Gene. "Whitehead and Hartshorne." *Journal of Religion,* 55, 1975, 125–137.

Method, metaphysical; God: Hartshorne's interpretation of, as dipolar, as actual entity, as living person; eternal objects; possibilities, as emergent; qualities, secondary; temporality; Hartshorne, Charles; Ford, Lewis S.; Fost, Frederic; Griffin, David.

Major areas of disagreement between Hartshorne and Whitehead have to do with the nature of metaphysical method, the temporality of God, and the nature of possibility.

1498   Reinelt, Herbert R. "God and Actuality: A Critical Interpretation of the Analogy Between God and the World in Terms of the Categoreal Scheme of Alfred North Whitehead." Unpublished Ph.D. dissertation Yale University, 1962.

God: and world, and categoreal scheme; analogy, and God; theology, philosophical.

1499   Reinelt, Herbert R.   "Whitehead and Theistic Language." *Christian Scholar*, 50, 1967, 222–234.

God: language about, experience of, and eternal objects: philosophy, linguistic.

Once it is seen that God and all other actual entities involve eternal objects, the basis for the interpretation of language about God is provided. Insofar as God and other actual entities participate in the same characteristics, the same assertion can be made about each of them and in the same sense of the term.

1500   Reinelt, Herbert R.   "A Whiteheadian Doctrine of Analogy." *The Modern Schoolman*, 48, 1970–1971, 327–342.

Analogy: with respect to concept, with respect to being, and God, as identity of eternal object in diverse occasions, as identity of function in diverse occasions; contrasts; multiplicities; eternal objects; language, philosophy of.

Whitehead's metaphysics presents basic tools for an analysis of language, as can be demonstrated through consideration of the concept and uses of analogy.

1501   Reitz, Helga.   "Was ist Prozeβtheologie?"   *Kerygma und Dogma*, 16, 1970, 78–104.

Process theology, summary of; God, concept of; church, and society; epistemology; ontology; theology, task of.

1502   Reitz, Helga.   "Wirklichkeit ist ein Prozess—Neue Impulse einer amerikanischen Theologie."   *Evangelische Kommentare*, 12, 1974, 741–743.

Process theology, summary of.

1503   Richmond, James.   "God, Time, and Process Philosophy." *Theology*, 68, 1965, 234–241.

God: temporality of, as living; time, and human experience; Ogden, Schubert M.; philosophical theology.

Ogden's concept of God offers clear philosophical and religious advantages; its major difficulty is the loss of ultimacy in the idea of God. (Written in response to Schubert M. Ogden, "The Temporality of God.")

1504   Riconda, Giussepe.   "L'empirismo radicale di W. James." *Filosofia*, 16, 1965, 291–332. Also in *La filosofia di William James.* Turin: Edizioni de Filosofia, 1965.

Empiricism, radical; James, William.

1505   Riconda, Giussepe.   "Il processo e la realta."   *Filosofia*, 18, 1967, 241–264.

Philosophy, speculative; metaphysics; actual entities; creativity; eternal objects; God.

(A sketch of Whiteheadian metaphysics written as a presentation of the Italian translation of *Process and Reality*.)

1506   Riker, John H.   "Ethics, Meta–Ethics, and Metaphysics: A Study in Whitehead's Cosmology." Unpublished Ph.D. dissertation, Vanderbilt University, 1969.

Ethics; metaphysics; beauty; value; morality; philosophy, analytical.

Whitehead's metaphysics supports an ethical theory which emphasizes the maximization of beauty as the criterion of moral obligation.

1507   Ritchie, A. D.   "Whitehead's Defence of Speculative Reason." *The Philosophy of Alfred North Whitehead.* Edited by Paul A. Schilpp.   La Salle, Illinois: Open Court Publishing Company, 1941, 329–349.

Reason: theoretical, practical; causation: final, formal; value; naturalism; supernaturalism; Plato.

As against the supernaturalist, for whom the distinction between the realm of value and fact is central, Whitehead is a naturalist.

1508   Riverso, E.   "Alfred North Whitehead oggi."   *Giornale Critico Della Filosofia Italiana*, 45, 1966, 274–277.

Philosophy: of Italian renaissance, of science; Bergson, Henri.

The value of the thought of Whitehead is in his early philosophy of science and not in his metaphysics which gives the impression of a philosophical fiction.

1509   Roberts, George W.   "A Problem in Whitehead's Doctrine of Abstractive Hierarchies."   *Philosophy and Phenomenological Research*, 28, 1967, 437–439.

Hierarchy, abstractive; *Science and the Modern World*; eternal objects, as abstractive hierarchy.

It can be established that, in Whitehead's defined senses for the expressions "finite abstractive hierarchy" and "infinite abstractive hierarchy," finite abstractive hierarchies are impossible, since every abstractive hierarchy is necessarily infinite.

1510   Robertson, Jr., John C.   "The Concept of the Divine Person in the Thought of Charles Hartshorne and Karl Barth." Unpublished Ph.D. dissertation, Yale University, 1967.

God, as living person; Hartshorne, Charles; Barth, Karl; theology.

1511   Robertson, John C., Jr.   "Rahner And Ogden: Man's Knowledge of God."   *Harvard Theological Review*, 63, 1970, 377–407.

Method, theological; God: knowledge of, as love, and world; Rahner, Karl; Ogden, Schubert M.; Thomism; theology, process.

Rahner and Ogden are in basic agreement on the fundamental issue of theological method.   Their basic difference is to be found in the way the God known according to this method is to be conceived.   The two positions should be brought into dialog with each other.

1512   Robertson, John C. "Does God Change?" *The Ecumenist*, 9, 1971, 61–64.

God: as becoming, and time, consequent nature of.

1513   Robinson, Daniel Somer. "Dr. Whitehead's Theory of Events." *Philosophical Review*, 30, 1921, 41–56.

Event, external; externality, constants of; ether; *Enquiry Concerning the Principles of Natural Knowledge*; philosophy, of science.

Chief among the obscurities in Whitehead's discussion of an event is the matter of the relation of an event to the continuous ether which he defines as the whole complex of events.

1514   Robinson, John A. T. *Exploration into God.* Stanford, California: Stanford University Press, 1967, 103.

Appetition; God, as persuasive power.

It is difficult to explain the momentum of the evolutionary process without reference to 'appetition'.

1515   Robson, J. W. "Whitehead's Answer to Hume." *Journal of Philosophy*, 38, 1941, 85–95.

Induction, ground of; anticipation; causation; Hume, David; epistemology.

Although Whitehead gives an account of our immediate experience and inductive procedure in some respects far more adequate than Hume's account, he fails to show how we can ever reasonably infer that a particular future probably will have specified characteristics. Such inference would require that the present have internal relational properties connecting them with the future.

1516   Root, Vernon M. "Alfred North Whitehead's Theory of Eternal Objects." Unpublished Ph.D. dissertation, Yale University, 1950.

Eternal objects: as abstractions, as essences, as forms of definiteness, as generic, mathematical basis of, ingression, in objectification, as pure possibilities; mathematics.

1517   Root, Vernon M. "Eternal Objects, Attributes, and Relations in Whitehead's Philosophy." *Philosophy and Phenomenological Research*, 14, 1953, 196–204.

Eternal objects: as abstractive hierarchy, objective species of, subjective species of; ingression; metaphysics.

If it is to be possible for Whitehead, within his own system, to characterize the basic entities of that system, a new primitive relation will have to be introduced, the relation of "exemplification."

1518   Rorty, Richard M. "Whitehead's Use of the Concept of Potentiality." M.A. Thesis, University of Chicago, 1952.

Potentiality: real, ideal; eternal objects: as potential, as abstractive hierarchy; God, primordial nature of; extensive continuum; pole, physical; subjective form.

Eternal objects, as ideal potentials, are the ground of order. Creativity, which is real potentiality, is the ground of freedom. The two kinds of potentiality depend for their meaning on two distinct intuitions—one of flux and one of permanence.

1519 Rorty, Richard M. "Matter and Event." *The Concept of Matter.* Edited by E. McMullin. Notre Dame, Indiana: Notre Dame University Press, 1963.

Matter; events, theory of; actuality.

1520 Rorty, Richard M. "The Subjectivist Principle and the Linguistic Turn." *Alfred North Whitehead: Essays on His Philosophy.* Edited by George L. Kline. Englewood Cliffs, New Jersey: Prentice–Hall, Inc., 1963, 134–157.

Language: ordinary, and referent, and philosophy, and subject–predicate mode of expression, Whitehead's use of; subjectivist principle; particular; actual entity; substance; prehension; philosophy, and language; philosophy, analytic.

Ordinary language philosophers agree with Whitehead that the attempt to conceive selves as substances with properties is largely responsible for traditional problems in epistemology, but they deny that ordinary language is committed to such a conception. Whitehead assumed too quickly that ordinary language is so committed.

1521 Rose, M. C. "Three Hierarchies of Value: A Study of the Philosophies of Value of H. Bergson, Alfred North Whitehead, and S. Kierkegaard." Unpublished Ph.D. dissertation, John Hopkins University, 1949.

Value: theory of; Bergson, Henri; Kierkegaard, Soren.

1522 Ross, S. D. "The Inexhaustibility of Nature." *Journal of Value Inquiry,* 7, 1973, 241–253.

Nature; philosophy, of nature.

1523 Rotenstreich, Nathan. "On Whitehead's Theory of Propositions." *Review of Metaphysics,* 5, 1952, 389–404.

Propositions: and eternal objects, and actual entities, and actuality, and potentiality; truth, and interest; eternal objects, and ingression; Plato; Plotinus; Kant, Immanuel.

Whitehead's doctrine of propositions aims to solve the problem concerning the transition from a neutral multiplicity of eternal objects to a specific nexus of actual entities.

1524 Rotenstreich, Nathan. "The Superject and Moral Responsibility." *Review of Metaphysics,* 10, 1956, 201–206.

Morality, and moral responsibility; identity; ethics.

Moral responsibility as accountability is not an outcome of the process. It presupposes the fact of consciousness which bridges over the different stages of personal existence.

1525 Rotenstreich, Nathan. *On the Human Subject.* Springfield, Illinois: Charles C. Thomas Publishers, 1966.

Subject; subjectivity; self.

1526 Roth, R. J. *American Religious Philosophy.* New York: Harcourt, Brace and World, 1967, 109–144.

Whitehead, Alfred North: introduction to his thought.

1527 Rovatti, Pier Aldo. "L'atteggiamento etico nella filosofia del proceso." *Aut Aut,* 1965, 43–67.

Ethics; process philosophy, summary of.

1528 Rovatti, Pier Aldo. "Logica e filosofia in Whitehead." *Aut Aut,* 1966, 76–100.

Whitehead, Alfred North: introduction to his thought; logic.

1529 Rovatti, P. A. "Whitehead e Husserl: una relazione." *Man and World,* 1, 1968, 587–603.

Phenomenology; science, and philosophy; existence; Paci, E.; Laszlo, I.

(The author compares Whitehead and Husserl on the topics Philosophy of Science and Philosophy of History, demonstrating the relation between the crisis in science and that in human existence.)

1530 Rovatti, Pier Aldo. *La dialettica del processo. Saggio su Whitehead.* Milan: Il Saggiatore, 1969.

Whitehead, Alfred North: introduction to his thought; process; as a model for philosophy, principle of.

1531 Royal, E. Peter. "Becoming, Causality, and Time." *New Scholasticism,* 39, 1965, 26–52.

Time: and causality, epochal theory of, indivisibility of; Plato; Galilie, Galileo; Newton, Isaac; physics.

The epochal theory of time not only leads to an infinite regress in becoming but also makes it impossible for what exists in any time to be something that was in its becoming in the immediately preceding time. And yet becoming in exactly this sense seems to be among the most conspicuous of facts.

1532 Ruggiero, G. de. "Whitehead e la dottrina delle scienze naturali." *Filosofi del novecento.* Bari: Laterza, 1934.

Science, and philosophy.

1533 Rusk, R. R. *The Doctrines of the Great Educators,* 4th ed. St. Martins, 1969, Ch. 14.

Philosophy, of education; rhythm: and generalization, and precision, and romance; education: aims of, organic theory of, purpose of.

1534 Russell, Bertrand. *Introduction to Mathematical Philosophy.* London: George Allen and Unwin Ltd., 1919.

Numbers; multiplication; *Universal Algebra; Principia Mathematica;* mathematics.

(This work does not contain a sustained discussion of Whitehead.)

1535   Russell, Bertrand.   "Whitehead and *Principia Mathematica*." *Mind*, 57, 1948, 137–138.

Principia Mathematica; Russell, Bertrand.

Russell indicates the method and division of labor involved in his collaboration with Whitehead on *Principia Mathematica*.

1536   Russell, Bertrand.   "Portraits from Memory: Alfred North Whitehead." *Harper's Magazine*, 205, #1231, 1952, 50–52.

Whitehead, Alfred North.

1537   Russell, Bertrand.   "Alfred North Whitehead." *Rivista Critica di Storia della Filosofia*, 8, 1953, 100–104.

Whitehead, Alfred North: philosophical development of.

1538   Russell, Bertrand.   *Portraits from Memory and Other Essays.* London: Allen and Unwin, 1956, 92–97. New York: Simon and Schuster, 1956, 99–104.

Whitehead, Alfred North: biography of.

(The author describes Whitehead as he knew him in England.)

1539   Russell, Bertrand.   *The Autobiography of Bertrand Russell: 1872–1914.* London: Allen and Unwin Ltd., 1961.

Whitehead, Alfred North: biography of.

(The author recounts numerous episodes in his relationship with Whitehead and publishes some of the letters they exchanged.)

1540   Russell, Bertrand.   *The Autobiography of Bertrand Russell: 1914–1944.* Boston: Little, Brown & Company, 1968. London: Allen & Unwin, 1968.

Whitehead, Alfred North: biography of.

1541   Rust, Eric C.   *Evolutionary Philosophies and Contemporary Theology.* Philadelphia: Westminster Press, 1969.

Evolution, and religion; theology: process, and metaphysics; religion, and science; Christianity; organism; God: and time, primordial nature of, consequent nature of, transcendence of, immanence of, as personal; person: as series of experiences, and personal identity, and personal immortality; Hartshorne, Charles; Cobb, John B. Jr.; Temple, William.

Because of problems in his doctrine of organism, Whitehead cannot ascribe personal being to God, nor can he adequately account for the transcendence of God.   Also problematic is Whitehead's account of personal identity.

1542   Rust, Eric C.   *Nature—Garden or Desert?: An Essay in Environmental Theology.* Waco, Texas: Word Books, 1971.

Ecology; God: as dipolar; person; panpsychism; Hartshorne, Charles; Teilhard de Chardin; theology.

Whitehead's difficulty in explaining personal identity has ramifications for his doctrine of God.   A better understanding of personal being would have supplemented Whitehead's contribution to theology and ecology.

1543 Ruytinx, Jacques. "Alfred North Whitehead: Une bibliographie." *Revue Internationale de Philosophie*, 15, 1961, 267–277.

Whitehead, Alfred North: bibliography of.

1544 Saatkamp, Herman Joseph, Jr. "Whitehead and the Concept of Memory." *The Modern Schoolman*, 49, 1972, 319–329.

Memory: forms of, and imagination, veridical; prehensions; past: and present, and causal efficacy, of personal experience; novelty, and imagination; Sherburne, Donald.

Whitehead's conceptual scheme allows an account of the process of memory, providing answers to difficulties associated with verifying memory and with distinguishing memory from imagination.

1545 Sahakian, W. S. and Sahakian, M. L. *Realms of Philosophy*. Schenkman, 1965, Chapter 40.

Whitehead, Alfred North: introduction to his thought.

1546 Santayana, G. *Lotze's System of Philosophy*. Bloomington: Indiana University Press, 1971, 68–83.

Being, relational concept of; God: as ground of values, as persuasive, as suffering, and the world; feeling, aesthetic; order; Lotze, Hermann; Santayana, George; metaphysics.

The parallelism of Lotze and Whitehead extends to some of the principles of Whiteheadian metaphysics and encompasses numerous details that seem to mark this off as a distinctive type of metaphysics.

1547 Sarkar, Anil K. "Whitehead's Conception of God." *Prabuddha Barata*, 44, 1939, 397–403.

God: concept of, primordial nature of, consequent nature of, and world.

1548 Sarkar, Anil K. *An Outline of Whitehead's Philosophy*. London: Stockwell, 1940.

Whitehead, Alfred North: introduction to his thought; actual entities; eternal objects; God: concept of, primordial nature of, consequent nature of; creativity; concrescence; space–time.

1549 Sarkar, Anil K. *Changing Phases of Buddhist Thought: A Study in the Background of East–West Philosophy*. Patna, India: Bharati Bhawan, 1968.

Whitehead, Alfred North: introduction to his thought; Buddhism; peace; philosophy, process; intellect; Nagarjuna.

Significant affinities exist between the thought of Nagarjuna and that of Whitehead. A comparison between the two thinkers prepares the ground for further research in comparative philosophy.

1550 Sarkar, Anil K. *Whitehead's Four Principles from West–East Perspectives*. Patna, India: Bharati Bhawan, 1974.

Buddhism; Hinduism; space–time; eternal objects; God; creativity; peace; experience, religious; Whitehead, Alfred North: introduction to his thought; Buddha; Nagarjuna; Radhakrishnan, Sarvepalli; Plato; Hartshorne, Charles.

Four of Whitehead's principles—space–time, eternal objects, God, and creativity—can be significantly related to kindred principles in thought forms of the East, particularly Buddhism.

1551   Saw, R. L. "An Aspect of Causal Connexion." *Proceedings of the Aristotelian Society,* 35, 1934–1935, 95–112.

Causation, and perception; sense–data; qualities, secondary; bifurcation, of nature; philosophy, of nature.

One of Whitehead's most significant contributions to the philosophy of nature is his rejection of secondary qualities.

1552   Saw, R. L. "The Grounds of Induction in Professor Whitehead's Philosophy of Nature." *Philosophical Studies.* Edited by Hannay et. al. London: Allen & Unwin, 1948, 129–139.

Philosophy, of nature; induction.

1553   Schabert, J. A. "The Organic Realism of Whitehead." *Proceedings of the 8th Annual Meeting of the American Catholic Philosophical Association,* December 1932.

Realism; organism, philosophy of.

1554   Schaper, Eva. "Aesthetic Perception." *The Relevance of Whitehead.* Edited by Ivor Leclerc. New York: Humanities Press Inc., 1961, 263–285.

Aesthetics: and sense perception, and objectivity, and subjectivity; symbolic reference; Plato, on aesthetics; Kant, Immanuel: on aesthetics.

In aesthetic experience, sense–perception symbolically brings to consciousness important factors of the initial and primary perceptual basis.

1555   Schild, A. "On Gravitational Theories of Whitehead's Type." *Proceedings of the Royal Society of London,* Series A, 235, 1956, 202–209.

Gravitation; relativity, theory of; mathematics; physics.

1556   Schild, A. "Conservative Gravitational Theories of Whitehead's Type." *Recent Developments in General Relativity.* Edited by S. Bazanski, et. al. Pergamon, 1962, 409–413.

Gravitation; relativity, theory of; mathematics; physics.

1557   Schild, A. "Gravitational Theories of the Whitehead Type and the Principle of Equivalence." *Proceedings of the International School of Physics,* "Enrico Fermi" Course 20, Academic, 1963, 69–115.

Gravitation; equivalence; mathematics; physics.

1558   Schilpp, Paul Arthur. "Present Problems and Mr. Whitehead." *New Humanist,* 7, 1934, 27–30.

Whitehead, Alfred North.

Philosophers must concern themselves with contemporary social problems as well as with theoretical concerns. Whitehead demonstrates both concerns. (Written in response to M. C. Otto, "A. N. Whitehead and Science.")

1559   Schilpp, Paul A., editor. *The Philosophy of Alfred North Whitehead*. New York: Tudor Publishing Company, 1941, 1951.

Whitehead, Alfred North: autobiography of, biography of, philosophical development of, bibliography of; philosophy: of science, of nature, of religion, of education; mathematics; logic; psychology; *Mathematics and the Good*; *Immortality*.

(See articles by J. S. Bixler, John Dewey, John Goheen, Charles Hartshorne, William E. Hocking, Henry W. Holmes, Percy Hughes, C. I. Lewis, Victor Lowe, Evander B. McGilvary, Bertram Morris, Arthur E. Murphy, Joseph Needham, F. S. C. Northrop, Willard V. Quine, A. D. Ritchie, Paul A. Schilpp, and Wilbur M. Urban.)

Reviews

Gross, M. W. *Journal of Philosophy*, 40, 1943, 271–278.

Hartshorne, C. *Religion in Life*, 11, 1942, 469–470.

Hartshorne, C. *Thought*, 17, 1942, 545–547.

Parker, D. H. *Philosophical Review*, 51, 1942, 608–612.

Roberts, Leo. *Isis*, 36, 1945, 78–81.

Sisson, E. O. *Review of Religion*, 8, 1944, 150–153.

Stace, W. T. *Mind*, 52, 1943, 54–75.

1560   Schilpp, Paul A. "Whitehead's Moral Philosophy." *The Philosophy of Alfred North Whitehead*. Edited by Paul A. Schilpp. La Salle, Illinois: Open Court Publishing Company, 1941, 561–618.

Morality; ethics, and aesthetics; value: and judgment, and relatedness, and mathematics; good, and order; subjective aim, and morality; person, and personal identity.

Whitehead's position in moral philosophy is largely determined by the nature of his metaphysics, his predilection for mathematics and mathematical pattern, his universalizing of feeling as the basic function of every actual entity, and his taking aesthetic experience as an ultimate category.

1561   Schilpp, Paul Arthur. "Homage to a Modern Metaphysician." *Christian Century*, 78, 1961, 203–205.

Whitehead, Alfred North.

1562   Schimtz, K. L. "Weiss and Creation." *Review of Metaphysics*, 18, 1964, 147–169.

Creation; Weiss, Paul.

1563   Schindler, David L. "Creativity as Ultimate: Reflections on Actuality in Whitehead, Aristotle, Aquinas." *International Philosophical Quarterly*, 13, 1973, 161–171.

Creativity: and Aristotle's prime matter, and *esse*, as substantial activity, as ultimate; actuality, ground of; many, and the one; Thomas Aquinas; Aristotle; metaphysics.

Whitehead's creativity is functionally equivalent to prime matter in Aristotle and the act of existence (*esse*) in Aquinas. However, unlike *esse*, creativity cannot ground the actuality of entities since it is not actual itself.

1564   Schmidt, P. F. "Perception, Science and Metaphysics: A Study in Whitehead." Unpublished Ph.D. dissertation, Yale University, 1951.

Perception: and science, and nature; causal efficacy; presentational immediacy; science; metaphysics, as descriptive.

1565   Schmidt, P. F. *Perception and Cosmology in Whitehead's Philosophy.* New Brunswick, New Jersey: Rutgers University Press, 1967.

Perception; cosmology.

1566   Schools, P. A. "The Problem of Memory in the Epistemology of Some Anglo–American Philosophers." Unpublished dissertation, University of Toronto, 1966.

Memory; perception; causal efficacy; epistemology.

1567   Schoonenberg, Piet. "Process or History in God?" *Theology Digest*, 23, 1975, 38–44.

Process theology, summary of; God: immutability of, and perfection, and history; analogy; Hartshorne, Charles; theology: Scholastic, process.

The many strengths of process theism are obscured by its lack of an eschatology, and its lack of the sense of mystery in God.

1568   Schrag, Calvin O. "Whitehead and Heidegger: Process Philosophy and Existential Philosophy." *Dialectica: Revue Internationale de Philosophie de la Connaissance*, Berne, 13, 1959, 42–56.

Method, philosophical; substance, and subjectivity; nature, and history; Heidegger, Martin; existentialism.

The philosophies of Whitehead and Heidegger are similar in philosophic intention as well as in specific points, such as the primacy of event and decision. Yet Whitehead tends to reduce human subjectivity to an instance of the cosmic life process, while Heidegger tends to reduce nature as a whole to a mode of historical being.

1569   Schrag, Calvin O. "Struktur der Erfahrung in der Philosophie von James . und Whitehead." *Zeitschrift für philosophisches Forschung*, 23, 1969, 479–494.

Experience, ontology of; prehension; feelings, non–conformal; sense–perception; perception, as non–sensuous; James, William.

As James and Whitehead recast the structure of experience, they revise its traditional subject–object model.

1570   Schroeder, W. Widick. *Cognitive Structures and Religious*

Research: Essays in Sociology and Theology. East Lansing, Michigan: Michigan State University Press, 1970.

Religion, and science, and society; ethics; society: and social organization, and social institutions, and religious institutions; church; ministry; value, and fact; justice; love; language, religious; sermon; God: language about, and world; Durkheim, Emile; Weber, Max; Parsons, Talcott; Warner, Loyd; Niebuhr, H. Richard; Niebuhr, Reinhold: Hartshorne, Charles; sociology of religion; theology, process.

The philosophical and theological conceptualities of Whitehead and Hartshorne are useful in analyzing problems in the social sciences. They free the social sciences from one illegitimate divorce of fact and value and aid in the empirical studies of religious phenomena.

1571   Sciacca, Michele Federico. *Il problema di Dio e della religione nella filosofia attuale.* Brescia: Morcelliana, 1946. Also in French, *Le problème de Dieu et de la religion dans la philosophie contemporaine.* Aubier: Montaigne, 1950, 98–104.

God: problem of, concept of.

1572   Sciacca, Michele Federico. *Philosophical Trends in the Contemporary World.* Notre Dame: University of Notre Dame Press, 1964.

Process philosophy, summary of.

Whitehead is not a metaphysician, but a cosmologist who, lacking a philosophical mentality, believes that metaphysics is only cosmology in the sense of a philosophy of nature.

1573   Seaman, Francis. "The Impact of the Theory of Relativity on Some Recent Philosophies." Unpublished Ph.D. dissertation, University of Michigan, 1950.

Relativity, theory of; Bergson, Henri.

1574   Seaman, Francis. "Whitehead and Relativity." *Philosophy of Science,* 22, 1955, 222–226.

Relativity, theory of; abstraction, extensive; geometry; philosophy, of science.

In *Process and Reality* Whitehead revised his early theory of relativity to accord with his new belief that creativity was atomic rather than continuous. This later view, plus his approach to geometry and his method of extensive abstraction, are in line with the directions of modern science.

1575   Seaman, Francis. "Discussion: In Defense of Duhem." *Philosophy of Science,* 32, 1965, 287–294.

Conventionalism, Duhem's; falsifiability; theories: physical, relativity; process: continuity of, as atomic; Duhem, P.; Grünbaum, A.; Einstein, Albert; physics, relativity; geometry, Euclidean.

Against Grünbaum's claim that, for the case of Euclidean geometry, Duhem's conventionality thesis is false, it can be shown, by reference to the physical theory found in *Process and Reality*, that Euclidean geometry can be preserved from falsifiability by making suitable modifications in the hypothesis of the continuity of physical processes.   Hence grünbaum has not shown that Duhem's thesis is false.

1576   Seaman, Francis.   "Note on Whitehead and the Order of Nature."   *Process Studies*, 5, 1975, 129–133.

Nature, order of; relativity; geometry; mathematics; physics.

1577   Seijas, R.   *Objetivismo teorico.*   Buenos Aires: Tiempos Modernos, 1959.

Objectivism.

1578   Sellars, Roy Wood.   "Concerning 'Transcendence' and 'Bifurcation'."   *Mind*, 31, 1922, 31–39.

Subject–object; perception, and nature; bifurcation; Locke, John; epistemology; realism.

Whitehead extrudes mind from nature in a very hasty fashion. The nature known in perception is identical with the nature which is one condition of the sense–objects by means of which we know it.

1579   Sellars, Roy W.   "Philosophy of Organism and Physical Realism." *The Philosophy of Alfred North Whitehead.*   Edited by Paul A. Schilpp.   La Salle, Illinois: Open Court Publishing Company, 1941, 405–433.

Substance; space–time; bifurcation, of nature; eternal objects; location, fallacy of simple; Santayana, George; realism, critical: Platonism.

Eternal objects are the factors in Whitehead's philosophy which make possible the participation of one actual occasion in another.   If there are no such eternal objects, but only sensations of a similar sort generated in organic selves, Whitehead's philosophy would have to be replaced by a critical realism.

1580   Sellars, Roy Wood.   "Querying Whitehead's Framework."   *Revue Internationale de Philosophie*, Brussels, 15, 1961, 135–166.

Perception: and sense data, and presentational immediacy, and causal efficacy; subjectivist principle; Hume, David; empiricism; epistemology.

Whitehead's construction rests on dubious premises concerning the nature of perceiving and conceiving.   His prehensive stress upon sensory data as terminal is particularly questionable.

1581   Sellars, Roy W.   *Reflections on American Philosophy From Within.*   Notre Dame, Indiana: University of Notre Dame Press, 1969.

Subjectivism, reformed; panpsychism; Tillich, Paul; Hartshorne, Charles; materialism; realism, critical.

Whitehead is a reformed subjectivist rather than a realist—a fact from which his philosophy suffers.

1582   Shahan, Ewing P. *Whitehead's Theory of Experience.* New York: King's Crown Press, Columbia University, 1950.

Experience: in Whitehead's early works, in Whitehead's later works, objects of, subjective aspects of; life; creativity, as ultimate; enjoyment, self; subjective aim; objects, of perception; extension; extensive continuum; presentational immediacy; eternal objects; God.

Whitehead's works exhibit two views of experience which are significantly different and which cannot co–exist without some modification of one or the other. In one case human experience is analyzed in terms of its objective content; in the other there is equal if not greater emphasis on the subjective aspects of experience. (This is the author's Ph.D. dissertation at Columbia University, 1951.)

Reviews

Cesselin, F. *Revue Philosophique*, 77, 1952, 88–95.

Leclerc, I. *Philosophical Quarterly*, 2, 1952, 82–84.

Mays, W. *Mind*, 61, 1952, 429–432.

1583   Shaw, D. E. D. "Perspective on Providence." *New College Bulletin*, 6, 1971, 9–20.

God: providence of, and history.

1584   Shearn, Martin. "Whitehead and Russell's Theory of Types: A Reply." *Analysis*, 11, 1951, 45–48.

Types, theory of; functions; Smart, J. C. C.; logic, mathematical.

Smart fails to notice that Whitehead and Russell do not always use the term "function of functions" in strict analogy to the term "function of individuals." Thus his objections to their theory of types is invalid. (Written in response to J. C. C. Smart, "Whitehead and Russell's Theory of Types.")

1585   Sheen, F. J. "Professor Whitehead and the Making of Religion." *New Schoolman*, 1, 1927, 147–162.

Religion in the Making; religion, Whitehead's view of.

(This is a review of *Religion in the Making*.)

1586   Sheen, F. J. *Philosophy of Science.* Beverly Hills, California: Bruce Publishing Company, 1934.

Philosophy, of science.

1587   Sheldon, Wilmon H. *America's Progressive Philosophy.* New Haven, Connecticut: Yale University Press, 1942.

Philosophy, process; process, as model for philosophy; experience, and nature; energy, and emotion; Dewey, John; Bergson, Henri; idealism; materialism.

Process philosophy is superior to other forms of thought, not because it proves them false, but because it shows how the rival views may all be compatible with one another and with itself. The notion of process or change, and that of the world as a continuum of experience, are among those within process philosophy from which philosophy as a whole can gain.

1588   Sheldon, Wilmon H.   *God and Polarity: A Synthesis of Philosophies.*   New Haven: Yale University Press, 1954, Chapter 7.

Process philosophy, evaluation of.

The main theses of process thought are: the notion of progress, of ubiquitous change, of nature as continuous with no inaccessible private minds, of the unforeseeable future details of progress, of the relational character of everything, and of the power of art and the lure of ideals.

1589   Sheldon, Wilmon H.   *Rational Religion: The Philosophy of Christian Love.*   New York: Philosophical Library, Inc., 1963.

Religion, and reason; love.

1590   Shepherd, John J.   "Panpsychism and Parsimony."   *Process Studies*, 4, 1974, 3–10.

Panpsychism; dipolarity; space, and panpsychism; Lawrence, Victor; Lawrence, D. H.; Hartshorne, Charles.

Whitehead's doctrine of panpsychism fails to account for the nature of spatial extension in the physical world.

1591   Sherburne, Donald W.   "For the Best Paper Showing that Motion is or is not Possible in Whitehead's Later Philosophy." *Review of Metaphysics*, 15, 1961, 142–144.

Motion: physical, telic; morality, and moral responsibility.

Whitehead can provide a reasoned account of motion as physical change, as a being acting telically, and as a person carrying out moral judgment.

1592   Sherburne, Donald W.   *A Whiteheadian Aesthetic: Some Implications of Whitehead's Metaphysical Speculation.*   New Haven: Yale University Press, 1961.

Whitehead, Alfred North: introduction to his thought; aesthetics: theory of, and aesthetic object; art: function of, performer, nonperformer, and artistic creation, and artistic expression, and aesthetic experience; poetry; music; propositions, and art; concrescence, phases of; feelings: intellectual, physical, propositional; beauty; subjective aim; subjective form; transmutation: horizontal, and artistic creation, and artistic expression; art, and God; creativity; eternal objects; reversion; Cobb, John B. Jr.; Leclerc, Ivor; Maritain, Jacques; Greene, Theodore M.; Forster, E. M.; Frost, Robert; Blyth, John W.; Bell, Clive; Bergson, Henri.

Whitehead's metaphysics successfully illumine the nature of artistic creation, aesthetic experience, and the ontological status of the aesthetic object. (This is the author's Ph.D. dissertation submitted to Yale Univeristy in 1960.)

Reviews

Aldrich, V. C.   *Journal of Philosophy*, 59, 1962, 325–328.

Johnson, A. H.   *Dialogue*, 2, 1963, 106–108.

Kennick, W. E.   *Philosophical Review*, 71, 1962, 399–401.

Reither, W. H.   *Philosophy and Phenomenological Research*, 22, 1961–1962, 424–426.

1593   Sherburne, Donald W.   "Responsibility, Punishment and Whitehead's Theory of the Self."   *Alfred North Whitehead: Essays on His Philosophy.*   Edited by George L. Kline. Englewood Cliffs, New Jersey: Prentice–Hall, 1963, 179–188.

Responsibility, moral; self, and self–identity; decision; Schlick, Morris.

Whitehead's theory of self enables one to reject the appeal to retribution as the basis for punishment, to incorporate the reformation theory of Schlick into a process perspective, and to retain in cosmology the notions of responsibility, judgment, freedom, and creativity.

1594   Sherburne, Donald W.   *A Key to Whitehead's Process and Reality.*   New York: Macmillan Company, 1966. Bloomington, Indiana: Indiana University Press, 1971.

Process and Reality; Whitehead, Alfred North: introduction to his thought, and other philosophers; actual entity; eternal objects; creativity; concrescence, phases of; nexus; perception; God: and the world, and classical theism, primordial nature of, consequent nature of; prehensions; datum; subjective form; satisfaction; superject; objective immortality; ontological principle; subjective aim; feelings: conformal, conceptual, propositional, complex, comparative; purpose, physical; reversion, conceptual; propositions; transmutation; physiology, psychological; order; substance; causation; causal efficacy; presentational immediacy; symbolic reference; philosophy: and science, aim of, purpose of, speculative; Descartes, Rene; Locke, John; Hume, David; Kant, Immanuel; Newton, Isaac.

(Sherburne reorganizes numerous quotations from *Process and Reality* into a topical survey.   The aim is to render the inter–related treatment of issues in *Process and Reality* more intelligible to the beginning student.   A helpful glossary appears at the end of the book.)

1595   Sherburne, Donald W.   "Whitehead Without God."   *Christian Schoolman*, 50, 1967, 251–272. Also in *Process Philosophy and Christian Thought*. Edited by Delwin Brown, Ralph E. James, and Gene Reeves.   Indianapolis, Indiana: Bobbs–Merrill Company, Inc., 1971, 305–328.

God: Whitehead without, and creativity, and eternal objects, and order, as source of initial aim; past, and present; objective immortality; novelty; region, and regional inclusion; initial aim; truth.

Whitehead's concept of God explains how the past can be preserved in the present, how eternal objects are ontologically grounded, and how temporal occasions receive their initial subjective aims. None of these explanatory roles are necessary to Whitehead's scheme. Hence the concept of God can be discarded from Whitehead's system and his scheme can be reinterpreted from a naturalistic perspective.

1596   Sherburne, Donald W. "Reply." *Christian Scholar*, 50, 1967, 316–319.

Christian, William A.; metaphysics; theology, and philosophy. Christian subordinates metaphysics to a single tradition's theological principles. This is too restricted a focus for the metaphysician, who must utilize data from every dimension of experience. (Written in response to William A. Christian, "The New Metaphysics and Theology.")

1597   Sherburne, Donald W. "Whitehead's Psychological Physiology." *Southern Journal of Philosophy*, 7, 1969, 401–407.

Society, personally ordered; nexus; non–social; freedom; Cobb, John B., Jr.; Pols, Edward; physiology, psychological.

Whitehead's concept of the personally–ordered society identified as the soul is illuminated by positing a non–social nexus as the immediate context of this society.

1598   Sherburne, Donald W. "The 'Whitehead Without God' Debate: The Rejoinder." *Process Studies*, 1, 1971, 101–113.

Inclusion, regional; actual entity: unity of, standpoint of; extensiveness of; extensive continuum; God, as ground; Cobb, John B., Jr.

Since a region originates with its entity, the region shares integrally in the actual unity and indivisibility of the occasion. This argues against regional inclusion, and hence against the possibility of God's prehension of occasions through regional inclusion.

1599   Sherburne, Donald W. and Cobb, John B., Jr. "Regional Inclusion and the Extensive Continuum." *Process Studies*, 2, 1972, 277–295.

Region, and regional inclusion; extensive continuum: atomization of, as real potentiality; standpoints.

Cobb's attempt to relate God and a particular actual entity via regional inclusion fails, in part, because Cobb fails to distinguish between regions and standpoints.

1600   Shimony, Abner. "Quantum Physics and the Philosophy of Whitehead." *Studies in the Philosophy of Science*, Volume 2. Edited by R. S. Cohen and M. W. Wartofsky. New York: Humanities Press, 1965, 307–330. Also in *Philosophy in America*. Edited by Max Black. Ithaca: Cornell University Press, 1965, 240–261.

Physics: quantum, microphysics, indeterminism in; waves, and particles; location, simple; Heisenberg, Werner; Schrödinger, E.

Contemporary quantum theory and microphysical theory offer only partial agreement with Whitehead's physics. Suggested modification would graft the radical elements of quantum theory onto the radical elements of the philosophy of organism by assuming that elementary entities have proto–mental characteristics while treating the states of these entities in accordance with the combinatory principles of quantum theory.

1601   Shive, J. R.   "The Meaning of Individuality: A Comparative Study of Alfred North Whitehead, Borden Parker Bowne, and Edgar S. Brightman."   Unpublished Ph.D. dissertation, University of Chicago, 1961.

Individuality; self; relatedness; Brightman, Edgar S.; Bowne, Borden Parker.

1602   Shouse, J. B.   "Some Modern Philosophers on Education." *Educational Forum*, 16, 1951, 55–63.

Dewey, John; Russell, Bertrand; philosophy, of education.

Despite the intimate relationship between education and philosophy, Whitehead did little to utilize this relationship.

1603   Sichel, Betty A.   "Alfred North Whitehead's Ethical Theory and the Implications of this Theory for Education."   Unpublished Ph.D. dissertation, New York University, 1967.

Ethics; education; aesthetics; value; education, and creativity; good; evil; rhythm.

From the speculative categories of Whitehead's philosophy an ethical theory can be formulated which has definite implications for educational method.

1604   Siegmund, G.   "Alfred North Whitehead."   *Philosophisches Jahrbuch*, 58, 1948, 177–178.

Whitehead, Alfred North: introduction to his thought.

1605   Simmons, James Robert.   "The Problem of Human Individuality with Emphasis on the Philosophy of Alfred North Whitehead." Unpublished Ph.D. dissertation, Columbia University, 1955.

Individuality, human; self; ego; society.

1606   Simmons, James Robert.   "Whitehead's Aesthetic of Nature." *Southern Journal of Philosophy*, 6, 1968, 14–23.

Whitehead, Alfred North, method of; nature, and human existence; feelings, universality of; aesthetics, and metaphysics.

Whitehead begins his metaphysics as introspective psychology, which he expands, with increasing abstractness, into aesthetics, biology, and then physics.   In the process, Whitehead teleologizes all of nature.

1607   Simmons, James Robert.   "Whitehead's Metaphysic of Persuasion."   *Philosophy and Rhetoric*, 2, 1969, 72–80.

Language, Whitehead's use of; propositions, as lures; rhetoric.

Whitehead transforms a complex of statements and tautologies into philosophical propositions.   He intends these propositions to conform to persuasive fact, to give significance to fact, and to persuade the reader to deeper experience.

1608   Simmons, James Robert.   "An Antinomy of Perishing in
        Whitehead." *Personalist*, 50, 1969, 559–566.

        Perishing, perpetual; location, simple; monism; pluralism.

        Whitehead cannot go from his monistic phase to his pluralistic
        phase except through appealing to the notion of perishing.
        But his monistic phase, wherein each entity is present in every
        entity, is such that he cannot justify his notion of perishing
        without first appealing to his pluralistic phase.

1609   Simonpietri, F. A. *Lo individual y su relación interna en Alfred
        North Whitehead.*   Pamplona: Ediciones Universidad de
        Navarra, forthcoming.

        Individual; relations, internal.

        (This is the author's dissertation at the Universidad de
        Navarra, Spain, 1967.)

1610   Singermann, O. "The Relation between Philosophy and Science"
        (in Hebrew). *Iyyun*, 19, 1968, 65–91.

        Science, and philosophy; objects, of science; perception;
        materialism; realism, scientific; Bergson, Henri.

1611   Sinha, Ajit Kumar. "For the Best Paper Showing that Motion is
        or is not Possible in Whitehead's Later Philosophy." *Review
        of Metaphysics*, 15, 1961, 144–147.

        Eternal objects; motion.

        Whitehead could not free his philosophical standpoint from the
        concept of static and changeless reality in the final stages of
        the development of his thought, even though he tried to
        reconcile the concept of change with the concept of
        permanence.

1612   Sini, C. *Whitehead e la funzione della filosofia.* Padova:
        Marsilio, 1965.

        Philosophy: aim of, method of, nature of, speculative.

1613   Sinisi, V. F.   "Lesniewski's Analysis of Whitehead's Theory of
        Events."   *Notre Dame Journal of Formal Logic*, 7, 1966,
        323–327.

        Event; philosophy, of nature.

1614   Singh, Satya Prakash. *Sri Aurobindo and Whitehead on the
        Nature of God.* Aligarh, India: Vigyan Prakashan Press, 1972.

        Saccidananda; God: consequent nature of, primordial nature of,
        superjective nature of, as becoming; creativity; space–time;
        harmony; Aurobindo, Sri; metaphysics.

        (Aurobindo's conception of the divine being–consciousness–bliss,
        or Saccidananda, is exhaustively compared with Whitehead's
        conception of God, while creativity is compared to
        consciousness–force.   Whitehead's system ultimately is
        considered inadequate because it fails to take account of yogic
        experience.)

1615   Sipfle, David A. "On the Intelligibility of the Epochal Theory of Time." *Monist*, 53, 1969, 505–518.

Time, epochal theory of; actuality, atomic; Zeno; Chappell, V. C.

The epochal theory of time is based on the atomic nature of actual occasions, and not on the Zenonian arguments. (Written in response to V. C. Chappell, "Whitehead's Theory of Becoming.")

1616   Sipfle, David A. "Henri Bergson and the Epochal Theory of Time." *Bergson and the Evolution of Physics.* Edited by P. A. Y. Gunter. Knoxville: University of Tennessee Press, 1969, 275–294.

Time, epochal theory of; duration; Bergson, Henri; Chappell, Vere C.

Just as Whitehead allows for both the separative and the prehensive aspects of time, so Bergson insists on the reality of both distinguishable temporal epochs and their profound interrelatedness. Thus for Bergson real time, whether endured by mind or matter, is epochal.

1617   Sisson, E. O. "Whitehead's Mysticism: A Review Article." *Review of Religion*, 8, 1944, 150–153.

Intuition; mysticism; religion, nature of; philosophy, of religion.

1618   Skutch, A. F. *The Quest of the Divine.* Meador, 1956.

God: nature of, concept of.

1619   Slater, R. H. L. *God of the Living or Human Destiny.* New York: Charles Scribner's Sons, 1939.

Process, as fundamental character of universe; change, meanings of; relatedness; God, religious availability of; Buddhism; theology.

1620   Smart, J. J. C. "Whitehead and Russell's Theory of Types." *Analysis*, 10, 1950, 93–96.

Types, theory of; functions: mathematical, propositional; Russell, Bertrand; logic, mathematical.

A latent confusion in Whitehead and Russell's symbolism seems to vitiate their entire theory of types.

1621   Smith, James. "Alfred North Whitehead." *Scrutiny*, 3, 1934, 2–21.

Whitehead, Alfred North; process philosophy, summary of.

The office of universal artist to which Whitehead aspires demands of its occupant that he recognize the better as better, and the best as best. By lack of this fastidiousness, Whitehead fails, for he reduces morality to zest, and has no true sense of tragedy.

1622   Smith, James L. "Aesthetics and Art within a Whiteheadian Cosmology." Unpublished Ph.D. dissertation, Tulane University, 1969.

Aesthetics; art, and creativity; beauty; music; Cobb, John B. Jr.; Sherburne, Donald W.

1623   Smith, John E. *Reason and God: Encounters of Philosophy with Religion.* New Haven, Connecticut: Yale University Press, 1961.

Christianity, and culture; human existence, social nature of; togetherness.

(The work contains no sustained discussion of Whitehead's philosophy, but uses a few of Whitehead's ideas in discussing the relation between religion and philosophy.)

1624   Smith, John E. "Purpose in American Philosophy." *International Philosophical Quarterly,* 1, 1961, 390–406.

Purpose: cosmic, human, physical; Royce, Josiah; Dewey, John; James, William; Peirce, Charles S.; philosophy, American.

American philosophy may be described as purposive. Whitehead's contribution was to consider nature in terms of a directional aim, and to emphasize purpose in the functioning of reason.

1625   Smith, John E. *The Spirit of American Philosophy.* New York: Oxford University Press, 1963, 1966, 1972.

Philosophy: in America, and science; education; experience, and science; knowledge, and specialization; value; purpose; mathematics: pure, applied, and quantity–quality distinction; pragmatism.

(This is an introduction to five American philosophers, among which Whitehead is included. The other four are Charles Peirce, William James, Josiah Royce, and John Dewey.)

1626   Smith, Raymond. *Whitehead's Concept of Logic.* ("Thomistic Studies") Westminster, Maryland: Newman Press, 1953.

Logic: mathematical, deductive, symbolic; mathematics.

1627   Smith, Mrs. Vernon H. "The Nature and Function of the Self as Developed in the Philosophy of Alfred North Whitehead." *Educational Theory,* 8, 1957–1958, 109–113.

Self, and self–creativity; God, and the world.

The process of self–creativity and the inseparability of creator and creature provide guidelines for a Whiteheadian understanding of the self.

1628   Smith, W. D. "The Doctrines of God in Whiteheadian Process Theologians: Whitehead, Hartshorne, Pittenger, Ogden, and Cobb." Unpublished dissertation, Southwestern Baptist Theological Seminary, 1972.

God: nature of.

1629   Snook, Lee E. "Luther's Doctrine of the Real Presence: Critique and Reconstruction from the View of Process Thought." Unpublished Th.D. dissertation, Union Theological Seminary in New York, 1971.

God, as absolute; sacrament; eucharist; redemption; Christ; Luther, Martin.

Luther's doctrine of a God who is for the world and yet who creates the world can be fruitfully interpreted from within a process perspective. In the process Luther's doctrine of the real presence of Christ in the eucharist can be better understood.

1630   Snyder, William S.   "Whitehead's Theory of Perception: An Epistemological Source of Speculative Philosophy." Unpublished Ph.D. dissertation, Princeton University, 1955.

Epistemology; knowledge, and perception; perception; mind; objects, scientific; causality; abstraction; *An Enquiry Concerning the Principles of Natural Knowledge; The Concept of Nature.*

Many epistemological issues can be resolved if the question concerning the relation between scientific knowledge and its understanding of reality is distinguished from the question concerning the nature of mind and its apprehension of reality. Whitehead deals with each of these questions, but fails to distinguish them.

1631   Sommers, Frederick T.   "An Empiricist Ontology: A Study in the Metaphysics of Alfred North Whitehead."   Unpublished Ph.D. dissertation, Columbia University, 1955.

Ontology; feeling; substance; being; concrescence; panpsychism; teleology; actuality; possibility; propositions; Plato; Aristotle; empiricism.

Whitehead's understanding of being integrates an Aristotelian functionalism and a Platonic realism.

1632   Soneson, J. M.   "The Individual: A Comparison of the Philosophical Anthropologies of Soren Kierkegaard and Alfred North Whitehead with Theological Implications." Unpublished Ph.D. dissertation, University of Chicago, 1969.

Individual; self; Kierkegaard, Soren; existentialism.

1633   Speck, J. editor.   *Grundprobleme der Grossen Philosophen.* Göttingen: Vanderhöck und Ruprecht, 1972.

Whitehead, Alfred North, introduction to his thought.

1634   Spencer, John B.   "The Ethics of Alfred North Whitehead." Unpublished Ph.D. dissertation, University of Chicago, 1966.

Concrescence; aesthetics, and ethics; morality; beauty; God; ethics.

1635   Spencer, Theodore.   "Portrait: Alfred North Whitehead." *American Scholar,* 16, 1947, 82–86.

Whitehead, Alfred North.

1636   Spivey, Mark A.   "Prehensions."   Unpublished Ph.D. dissertation, University of North Carolina at Chapel Hill, 1971.

Subject.

(The author employs the term 'prehension' for his own purposes. There is a brief criticism of Whitehead's notion of subject.)

1637 Sprague, S. R. "Shaping a Process Theology: The Theological Method of John B. Cobb, Jr." Unpublished dissertation, Southern Baptist Theological Seminary, 1975.

Theology: method of, natural, process; Cobb, John B. Jr.

1638 Sprinkle, H. C. "Concerning the Philosophical Defensibility of a Limited Indeterminism." Unpublished Ph.D. dissertation, Yale University, 1933.

Indeterminism; freedom; causality; determinism.

1639 Stace, W. T.; Blake, R. N. and Murphy, A. E. "Can Speculative Philosophy be Defended?" *Philosophical Review*, 52, 1943, 116–143.

Philosophy: speculative, method of, nature of.

1640 Stace, W. T. "Interestingness." *Philosophy*, 74, 1944, 233–241.

Interest; truth; beauty.

Interestingness is an ultimate value, coordinate with beauty, and independent of it.

1641 Stace, W. T. "The Problem of Unreasoned Beliefs." *Mind*, 54, 1945, 27–49, 122–147.

Intuition; knowledge, immediate; epistemology.

Whitehead's reliance on intuition is an excellent example of philosophers who use unreasoned beliefs as basic evidence. Such beliefs contain implicit reasoning processes which must be made explicit for critical investigation.

1642 Stahl, Roland Jr. "The Influence of Bergson on Whitehead." Unpublished Ph.D. dissertation, Boston University Graduate School, 1950.

Process; elan vital; creativity; novelty; feeling, and intuition; time, and duration; location, fallacy of simple; consciousness; mentality; Bergson, Henri.

Bergson's philosophy influenced Whitehead in numerous ways. Whitehead in turn modified many of Bergson's ideas in the direction of greater coherence and fuller development.

1643 Stahl, Roland Jr. "Bergson's Influence on Whitehead." *Personalist*, 36, 1955, 250–257.

Creative advance; duration; Bergson, Henri; Lowe, Victor.

Whitehead was considerably influenced by Bergson's notions of creative evolution, of time, durations, and intuition.

1644 Stallknecht, Newton Shelps. *Studies in the Philosophy of Creation, With Special Reference to Bergson and Whitehead.* Princeton, New Jersey: Princeton University Press, 1934.

God: as creator, primordial nature of, and order, and time, consequent nature of; consciousness; one, and many;

perception; nature, and consciousness; bifurcation; Bergson, Henri; Hocking, William E.; Plato.

Although Whitehead's deemphasis of the importance of consciousness raises several problems for his scheme of thought, his account of the relation between God and the world is admirable in that it is one of the first accounts in the history of metaphysics through which God can reasonably be conceived as personal.

1645   Stapledon, Olaf. "The Location of Physical Objects." *Journal of Philosophical Studies*, 4, 1929, 64–75.

Location, fallacy of simple; abstractions; qualities: primary, secondary.

Other than abstractions, the only simply located occurrence is the event's prehension of the rest of the universe.

1646   Stearns, Isabel. "The Person." *Review of Metaphysics*, 3, 1950, 427–436.

Person: and memory, and personal identity; self–transcendence.

If the definite and determined character of the person belongs primarily to its past, and if the indefinite and indeterminate character has to do primarily with its potentiality for the future, then we must discover in its moving present that concrete self within which these two characters are merged and mediated.

1647   Stearns, Isabel. "Time and the Timeless." *Review of Metaphysics*, 4, 1950, 187–200.

Time: and human experience, and timelessness, metaphysics.

The status of the past as a transcendent fact, the appearance of the eternal in the midst of the present, and the necessity for a timeless dimension of the individual, unite to establish the fact that the temporal cannot be isolated from the timeless.

1648   Stearns, J. Brenton. "On the Impossibility of God's Knowing That He Does Not Exist." *Journal of Religion*, 46, 1966, 1–8.

Proof, modal; argument, ontological; perfection; God: and divine knowledge, proofs of; necessity; contingency; possibility; Hartshorne, Charles; Ogden, Schubert M.; philosophical theology; logic.

Hartshorne's modal proof establishes, not the existence of an infallible knower, but rather the absolute necessity of infinite possibility.

1649   Stebbing, L. Susan. "Mind and Nature in Professor Whitehead's Philosophy." *Mind*, 33, 1924, 289–303.

Mind, and nature; bifurcation, of nature; perception, theory of; *Concept of Nature; Enquiry Concerning the Principles of Natural Knowledge*.

Whitehead's philosophy of nature requires further development with respect to the relation of mind to nature.

1650   Stebbing, L. Susan. "Universals and Professor Whitehead's Theory of Objects." *Proceedings of the Aristotelian Society*, 25, 1924–1925, 305–330.

Universals: status of, theory of; particulars; substance; language, and subject–predicate mode of expression.

There are significant resemblances between Whitehead's "object" and what is commonly called a "universal," but simply to substitute one for the other is misleading.

1651   Stebbing, L. Susan. "Professor Whitehead's 'Perceptual Object'." *Journal of Philosophy*, 23, 1926, 197–213.

Objects, of perception; sense–perception; universals, theory of; *Concept of Nature; Enquiry Concerning the Principles of Natural Knowledge.*

The perceptual object is an event controlling the ingression of sense objects in nature. This substitution of "event" and "object" for subject/predicate and particular/universal frees Whitehead's theory from the difficulties of a theory of universals.

1652   Stebbing, L. Susan; Braithwaite, R. B. and Wrinch, D. "Symposium: Is the 'Fallacy of Simple Location' a Fallacy?" *Proceedings of the Aristotelian Society Supplement*, 7, 1927, 207–243.

Location, fallacy of simple.

1653   Stebbing, L. Susan. "Concerning Substance." *Proceedings of the Aristotelian Society*, 30, 1929–1930, 285–308.

Substance, primary; particular; universal; actual entity, and substance; relatedness; Aristotle; monism.

Whitehead's criticism of philosophies of substance, and of the subject–predicate doctrine upon which they are based, leads him toward an uncompromising monism.

1654   Steffens, D. C. M. "La correlacíon entre la percepcíon sensorial y el pensamiento científico según Alfred North Whitehead." *Internacional Congreso Filosófico*, 1954.

Perception, and sense data; philosophy, of science.

1655   Stein, H. "On Einstein–Minkowski Space–Time." *Journal of Philosophy*, 67, 1968, 5–23.

Space–time, Einstein–Minkowski; Einstein, Albert; Minkowski, H.

1656   Stein, H. "A Note on Time and Relativity Theory." *Journal of Philosophy*, 67, 1970, 289–294.

Becoming, unison of; time; simultaneity; contemporaries, problem of; duration; loci, strain; Lango, John W.; Einstein, Albert.

(This is a reply to John Lango's criticism of Stein's analysis of the relativistic theory of time. Indirectly Stein criticizes Whitehead's theory of durations and strain loci.)

1657   Stevens, Edward I.   "Freedom, Determinism, and Responsibility:
         An Analysis and a Whiteheadian Interpretation."   Unpublished
         Ph.D. dissertation, Vanderbilt University, 1965.

         Freedom;   determinism;   responsibility;   ethics;   positivism;
         utilitarianism; psychology; science.

         From Whitehead's perspective, the evidence of science cannot
         be decisive in answering the question of freedom of choice in
         human existence.   Whitehead's cosmology accounts for freedom.

1658   Stiernotte, A. P., editor.   *Mysticism and the Modern Mind.*
         Berea, Ohio: Liberal Arts Publishing, 1959, 60–70.

         Mysticism; experience, religious; religion, nature of.

1659   Stokes, Walter E.   "The Function of Creativity in the
         Metaphysics of Whitehead."   Unpublished Ph.D. dissertation,
         St. Louis University, 1960.

         Creativity: as ultimate, as surd, and eternal objects, and time;
         God, and creativity; receptacle; Plato; Aristotle; Hartshorne,
         Charles; Leclerc, Ivor; Bidney, D.; Emmet, Dorothy; Mays,
         Wolf.

         Creativity is a metaphysical principle that is real,
         indeterminate, and infinite in itself, although non–being rather
         than being.   It is the ultimate surd or irrational element in
         the universe, expressive of the limit of the Platonic search for
         intelligible form.

1660   Stokes, Walter E.   "Recent Interpretations of Whitehead's
         Creativity."   *Modern Schoolman*, 39, 1962, 309–333.

         Creativity; Mays, Wolf; Johnson, A. H.; Hartshorne, Charles;
         Bidney, D.; Christian, William A.; Leclerc, Ivor; Rotenstreich,
         Nathan; Moxley, D. J.; Stebbings, L. Susan; Emmet, Dorothy.

         Interpretations of Whitehead's creativity range from "applied
         logic" to agency as such.   Frequently interpreters relate
         creativity to Plantonism.

1661   Stokes, Walter E.   "Whitehead's Prolegomena to Any Future
         Metaphysics."   *Heythrop Journal*, 3, 1962, 42–50.

         Concreteness, misplaced (fallacy of); substance, Cartesian;
         perception, sensationalist doctrine of; Locke, John; Descartes,
         Rene; Hume, David; Kant, Immanuel; metaphysics.

         Three interlocked and interrelated errors—the Cartesian
         substance–quality doctrine of actuality, the sensationalist
         doctrine of Locke and Hume, and the Kantian doctrine of the
         objective world—are instances of the Fallacy of Misplaced
         Concreteness.   Whitehead's criticism of these errors constitutes
         his own prolegomena to any future metaphysics.

1662   Stokes, Walter E.   "Freedom as Perfection: Whitehead, Thomas
         and Augustine."   *American Catholic Philosophical Association
         Proceedings*, 36, 1962, 132–142.

         God: freedom of, and creativity, primordial nature of;

creativity; ontological principle; Thomas Aquinas; Augustine; Thomism.

Whitehead's notion of the freedom of God can be unified with the notions of liberty found in the Augustinian and Thomistic traditions to emphasize the maximum freedom of God.

1663 Stokes, Walter E. "A Select and Annotated Bibliography of Alfred North Whitehead." *Modern Schoolman*, 39, 1962, 135–151.

Whitehead, Alfred North, bibliography of.

1664 Stokes, Walter E. "God for Today and Tomorrow." *New Scholasticism*, 43, 1963, 351–378. Also in *Process Philosophy and Christian Thought*. Edited by Delwin Brown, Ralph E. James and Gene Reeves. Indianapolis, Indiana: Bobbs–Merrill Company, Inc., 1971, 244–265.

God: and freedom, relations of, and world, experience of, as creator; peace; harmony; romanticism; Thomas Aquinas; Plato; Hegel, G. W. F.

For those asking if God's existence can be reconciled with persons' deepened understanding of themselves as free creators of the world, the Whiteheadian approach, with its notion of God's persuasive personal action in the world, and its discovery of God's presence yet absence in man's creative activity, combined with its stress on the mutual immanence of God and the world, offers pathways for further development.

1665 Stokes, Walter E. "Whitehead's Challenge to Theistic Realism." *New Scholasticism*, 38, 1964, 1–21.

Universe, solidarity of; God: of classical theism, and freedom; Thomas Aquinas; Thomism.

Whitehead's theory of knowledge, of God and freedom, and of the solidarity of the universe present constructive challenges to contemporary Thomism.

1666 Stokes, Walter E. "Is God Really Related to this World?" *American Catholic Philosophical Association Proceedings*, 39, 1965, 145–151.

God: and world, and classical theism; Thomas Aquinas; Hartshorne, Charles; Thomism; theology.

Between philosophies which exclude the possibility of the real relation of God to the world and those, such as Whitehead's, which demand reciprocal relations between God and the world lies a third position in which real but asymmetrical relations between God and the world are posited.

1667 Stokes, Walter E. "Alfred North Whitehead." *New Catholic Encyclopedia*. New York: McGraw–Hill, 1967, Volume 14, 896–897.

Whitehead, Alfred North, introduction to his thought.

1668 Stokes, Walter E. "Truth, History, and Dialectic." *American Catholic Philosophical Association*, 43, 1969, 85–90.

Creativity; God, and value; truth; beauty; peace; ontological principle; solidarity, of world.

The human drive toward truth and beauty reveals the presence of God as the source of value.

1669 Stone, R. H. "Essence of Education: Alfred North Whitehead." *Union Seminary Quarterly Review*, 19, 1963, 35–47.

Education: stages of, religious; philosophy, of education.

1670 Strain, John P. "Whitehead's Concept of Human Experience as it Clarifies Educational Precision." Unpublished Ph.D. dissertation, George Peabody College, 1961.

Education; rhythm; reason; experience, and time.

Whitehead's philosophical system implies a philosophy of education in which thought, action, and aesthetics play complementary roles.

1671 Streng, Frederick J. "Metaphysics, Negative Dialectic, and the Expression of the Inexpressible." *Philosophy East and West*, 25, 1975, 429–447.

Propositions: function of, and reality; causal efficacy; individuality; dependent coorigination; values; awareness, states of; Nagarjuna; Buddhism.

Nagarjuna and Whitehead use concepts for fundamentally different purposes: Whitehead, for the sake of speculative understanding, and Nagarjuna, in order to overcome such speculation.

1672 Stumpf, S. E. *Socrates to Sartre: A History of Philosophy.* New York: McGraw–Hill Co., 1966, Chapter 19.

Process philosophy, summary of.

Whitehead sought to show just what the limits of science are and what unique insights could be provided by metaphysics.

1673 Suchocki, Marjorie. "Conference on Mahayana Buddhism and Whitehead." *Process Studies*, 4, 1974, 305–307.

Buddhism: Mahayana, and substance, and perception, and history, and time, and God, and interrelatedness; dependent coorigination.

(The author reviews the topics discussed at a conference on Mahayana Buddhism and Whitehead held in 1974. Affinities between Whitehead's thought and Mahayana Buddhist thought pertain to perception, nonsubstantiality, and interrelatedness. Differences concern God, the importance of history, and the nature of time.)

1674 Suchocki, Marjorie. "The Metaphysical Ground of the Whiteheadian God." *Process Studies*, 5, 1975, 237–246.

God: as actual entity, as a society, as lure for feeling; satisfaction; novelty; unity, of occasion; Cobb, John B., Jr.

The 'societal' view of God results in a separation of first principles in Whitehead's system. Such a view fails to account for a unitive ground to possibility and, thus, for relevant novelty.

1675   Sullivan, William M. "The Process Social Paradigm and the Problem of Social Order." Unpublished Ph.D. dissertation, Fordham University, 1971.

Civilization; society; government; democracy; Marxism; alienation; symbolism; Weber, Max; Dewey, John; Mead, George H.; Marx, Karl; sociology; psychology.

A social paradigm based on Whitehead's philosophy can both incorporate Max Weber's emphasis on the role of coercive power in society and also emphasize the importance of symbolic legitimation in accounting for the stability and change of coercive institutions.

1676   Sun, George C. "Chinese Metaphysics and Whitehead." Unpublished Ph.D. dissertation, Southern Illinois University, 1971.

Philosophy, Chinese; Buddhism; Confucianism; Taoism; I Ching; Confucius; Chuang Tzu; Leibniz, G. W.; Pepper, Stephen.

By virtue of significant affinities between Whiteheadian thought and Chinese philosophy, much of Confucianism, Taoism, and Buddhism can be interpreted in Whiteheadian terms.

1677   Susinos, Franciso. "Apuntes para una valoracion critica del organicismo cosmologico de Whitehead." Salmanticensis, 8, 1961, 337–393.

Process philosophy, summary of; categoreal scheme; God: doctrine of, primordial nature of, consequent nature of, and world; process.

Whitehead's philosophy of organism achieves a radical revolution in modern philosophy comparable to that of Heidegger's Sein und Zeit.

1678   Svensson, Francis E. "The Concept of Change: Alternative Perspectives." Unpublished Ph.D. dissertation, University of Washington, 1970.

Society; Thompson, James C.; Dewey, John; political science.

Political and social models presuppose cosmology. Whitehead's 'process' cosmology serves as a foundation for social theories of the type endorsed by John Dewey.

1679   Swabey, M. C. The Judgment of History. New York: Philosophical Library, 1954, 205–213.

History: and reason, and transcendent aim, and tragedy; Adventures of Ideas; philosophy, of history.

For Whitehead history is profoundly metaphysical; the force and grandeur of the ideas exemplified in different cultural fields drive human life forward toward the source of all harmony.

1680   Swyhart, Barbara A. D. *Bioethical Decision–Making.* Philadelphia: Fortress Press, 1975.

Ethics: and psychology, and medicine, and sociology; abortion; decision–making; value; importance; Buddhism, and ethics; religion, and value.

(The author's primary interest is in bioethics with special reference to the problem of abortion. The methodology used is adapted from Whitehead's philosophy.)

1681   Synge, John L. *The Relativity Theory of A. N. Whitehead.* Baltimore: University of Maryland, 1951.

Cosmology; physics, relativity theory in; acceleration; fields; mechanics; gravitation; light, velocity of; Maxwell, J. C.; Einstein, Albert.

This work provides a brief comparison of Einstein's and Whitehead's relativity theories with a detailed derivation of Whitehead's, showing the application of Whitehead's theory to problems in celestial mechanics and electromagnetism.

1682   Synge, John L. "Orbits and Rays in the Gravitational Field of a Finite Sphere According to the Theory of Alfred North Whitehead." *Proceedings of the Royal Society of London*, Ser A 211, 1952, 303–319.

Orbit; gravitation; relativity, theory of; philosophy, of science; physics.

1683   Synge, John L. "Note on the Whitehead–Raynor Expanding Universe." *Proceedings of the Royal Society of of London*, Ser A 224, 1954, 336–338.

Universe, expanding; Raynor, C. B.; physics.

1684   Synge, John L. *Relativity: The Special Theory.* London: North–Holland Publishing Company, Ltd., 1955, 1958, 1964, 1972.

Relativity, special theory of; fields; mechanics; gravitation; light, velocity of; Einstein, Albert.

1685   Tagaki, S. "Whitehead: Shizen Ninshiki No Shogenri (An Enquiry Concerning the Principles of Natural Knowledge)." *Gendai Shizenkagaku Koza 8.* Tokyo: Kobundo, 1952, 125–128.

Philosophy, of nature; knowledge, and perception; epistemology.

1686   Takenaka, N. "Whitehead No Shukyoron (Whitehead and Religion)." *Chugai Nippo*, March 8–15, 1947.

Religion: nature of, and reason, and science; philosophy, of religion.

1687   Tanaka, Takao. "Dogen no Shukyoteki sekaikan to Howaitoheddo no keijijogakuteki uchuron ('Dogen's Religious World View and Whitehead's Metaphysical Cosmology')." *Zen no honshitsu to ningen no shinri (The Essence of Zen and the Truth of Man).* Edited by K. Nishitani and S. Hisamatsu. Tokyo: Sobunsha, 213–271.

Creativity, and Buddhist dependent coorigination; time: as

momentary, as perpetually perishing; mind, mind–body; self–enjoyment; Dogen; Buddhism.

With respect to creativity, time, causality, relatedness, and self–enjoyment, Whitehead's philosophy has significant affinities to the thought of the Japanese Buddhist philosopher, Dogen.

1688   T'ang Chun–i.   *Che–hsueh kai–lun* (A General Outline of Philosophy).   Taipei, Taiwan: Student Book Company, 1974, 934–960.

Whitehead, Alfred North: introduction to his thought, bibliography of; location, fallacy of simple; actual occasion; feelings; prehensions: physical, conceptual; presentational immediacy; causal efficacy; abstraction, extensive; God: primordial nature of, consequent nature of; value.

(This is one chapter of a multi–volume work that seeks to explain the fundamentals of Whitehead's philosophy of organism within the larger context of a study of comparative philosophy.   Whitehead is taken as the main thinker in Western theories of organic philosophy.)

1689   Taube, M.   *Causation, Freedom, and Determinism.*   London: Allen & Unwin, 1936.

Causation: efficient, final; determinism, and indeterminism; freedom; novelty.

1690   Taylor, A. E.   "Dr. Whitehead's Philosophy of Religion."   *Dublin Review*, 181, 1927, 17–41.

God: functions of, and evil; Thomas Aquinas; philosophy: and science, of religion.

The importance of Whitehead's work for theism is that he is basing his case directly on analysis of the natural world of becoming itself, and not on more general theorems of epistemology.   However, Whitehead is unwilling to call God the source of all being.   (This essay is based on *Science and the Modern World.*)

1691   Taylor, A. E.   "Some Thoughts on *Process and Reality*."   *Theology*, 21, 1930, 66–79.

Process and Reality; God, Whitehead's arguments for; metaphysics.

In the main, *Process and Reality* is one long discussion of such notions as God, substance, potentiality and act, final causality, contingency, quality.   The account of God as the ultimate source of the historical world of becoming comes back into cosmology, yet this account may not satisfy the theological reader.

1692   Taylor, Harold.   "Hume's Answer to Whitehead."   *Journal of Philosophy*, 38, 1941, 409–416.

Causation; perception, theory of; belief; Hume, David; Gross, M. W.; empiricism.

Power, causal energy, and creative process are products of the mind itself, not of natural objects, and to speak as if the objects themselves were behaving rationally is to mistake internal for external objects. (Written in response to J. W. Robson and M. W. Gross, "Whitehead's Answer to Hume.")

1693 Taylor, John F. A. "Perception and Nature: A Monograph on Whitehead." Unpublished Ph.D. dissertation, Princeton University, 1940.

Nature; perception; sensationalist principle; presentational immediacy; causal efficacy; Hume, David; Descartes, Rene.

1694 Temple, G. "A Generalisation of Professor Whitehead's Theory of Relativity." *Proceedings of the Physical Society of London*, 36, 1923–1924, 176–193.

Relativity, theory of; Einstein, Albert.

1695 Temple, G. "Central Orbits in Relativistic Dynamics Treated by the Hamilton–Jacobi Method." *Philosophical Magazine*, Ser 6, 48, #284, 1924, 277–292.

Relativity, theory of; orbits; acceleration; physics.

1696 Temple, William. *Nature, Man, and God.* London: Macmillan and Company, Ltd., 1934.

God: primordial nature of, consequent nature of, as personal; consciousness; panpsychism; value, and beauty; philosophical theology.

Whitehead's concept of God does not explain all that it is meant to explain. This situation could be modified if Whitehead would attribute more transcendence and personality to God.

1697 Teo, W. K. H. "Heidegger on *Dasein* and Whitehead on Actual Entities." Unpublished Ph.D. dissertation, Southern Illinois University, 1969.

Dasein; actual entities; existence; Heidegger, Martin; existentialism.

1698 Thomas, George F. "The Philosophy of Religion: Can the Philosophy of Religion be Theologically Neutral?" *Protestant Thought in the Twentieth Century: Whence and Whither?* edited by Arnold S. Nash. New York: Macmillan Company, 1951, 73–101.

God: nature of, religious availability of; Christianity; religion; philosophical theology; Hartshorne, Charles.

Whitehead's emphasis on the individual as opposed to the religious community renders his view of religion inadequate from the Christian point of view. The question as to whether Whitehead's view of God is adequate to Christianity depends upon whether his view holds God to be personal or not. The latter issue is a matter of debate.

1699 Thomas, George F. *Religious Philosophies of the West.* New York: Charles Scribner's Sons, 1965, Chapter 13.

Whitehead, Alfred North: introduction to his thought; actual entities; eternal objects; God: nature of, primordial nature of, consequent nature of, as creator; philosophy, of religion.

1700   Thomason, O. S. U., Adelaide. "An Examination of the Law of Contrast in Charles Hartshorne's Panentheism." Unpublished Ph.D. dissertation, Fordham University, 1969.

Panentheism; Hartshorne, Charles.

(This dissertation is on Charles Hartshorne and contains only indirect reference to Whitehead.)

1701   Thompson, Edmund J. "An Analysis of the Thought of Alfred North Whitehead and William Ernest Hocking Concerning Good and Evil." Ph.D. dissertation, University of Chicago, 1935; University of Chicago Press, 1935.

Good; evil; God, goodness of; Christianity; Jesus Christ; Hocking, William E.

'Good' and 'evil' are descriptive adjectives which apply to processes in accordance with the extent to which those processes support or obstruct the actualization of progressively more comprehensive patterns for existence. God encourages the actualization of the most comprehensive and mutually sustaining system of patterns, and therefore it is appropriate to describe God as good. (This is the author's Ph.D. dissertation at University of Chicago in 1935.)

1702   Thompson, Kenneth F., Jr. *Whitehead's Philosophy of Religion.* The Hague: Mouton, 1971.

Philosophy, of religion; God: and evil, Whitehead's arguments for, nature of, and the world, and creatio ex nihilo, as creator, of classical theism; morality, and God; religion: and morality, and civilization.

Whitehead's doctrine of God can be looked upon as a philosophical contribution to the arrest of the decay of religion, especially in its role as an alternative to the picture of God as an Absolute Monarch. (This is the author's Ph.D. dissertation at Columbia University in 1964.)

1703   Thonnard, F. J. "El mundo inteligible según Alfred North Whitehead y San Agustín." *Sapientia*, 19, 1964, 205–209.

World; God, and world; Agustine.

Since mind and body are in fact distinct substances, Whitehead's philosophical position is clearly counter–intuitive.

1704   Thornton, Lionel S. *The Incarnate Lord: An Essay Concerning the Doctrine of the Incarnation in its Relation to Organic Conceptions.* New York: Longmans, Green and Company Ltd., 1928.

Christology; incarnation; objects: and events, physical; organism; eternal objects, and the Trinity; God, as concrete; theology.

Whitehead's notion of event and object in cosmology can be used to explain how the incarnation of Christ is the culmination of a complex evolutionary process. As 'the eternal object incarnate,' Christ is the source of all revelation and the center of cosmological history. (Written prior to *Process and Reality*.)

1705   Tiebout, Harry M., Jr. "Appearance and Causality in Whitehead's Early Writings." *Philosophy and Phenomenological Research*, 19, 1958, 43–52.

Perception, Whitehead's early theory of; bifurcation, of nature; qualities, secondary.

Whitehead's extended analysis of the problem of perception in his later works leads him to draw certain fundamental distinctions that were ignored in the early writings. Nevertheless, the doctrines set forth in the early works take their places in the cosmology of *Process and Reality* with very little modification.

1706   Tiebout, Harry M., Jr. "Subjectivity in Whitehead: A Comment on 'Whitehead and Heidegger'." *Dialectica: Revue Internationale de Philosophie de la Connaissance* (Berne), 13, 1959, 350–353.

Subjectivity: human, general; Schrag, C. O.; Heidegger, Martin; existentialism.

Whitehead's existentialist cosmology adequately distinguishes between human subjectivity as opposed to subjectivity in general. (Written in response to C. O. Schrag, "Whitehead and Heidegger: Process Philosophy and Existential Philosophy.")

1707   Todd, Quintin. "James, Whitehead, and Radical Empiricism." Unpublished Ph.D. dissertation, Pennsylvania State University, 1969.

Experience, appeal to; society; eternal objects; actual entities; connection, extention; God: as finite, as persuasive; reason, function of; necessity; eros; James, William; Plato; empiricism, radical.

Whitehead and James each attempt, and fail, to achieve the goals of radical empiricism. What is required to fulfil the goals of radical empiricism is an adequate formulation of the concept of society.

1708   Tong, Lik K. "Context and Reality: A Critical Interpretation of Whitehead's Philosophy of Organism." Unpublished Ph.D. dissertation, New School for Social Research, 1969.

Ontology; being; agency; philosophy, method of; relativity; experience; Aristotle; Leibniz, G. W.; Kant, Immanuel; phenomenology.

Whitehead's mature philosophy is essentially an ontology rather than a cosmology, although Whitehead failed to clarify the difference. Central to Whitehead's conceptuality is a functional conception of existence, as theory of forms, and the notion of perspective. The basic weakness of Whitehead's thought lies in his methodology, which needs a more rigorous phenomenological foundation.

1709   Tovo, Jerome C.   "The Experience of Causal Efficacy in Whitehead and Hume."   Unpublished Ph.D., Indiana University, 1964.

Causation; causal efficacy; Aristotle, and four causes; Hume, David.

In his doctrine of causal efficacy, Whitehead exploits Hume's doctrine of force and vivacity in order to reverse Hume's own skepticism regarding causality.   However, Whitehead fails to overcome Hume's basic criticisms of realistic views of causality.

1710   Towne, Edgar A.   "Metaphysics as Method in Charles Hartshorne's Thought."   Southern Journal of Philosophy, 6, 1968, 126–142.

Method, metaphysical; metaphysics: principles of, verification of, necessity of; Hartshorne, Charles; metaphysics.

Hartshorne considers metaphysics to be a distinct type of reasoning which is integral to the methods both of philosophy and theology.   His own method is to treat the logical character of metaphysical concepts as categorically universal, then as necessary.   Metaphysical method has logical integrity, and is subject to verification.

1711   Towne, Edgar A.   "Henry Nelson Wieman: Theologian of Hope." Iliff Review, 27, 1970, 13–24.

Hope: theology of, ground of, as creativity; Marxism; Wieman, Henry N.; theology.

Wieman's theology is a theology of hope in that it specifies the possibility of an openness to the future of humanity as a whole.

1712   Tracy, David.   "God's Reality: The Most Important Issue." Anglican Theological Review, 55, 1973, 218–224.

Process philosophy, evaluation of; God, doctrine of; secularism.

Process thinkers have articulated a challenge to our usual way of thinking, particularly on the question of God, which no serious participant in our present moment can long ignore. (Written in response to Process Theology, edited by E. Cousins, and Process Philosophy and Christian Thought, edited by Brown, James, and Reeves.)

1713   Treash, Gordon S.   "Actuality and Social Order: Whitehead's Theory of Societies."   Unpublished Ph.D. dissertation, Emory University, 1968.

Societies: corpuscular, living, serially ordered, non–serially ordered; measurement.

The notion of social order is important because it is a direct consequence of Whitehead's theory of actuality.   Societies are the entities which human beings encounter in ordinary conscious awareness and scientific inquiry.

1714   Treash, Gordon S. "Whitehead and Physical Existence: A Reply to Professor Leclerc." *International Philosophical Quarterly*, 10, 1970, 118–125.

Societies; ontological principle; actuality; Leclerc, Ivor.

Leclerc argues that the indivisibility of the ultimately real fails to account for the pluralities which are the physical existents. On the contrary, Whitehead's doctrine of societies allows for the emergence of societal qualities which are not reducible to qualities possessed by every member of the society. (Written in response to Ivor Leclerc, "The Problem of the Physical Existent.")

1715   True, Isaac D. "Whitehead on Truth." Unpublished Ph.D. dissertation, St. Louis University, 1972.

Truth: correspondence theory of, coherence theory of, pragmatic meaning of; propositions; judgments; feelings, comparative; imagination.

Whitehead's is a correspondence theory of truth, with truth relations occuring only in comparative feelings, specifically propositions.

1716   Tsanoff, Radoslav A. *The Great Philosophers.* New York: Harper & Row, 1964, 565–569.

Process philosophy, summary of.

1717   Turner, J. E. "Dr. A. N. Whitehead's Scientific Realism." *Journal of Philosophy*, 19, 1922, 146–157.

The Concept of Nature; events; objects; duration; realism.

The Concept of Nature constitutes a distinct advance in the discussion of ontology, despite Whitehead's over–emphasis upon sense–awareness. By supplementing the work from a strictly philosophic standpoint, we should be much nearer a lasting and satisfactory realism.

1718   Udert, Lothar. "Zum Begriff der Zeit in der Philosophie Alfred North Whiteheads." *Zeitschrift für philosophische Forschung*, 21, 1967, 409–430.

Time: as absolute, and human experience, measurement of, and memory, relativity of; duration; bifurcation: of nature, theory of; space; *The Concept of Nature*.

The primary theme in Whitehead's *The Concept of Nature* is the problem of time and its relation to space and events.

1719   Ueda, S. "Whitehead No Shizen Tetsugaku (The Whiteheadian Philosophy of Nature)." *Anglo–Saxon Tetsugaku No Dento* (The Tradition of Anglo–Saxon Philosophy)." Tokyo: Tokyodo, 1947, 161–213.

Philosophy, of nature; nature.

1720   Underhill, L. "The Problem of Evil in the Philosophy of Alfred North Whitehead." Unpublished Ph.D. dissertation, Drew University, 1955–1956.

Evil; disorder; God, and evil.

1721   Urban, Wilbur M. "Elements of Unintelligibility in Whitehead's Metaphysics: The Problem of Language in *Process and Reality.*" *Journal of Philosophy,* 35, 1938, 617–637.

Language: uses of, Whitehead's uses of.

If the fundamental principle of intelligibility is the primacy of value, then dramatic, subject–predicate language must be used. If the principle is that of functional relations, then mathematics will be the linguistic ideal. The two principles struggle for supremacy in Whitehead's cosmology, with a resultant obscurity and blatant unintelligibility.

1722   Urban, Wilbur M. *Language and Reality: The Philosophy of Language and the Principles of Symbolism.* New York: Macmillan, 1939. Freeport, New York: Books for Libraries Press, 1971.

Language; symbolism; metaphysics, and metaphor; *Symbolism, Its Meaning and Effect.*

An inconsistency exists between Whitehead's claim that language and reality are disjunctive and his own attempt to verbally articulate the nature of reality.

1723   Urban, Wilbur M. "Whitehead's Philosophy of Language and its Relation to his Metaphysics." *The Philosophy of Alfred North Whitehead.* Edited by Paul A. Schilpp. La Salle, Illinois: Open Court Publishing Company, 1941, 301–327.

Language: and reality, and subject–predicate mode of expression, and intelligibility, and process, and evolution; substance, and language; Bergson, Henri; naturalism; idealism.

Whitehead is a naturalist in interpreting language as an extension of the tool–making function of the intelligence. Since the function of language is purely pragmatic, he deems it possible and advisable to redesign much of traditional language for purposes of metaphysics.

1724   Usai, R. "Nota bigrafica." *Aut Aut,* 1965, 85–89.

Whitehead, Alfred North: biography of.

1725   Ushenko, Andrew P. "The Logic of Events: An Introduction to a Philosophy of Time." *University of California Publications in Philosophy,* 12, 1929, 1–180.

Time; simultaneity; space–time; present, as specious; rhythm; continuity.

(Drawing on implications in Whitehead's theory of time as an organism of organisms, the author shows how both continuity and discreteness are explained by means of an heirarchy of organisms.)

1726   Ushenko, Andrew P. "Negative Prehension." *Journal of Philosophy,* 34, 1937, 263–267.

Prehensions, negative: of concepts, of individuals; idealism.

The doctrine of negative prehension as a process of adaptation overcomes the difficulties of idealism by making a distinction between negative prehension of concepts and of individuals. Epistemological and ontological monism are thus avoided.

1727   Ushenko, Andrew P. *Power and Events: An Essay on Dynamics in Philosophy.* Princeton, New Jersey: Princeton University Press, 1946. New York: Greenwood Press, 1969.

Actuality; activity; power; potentiality; extension; sense–perception; perspective; standpoint; strain feelings; contemporaneity; space–time; location, simple; causation, efficient; geometry; Bergson, Henri; Russell, Bertrand.

Although Whitehead has much to say about potentiality, he fails to construe it as an active power to affect others. The result is that agency lies only in the act of perception. This identification of action with perception is the key to his philosophy.

1728   Ushenko, Andrew P. "A Note on Whitehead and Relativity." *Journal of Philosophy*, 47, 1950, 100–102.

Relativity, special theory of; perception, theory of; relativism, objective.

The complexity of Whitehead's theory of perception is fully justified on the grounds of the theory of relativity; in fact, no other general treatment of visual perception agrees with the concept of physical space–time.

1729   Van der Horst, J. W. "De methode van de metafysica volgens Alfred N. Whitehead." *Annalen van het Genootschap voor wetenschappelijke philosophie*, 31. Also in *Algeheen Nederlands tijdschrift voor wijsbegeerte en psychologie*, 52, 1959–1960, 103–111.

Philosophy, speculative; metaphysics; adequacy; intuition; imagination.

(This work examines the requirements set by Whitehead for a speculative philosophy. Special attention is devoted to the relation between adequacy and experience.)

1730   Van der Veken, Jan. "Can the True God be the God of One Book?" *Ephemerides Theologicae Lovanienses*, 51, 1975, 35–48. Also in *Religious Experience and Process Theology*. Edited by Harry J. Cargas and Bernard Lee. New York: Paulist Press, 1976.

Religion, and reason; romance; God, doctrine of; Jesus: as Christ, as unique; culture; ecumenism; Hegel, G. W. F.

Whitehead's philosophy is subtle enough to illumine the old problem of the God of religion and the God of philosophy in a new way.

1731   Van Hecke, Lode. "De notie 'subjectief doel' in de filozofie van A. N. Whitehead." Unpublished M.A. dissertation, Katholieke Universiteit t Leuven, 1975.

Subjective aim; God, and world; initial aim; Kant, Immanuel; Merleau–Ponty, Maurice.

The notion of subjective aim is an essential explanatory principle expressing the link between God and the world. It is also the basis for freedom and order.

1732 Van Nuys, Kelvin. *Is Reality Meaningful? Static Contradictions and Dynamic Resolutions between Facts and Value.* New York: Philosophical Library Inc., 1966.

Value: theory of, and fact, and feeling, and process, and self–enjoyment; aesthetics; subjective aim; evil; matter; materialism; process; feeling; body, human; freedom, and determinism.

Certain of Whitehead's notions are helpful in shaping a theory of value which emphasizes process over static existence.

1733 Van Nuys, Kelvin. *Science and Cosmic Purpose.* New York: Philosophical Library, 1966.

Teleology; cosmos; God, primordial nature of; science, and religion; meaning; determinism, and indeterminism.

1734 Van Os, C. H. "Over de Philosophie van A. N. Whitehead." *Synthese*, 4, 1939, 221–238.

Relativity, principle of; philosophy, and mathematics; Spinoza, Benedict; Leibniz, G. W.; Berkeley, George; neo–realism.

(The author uses the principle of relativity as a key for introducing Whitehead's philosophy in a non–technical manner.)

1735 Van Os, C. H. *Aspecten der Evolutie in het bi jonder aan de Hand van de Denkbeelden van P. Teilhard de Chardin en Alfred North Whitehead.* Amsterdam: Uitgeverij der Theosofisch Vereniging Netherlands Afdeling, 1965.

Evolution, and human existence; eschatology; Teilhard de Chardin.

1736 Van Wesep, H. B. *Seven Sages: The Story of American Philosophy.* London: Longmans, Green, 1960, 393–415.

Whitehead, Alfred North, introduction to his thought.

1737 Veatch, Henry. "The Truths of Metaphysics." *Review of Metaphysics*, 17, 1964, 372–395.

Language, and metaphysics; judgments: synthetic a priori, metaphysical; truth, analytic; Kant, Immanuel; linguistic analysis; metaphysics.

The necessary truths of traditional metaphysics are self–evident in terms of the things to which the truths correspond, and not in terms of the mere words and concepts through which the truths are articulated. Thus Kant's critique that only synthetic propositions can have existential import is unfounded.

1738 Veca, S. "Tempo ed astrazione estensiva nel concetto di natura di Whitehead." *Aut Aut*, 1965, 17–42.

Abstraction, extensive; nature.

1739 Verghese, Paul. "God's Survival and the Future of the Universe." *Anticipation*, 16, 1974, 35–36.

Self: as primal phenomenon, as relational, as analogy for God; future: of God, of human existence, of universe; Ogden, Schubert M.; ecology.

The future of man is but part of the future of the universe, which in fact is the future of God.

1740   Verschueren, Jan. "La 'théologie naturelle chrétienne' de John B. Cobb, Jr.: Une approche méthodologique." Unpublished dissertation, Pontificia Universitas Gregoriana, 1976.

Theology, natural; philosophy, the "right" one for theology; God: problem of, doctrine of, adequacy of.

1741   Virtue, Charles F. Sawhill. "General Philosophy and Philosophy of Education: A Word from an Academic Philosopher." *Educational Theory*, 8, 1958, 203–212.

Dewey, John; philosophy, of education.

Whitehead and Dewey are among those who illustrate the sense in which educational philosophy is rooted in a general philosophic commitment.

1742   Vlastos, Gregory. "Whitehead, Critic of Abstractions (Being the Story of a Philosopher Who Started with Science and Ended with Metaphysics)." *Monist*, 39, 1929, 170–203.

Whitehead, Alfred North, method of; prehension; induction; eternal objects; metaphysics.

The most striking feature in the transition of Whitehead's thought is the fateful unavoidableness of the development of metaphysics, as a synthesis of knowledge. Whitehead bases his metaphysics on a single generalization: prehension.

1743   Vlastos, Gregory. "The Problem of Incompatibility in the Philosophy of Organism." *Monist*, 40, 1930, 535–551.

Incompatibility: logical, in concrescence; metaphysics.

Logical incompatibility indicates the importance of a proposition's determinative, concrete context for judgment concerning real or apparent incompatibility. It is questionable whether value in the generalizations of metaphysics for the concrete problem of incompatibility.

1744   Vlastos, Gregory. "Organic Categories in Whitehead." *Journal of Philosophy*, 34, 1937, 253–262. Also in *Alfred North Whitehead: Essays on His Philosophy*. Edited by George L. Kline. Englewood Cliffs, New Jersey: Prentice–Hall, Inc., 1963, 158–167.

Individuality, and community; dialectic, Hegelian; causation: efficient, final; mind, and matter in nature; Hegel, G. W. F.

By interpreting all process as an interplay of matter and idea in temporal actualities, and of idea and matter in a nontemporal actuality, Whitehead employs a unique variant of the Hegelian dialectic.

1745   Voskuil, Duane M. "Whitehead's Metaphysical Aesthetic." Unpublished Ph.D. dissertation, University of Missouri, 1969.

Aesthetics, and metaphysics; beauty; art; subjective aim; synthesis; contrasts; prehensions, negative; transmutation; purpose, physical.

The conditions to which aestheticians appeal in specifying aesthetic experience are identical to those to which the philosopher must appeal in specifying the nature of experience in general. Insofar as Whitehead's list of categoreal obligations is adequate to interpret experience in general, it characterizes aesthetic experience.

1746   Waddington, C. H. "The Practical Consequences of Metaphysical Beliefs on a Biologist's Work: An Autobiographical Note." *Towards a Theoretical Biology, Volume II.* Edited by C. H. Waddington. Chicago: Aldine Publishing Company, 1969, 72–81.

Metaphysics, and scientific experiment; biology: and metaphysics, and process, and event, and concrescence; Bohm, David.

Review

Martin, F. D. *Process Studies*, 4, 1974, 51–55.

1747   Waddington, C. H. *Behind Appearance: A Study of the Relations Between Painting and the Natural Sciences in This Century.* Edinburg: Edinburg University Press, 1969. Cambridge, Massachusetts: M. I. T. Press, 1970, 109–120.

Art, and nature; painting; science; beauty; aesthetics.

1748   Wagner, Hilmar. "A Comparison of Bertrand Russell and Alfred North Whitehead on Education." *Journal of Thought*, 2, 1967, 65–74.

Education, philosophy of; Russell, Bertrand; education.

Both Whitehead's and Russell's paths lead toward an educational theory directed toward student involvement in the subject rather than with the subject.

1749   Wahl, Jean. "La philosophie speculative de Whitehead." *Revue Philosophique*, 2, 1931, #111, 341–378; #112, 108–143. Also in *Vers le concret.* Paris: Vrin, 1932, 127–221.

Philosophy, speculative.

1750   Ward, Benjamin F. "Aim, Decision, Adventure: An Inquiry into Whitehead's Metaphysics of Creative Purpose." Unpublished Ph.D. dissertation, Yale University, 1972.

Freedom; decision; subjective aim; adventure; contingency; *causa sui.*

1751   Ward, F. C. *Mind in Whitehead's Philosophy.* New Haven, Connecticut: Yale University Press, 1937.

Mind; self; consciousness; experience; prehensions; society: human, personally ordered.

(This is the author's Ph.D. dissertation submitted to Yale University in 1937.)

1752   Ward, Leo R. "Whitehead on Joy in Learning." *The Review of Politics*, 32, 1970, 490–502.

Philosophy, of education; learning, and adventure; education, stages of.

From Whitehead's perspective the process of learning should be characterized by a spirit of joy and adventure.

1753   Watson, John. "A Discussion of Dr. Whitehead's Philosophy of Nature with Special Reference to His Work, *Concept of Nature.*" *Actes 8 Congress of International Philosophy* (Prague), 1936, 903–909.

Concept of Nature; mind, and nature; realism; idealism; Turner, J. E.

So far as the denial of any substratum and the rejection of bifurcation are concerned, there is nothing to show that Whitehead is either a neo–realist or an idealist.

1754   Watt, T. L. "The Freedom of God in the Philosophy of Alfred North Whitehead and Its Theological Implications." Unpublished Th.D. dissertation, Union Theological Seminary, 1967.

God: freedom of, nature of; theology, philosophical.

1755   Weatherly, O. H. "The Problem of Epistemology in Contemporary American Theism." Unpublished Ph.D. dissertation, University of Chicago, 1953.

Epistemology; theism, American.

1756   Weber, Pearl Louise. "Significance of Whitehead's Philosophy for Psychology." *Personalist*, 21, 1940, 178–187.

Perception, and causal efficacy; emotion, primacy of; consciousness; psychology.

Whitehead's philosophy suggests a primacy of affectivity, a new primitive factor in perception, and mind as a function of organism. Psychology will not have reached its goal until it shall have made a thorough study of these suggestions.

1757   Wedd, D. L. "God the Redeemer: Sovereignty and Suffering." *Christianity Today*, 13, August 1, 1969, 13–15.

God: as suffering, sovereignty of; redemption.

1758   Wegener, Frank C. *The Organic Philosophy of Education.* Dubuque, Iowa: Wm. C. Brown Company, 1957; Westport, Connecticut: Greenwood Press, 1974.

Education: aims of, and social process, and cosmology, and social sciences, and concrescence, organic theory of; philosophy, of education; creativity, and education; bipolarity; art, and education; concrescence, and education; God; knowledge; learning; teaching; value, and education; truth; Dewey, John; Aristotle, on education; Plato, on education; Peirce, Charles; pragmatism.

1759   Wegener, Frank C. "A. N. Whitehead: An Implied Philosophy of School and Society." *Educational Theory*, 11, 1961, 194–208.

Philosophy: of education, social.

An application of Whitehead's thought to philosophies of school and of society would be most comprehensive, insisting upon the complementary relations of opposing views.

1760 Wein, Hermann. "Métaphysique et anti–métaphysique accompagné de quelques réflexions pour la défense de l'oeuvre de Nietzsche." *Revue de Métaphysique et de Morale*, 63, 1958, 385–411.

Metaphysics, and anti–metaphysics; continuum, extensive; connection, extensive; societies, structured; hierarchy; Kant, Immanuel; Hartmann, Nicolai; Nietzsche, Friederich.

1761 Wein, Hermann. "In Defence of the Humanism of Science: Kant and Whitehead." Translated by Eva Schaper. *The Relevance of Whitehead.* Edited by Ivor Leclerc. New York: Humanities Press Inc., 1961, 289–315.

Science: and technology, and humanism, and subjectivity, and objectivity; Kant, Immanuel; Marx, Karl; Heidegger, Martin; Hartmann, Nicolai.

Whitehead is related to the theme of the Kantian *Critiques* as the only philosopher of the twentieth century who, after Hegel and Schelling, confesses to 'speculative philosophy', and as the only philosopher who attempts to reunite science and religion through philosophy.

1762 Weinberg, J. "The Idea of Causal Efficacy." *Journal of Philosophy*, 47, 1950, 397–407.

Causal efficacy; causation.

1763 Weingart, Richard E. "Process or Deicide?" *Encounter*, 29, 1968, 149–157.

God: doctrine of, experience of; Altizer, Thomas J. J.; theology: radical, process.

Loss of the traditional doctrine of God engenders an experience of chaos. Process theology must speak to this dimension of experience if it is to meet the test of comprehensiveness required of a contemporary doctrine of God.

1764 Weisenbeck, Jude D. *Alfred North Whitehead's Philosophy of Values.* Waukesha, Wisconsin: Thomas Press, Inc., 1969.

Value: aesthetic, religious, moral, intrinsic, objective, and eternal objects; God: and value, objective immortality in; ethics; beauty; contrast; discord; morality; creativity, and value; process, and value; causation, final; Whitehead, Alfred North: philosophical influences on.

Probably the strongest point in favor of Whitehead's general theory of values is his defense of final causation. One weakness in his theory is his failure to explain the nature of ideals of perfection. Another weakness is his inadequate explanation of how values are objectively immortalized in God.

Review,

Spencer, J. B. *Process Studies*, 1, 1971, 66–68.

1765 Weiss, Paul. "The Nature and the Status of Time and Passage." *Philosophical Essays for Alfred North Whitehead.* Edited by F. S. C. Northrop et al. London: Longmans, Green, 1936, 153–173.

Time: and transition, and temporality, and nature.

1766 Weiss, Paul. *Reality.* Carbondale, Illinois: Southern Illinois University Press, 1938.

Time: as momentary, and extension, and perishing; Descartes, Rene.

Whitehead stands within the Cartesian tradition which identifies the temporal with the momentary. As a consequence his view of time is problematic.

1767 Weiss, Paul. "Alfred North Whitehead, 1861–1947." *Atlantic Monthly*, 181, 1948, 105–107.

Whitehead, Alfred North, biography of.

1768 Weiss, Paul. *Modes of Being.* Carbondale, Illinois: Southern Illinois University Press, 1958.

Substance; endurance; perishing; possibilities, real; creativity: as field, as existence.

1769 Weiss, Paul. "History and Objective Immortality." *The Relevance of Whitehead.* Edited by Ivor Leclerc. New York: Humanities Press Inc., 1961.

Objective immortality; ethics.

Whitehead's doctrine of objective immortality maintains that the past is now an active component in the present. His account is closely tied to his thesis that actual occasions perish when and as they become. Held too tenaciously, the view would prevent Whitehead from affirming that there were any beings, other than God, which actually persist. As a consequence there could be no ethics of obligation, political action, artistic production, or historical process.

1770 Weiss, Paul. *Philosophy in Process, Volume I.* Carbondale, Illinois: Southern Illinois University Press, 1963.

Location, simple; objects, of science; substance; past, and future; Aristotle; Buddhism.

Whitehead's categories confound the nature of and relationships between actualities, eternal objects, formal structures, and creative energies.

1771 Weiss, Paul. *Philosophy in Process, Volume II: 1960–1964.* Carbondale, Illinois: Southern Illinois University Press, 1966.

Perishing; perception, and science; substance; wholes, temporal; mind, mind–body problem; Peirce, Charles S.; Neoplatonism.

1772 Weiss, Paul. *Philosophy in Process, Volume III: March–November, 1964.* Carbondale, Illinois: Southern Illinois University Press, 1968.

God: nature of, and Being; substance, and inheritance; concrescence, and coming to be; Hegel, G. W. F.; Hartshorne, Charles; existentialism.

1773   Weiss, Paul. *Philosophy in Process, Volume IV: November 26, 1964–September 2, 1965.* Carbondale, Illinois: Southern Illinois University Press, 1969.

Societies, and actual occasions; religion, nature of; Mead, George H.; Thomism.

1774   Welch, C. "Theology." *Religion.* Edited by P. Ramsey. Englewood Cliffs, New Jersey: Prentice–Hall, Inc., 1965.

Theology.

1775   Wells, David F. "George Tyrrell: Precursor of Process Theology." *Scottish Journal of Theology*, 26, 1973, 71–84.

Theism: classical, dipolar; God, immanence of; incarnation, universal; faith, and reason; revelation, emergent; Tyrrell, George; Blondel, Maurice; Ogden, Schubert M.; theology.

The vigorous restatement of Christian theology in terms of process thought both now and earlier through George Tyrrell raises questions concerning the sufficiency of process philosophy for theological use.

1776   Wells, Harry K. *Process and Unreality.* London: Kings Crown Publishers, 1950; Staten Island, New York: Gordian Press, Inc., 1975.

Process philosophy: summary of; Whitehead, Alfred North: evaluation of; bifurcation; abstraction, extensive; objects; God, concept of; rhythm; flux; permanence; Hegel, G. W. F.

Whitehead's failure was to develop a speculative cosmology which could never, as a philosophical method, deal with process on its own terms.

Reviews

Leclerc, I. *Philosophical Quarterly*, 1952.

Mays, W. *Mind*, 61, 1952, 429–432.

1777   Wells, Harry K. "Les tendances de la philosophie contemporaine en Amerique." *Pensée*, 30, 1950, 44–56.

Philosophy, in America: eternal objects.

1778   Wells, Harry K. "The Philosophy of A. N. Whitehead." *Science and Society*, 16, 1951–1952, 27–43.

Process philosophy, summary of; abstraction, extensive; Marxism.

The method of extensive abstraction is an attempt to reduce nature from processes to things. The method succeeds only at the expense of a bifurcation of nature into events and eternal objects. Thus the single attempt Whitehead made to stay within the bounds of the natural world, without appeal to the supernatural, collapses, as do all attempts other than the Marxist dialectical method.

1779 Wendler, Herbert W. "Alfred North Whitehead: A Shift of Emphasis." *Texas Quarterly*, 8, 1965, 39–45.

Science, and philosophy; language, Whitehead's use of; Aristotle.

Whitehead's shift of emphasis to process signifies that the most fundamental modes of thought for over 2,000 years are now at the eve of their displacement. Yet Whitehead was required to state his scheme of notions in a language whose very structure presupposes and depends upon the Aristotelian concepts which the Whiteheadian scheme contradicts.

1780 Werkmeister, W. H. *A History of Philosophical Ideas in America*. New York: The Ronald Press, 1949, 343–366.

Process philosophy, summary of.

Whitehead's philosophy, although fundamentally a form of idealism, makes nature the central issue and thus represents a unique basic orientation within the general framework of idealistic thought.

1781 Wesep, H. B. Van. *Seven Sages: The Story of American Philosophy*. New York: Longmans, Green, and Co., 1960, 393–445.

God; feeling; perception; actual occasions; actuality, and potentiality; enjoyment; civilization; art; bifurcation; eternal objects; time; mind, mind–body; Peirce, Charles S.

(This work is a non–technical introduction to seven American philosophers, with Whitehead among them. The other philosophers are Benjamin Franklin, Ralph Waldo Emerson, William James, John Dewey, George Santayana, and Charles Peirce. In discussing the seven thinkers the author attempts to show a line of development in the history of American philosophy.)

1782 Westphal, Merold. "Temporality and Finitism in Hartshorne's Theism." *Review of Metaphysics*, 19, 1966, 550–564.

God: as relative, and time, of classical theism, Hartshorne's interpretation of; Thomas Aquinas; Hartshorne, Charles; Leibniz, G. W.; theology.

Hartshorne misinterprets Thomas. Thomas asserts that God is related to creatures, but in such a manner as to render invalid any inference of dependence on them. God is related to creatures in idea.

1783 Whitbeck, Caroline. "Simultaneity and Distance." *Journal of Philosophy*, 66, 1969, 329–340.

Simultaneity; space–time; relativity, theory of; conventionalism; Grünbaum, A.; Reichenbach, Hans; Poincaré, H.; physics.

The Whiteheadian view that nature exhibits a system of uniform relations, metrical as well as topological, which constitute space and time, is compatible with Poincaré's thesis of conventionalism with respect to natural knowledge in general.

1784 White, Morton. *The Age of Analysis: 20th Century Philosophers.* New York: The New American Library, 1955, 81–100.

Nature, as alive; matter, dead; qualities: primary, secondary.

(This work consists of selections from the works of various twentieth century philosophers, plus brief commentaries by the editor. In the case of Whitehead, the selections are from the eighth lecture of *Modes of Thought*, "Nature Alive".)

1785 White, W. "The Idea of God in the Philosophies of Spinoza and Whitehead." Unpublished M.A. thesis, University of Chicago, 1953.

God: concept of, freedom of; monads; Spinoza, B.

1786 Whitla, William. "Sin and Redemption in Whitehead and Teilhard de Chardin." *Anglican Theological Review*, 47, 1965, 81–93.

Evil; sin; redemption; God, and evil; Teilhard de Chardin; theology, process.

Process philosophy offers fresh interpretations of the pattern of biblical revelation, with its insistence upon the essentially optimistic dynamism of created order, and the supremacy of the mind and love which are at the goal and center of the whole process.

1787 Whitrow, G. J. and Morduch, G. E. "General Relativity and Lorentz–Invariant Theories of Gravitation." *Nature*, 188, 1960, 790–804.

Relativity, theory of; gravitation; Lorentz.

1788 Whitrow, G. J. and Morduch, G. E. "Relativistic Theories of Gravitation." *Vistas in Astronomy*, Volume 6. Edited by A. Beer. New York: Pergamon Press, 1965.

Motion; acceleration; space–time; relativity, general theory of; Einstein, Albert; astronomy; physics.

(This paper compares Lorentz's invariant theories of relativity, of which Whitehead's theory is an example, with Einstein's general theory of relativity by considering seven possible tests.)

1789 Whittaker, E. "Alfred North Whitehead, 1861–1947." *Obituary Notices of Fellows of the Royal Society of London*, 6, 1948, 281–296.

Whitehead, Alfred North: obituary notice.

1790 Whittaker, E. "Professor A. N. Whitehead, O. M., F. R. S." *Nature*, 161, 1948, 267–268.

Whitehead, biography of; event; abstraction, extensive; *Principia Mathematica*; mathematics; philosophy, of science; metaphysics.

(This is an obituary for Whitehead tracing aspects of his life and thought.)

1791   Whittemore, Robert C.   "Panpsychism and the Function of God."
        Unpublished Ph.D. dissertation, Yale University, 1953.

        Panpsychism; panentheism; religion, and science; Hartshorne,
        Charles; Hegel, G. W. F.; Schelling, F. W. J.; Royce, Josiah;
        Fechner, Gustav T.; Lotze, Rudolph; Leibniz, Gottfried;
        Paulsen, Friedrich; Ward, James.

        Divisions between religion and science can only be solved by
        an adoption of panpsychism and panentheism.   Whitehead's
        philosophy gives the first clear expression to this alternative,
        although the seeds of panpsychism and panentheism can be
        traced to thinkers prior to Whitehead.

1792   Whittemore, Robert C.   "Whitehead's Process and Bradley's
        Reality."   Modern Schoolman, 32, 1954–1955, 56–74.

        Process, principle of; Bradley, Francis H.

1793   Whittemore, Robert C.   "Time and Whitehead's God."   Tulane
        Studies in Philosophy, 4, 1955, 83–92.

        God: and time, primordial nature of, as eternal.

1794   Whittemore, Robert C.   "Hegel's 'Science' and Whitehead's
        'Modern World'."   Philosophy, 31, 1956, 36–54.

        Dialectic, Hegelian; logic, as process; Hegel, G. W. F.;
        metaphysics.

        At every significant point—particularly in a comparison of
        "dialectic" and "process"—the system of Hegel is in accord
        with the cosmological scheme of process philosophy.   With
        regard to the continuity of history and the concept of God,
        Hegel provides an improvement on the process scheme.

1795   Whittemore, Robert C.   "Prolegomena to a Modern Philosophical
        Theism."   Tulane Studies in Philosophy, 5, 1956, 87–93.

        God, nature of; theology, philosophical.

1796   Whittemore, Robert C.   "Philosophy as Comparative Cosmology."
        Tulane Studies in Philosophy, 7, 1958, 135–146.

        Philosophy, task of; method, philosophical.

        Philosophy today lacks, yet must develop, a methodology for
        the criticism of its ultimate notions and presuppositions.

1797   Whittemore, Robert C.   "Metaphysical Foundations of Sartre's
        Ontology."   Tulane Studies in Philosophy, 8, 1959, 111–121.

        Self: and   self–creativity,   and   self–transcendence;   Sartre,
        Jean–Paul; existentialism; metaphysics.

        Whitehead's theory of feelings is a genetic description of
        Sartre's being–for–itself.   Whitehead may well provide a
        metaphysics for Sartre's ontology.

1798   Whittemore, Robert C.   "The Metaphysics of Whitehead's
        Feelings."   Tulane Studies in Philosophy, 10, 1961, 109–113.

        Emotion; causation, final; psychology; metaphysics.

        If Whitehead's cosmology is implicit in his theory that the
        basis of experience is emotional, then adoption of that

psychology must imply adoption of that cosmology which is its consequence.

1799   Whittemore, Robert C. *Makers of the American Mind.* New York: W. Morrow, 1964, 463–481.

Whitehead, biography of; God, nature of; creativity; actual entities; process; philosophy: of nature, of science.

If philosophy fails to incorporate the insights of science, it becomes ancillary to science. The value of Whitehead's philosophy lies in its attempt to interpret and explain scientific as well as personal experience.

1800   Whittemore, Robert C. "The Americanization of Panentheism." *Southern Journal of Philosophy*, 7, 1969, 25–35.

God: doctrine of, as actual entity, Hartshorne's interpretation of; panentheism; Hartshorne, Charles; Christian, William; Royce, Josiah; philosophy, American.

Panentheism has been a theme in American philosophy and theology from the colonial protounitarian period through the present.

1801   Wickham, Harvey. *The Unrealists: James, Bergson, Santayana, Einstein, Bertrand Russell, John Dewey, Alexander, and Whitehead.* Macveagh: Dial Press, 1930; London: Sheed and Ward, 1933; Freeport, New York: Books for Libraries Press, 1970, 244–258.

Perception, and the external world; presentational immediacy; causal efficacy; symbolic reference; inference; *Symbolism, Its Meaning and Effect.*

Whitehead's analysis of perception is plagued by confusion of thought.

1802   Wiehl, Reiner. "Der Begriff in den Anschauungsformen der Mittelbarkeit und Unmittelbarkeit: Nebst einem Anhang über die Kategorien in Whitehead's "Process and Reality"." Unpublished dissertation, Frankfurt, 1959.

Feeling; immediacy; experience; categoreal scheme.

1803   Wiehl, Reiner. "Zeit und Zeitlosigkeit in der Philosophie A. N. Whiteheads." *Natur und Geschichte: Karl Löwith zum 70 Geburtstag.* Stuttgart: W. Kohlhammer, 1968, 373–405.

Becoming; time; events; concrescence; temporality; existence, category of; explanation, category of; possibility; concreteness.

Translation

"Time and Timelessness in the Philosophy of Alfred North Whitehead." *Process Studies*, 5, 1975, 3–30.

1804   Wieman, Henry Nelson. *Religious Experience and Scientific Method.* New York: Macmillan Company, 1926; Carbondale, Illinois: Southern Illinois University Press, 1971.

Religion: and religious experience, and science; materialism; God, experience of; event, perceived; bifurcation, of nature; metaphysics, Whitehead's early avoidance of; theology, empirical.

Whitehead's early philosophy of science provides a framework in which to understand the relation between religious experience and scientific method.

1805   Wieman, Henry Nelson.   "Professor Whitehead's Concept of God."   *Hibbert Journal*, 25, 1926–1927, 623–630.   Also in *The Wrestle of Religion with Truth.*   New York: MacMillan Company, Inc., 1927, Chapter 11.

God: as principle of concretion, and order, and evil; panentheism; aesthetics, and religion; *Religion in the Making.*

For three reasons Whitehead's God cannot be regarded as pantheistic.   First, God is not the totality of all being, but rather a sustaining character or order of all being.   Second, God does not include evil, since evil has its own force independently of God.   And third, God transcends the world of actuality by being equally operative in the world of potentiality.

1806   Wieman, Henry Nelson.   *The Wrestle of Religion with Truth.* New York: MacMillan Company, Inc., 1927, Chapters 11–13.

God: as principle of concretion, and order, and evil; panentheism; space; time; aesthetics, and religion; religion: nature of, and science, and value, and religious experience, and philosophy; good; evil; morality; value; philosophy, of religion; *Principles of Natural Knowledge; The Concept of Nature.*

Providing Whitehead's definition of God is accepted, his thought gives a scientific demonstration of God as the principle of concretion in the universe.   This demonstration consists of the analysis of space and time in *Principles of Natural Knowledge* and *The Concept of Nature.*

1807   Wieman, Henry Nelson.   "Value and the Individual."   *Journal of Philosophy*, 25, 1928, 233–239.

Individual: and values, and possibilities; God, as source of value.

The universe has a basic principle of organization which provides for all those reorganizations which the universe must undergo in order to become more completely individual and of greater value.

1808   Wieman, Henry Nelson and Meland, Bernard E.   *American Philosophies of Religion.* Chicago and New York: Willet, Clark and Company, 1936; New York: Harper and Brothers, 1948.

Philosophy, of religion; Whitehead, Alfred North: introduction to his thought.

1809   Wieman, Henry Nelson.   *Now We Must Choose.* New York: Macmillan Company, 1941.

Value, structural theory of; God, and nature; theology.

1810   Wieman, Henry Nelson.   *The Source of Human Good.* Carbondale, Illinois: Southern Illinois University Press, 1946.

God: and creativity, primordial nature of, consequent nature of, and evil, and novelty, and potentiality, and order; order; creativity; value, preservation of; theology.

(The author develops a metaphysical position which, while influenced by Whitehead, differs from Whitehead's thought with respect to God, order, creativity, and the preservation of value.)

1811　Wieman, Henry Nelson. *The Intellectual Foundation of Faith.* New York: Philosophical Library, 1961.

Theology, empirical; process theology.

1812　Wieman, Henry Nelson. "Concerning the Intellectual Foundation of Faith—An Exchange of Views." *Iliff Review*, 18, 1961, 51–53.

God, creativity of; human existence, and creativity; Milligan, Charles S.; Wieman, Henry Nelson.

The purpose of *The Intellectual Foundation of Faith* (Wieman) is to find out what is the enduring structure of the divine creativity and what are the obstructions to this creativity. (Written in response to C. S. Milligan's review of *The Intellectual Foundation of Faith.*)

1813　Wieman, Henry Nelson. "The Structure of the Divine Creativity: An Exchange of Views, II." *Iliff Review*, 19, 1962, 37–42.

Creativity; God, creativity of; evolution, as creative; Wieman, Henry Nelson; Milligan, Charles S.

The structure of divine creativity involves: 1) two or more individuals in an open relationship; 2) with mutual understanding; 3) and mutual integration of the other's perspective; 4) resulting in a wider and deeper community between participant individuals; 5) and an expanded range of vision. (Written in response to Charles S. Milligan, "A Rejoinder to Professor Wieman.")

1814　Wieman, Henry Nelson. "The Ways of God with Man." *Iliff Review*, 20, 1962, 37–41.

God: experience of, as Being; Jesus, as revelation; evil; Wieman, Henry Nelson; Milligan, Charles S.

That which saves humanity must be found operating at the levels of human existence in such a way as to transform human existence from the evil to the good. (Written in response to Charles S. Milligan, "Broader than the Measure of Man's Mind, But.")

1815　Wieman, Henry N. "A Waste We Cannot Afford." *Unitarian Register and Universalist Leader*, 143, 1962, 11–13.

Religion, and science; technology; God, nature of.

Whitehead has helped to bring science into the service of religious commitment by showing that human life is created and sustained by creativity. He has hindered the relation between religion and science by failing to clarify the radical difference between creativity at the human and subhuman levels.

1816   Wieman, Henry Nelson. "Intellectual Biography." *The Empirical Theology of Henry Nelson Wieman.* Edited by Robert W. Bretall. New York: Macmillan Company, 1963; Carbondale, Illinois: Southern Illinois University Press, 1969, 1–18.

God, and creativity.

Although Whitehead applies the term 'God' to the primordial order of the universe rather than to the creativity which operates in human life, an analysis of his thought shows that the primordial order is itself an ingredient in the creativity.

1817   Wiener, N. "A Comparison Between the Treatment of the Algebra of Relations by Schroeder and That by Whitehead and Russell." Unpublished Ph.D. dissertation, Harvard University, 1913.

Algebra; relations; Russell, Bertrand.

1818   Wightman, William P. D. "Whitehead's Empiricism." *The Relevance of Whitehead.* Edited by Ivor Leclerc. New York: Humanities Press Inc., 1961, 335–350.

Philosophy: method of, of science; experience, as datum for philosophy; empiricism.

The fact that the empirical character of Whitehead's philosophy has not been fully explored has resulted in insufficient exegesis of his philosophy of science.

1819   Wilcox, John T. "Relativity, Simultaneity, and Divine Omniscience." Unpublished M.A. thesis, Emory University, 1956.

Relativity; simultaneity; omniscience.

1820   Wilcox, John T. "A Question from Physics for Certain Theists." *Journal of Religion,* 41, 1961, 293–300.

Simultaneity, relative; relativity, theory of; God, and time; Hartshorne, Charles; Christian, William; physics; theology.

The relativity of simultaneity throws a great deal of doubt upon any theory of temporalistic theism, for the latter calls for a privileged time frame which contradicts relativity theory.

1821   Wild, John. "The Divine Existence: An Answer to Mr. Hartshorne." *Review of Metaphysics,* 9, 1950, 61–84.

God: Hartshorne's interpretation of, proofs of, freedom of; Hartshorne, Charles.

Hartshorne's surrelativist reconstruction results in an anthropomorphic deity which can satisfy neither the demands of philosophy nor those of religion. There is no defensible argument for the existence of such a deity.

1822   Will, Clifford M. "Relativistic Gravity in the Solar System, II: Anistropy in the Newtonian Gravitational Constant." *Astrophysical Journal,* 169, 1971, 141–156.

Gravitation; relativity, theory of, Newton, Isaac; physics.

1823   Will, Clifford M. "Einstein on the Firing Line." *Physics Today*, 25, 1972, 23–29.

Relativity, theory of; Einstein, Albert; physics.

1824   Williams, Daniel Day. "The Victory of Good." *Journal of Liberal Religion*, 3, 1942, 171–185.

God, goodness of; love; evil; theology.

1825   Williams, Daniel Day. "Truth in the Theological Perspective." *Journal of Religion*, 3, 1948, 242–254.

Method, theological; truth–claims: criterion for, perspectival; theology, and philosophy.

The criterion of truth is the achievement of a growing coherence of perspectives.

1826   Williams, Daniel Day. *God's Grace and Man's Hope.* New York: Harper and Row, 1949, 1965. Chapter 5 reprinted in *Process Philosophy and Christian Thought.* Edited by Delwin Brown, Ralph E. James, and Gene Reeves. Indianapolis, Indiana: Bobbs–Merrill Company, Inc., 1971, 441–463.

God, as persuasive power; grace, of God; history: as conflict, as teleological, and values; *Adventures of Ideas*: kingdom of God.

Whitehead's optimism concerning the victory of persuasion over brute force conflicts with his own insights that life is robbery and that tragedy is involved in the vision of God.

1827   Williams, Daniel Day. *What Present–Day Theologians are Thinking.* New York: Harper and Row, 1952, (revised) 1959, (revised) 1967.

God: and process, personal character of, immutability of, of classical theism; Hartshorne, Charles; Wieman, Henry Nelson; Ferre, Nels; theology, process.

(The author reviews major trends in twentieth century theological thought, with process theology among them.)

1828   Williams, Daniel Day. "Christianity and Naturalism: An Informal Statement." *Union Seminary Quarterly Review*, 12, 1957, 47–53.

Nature, and history; God, and the world; mind, and mind–body problem; Hartshorne, Charles; naturalism.

Naturalism can provide an intelligible way to speak about God's relationship to the world, and of history as the field of his redemptive activity.

1829   Williams, Daniel Day. "Moral Obligation in Process Philosophy." *Journal of Philosophy*, 56, 1959, 263–270. Also in *Alfred North Whitehead: Essays on His Philosophy.* Edited by George L. Kline. Englewood Cliffs, New Jersey: Prentice–Hall, Inc., 1963, 189–195.

Morality, and moral responsibility; evil; decision, moral; Wieman, Henry Nelson; ethics.

Process philosophy offers a metaphysics and theory of value which holds together absoluteness of moral obligation with acknowledgement of the creative and the tragic factors which attend ethical decision in an unfinished world.

1830   Williams, Daniel Day. "God and Time." *Southeast Asia Journal of Theology*, 2, 1961, 7–19.

God, and time; biblical studies; existentialism; eschatology.

Interpretation of biblical faith in its own terms, and advances in modern science and metaphysics, present theology with the demand to reformulate the question of time and its relation to God.

1831   Williams, Daniel Day. "Deity, Monarchy, and Metaphysics: Whitehead's Critique of the Theological Tradition." *The Relevance of Whitehead*. Edited by Ivor Leclerc. New York: Humanities Press Inc., 1961, 353–372.

God: and classical theism, doctrine of, as principle of concretion, primordial nature of, as persuasive, as divine despot; theology, process.

(This paper examines Whitehead's critique of certain doctrines in Christian theology and explores Whitehead's alternative to the traditional way in which God is understood to act in the world.)

1832   Williams, Daniel Day. "How Does God Act?: An Essay in Whitehead's Metaphysics." *Process and Divinity*. Edited by William L. Reese and Eugene Freeman. La Salle, Illinois: Open Court Publishing Company, 1964, 161–180.

God: and world, primordial nature of, consequent nature of, as principle of concretion, as cause, and categoreal scheme, function of; verifiability; causation.

In relating a theological doctrine of God's action to scientific understanding, the greatest difficulty lies in assigning specific, observable consequences in the world to divine causality. From a Whiteheadian perspective specific instances of divine causality can be determined according to the manner in which the consequent nature of God is experienced by the world.

1833   Williams, Daniel Day. "The Theology of Bernard E. Meland." *Criterion*, 3, 1964, 3–9.

Faith, and culture; evil; Meland, Bernard E.; theology.

Three main motifs characterize Meland's theology: persistent, critical reflection on the American experience with its interweaving of secular and religious elements; protest against the disavowal of responsibility for culture; protest against a theology which knows nothing of the depths of anguish in life.

1834   Williams, Daniel Day. "The New Theological Situation." *Theology Today*, 24, 1968, 444–463.

Theology, twentieth century; Barth, Karl; Ebeling, Gerhard; Hartshorne, Charles.

Theology is distinguished today almost universally by the search for a genuinely social conception of man, of God, and of reality.

1835   Williams, Daniel Day. *The Spirit and the Forms of Love.* New York: Harper and Row, 1968.

Love: Christian, and Christ, types of, in the Biblical tradition, in the Augustinian tradition, in the Franciscan tradition, in the Christian evangelical tradition, and being, and self-sacrifice, and sexuality, and social justice, and the intellect; God: as love, experience of (in human experience), and creativity, and incarnation, and time, suffering of, and Christ, immutability of, power of, classical view of; Imago dei; Christ: and historical Jesus, and traditional Christology, suffering of, resurrection of, and atonement; Augustine; D'Arcy, Martin; Schweitzer, Albert; Niebuhr, Reinhold; Hartshorne, Charles; Nygren, Anders; theology, process.

(The author reviews the biblical way of thinking about love, and describes the major interpretations of love in the Christian tradition.   He then interprets love in light of process philosophy, relating it to such areas as self-sacrifice, sexuality, the struggle for social justice, and the intellectual life.   He argues that the understanding of God's love has been thwarted in the classical Christian tradition by the doctrine of divine immutability, and that the process view of God is more amenable to the appreciation of God as love.)

Review

Woodhouse, H. F. *Church Quarterly*, 2, 1969, 90.

1836   Williams, Daniel Day.   "Suffering and Being in Empirical Theology."   *The Future of Empirical Theology.*   Edited by Bernard E. Meland.   Chicago: University of Chicago Press, 1969.

Suffering; being; theology, empirical.

1837   Williams, Daniel Day. "Prozeß–Theologie: Eine neue Möglichkeit für die Kirche." Translated by Helga Krüger. *Evangelische Theologie*, 30, 1970, 571–582.

God: as primordial, knowledge of, of classical theism, and the future; Schleiermacher, Friederick; Kant, Immanuel; hermeneutic, process; metaphysics, and theology.

1838   Williams, Daniel Day. "Philosophy and Faith: A Study in Hegel and Whitehead." *Our Common History as Christians Essays in Honor of Albert C. Outler.* Edited by John Deschner et. al., 1975.

Hegel, G. W. F.; Christianity; faith; reason; religion, philosophy of.

Both Hegel and Whitehead share a conviction in the power of reason, but Whitehead is unwilling to extend it to encompass the whole as did Hegel.   Accordingly, in the area of religion Whitehead leaves the final role to vision and insight which can run beyond adequate rational articulation. (This is the last article written before the author's death in December, 1973.)

1839   Williams, Donald Cary. "La probabilité, l'induction et l'homme prévoyant." *L'Activité philosophique contemporaine en France et aux États-Unis.* Edited by Marvin Farber. Paris: Presses Universitaires de France, 1950, 197–219.

Relations, internal; epoch, cosmic; Hume, David; Kant, Immanuel.

1840   Williamson, Clark M. "God Acts in History." *Quest,* 8, 1964, 33–49.

History, relativity of; God, as acting in history; relativism, historical; Meland, Bernard E.; Dilthey, Wilhelm; Troeltsch, Ernst; theology.

Meland is able to talk about God's revelation in history without 1) bifurcating history into two kinds of history, and without 2) escaping from history or seeking to avoid it.

1841   Williamson, Clark M. "God and the Relativities of History." *Encounter,* 28, 1967, 199–218.

History, relativity of; Jesus, of history; Troeltsch, Ernst; theology.

The historicization of religion and values presents a major problem for theology. Recognition of our full participation in history, and acceptance of our full involvement in historical relatedness, must form part of our response to the problem.

1842   Williamson, Clark M. '"A Response to Professor Cotton." *Encounter,* 29, 1968, 141–148.

Language, Whitehead's use of; Cotton, J. H.; theology, and philosophy; positivism.

Cotton errs in understanding Whitehead's language to be largely metaphorical, lacking cognitive meaning. (Written in response to J. H. Cotton, "Theology and Philosophy: A New Phase of the Discussion.")

1843   Williamson, Clark M. "Paul Tillich's 'Two Types of Philosophy of Religion': A Reconsideration." *Journal of Religion,* 52, 1972.

Philosophy, of religion; Tillich, Paul.

1844   Williamson, Clarke. "Whitehead as Counterrevolutionary? Toward Christian–Marxist Dialogue." *Process Studies,* 4, 1974, 176–186.

Ethics; justice; philosophy, political; society; individuality; Christianity, and culture; Marx, Karl; Marxism.

Marxism and process thought each view metaphysics as a 'social requirement', and represent a materialistic philosophy of history. They each accept the premise of relativism with regard to established social order, and have a doctrine of human existence which can be called 'negative anthropology'. Both affirm transcendence as a fundamental dimension of reality, and each takes a dialectical approach to religion with regard to its relation to society.

1845 Wilson, C. *Religion and the Rebel.* Boston: Houghton Mifflin Company, Inc., 1957, 290–322.

Whitehead, Alfred North: introduction to his thought, philosophical development of.

1846 Wilson, C. *Beyond the Outsider.* Boston: Houghton Mifflin, 1965.

Civilization; peace; literature.

1847 Wilson, Edmund. "A. N. Whitehead and Bertrand Russell." *New Republic*, 45, 1925, 161–162.

Russell, Bertrand.

Whitehead and Russell, former collaborators, present striking contrasts of personality and philosophical approach in their separate publications.

1848 Wilson, Edmund. "A. N. Whitehead: Physicist and Prophet." *New Republic*, 51, 1927, 91–96.

Whitehead, Alfred North, biography of; Bergson, Henri; metaphysics.

Whitehead manages to preserve the theories of science by working out a metaphysic of the creative advance of nature which, unlike Bergson's creative evolution, admits scientific theories. He has saved logic along with God.

1849 Wilson, Edmund. "Portrait of a Sage." *New Republic*, 58, 1929, 300–305.

God, nature of; Whitehead, biography of.

(This is a farcical treatment of an evening dinner at the Whitehead's wherein Whitehead is referred to as Professor Grosbeake and humor is poked at his neologisms. In a lighthearted way both the novelty and insight of Whitehead's thought are presented.)

1850 Wind, Edgar. "Mathematik und Sinnesempfindung: Materialien zu einer Whitehead–Kritik." *Logos*, 21, 1932, 239–280.

Events, concept of; objects: concept, of perception; abstraction, extensive; cogredience; parallelism; sense–perception; time, epochal theory of; Kant, Immanuel; Hume, David; mathematics; physics.

1851 Windsor, A. C. A. "Natural History and Human History." *Downside Review*, 83, 1965, 131–144.

Induction; nature, and history; causality; Hume, David; empiricism.

Dissolution of the inductive problem as formulated by Hume leaves untouched and still to be performed the correct analysis of induction and of the empirical thinking of which it is a part. Whitehead did not go far enough in naturalizing our ordinary beliefs.

1852 Winn, Ralph B. "Whitehead's Concept of Process: A Few Critical Remarks." *Journal of Philosophy*, 30, 1933, 710–714.

Process philosophy, criticisms of.

Whitehead brings us back in some respects to the days of Newton, since he creates, on the one hand, the doctrine of the absolute space–time and, on the other hand, the doctrine of relative space and time, the latter being "simply expressions for a certain observed ordering of events."

1853   Winquist, Charles E. "Reconstruction in Process Theology." *Anglican Theological Review*, 55, 1973, 169–181.

Method, theological; language, religious; secularism; theology, empirical.

Process philosophy provides methodological structures which can be used by the theologian in defining his task. Rather than adopting a metaphysics, the process theologian is adopting an empirical method.

1854   Wolterstoff, Nicholas P. "Whitehead's Theory of Individuals." Unpublished Ph.D. dissertation, Harvard University, 1956.

Actual entity, unity of; events, and actual entities; eternal objects; concreteness; relativism, and prehensions; unity, and disunity; perspective.

(This work is a commentary on Whitehead's notions of concreteness, particularity, and intrinsic unity.)

1855   Wood, F. "A Whiteheadian Concept of the Self." *Southwestern Journal of Philosophy*, 4, 1973, 57–65.

Self: as society, process model of.

1856   Woodbridge, Barry A. "The Role of Text and Emergent Possibilities in the Interpretation of Christian Tradition: A Process Hermeneutic in Response to the German Hermeneutical Discussion." Unpublished Ph.D. dissertation, Claremont Graduate School, 1976.

Hermeneutics: process, as social, German; propositions: and text, and emerging possibilities, as lure for feeling; Christianity: essence of, interpretation of; interpretation: criteria for, God's role in, community of, of past; society: living, dying; novelty; route, historical; understanding; Royce, Josiah; Troeltsch, Ernst; Robinson, James M.; Ebeling, Gerhard.

Whitehead's understanding of propositions and historical routes clarifies the function of the text in eliciting new understandings and appropriations of Christian tradition, thereby supplementing the conceptuality of the German hermeneutical discussion and enhancing the creative transformation of the Christian community.

1857   Woodhouse, H. F. "Pneumatology and Process Theology." *Scottish Journal of Philosophy*, 25, 1972, 383–391.

God: consequent nature of, as Holy Spirit, relatedness of, as love, as suffering, creativity of; Hartshorne, Charles; pneumatology; theology.

Certain ideas linked with process theology can be expanded to develop a more realistic pneumatology.

1858   Wyman, Mary A.   "Whitehead's Philosophy of Science in the Light of Wordsworth's Poetry."   *Philosophy of Science*, 23, 1956, 283–296.

Creativity, in art; God, and creativity; Wordsworth, William; poetry.

Wordsworth's influence on Whitehead might be seen in the resemblance of Wordsworth's ideas on the creative process to the metaphysical theories of Whitehead—a resemblance in which the function of God in the world is particularly emphasized.

1859   Wyman, Mary A.   *The Lure for Feeling in the Creative Process.* New York: Philosophical Library, 1960.

Creativity: and creative process, and value; aesthetics; art: and creativity, and creative process; proposition, as lure for feeling; God: as eros, primordial nature of, consequent nature of; beauty; contrast; intensity; subjective aim; concrescence; mysticism: Chinese, and nature; causation: final, efficient; subjective form; Taoism; Neo–Confucianism; Buddhism, Ch'an; Wordsworth, William; Plato; Spinoza, B.; Emerson, Ralph Waldo; Chu Hsi; Goethe, J. W. van.

There are essential connections between the artistic and mathematical sweep of Whitehead's philosophy and some of the major literary figures of European, American, and Oriental culture.   Like these figures, Whitehead recognizes a transcendent lure for feeling which guides all becoming to enduring value.

1860   Xirau, Ramon.   "Alfred North Whitehead: Tres categorías fundamentales."   *Filosofía y Letras*, 23, 1952, 311–325.

Whitehead, Alfred North: introduction to his thought.

1861   Yakushev, A. A.   "Subektivno–Idealisticheskii Smysl Teorii Simvolizma A Uaitkheda (The Subjectivist–Idealist Significance of Alfred Whitehead's Theory of Symbolism)."   *Voprosy Filosofi*, 12, 1962, 117–128.

Symbolism; subjectivism; idealism.

1862   Yakushev (Jakuszew), A. A.   "Zarys Systemy Metafizyki A. N. Whiteheada."   *Studia Filozoficzne*, 32, 1963, 191–210.

Metaphysics, method of.

1863   Yamamoto, Seisaku.   "The Philosophy of Pure Experience." Unpublished Ph.D. dissertation, Emory University, 1961.

Experience; representation; time, and human existence; Descartes, Rene; Kant, Immanuel; James, William; Bergson, Henri; Heidegger, Martin; Nishida, Kitaro; phenomenology.

Whitehead's insights into the subjective ground of time are not carried through.   As a result he fails to clearly distinguish physical time from time as it is lived in human existence.

1864   Yarros, Victor S.   "Dr. Whitehead and Professor Mather on Religion." *Open Court*, 42, 1928, 733–740.

Religion in the Making; God, concept of; Mather, K. F.; religion.

Two men of science, Whitehead and Mather, have written books on religion. Weak points in Whitehead's book concern his anthropomorphic attribution of moral order to God, his notion of the elimination of evil, and insufficient data for his ideal of goodness and harmony.

1865   Yezzi, R. D.   "The Application of Mathematics to Concepts in Physics: Four Theories."   Unpublished Ph.D. dissertation, Southern Illinois University, 1968.

Relativity, theory of; mathematics; physics.

1866   Young, Theodore A.   "Change in Aristotle, Descartes, Hume, and Whitehead: An Essay in Philosophy of Nature." Unpublished Ph.D. dissertation, Indiana University, 1964.

Change; continuity; succession; potentiality, and change; causation: efficient, final; repetition; time, and causality; locomotion; Aristotle; Descartes, Rene; Hume, David.

1867   Yu, David.   "A Comparison of the Metaphysics of Chu Hsi and Alfred North Whitehead."   Unpublished Ph.D. dissertation, University of Chicago, 1958–1959.

Philosophy, Chinese; God, and creativity; process; Chu Hsi.

1868   Zuurdeeg, W. F.   *An Analytical Philosophy of Religion.* Nashville: Abingdon Press, 1958; London: Allen & Unwin, 1959, 143–149.

Whitehead, Alfred North, method of; mechanism, organic; materialism, scientific; metaphysics.

Whitehead correctly accuses scientific materialism of encumbering the recognition of new scientific theories. However, his own views also contain an implicit convictional world view.

SECTION IV

DESCRIPTOR INDEX

(Please Note: The Numbers In This Index Refer To The *Entry Numbers* Of The Citations In The Secondary Bibliography. For Further Information On The Organization Of This Index, Refer To The Introduction.)

, and Four Causes 543, 1709
, and Ousia 638, 1021
, and Substance 626, 1021
Arithmetic 1473
Armstrong, D. M. 1242
Art 147, 200, 293, 437, 439, 488, 687, 704, 790, 913, 1128, 1285, 1460, 1622, 1745, 1781
, and Aesthetic Experience 1592
, and Artistic Creation 1592
, and Artistic Expression 1592
, and Christ 391
, and Coordinate Analysis 1234
, and Creative Process 1851
, and Creativity 1234, 1859
, and Education 1758
, and Form 148
, Function of 1592
, and Genetic Analysis 1234
, and God 1592
, and Nature 148, 684, 1747
, Nonperformer 1592
, Performer 1592
, and Science 148
, and Social Life 148
Associationism 308
Assymetry 310, 767, 1265
, Temporal 308
Astronomy 721, 1788
Atheism 512, 1302
, Arguments for 722
Atom 848
Atomicity 329, 858, 1021
Atomism 308, 490, 628, 672, 713, 861, 930, 1040, 1159
, Metaphysical 280
Atonement 885
, Theories of 361
Augustine 246, 310, 406, 667, 732, 1103, 1662, 1703, 1835
, and Evil 639
Augustus 1151
Aulen, Gustaf 361
Aurobindo, Sri 1118, 1614
Austin, J. L. 811

, and God (*see* God and Eternal Objects) 997, 1145
, as Ideal Continuum 447, 1219
, and Ingression 283, 336, 340, 382, 502, 997, 1145, 1219, 1449, 1516, 1523
, Individual Essence of 404, 448, 504, 542, 1051, 1145, 1219
, as Individuals 1219
, Locus of 382
, as Logical Forms of Events 1150
, Mathematical Basis of 808, 1516
, as Mathematical Forms 1104
, as Multiplicity 447
, in Objectification 336, 1145, 1516
, Objective Species of 180, 490, 504, 654, 1145, 1219, 1449, 1517
, Ontological Status of 1449
, Ordering of 382
, as Patterning 997
, as Personal 1145
, and Platonic Forms 340, 614, 1449
, and Plato's Ideas 1281
, as Potential 448, 490, 502, 504, 519, 1021, 1027, 1145, 1219, 1449, 1518
, and Power 1449, 1450
, as Predicate of Proposition 180
, Propositional 180
, as Pure Possibilities 336, 340, 1070, 1103, 1105, 1516
, as Relational 120, 997
, Relational Essence of 120, 404, 448, 488, 504, 542, 997, 998, 1024, 1051, 1104, 1145, 1219
, Relations Between 1027, 1145, 1449
, Relevance of 382
, and the Trinity 1024, 1704
, Structure of 336, 1024
, Subjective Species of 180, 490, 504, 654, 1145, 1219, 1449, 1517
, and Type Theory 1134
, Universal Relativity of 997
, as Universals 120, 340, 519, 614, 688, 703, 767, 1219, 1356
, Whitehead's Arguments for 1219
Eternalism 1198
Eternity 550
Ether 1513
Ethics 187, 188, 190, 219, 220, 234, 263, 272, 294, 360, 364, 390, 439, 607, 660, 661, 710, 769, 779, 791, 843, 890, 900, 956, 974, 1050, 1068, 1119, 1121, 1204, 1223, 1229, 1275, 1441, 1446, 1461, 1468, 1506, 1524, 1527, 1570, 1603, 1634, 1657, 1764, 1769, 1829, 1844

God

, as Conscious 732

, Consequent Nature of (as Consequent) 132, 137, 168, 170, 182, 188, 206, 220, 222, 251, 313, 320, 340, 367, 375, 384, 388, 390, 391, 392, 396, 402, 438, 444, 445, 504, 510, 524, 541, 549, 577, 579, 586, 619, 623, 667, 702, 716, 731, 732, 744, 746, 752, 760, 780, 793, 795, 858, 877, 882, 923, 980, 982, 991, 1015, 1021, 1061, 1062, 1071, 1073, 1075, 1116, 1118, 1187, 1188, 1238, 1288, 1359, 1371, 1380, 1395, 1423, 1425, 1459, 1477, 1512, 1541, 1547, 1548, 1594, 1614, 1644, 1677, 1688, 1696, 1699, 1810, 1832, 1857, 1859

, and Contingency 576, 621

, and Cosmic Order 268

, and Creatio Ex Nihilo 168, 367, 473, 653, 992, 1213, 1260, 1702

, and Creativity (Category of) 154, 248, 367, 406, 543, 556, 557, 562, 577, 581, 594, 598, 732, 1133, 1172, 1213, 1215, 1238, 1263, 1495, 1595, 1659, 1662, 1810, 1816, 1835, 1859, 1867

, Creativity of 214, 1272, 1372, 1812, 1813, 1857

, as Creator (Creating) 168, 215, 222, 367, 473, 529, 620, 653, 667, 716, 725, 749, 794, 1031, 1062, 1071, 1187, 1258, 1260, 1321, 1322, 1398, 1405, 1433, 1495, 1644, 1664, 1699, 1702

, Death of 138, 251, 365, 375, 431, 528, 692, 815, 938, 1195

, Decision of 558, 563, 567, 756

, as Deus Ex Machina 128, 314, 320, 510, 653, 707

, as Dipolar (Bipolar) 138, 251, 261, 313, 392, 565, 584, 654, 727, 730, 738, 759, 817, 883, 938, 1039, 1208, 1265, 1288, 1296, 1410, 1445, 1459, 1497, 1542

, Discovery of 1362, 1400, 1435, 1831

, as Divine Despot 1400, 1435

, and Divine Knowledge 406, 431, 732, 1071, 1380, 1648

, Doctrine(s) of 128, 347, 358, 529, 691, 731, 1156, 1298, 1301, 1370, 1440, 1677, 1712, 1730, 1740, 1763, 1800, 1831

, Emotional Intensity of 524

, as Eros 614, 623, 946, 1039, 1213, 1214, 1359, 1859

, and Eschatology 137

, as Eternal 530, 618, 725, 732, 763, 792, 987, 1212, 1793

, and Eternal Objects 367, 382, 448, 567, 688, 716, 1395, 1449, 1499, 1595

, and Evil (*see also* Theodicy) 170, 171, 206, 340, 406, 444, 489, 549, 639, 653, 667, 705, 716, 732, 762, 794, 819, 1075, 1116, 1117, 1238, 1263, 1273, 1359, 1395, 1399, 1405, 1414, 1445, 1690, 1701, 1702, 1720, 1786, 1805, 1806, 1810

, Existence of 1362

, Experience of (in Human Experience) 213, 274, 657, 660, 714, 1077, 1139, 1212, 1445, 1449, 1455, 1499, 1664, 1763, 1804, 1814, 1835

, Faithfulness of 267

, Finitude of 749, 1116, 1117, 1707

God

God